MULTICULTURALISM IN CANADA

Evidence and Anecdote

ANDREW GRIFFITH

Published by Anar Press

Library and Archives Canada Cataloguing in Publication
Griffith, Andrew, author
Multiculturalism in Canada : evidence and anecdote / Andrew Griffith.

Includes bibliographical references.
Issued in print and electronic formats.
ISBN 978-0-9880640-9-6 (paperback).--ISBN 978-0-9880640-8-9 (pdf)

1. Multiculturalism--Canada. I. Title.

FC105.M8G75 2015   *305.800971*   *C2015-905157-6*
C2015-905158-4

To Nazanine, Alex and Roxanne for their ongoing encouragement, support and love.

Preface

I have always had a fascination with how to visualize data to help tell a story about what the data means, its significance and the policy implications of any trends or tendencies shown.

This book came about after a number of roller-coaster years when I was in and out of cancer treatment and suddenly, to my surprise, having a good period, becoming somewhat bored, and looking for something to engage me. Given my interest in multiculturalism and data, I started playing around with some of the 2011 National Household Survey (NHS) data to see what it showed about multiculturalism in Canada, updating some of the work that my former team in the multiculturalism program had carried out a number of years earlier.

That project had been lead by Kamal Dib. I showed him my preliminary work and he suggested that I take it further and write a book. This book is the result of Kamal's initial and ongoing encouragement, and like many such endeavours, it took on a life of its own.

Fundamentally, multiculturalism is one of Canada's defining characteristics and an icon of Canadian identity. Canada's relative success in building an inclusive and welcoming society, and the need given ongoing immigration to maintain this relative success, is central to Canada's future as a country. Looking at some of the poisonous debates south of the border, and many of the divides in Europe, underlines the importance of getting multicultural and integration policies and programs right.

The book focusses on what the data shows, first in terms of the basic demographics. More importantly, however, it integrates economic outcomes, social indicators and political measures to provide a comprehensive overview of how effectively multiculturalism is facilitating equality of opportunity and mobility.

In the end, while the majority of the data came from the NHS, I drew from a variety of other sources to provide as comprehensive a portrait as possible. The book also includes an extensive theory, policy and practice chapter, given that the origins and original objectives of multiculturalism are often forgotten or ignored, thus leading to poorer quality of public understanding and debate. I want us to consider what multiculturalism means in the Canadian context, rather than import debates from elsewhere.

In addition to summarizing the findings, the conclusion highlights some ongoing policy issues that merit attention.

This book is written for those who love data, charts and tables. However, I hope all readers will find the analysis and insights of interest, and helpful to ongoing discussion and debate on multiculturalism and related immigration, citizenship and integration issues.

Table of Contents

TABLE OF CONTENTS

List of Charts and Tables

Executive Summary

Canada is one of the world's most multicultural societies. Of its population of almost 33 million people, 20.6 percent are foreign-born, and more than 250 ethnic origins are represented. The current ethnic and religious diversity is expected to continue growing alongside immigration in the coming years.

Multiculturalism, and the integration of newcomers and their descendants, has been part of our past, is part of our present, and will be part of our future, as Canada continues to receive more than 250,000 immigrants per year.

Given that multiculturalism and diversity are central to Canada's past, present and future, Canada's overall success is linked to its ongoing ability to integrate newcomers and their families, ensuring social inclusion and equality of opportunity. "Getting it right" matters.

Current and future policy choices should be largely based on an evidence-based analysis of the impact and outcomes from previous policy choices. This book aims to bring together the key data from a variety of sources to provide an overall portrait of the present as well as the likely impact of recent policy choices that have emphasized integration over accommodation in multiculturalism, and meaningfulness over facilitation in citizenship.

The data focus of this book provides a backdrop to current and future policy debates, hopefully resulting in more informed and balanced discussion. The story-telling power of anecdotes means that these also form part of the evidence base given their impact on public debate. However, having an overall sense of what the data shows should hopefully attenuate some of the tensions and rhetoric that can emerge.

On the whole, the data shows that Canada has been remarkably successful in integrating its large number of immigrants and diverse population, although not without challenges.

In many ways, this success reflects a mixture of history and luck. Our history is one of early accommodation between Aboriginal Peoples and Europeans and between French and English. Moreover, unlike many other countries, geography provides a barrier to large numbers of illegal and irregular immigrants, thus reducing the risk of poisonous debates as seen in other countries.

Moreover, initial advocacy of multiculturalism in the 1960s was by European and Christian groups, such as Ukrainian Canadians, who wanted their contribution to the building of Canada to be recognized alongside Aboriginal, French and British contributions. As a result, multiculturalism emerged almost organically from this mix of history and political requirement to compromise and to accommodate differences.

But it was not only history and luck. Canada made a deliberate political choice in favour of integration instead of assimilation, first articulated in the fourth volume of the *Bilingualism and Biculturalism Commission* report on ethnic groups other than English or French. Successive Conservative and Liberal governments liberalized immigration in the 1960s, removing race-based criteria in favour of a colour-blind point system. A strong political consensus emerged over time in favour of large-scale immigration, a relatively easy and direct pathway to citizenship, and an embrace of multiculturalism as part of Canadian identity, although concerns remained about how well different groups were integrating.

Partially as a result of this choice, a lively intellectual debate emerged, flourished and contributed to national discourses on multiculturalism. Canada developed some of the leading theorists of multiculturalism, producing people like Charles Taylor, Will Kymlicka and for the Quebec variant "interculturalisme," Gérard Bouchard, as well as a lively group of authors, pundits and academics with a wide range of perspectives on whether or not multiculturalism strengthened or weakened Canadian society.

Certainly compared to most other countries, Canada has been successful in creating an overall inclusive society, one that encourages participation and equality of opportunity.

The available data from Statistics Canada, Citizenship and Immigration Canada operational statistics, employment equity figures and other sources helps us understand both the strengths and weaknesses of multiculturalism in Canada.

In this book, over 200 charts and tables are used to highlight what the data and analysis show, particularly variations between groups, generations, genders and regions.

In addition to covering the demographic characteristics at the national, provincial and municipal levels, this book assesses economic outcomes (for example, low-income cut-off prevalence, participation, unemployment, income and the federally regulated sectors of banking, communications and transport), social indicators (education levels, hate crimes and discrimination, healthcare and education sector workforce representation, and ethnic enclaves) and political and public sector indicators (citizenship, political party competition for the ethnic vote, judicial appointments, and public service representation).

What the Data Shows

This integrated assessment of demographic, economic, social and political indicators shows:

Greater and more varied diversity: Diversity within Canada continues to evolve and become more complex and varied, with over 250 ethnicities, an ever-larger visible minority population (19.1 percent) and increased religious diversity (8.8 percent). The broad visible minority and ethnic origin categories, while useful for group comparisons, understate the degree of diversity within these categories, whether in terms of religion, country of origin, time of immigration to Canada, or individual values and perspectives. And while there are commonalities across most regions, each province has its own particular "flavour" of diversity. British Columbia is more heavily Asian, Ontario has the greatest diversity, Alberta has overtaken Quebec both in numbers and diversity, and Quebec reflects the preference for French-speaking immigrants.

Changing urban mix: MTV (Montreal, Toronto, Vancouver) has been replaced by TVC (Toronto, Vancouver, Calgary), and Alberta (18.4 percent visible minorities) has displaced Quebec (11.0 percent visible minorities) as Canada's third most diverse province, reflecting Alberta's greater economic growth. Moreover, diversity continues to expand outwards from the largest cities and their suburbs, particularly in British Columbia, Ontario and Alberta, to more medium-sized cities. Religious diversity is particularly high in the Census Metropolitan Areas of Toronto (22.2 percent), Vancouver (16.9 percent) and Calgary (12.0 percent).

Historically, Quebec has been an exception to this trend, with new Canadians concentrated on the island of Montreal, but this is changing as the suburbs of Laval and Longueuil become more diverse.

Economic differences persist: Economic differences persist between visible minorities and those of Canadian or European origin, whether viewed by LICO prevalence, unemployment rates, or median income, even if participation rates for visible minorities are stronger. This is also the case for most second-generation immigrants who have been schooled in Canada, although all indicators show improvement for the second-generation. Median incomes of visible minorities (all generations) are 83.4 percent of non-visible minority median incomes. But second-generation visible minority median incomes are 91.0 percent compared to non-visible minorities. Moreover, second-generation university-educated visible minorities aged 25 to 34 show many groups doing as well or better than non-visible minorities, with median income of all visible minorities being 101.1 percent of non-visible minority median income. This pattern persists across the country, although visible minorities in Quebec are not doing as well.

Strong educational performance: Education outcomes for most visible minority groups are significantly stronger than non-visible minority groups in terms of university diplomas (38.2 percent compared to 23.0 percent). Most groups have relatively minor differences between men and women in terms of levels of education. Canada continues to do well in integrating new Canadians in primary and secondary education.

Discrimination remains an issue: Reported hate crimes and perceived discrimination remain an issue. The official statistics have been largely stable over the past four years, with Blacks being subject to relatively more hate crimes (0.28 per thousand Blacks) compared to other ethnic origins, as are Jews in comparison to other religions (0.66 per thousand Jews). Hate crimes are generally more common in provinces with greater numbers of visible minorities and religious minorities. However, these statistics do not account for other forms of religious and racial intolerance and discrimination, which account in part for the persistent differences in economic outcomes.

Improved representation in public services: Representation of visible minorities in the public institutions that Canadians interact with the most — healthcare, social services and education (particularly higher education) — is relatively close to representation in the general population in the larger provinces. In healthcare, visible minorities form 26.3 percent of the workforce in British Columbia, 21.8 percent in Alberta, 24.2 percent in Ontario, and 10.4 percent in Quebec, with broadly comparable figures in social services. While many visible minorities in these sectors are in more junior positions, a number of communities have strong representation in more highly paid occupations. Visible minorities accessing healthcare are more often than not served by a mix of visible minorities and non-visible minorities.

Ethnic enclaves at the riding level: While there are areas of ethnic group concentration, most ridings at the federal level have a mix of communities, some larger than others (in 2015, 33 ridings, mainly in Ontario and British Columbia, have more than 50 percent visible minorities). Typically — but not universally — visible minority MPs elected in the 2011 election tended to represent ridings with large populations of their minority group.

Declining naturalization: The Canadian model of immigration leading to citizenship is at risk given declining naturalization rates, reflecting policy and program changes that have made citizenship "harder to get and easier to lose." Changes to the citizenship study guide and test had a disproportionate effect on visible minorities, with a 14.7 percent decline in the pass rates compared to a 4.2 percent decline for European and North American ethnic origins. The 85.6 percent *overall* naturalization rate of all immigrants hides the more recent trend towards declines in naturalization.

Political under-representation: Visible minorities and women continue to be under-represented in our federal and provincial political representatives, with the number of visible minority candidates relatively stable at 10 percent among all major parties since 2004. At the federal level, visible minorities represented 9.4 percent of all MPs elected in 2011 compared to the 15 percent of the total population who are visible minority Canadian citizens. Even the most diverse provinces, British Columbia and Ontario, have significant under-representation at both the federal and provincial levels. However, Canada has no anti-immigration party and all parties are competing for the ethnic vote. Visible minorities and women are also seriously under-represented in judicial appointments.

Public sector representation reasonably strong: Core public service employment of visible minorities is roughly in line with labour market availability (LMA) for the federal government (14.1 percent compared to 15.0 percent LMA). However, some federal departments and agencies (e.g., Canadian Forces, RCMP) have significant under-representation (less than 10 percent visible minorities). The larger provincial governments also have reasonable representation, with the exception of Quebec.

Implications and Reflections

Multiculturalism in Canada also includes personal reflections on some of the possible policy implications and ongoing issues related to these findings. The concluding chapter recommends areas where further attention is required, both in terms of improved research as well as policy options and actions. Areas that need to be addressed include the following:

Settlement patterns, enclaves and social media: Will current patterns of ethnic neighbourhoods and concentration of ethnic communities continue to increase or will immigrants and their children will disperse to other communities for economic or other reasons? Will media fragmentation and social media increase silos between communities?

Integration and accommodation balance: Will the dynamic between integration and accommodation continue in reasonable balance? What about the challenges posed by increased demands for religious accommodation?

Discrimination remains an issue: Will implicit bias and discrimination continue to impact the economic participation and outcomes of visible minorities? More broadly, what will be the impact on civic participation and social inclusion?

Radicalization and extremism: Will radicalization and extremism, both violent and non-violent, remain relatively manageable?

Dual loyalties, foreign policy and diaspora politics: Will Canadians continue to find a reasonable balance between diaspora politics and loyalty to Canada and countries of origin? Will governments be able to balance coherently the range of different interests among communities with broader Canadian interests?

Declining citizenship: Will "harder to get and easier to lose" citizenship continue to result in a decreasing naturalization rate and consequently a larger disenfranchised population that undermines the Canadian social fabric and our model of integration?

Political representation: Will Canadian political institutions and public services become more representative of the population they serve?

Multiculturalism focus: Will governments maintain a policy and program focus on longer-term multiculturalism-generational integration?

Public discourse: Will media and public debate on reasonable accommodation and communities remain respectful and inclusive, while allowing for open and frank discussion?

Chapter 1 — Introduction

Canada is known for its inclusive citizenship, immigration and multiculturalism policies that have been largely successful in integrating millions of new Canadians over the decades. These policies have reflected Canada's history, identity and values as they have evolved and continue to evolve.

But why yet another book on multiculturalism? Why a book focussed on data and statistics, rather than the rich examples of where multiculturalism is succeeding or failing? Why does it matter? After all, Canada is diverse and is generally portrayed as one of the most successful societies in "managing" diversity. Multiculturalism is largely accepted by Canadians, with most having adjusted to the impact of greater diversity.

Why "Getting it Right" Matters

It matters because Canada continues to become more diverse, with more aspects of diversity, such as religion, coming to the fore. It matters because the balance between integration — or "fitting in" — and accommodation — or society adapting to new and old requests for consideration — can only continue to grow, whether in the form of issues related to university mixed-gender coursework or the wearing of the niqab at citizenship ceremonies.

It matters because we are living with consequences of previous policy choices, ones that need to be re-examined from time to time to ensure their continued relevance and appropriateness. It matters given that future policy choices should be informed by as strong an evidence base as possible.

My general thesis starting out was that multiculturalism in Canada was working well, both in relation to other countries as well as within Canada itself, but that challenges remained particularly with respect to economic outcomes, political representation and public sector diversity for more recent visible minority immigrant communities.

Looking at ethnic origin, visible minority and religious minority views, separated out by gender and generation, and the respective relative outcomes, provides different views of how outcomes vary by group characteristics, both absolutely and in relative terms. Provincial breakdowns provide a further view to assess the relative success of communities between provinces.

The data reinforces this overall assessment, highlighting both areas where Canada is relatively strong and areas of concern: on the national, regional, and group levels, particularly when it comes to ensuring greater equality of opportunity.

Areas where the data suggests we need to focus include the following:

• Diversity is more varied and complex, with concentration in existing cities and dispersion to more centers, as well as the more varied challenges related to the balance between integration and accommodation;

- While educational outcomes are strong, poorer economic outcomes for visible minorities persist, including for second-generation immigrants. Some visible minority groups are doing relatively better than others;

- Provincial public services are reasonably representative (healthcare, education) although most visible minority groups are overly represented in support or more junior positions;

- Neighbourhoods are more mixed visible minority than one community being in a majority but, at the federal riding level, the number of ethnic enclaves continues to increase;

- A declining naturalization rate means the immigrant-to-citizen model is at risk;

- Under-representation among elected officials and judges remains; and,

- The federal public service is reasonably representative compared to the number of visible minority citizens, less so compared to the total visible minority population. Provincial and municipal governments are less representative even in the more diverse and larger provinces.

In identifying these and other issues in some depth, this book highlights areas where further policy work and research is required.

My bias is towards more flexible and inclusive approaches over more defined approaches that stress social cohesion, which the data largely supports and which generally has served Canada well. Others may have different views but I have tried to select data to provide a neutral evidence base that readers can interpret as they see fit.

Much of the book aims to provide an evidence-based backdrop to public debates over citizenship, immigration and multiculturalism, and the regular discussions regarding the balance between integration and accommodation.

Public debate is necessary and good, and is part of the process of generating national (and regional) consensus. While there will and should be ongoing debate over whether some accommodation requests go too far in the accommodation direction, neglecting integration, how Canada handles these requests and related debates matters. Treating individual requests with respect and understanding, rather than dismissal, matters (but does not mean accepting each and every request). Similarly, engaging in public debate with respect and understanding, rather than a lack of openness to listen to (if not to accepting) different perspectives matters. In the end, it is how successfully we as Canadians live and relate together, with all the richness and challenges that diversity brings.

> **Multiculturalism and Pluralism**
>
> Multiculturalism: Recognition of diversity and focus on equal participation.
>
> Pluralism: Mutual respect and civic inclusion. Peace, prosperity and security accessible to all.
>
> *Both take deep forms (e.g., separate education, health, political institutions) and shallow forms (e.g., common public education)*

Making sure that the vast majority of Canadians, whatever their origin and background, feel included in Canadian society and fully able to participate economically, socially and politically: this matters. It is a necessary, if not sufficient condition, for a well-functioning society. One only needs to look at the European failure to integrate minority communities to appreciate the risk.

Given continued immigration and the increasing diversity that results, this snapshot of Canada's performance in 2011 should help inform discussion and debate about the effectiveness of current and future policies. While Canada continues to compare well to other countries, this book highlights areas where the traditional Canadian model of immigration leading to citizenship is at risk, with a view to prompting discussion on whether or not the current suite of policy instruments and programs is adequate to address the challenge of ensuring as full and equitable participation in Canadian society as possible.

The Uniqueness of Canada

Unique among immigration-based countries, Canada is made up of a mix of Aboriginal Peoples, the two founding nations (French and British), and successive waves of other peoples.[1] This history has allowed Canada to develop more of a culture of accommodation and acceptance of diversity from its inception. The development of universal and national human rights frameworks and legislation further strengthened this trend, as did the growing civic participation of established and newer immigrant populations, making Canadian political parties responsive to and reflective of increased diversity.[2]

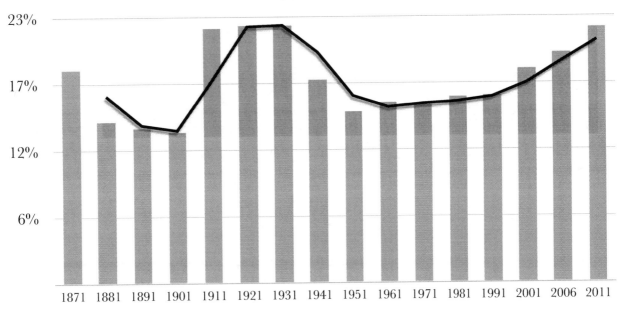

As an immigration-based country, Canada has always had high levels of foreign-born residents as the chart above shows.

While these successive waves of immigration and integration have been by and large successful, each new community has struggled with acceptance by those already in Canada.

This is nothing new. Black Loyalists fleeing the American Revolution, Irish fleeing the potato famine, Eastern Europeans coming to settle Western Canada, and restrictions on early waves of Chinese, Indian and Jewish immigration are part of Canadian history. Wartime internment of Ukrainian, Japanese, Italian and German Canadians is equally an instance of the historic tensions that came with immigration.

---

[1] See Ralston Saul, in his books *The Comeback* and *A Fair Country: Telling Truths about Canada,* for his insights into the Aboriginal contribution to Canadian history.

[2] Andrew Griffith, *Policy Arrogance or Innocent Bias: Resetting Citizenship and Multiculturalism* 5.

But Canada has largely managed to surmount these tensions and create a remarkably successful diverse society, without the major tensions present in other countries.

While the culture of accommodation that emerged from the interaction and interdependence among Aboriginal, French and English inhabitants was far from perfect, it is largely unique in relation to other countries, which had a stronger national monoculture and thus were not forced to find ways of living together and compromising. Our initial diversity among these three founding groups, while challenging and unevenly balanced, meant that early Canadian history involved accommodation and compromise, setting the stage for the increased diversity of subsequent waves of immigration. This set the template for how Canada would, over time, develop policies, laws and ways of being that would value diversity, not just tolerate it.

Immigration, integration and citizenship policies reflect this unique Canadian experience. Canada has always been an immigration-based country, with an expectation that people settle here permanently and become citizens, with a less fixed and more fluid sense of identity given Canada's intrinsic diversity. As a result, Canada has been relatively accepting and accommodating of the complex and diverse identities that people have.

As the graphic below shows, while there is a certain 'linear nature' to the immigration journey — one comes to Canada, one benefits from language training and other integration programs, one becomes a citizen — these steps, and the expectation of becoming a citizen, reflect the underlying view of Canada as a multicultural society, anchored by Canada's history, identity and values.

The Immigration, Integration, Citizenship and Multiculturalism Continuum

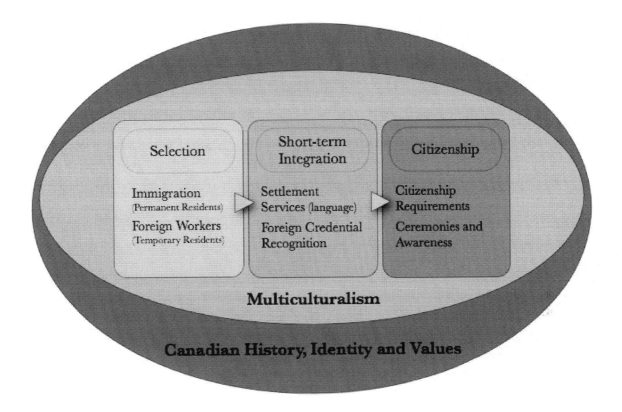

While the first hundred years of Canada (1867-1965) can best be described as having a "white only" immigration policy, with the restrictions on non-whites mentioned earlier, this started to change in the 1960s as Canada opened its doors to the world, in response to a relative decline in European immigrants (due, in part, to Europe's increasing prosperity). The diversity Canada has today — some 250 different ethnic origins — reflects this openness, with European immigrants only accounting for approximately 16 percent of total immigrants over the past 25 years.

As is normal in all countries, Canada's history, identity and values are not immutable but develop and evolve with time. These three fundamentals have informed the theoretical framework behind multiculturalism.

An Evidence-Based Approach

I have chosen a statistics — and data-heavy — approach to help inform the more anecdotal examples and cases on where multiculturalism is succeeding and where it faces challenges.

I have used the latest evidence and data is used in my assessment, drawing from the 2011 National Household Survey and other pertinent data sources, such as operational statistics from Citizenship and Immigration Canada (CIC), employment equity reports from the Public Service Commission (PSC), Treasury Board Secretariat (TBS) and Labour Canada, and hate crimes reporting from Canadian police forces.

Combining these various information sources, this book provides a comprehensive portrait of how the diverse groups that make up Canada, how well they are doing in terms of economic and social outcomes, and how effective is their participation in Canadian political processes. Others may have chosen a different mix of statistics and indicators to capture the various aspects of multiculturalism in Canada than used in this book. Appendix C outlines the methodology used and the rationale for the choices made.

These data sets are the best available and, given my focus on the national, provincial and large municipality levels, are more than adequate for my purposes (most concerns regarding the NHS pertain to the census tract and small municipality level). However, given that comparing the NHS with earlier Censuses is problematic from a data-integrity point of view, I simply present the most current snapshot possible, with limited use of historic data. Appendix C provides details on the methodology I have used and the assumptions I have made.

I make extensive use of charts and tables to demonstrate how well Canada is doing in its integrative multiculturalism, and to highlight some of the historic and ongoing issues. I use a mix of visible minority, ethnic origin and religious views to contrast and compare how different communities are doing. The term "non-visible minorities" or "Not VisMin" is used to cover the Statistics Canada term "not a visible minority" for readability reasons.[3] Aboriginal people, although part of the "non-visible minorities" category, are included separately in some charts for comparison purposes. At the same time, I try to identify and focus on the key indicators that best capture how multiculturalism and integration are working.

Most visible minority focussed charts include both non-visible minorities (labelled as Not VisMin) and Aboriginal Peoples (labelled as Aboriginal) for comparison purposes. These are placed as the last two categories for consistency and readability purposes.

I link throughout, where appropriate, to citizenship and immigration data and issues, given the close connections between immigrant selection, short-term integration and citizenship acquisition, and the longer-term, multi-generational integration objective of multiculturalism.

---

[3] Statistics Canada definition: "Includes respondents who reported 'Yes' to the Aboriginal identity question (Question 18) as well as respondents who were not considered to be members of a visible minority group."

To my knowledge, an integrated approach to multiculturalism and related indicators has not recently been undertaken, and it provides a more accurate assessment of how well Canadian citizenship, immigration and multiculturalism policies are working in practice.

The evidence I have, while not perfect, provides a reasonable basis for assessing the many commentaries, media stories and anecdotes regarding the success (or failure) of multiculturalism.

One of our fundamental premises is that a measure of success or failure is the degree to which outcomes are comparable across ethnic groups. Persistent gaps in unemployment rates, median income and low-income prevalence, particularly if these continue over generations, signal integration issues. Does our education system provide equal opportunities for success? To what extent does our political system (both in terms of elected representatives and the public service) reflect the demographics of the general population? In other words, can the "life chances" of minority groups be delinked from their ethnic, racial, religious backgrounds?

While it is utopian to aim for perfectly equivalent outcomes for all ethnic communities — the same chance of being in prison as being a Member of Parliament — considering this data nevertheless provides a measure of how open, welcoming, and inclusive a society we live in.

As noted above, our base assumption is that overall Canada has been remarkably successful in its "multicultural experiment" but that we need to avoid complacency in light of ongoing economic and social challenges.

This 'snapshot' looks at multiculturalism from a variety of aspects:

- Economic: How well are communities doing with respect to employment and income? How do economic outcomes compare by generation? By gender?

- Social: How well are new Canadians doing in terms of education levels and outcomes? Are ethnic enclaves or concentration becoming a more significant issue or are they part of the normal historic patterns of immigrants and their descendants? What is the impact of community-based and internet-based social networks on integration?

- Political: What is the medium-term impact of a declining citizenship naturalization rate? How well do Canadian political institutions reflect Canada's increased diversity? What about the public service, both in the narrow core government administration as well as the broader public sector (for example, education and healthcare)?

Outline of the Book

In order to frame this analysis, *Chapter 2 — Theory, Policy and Practice* provides a summary of the evolution of multiculturalism and how the policy developed, capturing some of the major — and ongoing — debates. A brief comparison of multiculturalism and diversity policies in other countries helps capture both the uniqueness of the Canadian variant as well as some of its similarities with other approaches. The chapter concludes with a summary of some of the key issues facing Canada from a multiculturalism and integration perspective.

Chapter 3 — Canada: A National Perspective examines the demographics and economic, social and political outcomes at the national level. It provides a number of different views that allow regional comparisons, as well as visible minority, ethnic origin and religion views, to help understand the strengths and weaknesses of multiculturalism. Considerable emphasis is placed on both political representation and public service representation given the importance these have in creating and sustaining belonging. This chapter is the core of the book and is the most detailed.

Subsequent chapters provide lighter regional views, including diversity within our largest cities. The regional views focus more on visible minority comparisons with non-visible minorities and, where appropriate, Aboriginal Peoples to highlight areas of relative success and particular challenges.

Chapter 4 — British Columbia: Or Should it be Asian Columbia? assesses how well the various Asian (and other origin) communities are doing, including breaking down the various communities of the lower mainland. *Chapter 5 — Alberta: The New Face of Diversity* notes how economic growth has resulted in Alberta becoming the third-most-diverse province. *Chapter 6 — Saskatchewan: Steady Growth* and *Chapter 7 — Manitoba: Quiet Success* each cover regions characterized by large aboriginal populations, but which stand in contrast to each other given Saskatchewan's stronger economic growth and Manitoba's greater historic and current diversity.

Chapter 8 — Ontario: Multiculturalism at Work discusses Canada's most diverse province and the increased challenges facing many of the urbanized poor visible minorities, particularly in the Greater Toronto Area and some of the other larger cities. *Chapter 9 — Quebec: Impact of a Complex Identity* outlines how relative economic stagnation along with persistent and polarizing identity debates have hampered integration, reflecting in part the contrast between relatively diverse Montreal and other regions of Quebec.

Chapter 10 — Atlantic Canada: Immigrants Wanted but Will They Come and Stay? contrasts the different Atlantic provinces, noting that that only Nova Scotia has significant immigration and diversity, partly due to its historic Black community. *Chapter 11 — The North: Aboriginal Nations and New Canadians* briefly looks at how issues related to Aboriginal Peoples make those related to visible minorities relatively inconsequential.

Lastly, *Chapter 12 — Policy Reflections and Implications* attempts to provide an overall assessment of how Canadian multiculturalism is working, and what the evidence suggests as possible implications of and policy responses to issues facing Canadian multiculturalism as Canada approaches its 150th anniversary in 2017.

An extensive set of appendices provides further background and data for reference purposes.

Chapter 2 — Theory, Policy and Practice

Canada was the first country to develop multiculturalism policies, a step that reflected its unique condition as a locus of both historical diversity (Aboriginal, French, British, and other European populations) and new diversity (as immigrants began arriving from around the world). It is also no surprise that Canada has some of the world's leading theorists on multiculturalism, with an active, ongoing academic and popular debate over multiculturalism in theory and in practice.

This chapter provides the theoretical and policy framework of multiculturalism that underpins the analysis of what the data and statistics show. It starts off with a discussion of the theory of multiculturalism, drawing heavily on Canadian academics and commentators. This leads to a discussion of the history and developments of the constitutional and legal framework underlying Canadian multicultural policies. The next section outlines how multiculturalism policy and programs have evolved within the overall context of encouraging integration.

The chapter then discusses the counter-narrative against multiculturalism that developed in the 1990s and related debates that continue to this day. Brief comparisons with diversity policies and approaches in Australia, the United States, the United Kingdom, France, Germany and the Netherlands follow. Canadian public attitudes towards immigration, citizenship and multiculturalism are then explored, highlighting the uniqueness of Canadian general public support. The Conservative government's multiculturalism policy and program review emphasizing integration is reviewed, underlining how the changes in many ways return to some of the roots of multiculturalism.

The chapter concludes by highlighting a number of current and ongoing policy issues around the Canadian model of citizenship, immigration and multiculturalism that will be further explored in chapter 12.

CANADA'S MODEL OF MULTICULTURAL CITIZENSHIP

Charles Taylor and Will Kymlicka gave the theory of multicultural citizenship depth and texture. Gérard Bouchard, in his work on defining *interculturalisme*, refined the general Canadian approach for the Quebec context.

Culture by definition is a carrier of many elements, such as ethnicity, language, religion, arts, cuisine, leisure and sports. While multiculturalism as originally envisaged in Canada primarily took the form of ethnocultural diversity among different European ethnic origins and variants of Christianity, the framework was broad enough for the increased ethnic and religious diversity that followed the removal of remaining race-based immigration restrictions. Invariably, multiculturalism provoked discussion and debate around issues of identity and belonging, and what it means to be Canadian.

The work of Taylor and Kymlicka helped address these issues.

First was the issue of minority rights of groups and not just of individuals. In 1992, Taylor argued that societies, such as Canada, have become increasingly multicultural and more open to migration. This has led to a situation where some cultures in Canada imposed themselves on others (with the assumed superiority of a hegemonic culture) placing minority cultures in danger of vanishing within the mainstream. He adds that the recognition or non-recognition of minority cultures has influenced identity formation; non-recognition has caused damage and pain and has oppressed people (e.g., African Americans and women in history). Recognition became a basic human need.

Recognition has two aspects: first, the degree to which society accepts that every individual is *original;* and secondly, as an ethical ideal for everyone to be true to his or her identity and culture.

These principles of originality are not only for individuals but also for groups of people as carriers of culture.[4] But recognition should be limited to a combination of shareable rights and cultural traditions, since the state cannot be made responsible for enforcing equal recognition of private group interests:

> "...it (the politics of difference) asks that we give acknowledgement and status to something that is not universally shared. Or, otherwise put, we give due acknowledgement only to what is universally present – everyone has an identity – through recognizing what is peculiar to each. The universal demand powers an acknowledgement of specificity"[5]

But culture is also about groups not just individuals, and many have rejected group rights within the state[4]. Can a constitutional democracy based on individual rights and freedoms also recognize group rights? Would this not risk what the French call *communautarisme,* creating a cleavage between individual *and* universal rights vs. the collective goals of the state? Were equality

---

[4] Charles Taylor et al, *Multiculturalism: Examining the Politics of Recognition* 36.

[5] Ibid. 39.

rights compatible with the recognition of difference and the granting of 'special' rights or restrictions to accommodate difference?

The debate involved people from Canada and Europe. For example, Jurgen Habermas asked:

> "Should citizens' identities as members of ethnic, cultural, or religious groups publicly matter? And if so, how can collective identities make a difference within the frame of a constitutional democracy? Are collective identities and cultural memberships politically relevant, and if so, how can they legitimately affect the distribution of rights and the recognition of legal claims?" [6]

For Habermas, religion and ethnic identities were private matters and had no place in the public sphere. He argued that it is harmful to bring forward group rights in a constitutional democracy based on individual rights and responsibilities; the state cannot allocate claims when religious or ethnic identities are forced upon the public sphere. Habermas criticized attempts in Western democracies to revive ethnic nationalist dogmas — whose disastrous outcome is a painful matter of historical record. They must be combated by constitutional or civic citizenship that respects democratic principles and evaluated in light of universal normative precepts embodied in the constitution itself:[7]

> "Laws are legitimate only if they are in tune with the opinions, values, and norms generated discursively in civil society... Legitimate laws must be consistent with moral, ethical, and pragmatic considerations and serve the good of the legal community"[8]

Will Kymlicka advanced the debate by arguing that the Canadian brand of *multicultural citizenship* recognizes minority rights without unreasonable complexity. Kymlicka notes that for years the central critique of multiculturalism and minority rights theory was based on the argument that justice required state institutions to be "colour-blind." As a result, the onus remained firmly on proponents of minority rights "to show that deviations from difference-blind rules that are adopted in order to accommodate ethnocultural differences are not inherently unjust".[9]

But this onus shifted after the year 2000 as Western democracies came to recognize, at least in theory if not always in practice, the legitimacy of minority group rights and policies with respect

---

[6] Jurgen Habermas, "Struggles for Recognition in Constitutional States," *International European Journal of Philosophy*, No. 128, 1993.

[7] Habermas, particularly his essays "Apologetic tendencies" and "Historical Consciousness and Post-Traditional identity: Orientation Towards the West in West Germany," *The New Conservatism: Cultural Criticism and the Historians' Debate.*

[8] James Gordon Finlayson, *Habermas: A Very Short Introduction* 141-142.

[9] Will Kymlicka, "The New Debate on Minority Rights," *Multiculturalism and Political Theory* 42.

to both ethnic communities and Aboriginal Peoples. This marked the beginning of a more multicultural approach, with national minorities in some countries gaining various degrees of self-governance.

The "burden of proof" became much more balanced, with defenders of so-called colour-blind institutions now having to demonstrate that maintaining such institutional arrangements would not lead to injustices for minority groups.

This balance has, in turn, forced critics of multiculturalism and minority rights to search for a new basis for their critique. Kymlicka claims the standard depiction of the so-called "normal" state has shifted away from the centralized and homogenous model of the past, toward a multicultural ideal.[10]

Throughout much of the 20th century, Kymlicka writes, the most influential example of a *normal* state was France — i.e. a highly centralized state with an undifferentiated conception of republican citizenship and single official language. France had no room for, or recognition of, minority rights.

But this has changed dramatically since the 1990s. The best example was the European Union's decision to make respect for minority rights one of the assessment criteria for would-be member countries.

Kymlicka sees in this shift a moral redefinition of the modern state ideal wherein denying the existence of minorities or treating them as politically inconsequential is seen as evidence that one is not yet ready to become a member in good standing of the club of democracies. He then lists three key features that mark the shift away from the older ethnic citizenship to multicultural citizenship. These three features are:

1. The repudiation of the idea of the state as belonging to a dominant group.

2. The replacement of assimilationist and exclusionary nation-building policies with policies of recognition and accommodation.

3. The acknowledgement of historic injustices and offering amends for them. Canada was indeed moving forward as an example to the world of a successful democracy that respects all its citizens.

If Taylor and Kymlicka are largely the parents of the theory of multicultural citizenship, Gérard Bouchard is the main theorist who has articulated the Quebec version of multiculturalism, *interculturalisme*. In essence, he rebalances the emphasis on recognition of minorities in countries or regions when the majority itself is a minority, what he calls dual societies:

> In dual societies, therefore (or more precisely: in societies where ethnoculturality is addressed through the lens of a duality), a balance must

---

[10] Drawn from Will Kymlicka, *Multicultural Odysseys: Navigating the New International Politics of Diversity.*

be struck between the perpetuation and development of majority cultures, taking into account their ongoing history and founding myths, and the integration of minorities, taking into account their rights. The main challenge is to arbitrate between majorities and minorities in a spirit of conciliation, interaction and negotiation that respects ethnocultural diversity, while providing for the continuing cultural identity of founding groups and their heritage. Respect for the fundamental values of host societies and the emergence of shared cultural expressions and practices, as part of the process of integration, also are at the heart of interculturalism. [11]

But the difference is one of nuance and emphasis. Canadian multiculturalism, and Quebec *interculturalisme*, are both exist in the context of a history that is itself the product of dominant groups. Minorities integrate within that context. After all, the Constitution and Charter include historic collective rights for Aboriginal people (which continue to be elaborated by the Courts) and the founding French and English groups (in the form of language rights).

> Let them look to the past, but let them also look to the future; let them look to the land of their ancestors, but let them look also to the land of their children.
>
> *Wilfred Laurier*
> *September 2, 1905, Toronto Globe*

Underlying multiculturalism (and *interculturalisme*) is integration and acculturation, which is an ongoing process of compromise and negotiation at both the individual and societal levels. John Berry's work is but one example of this process:

> This vision of how to live in plural societies incorporates two basic social processes. The first is the acceptance of the value of cultural diversity for a society by all constituent cultural communities. Such diversity is to be seen as a resource, to be prized and nurtured. The second is the promotion of equitable participation by all groups in the larger society. All groups have the right to access all aspects of the larger society, including culturally appropriate education, work, health care, and justice. These two components are the basis of the Canadian multicultural policy....
>
> In order to accomplish these two goals, multiculturalism involves social change to meet the needs of all the groups living together in the plural society. All groups should be prepared to constantly reassess their ways of living together, and to engage in compromise. That is, attaining the multicultural vision requires mutual accommodation, rather than change on the part of only one of the groups. This accommodation requires that the institutions of the dominant group/larger society should evolve, so that

---

[11] Gérard Bouchard, <u>Steering Paper, International Symposium on Interculturalism</u>. This has subsequently been expanded into a book, *Interculturalism: A View from Quebec*.

the needs of all (dominant and non-dominant) groups can be met. It also requires that the non-dominant groups adopt the basic (but evolving) values of the larger society, and adapt to the existing (but evolving) social institutions and structures.[12]

While maddening to some who prefer a more Cartesian, fixed approach to this never-ending process of negotiation and compromise, with its perceived cultural relativism and "anything goes" approach, a deeper look at multiculturalism as implemented in policy and program terms reinforces the deep anchoring of multiculturalism within the overall Canadian constitutional, legal and cultural framework.

---

[12] John Berry, "Integration and Multiculturalism: Ways towards Social Solidarity," *Papers on Social Representations* 2.1-2.21.

INTEGRATION, NOT ASSIMILATION — CONSTITUTIONAL AND LEGISLATIVE FRAMEWORK

From a constitutional perspective, immigration is a shared jurisdiction with the provinces, as is multiculturalism; whereas citizenship (in the narrow sense of *granting* citizenship) is exclusively federal.

While Canadian immigration policy has a history as long as Canada itself, citizenship policy emerged post-World War II with the Citizenship Act of 1947. Multiculturalism, in contrast, is relatively recent, with the original policy dating from 1971.

The relationship between all three policy and program areas is close. Immigration was originally for permanent settlement and, since the original Citizenship Act of 1947, the focus has been on encouraging immigrants to take up citizenship. Until the 2014 changes, the emphasis was on facilitation, making it easy to become Canadian, viewing citizenship more as a 'way-station' to integration rather than being an end-point. No distinction was made between those born in Canada and those naturalized until the 2014 change allowing for revocation in the case of terror or treason.

Multiculturalism policy was a way to recognize the ever-increasing diversity of Canadians, their contribution to the building of Canada, and to facilitate their integration and participation in Canadian society.

> Freedom includes the right to say what others may object to and resent... The essence of citizenship is to be tolerant of strong and provocative words.
>
> *John Diefenbaker*
> *April 9, 1970, House of Commons*

The 1969 *Report of the Royal Commission on Bilingualism and Biculturalism* (the Laurendeau-Dunton or B&B Commission) provided the original policy framework and objectives for multiculturalism, or recognizing 'the cultural contribution of the other ethnic groups." In essence, the Commission was responding to the increased diversity of Canadians of European origins, beyond the traditional French and British ethnic origins. Visible and religious minorities represented some two percent of the population, and thus multiculturalism policy and ideas were largely being applied to European, white and Christian communities. This does not diminish the importance of recognizing diversity within those groups, but this embryonic multiculturalism operated in a society much more homogenous than our present one.[13]

---

[13] For example, differences among Christian sects (e.g., Catholics, Baptists, Anglicans, etc.), as well as among European ethnic origins (e.g., English, Scottish, Irish, French, Polish, etc.), were important and figured prominently in earlier manifestations of multiculturalism in Canada. Today, those differences are less prominent given that visible minorities form close to 20 percent of the population, resulting in more use of the general categorizations of "European" and "Christian."

Ukrainian Canadians were among the strongest proponents of this recognition, viewing their contribution to the settling of the West as equivalent, in nation-building terms, to that of the French in Quebec or the English in Ontario.[14]

The *Report* made a conscious and deliberate decision to contrast assimilation — the "melting pot" approach — with integration. Integration meant recognizing cultural diversity, language and histories, rather than denying these aspects of identity. The *Report* acknowledges that the vast majority of ethnic groups prefer integration, preserving their original culture and language, to assimilation and losing this important aspect of their identity:

> 8. Integration, in the broad sense, does not imply the loss of an individual's identity and original characteristics or of his original language and culture. Man is a thinking and sensitive being ; severing him from his roots could destroy an aspect of his personality and deprive society of some of the values he can bring to it. Integration is not synonymous with assimilation. Assimilation implies almost total absorption into another linguistic and cultural group. An assimilated individual gives up his cultural identity, and may even go as far as to change his name. Both integration and assimilation occur in Canada, and the individual must be free to choose whichever process suits him, but it seems to us that those of other than French or British origin clearly prefer integration.[15]

The report continues with a sophisticated discussion of the process of acculturation:

> 11. The process of integration goes hand in hand with what anthropologists call "acculturation." Anyone who chooses Canada as his adopted country adopts a new style of life, a particular kind of existence. This phenomenon is easily visible in the immigrant's experience in the work world, in his social contacts with other people, in the schools, where children acquire a major part of their preparation for life, and in all his contact with other citizens and public institutions. In office and factory, train and plane, in court and Parliament, the process of acculturation can be seen, despite the obstacles facing an individual as he becomes acquainted with his new environment, in which he is exposed to so many influences. Acculturation is the process of adaptation to the environment in which an individual is compelled to live as he adjusts his behaviour to that of the community.

---

[14] Manoly Lupul, *The Politics of Multiculturalism: A Ukrainian Canadian Memoir* and Daniel Westlake, "Building Multiculturalism: The Contribution of the Ukrainian Canadian Community to a Re-Thinking of Canadian Identity," outline the Ukrainian Canadian contribution to multiculturalism.

[15] Royal Commission on Bilingualism and Biculturalism Volume IV, *The Cultural Contribution of the Other Ethnic Groups* 5.

12. Acculturation is inevitable in a multi-ethnic country like Canada, and the two main societies themselves are open to its influence. The integration of immigrants into the life of the country, with the help of its institutions, is surely the road to their self-fulfilment. But in adopting fully the Canadian way of life, sharing its advantages and disadvantages, those whose origin is neither French nor British do not have to cast off or hide their own culture. It may happen that in their determination to express their desire to live fully in this mode, their culture may conflict with the customs of their adopted society. But Canadian society, open and modern, should be able to integrate heterogeneous elements into a harmonious system, to achieve "unity in diversity."[16]

The original multiculturalism policy statement of 1971 built upon the B&B Commission's work. Recognition of cultural and linguistic heritage was to increase the sense of belonging to Canada and their integration into Canadian society without requiring people to give up their historic, and intrinsic, sense of who they were. The precise objectives of the policy were:

- To assist cultural groups to retain and foster their identity;

- To assist cultural groups to overcome barriers to their full participation in Canadian society. (Thus the multiculturalism policy advocated the full involvement and equal participation of ethnic minorities in mainstream institutions, without denying them the right to identify with select elements of their cultural past if they so chose.);

- To promote creative exchanges among all Canadian cultural groups;

- To assist immigrants in acquiring at least one of the official languages.[17]

The 1988 *Canadian Multiculturalism Act* essentially codified the 1971 policy statement, recognizing the changing demographics and increased diversity of Canada.

The *Act* is clearly situated in the overall constitutional and legal framework of Canada. Its preamble cites the *Constitution of Canada*, the *Canadian Charter of Rights and Freedoms*, the *Official Languages Act*, the *Citizenship Act* and the *Canadian Human Rights Act*, the *International Convention on the Elimination of All Forms of Racial Discrimination*, and the *International Convention on Civil and Political Rights*.

---

[16] Ibid. 7.

[17] Marc Leman, "Canadian Multiculturalism," provides a good outline and overview of the policy.

Moreover, the *Act* is within the broader international human rights framework and is signatory to six United Nations conventions pertaining to human rights and diversity[18]. The increasing complexity of economic and social issues, along with the persistence of racism and discrimination in old and new forms, is reflected in the web of Canadian and international laws and conventions.

The Preamble of the *Act* states that:

> "the Government of Canada recognizes the diversity of Canadians and regards race, national or ethnic origin, colour and religion as a fundamental characteristic of Canadian society and is committed to a policy of multiculturalism designed to preserve and enhance the multicultural heritage of Canadians while working to achieve equality of all Canadians in the economic, social, cultural and political life of Canada."[19]

> **Key provisions of the *Multiculturalism Act***
> - Recognize and promote diversity
> - Fundamental characteristic of Canada
> - Full and equitable participation
> - Recognize contribution to Canada
> - Equal treatment and protection
> - Respectful and inclusive institutions
> - Promote interaction
> - Foster recognition and appreciation
> - Preserve and enhance other languages in harmony with official languages
> - Responsive federal institutions

The *Act* thus emphasizes both the recognition of diversity and the achievement of equality as its fundamental objectives. And while the *Policy* and the *Act* were largely conceived in an era when religious diversity was relatively small, and accommodation issues less prevalent, the principles of recognition and equality applies to both religious and non-religious diversity.

The *Act* clearly states that multiculturalism also takes place within the context of aboriginal and official language rights, and that all Canadians, "whether by birth or choice, enjoy equal status, are entitled to the same rights, powers and privileges and are subject to the same obligations, duties and liabilities."[20] In other words, the universality of rights was maintained; accommodation was not derogation from fundamental rights.

---

[18] *The International Convention on the Elimination of All Forms of Racial Discrimination, the International Covenant on Economic, Social and Cultural Rights, the Convention on the Elimination of All Forms of Discrimination against Women, the Convention against Torture and Other Cruel, Inhuman or Degrading Treatment or Punishment, the Convention on the Rights of the Child.* In addition to these established conventions, the U.N. is developing a Disability Convention.

[19] Canadian Multiculturalism Act - Lois du Canada - Justice. Web.

[20] Ibid. It is noteworthy that the 2014 changes to the *Citizenship Act* mark a fundamental change, one that will likely be challenged in the courts.

But the *Act* is more 'aspirational' and enabling rather than operational in setting out its vision for Canadian multiculturalism. The only one firm requirement of the *Act* is for the Minister to table an *Annual Report on the Operation of the Canadian Multiculturalism Act*. Otherwise, the *Act* enables the Minister to undertake a range of activities in support of the objectives and provisions of the *Act*.

Integration Always Central to Multiculturalism

Successive governments have emphasized different aspects of the *Policy* and *Act*, reflecting the ongoing evolution of Canadian diversity and society. Since 1971, policy has evolved from ethnicity-focused "celebrating our difference" in the 1970s, to "managing diversity" in the 1980s, "constructive engagement" in the 1990s, "inclusive citizenship and integration" at the turn of the millennium, to the current emphasis on "social cohesion."

TABLE 1: MULTICULTURALISM POLICY CHANGES - 1970S TO PRESENT					
	Ethnicity Multi (1970s)	**Equity Multi (1980s)**	**Civic Multi (1990s)**	**Integrative Multi (2000s)**	**Social Cohesion (present)**
Focus	Celebrating differences	Managing diversity	Constructive engagement	Inclusive citizenship	Social cohesion
Reference Point	Culture	Structure	Society building	Canadian identity	Canadian values
Mandate	Ethnicity	Race relations	Citizenship	Integration	Cohesion
Magnitude	Individual adjustment	Accommodation	Participation	Rights and responsibilities	Responsibilities and rights
Problem Source	Prejudice	Systemic discrimination	Exclusion	Unequal access, "clash" of cultures	Faith and culture clashes
Solution	Cultural sensitivity	Employment equity	Inclusiveness	Dialogue/ mutual understanding	Shared values
Key Metaphor	"Mosaic"	"Level playing field"	"Belonging"	"Harmony/ jazz"	"Conforming"

The above table highlights these changes over the past five decades.[21] Following the events of 9/11, attention shifted towards integration and cohesion around Canadian identity and values as a way to reduce faith and culture clashes. The Conservative government further shifted multiculturalism towards integration, stressing responsibilities over rights, shifting from mutual understanding to a more explicit articulation of shared values. The metaphor shifted from the improvisational, "harmony/jazz" approach to a greater expectation of conformity.

---

[21] Adapted from A. Fleras and Jean Kunz, *Media and Minorities: Representing Diversity in a Multicultural Canada.*

Moreover, following the *Charter*, the Courts became more involved in resolving disputes over reasonable accommodation, and the balance between conflicting rights, with virtually all cases regarding requests to accommodate religious practices.[22]

However, Section 27, the multiculturalism provision of the *Charter* "consistent with the preservation and enhancement of the multicultural heritage of Canadians" was given only moderate weight and interpreted narrowly, being used only to ensure religious neutrality and the right to interpreters. Moreover, Section 27 was not used in some of the major cases on religious accommodation, nor was it used to justify positive entitlements for cultural communities, particularly funding for independent religious schools (unlike the historic rights of official language minorities):

> Overall, the multiculturalism jurisprudence, as well as its reception by governmental authorities, has tended to promote liberal pluralism with its emphasis on liberal neutrality, its refusal to see cultural diversity as a ground for entitlement and its plea for a tolerant society.[23]

Charter of Rights and Freedoms

2. Everyone has the following fundamental freedoms:

   (a) freedom of conscience and religion;

   (b) freedom of thought, belief, opinion and expression, including freedom of the press and other media of communication;

   (c) freedom of peaceful assembly; and

   (d) freedom of association

15. (1) Every individual is equal before and under the law and has the right to the equal protection and equal benefit of the law without discrimination and, in particular, without discrimination based on race, national or ethnic origin, colour, religion, sex, age or mental or physical disability.

    (2) Subsection (1) does not preclude any law, program or activity that has as its object the amelioration of conditions of disadvantaged individuals or groups including those that are disadvantaged because of race, national or ethnic origin, colour, religion, sex, age or mental or physical disability.

27. This Charter shall be interpreted in a manner consistent with the preservation and enhancement of the multicultural heritage of Canadians.

With respect to religious freedom and reasonable accommodation, the general legal approach has been:

- religious freedom should be granted if reasonable (expansive interpretation);

---

[22] For a high-level summary of how accommodation issues are handled, see the Library of Parliament's *An Examination of the Duty to Accommodate in the Canadian Human Rights Context* and Sujit Choudhry's *Rights Adjudication in a Plurinational State: The Supreme Court of Canada, Freedom of Religion, and the Politics of Reasonable Accommodation*, the latter for a more detailed discussion of accommodation cases and the divide between Supreme Court and Quebec Court of Appeal jurisprudence.

[23] Emanuelle Richez, *The Impact of Constitutional Multiculturalism after Three Decades of Existence*.

- rejection of a hierarchy of rights in favour of a "balance ... that fully respects the importance of both sets of rights";
- differentiation between the freedom to believe and the freedom to act upon those religious beliefs, with the latter "inherently limited by the rights and freedoms of others";
- caution against the "tyranny of the majority," protecting unpopular or distasteful practices.[24]

This more *ad hoc* approach has been mirrored at the political level. The practice of multiculturalism thus varies across the country, reflecting the political balance within each province among the various communities. The original balance of powers between federal and provincial governments, and the flexibility it provides, is reflected in these different approaches to multiculturalism.

Some examples are revealing. British Columbia grants Sikh motorcyclists a waiver from the helmet requirement, Ontario does not. Some provinces, like Quebec, provide subsidies to private faith-based schools; Ontario's 2007 election campaign was largely decided on that issue, with voters soundly rejecting the Progressive Conservative party and its proposal that funding be extended to such schools. And of course, Quebec, for reasons discussed in Chapter 9, has its own variant of multiculturalism, *interculturalisme*, and tends to take a more prescriptive approach to reasonable accommodation issues compared to most other provinces.

But beyond the broad federal framework of the Act, related legislation (e.g., employment equity) and the *Charter*, the day-to-day living of multiculturalism happens in our cities and communities. Whether this be in the workforce, in our education and health systems, or policing and law enforcement, the success or failure of multiculturalism is measured by the day-to-day experience of the diverse ethnic communities of Canada.

---

[24] Derek J. Bell, "York University, Religious Accommodation, and the Absence of Bright Lines."

Separation, not Integration — The Counter-Narrative

As one would expect in any area of public policy, there is a rich body of criticism and debate on the Canadian approach to citizenship, immigration and multiculturalism. Depending on the times, and the issues of the day, the nature of these critiques have either been expressed in terms of broad concerns regarding identify and democracy or more narrow concerns over foreign policy or terrorism. This section gives a sampling of some of the more well-known and common critiques.

One of the more interesting critics, Neil Bissoondath, argues that multiculturalism diminishes individual identity in its emphasis on group identity, and "betrays" the individual in so doing:[25]

> My point is simple, but it is one usually ignored by multiculturalism and its purveyors – for to recognize the complexity of ethnicity, to acknowledge the wild variance within ethnic groups, would be to render itself and its aims absurd. The individuals who form a group, the "ethnics" who create a community, are frequently people of vastly varying composition. Shared ethnicity does not entail unanimity of vision. If the individual is not to be betrayed, a larger humanity must prevail over the narrowness of ethnicity.
>
> To preserve, enhance and promote the "multicultural heritage" of Canada, multiculturalism must work against forces more insistent than any government policy. If a larger humanity does not at first prevail, time and circumstance will inevitably ensure that it does.

Bissoondath, given his own rich and diverse heritage, understandably chafes at being pigeon-holed into a single ethnic origin, which he considers akin to 'ghetto-ization' at both the community and individual levels.

But more importantly, his focus on the diversity within communities, is a caution against oversimplifying identity and treating community leaders as representative of their communities, reminds Canadians of the importance of individual, not just group, rights and identities. However, Bissoondath fails to acknowledge that individuals retain the choice of whether they adapt a 'group' identity or not: whether to live within their community or the 'mainstream,' or, as many do, find their personal mix of ethnic and mainstream identities.

The multiculturalism in question exists in the context of a liberal democratic society that emphasizes individual rights. It does not force individuals to assume group identities, but allows some expression of these identities as part of a more flexible approach to encouraging their participation in and integration with broader society. Some will, of course, prefer not to integrate, whether for traditional or faith-based reasons. This is not new as many earlier waves of immigrants have had elements that prefer to maintain a separate identity (e.g., Mennonites, Hutterites).

---

[25] Neil Bissoondath, *Selling Illusions: The Cult of Multiculturalism in Canada* 98.

Like Bissoondath, Lawrence Hill rightly cautions us against the risks of reducing identity to ethnic origin or faith in his Massey Lectures on *Blood*. Hill notes that our origins, and our identities, are complex and varied, and should not be constrained:

> If we were not so wedded to the arcane notions of blood, we would be freer to celebrate our various, complex and divergent identities relating to family and notions of talent and ability, citizenship and race. We would be more whole, self-accepting people, and less judgmental of others. In this day and age, who among us is not all mixed up? [26]

Philip Resnick, in his reflections on what makes Canada different from the United States, highlights the culture of accommodation that resulted from dual English and French identities and communities:

> For Canadians, because of the European-derived dualism built into their country from its foundations, have never known a seamless version of national unity. There has been lots of backsliding resistance to accommodation at various moments in Canadian history. Battles over recognition have not been lacking, nor are they likely to disappear in the future. But increasingly, both English Canada and Quebec have become more open and tolerant societies, where the markers of national identity are less weighed down by ethnic or racial stereotypes, or there is more opening to the linguistic and cultural "other."[27]

But Resnick reminds us that Canada's historical origins were and remain significant to the kind of country we have become:

> Canada is not a blank slate to be reinvented with each new immigrant or group of immigrants that arrives at our airports. Its underlying political and social values are ultimately European-derived ones: peace, order, and good government, constituted authority, political community, individual liberty, and citizenship equality.[28]

Multiculturalism "represents enormous progress," redefining "the national 'we' in a more universalistic way, rejecting ethnic origin, race, colour, or religion as criteria for inclusion."[29] However, while recognizing this, Resnick legitimately cautions:

---

[26] Hill, *Blood* 214.

[27] Philip Resnick, *The European Roots of Canadian Identity* 47.

[28] Ibid. 61.

[29] Ibid. 58.

31

> Nor should multiculturalism become a substitute for a sense of history and
> of the historical origins of modern-day Canada; for a sense of our
> multinational complexity (English-Canadian, Quebecois, aboriginal); for a
> civic consciousness in which ethnic, religious, or racial origins take second
> place to the things we share as Canadians; or for core political values.[30]

His emphasis on the historical origins of Canadian core political values, and his implicit recognition of how our values have changed to create a more inclusive society, are helpful to understanding present-day Canada. But beyond the high-level naming of Canadian (and liberal democratic) political and social values, he provides relatively little insight into how these should be translated into practice.

After all, just as Canada is not a blank slate, it is not a fixed slate. How Canada's underlying values continue to evolve, how Canada continues to balance integration and accommodation, what measures if any are needed to improve equality of opportunity, and the current focus on balancing individual liberty with security, are all challenges to the implementation of these high level values.

Salim Mansur, lacking the nuance of Resnick, focuses on his concern for Canada's political framework, democracy and culture, painting this in almost apocalyptic concerns regarding what he perceives as the erosion of freedom and liberal democracy through cultural relativism:

> … multiculturalism, in espousing acceptance of other cultures, irrespective
> of how such acceptance diminishes liberal democracy's unique set of
> values — most importantly the place of the individual citizen as a minority
> of one protected by the full panoply of the state's power based on the rule
> of law — has turned out to be an insidious assault on freedom in the
> West.[31]

He appears to be arguing that multiculturalism "trumps" the Constitution, the Charter, and the body of laws that anchor Canada as a liberal democracy, and that require requests for accommodation, religious or otherwise, to be balanced against other rights. He also, in contrast to Bissoondath, has a almost monochromatic view of identity, appearing to argue that civic identity and citizenship are incompatible with any expression of cultural or religious identities.

Mansur even goes so far as to argue that freedom and equality are almost intrinsically opposed: "[freedom's] quest has been regularly frustrated by the more immediate needs of equality in society." Historically, of course, this is inaccurate. Freeing slaves improved equality. Freeing women from traditional roles is improving gender equality.

It is hard to see how most demands for reasonable accommodation (e.g., wearing religious headgear, availability of *kosher* or *halal* food) reflect such an opposition. One person's enjoyment of the freedom to wear a *kippa*, turban or *hijab* does not impact the freedom of others not to do

---

[30] Ibid. 62.

[31] Salim Mansur, *Delectable Lie: A Liberal Repudiation of Multiculturalism* 138, 162 and 2 respectively.

so. Some requests for gender segregation are likewise innocuous (e.g., swimming classes) but others are not (e.g., not willing to be in mixed university classes).

And should the ideal of freedom include the freedom to discriminate? While one can debate the value of affirmative action and employment equity programs, these are efforts to increase equality of opportunity, and the freedom to participate fully in society.

In many ways, the critics just covered, and others, are overly influenced by the European context. Some, reflecting an almost colonial perspective, seem to delight in pronouncements from Europe that "multiculturalism is dead," whether from British Prime Minister David Cameron, German Chancellor Angela Merkel and former French President Nicholas Sarkozy, without acknowledging the distinct history and cultures that we have as a country based on immigration.[32]

Canada's immigration policies and context are equally distinct. Skilled rather than guest workers. A limited colonial past. A relatively impervious border. A clear — and relatively easy — path to citizenship. An expectation of participation. And, while Canada has both French and English variants of a dominant culture, we, apart from Aboriginal Peoples, are all immigrants, the main difference being how long ago we came here.

As a result, our dominant cultures are less dominant, less uni-dimensional, than in Europe. Moreover, European variants of multiculturalism have by and large taken deeper forms, with more separate public institutions (i.e., schools, political parties, etc.) than in Canada exacerbating integration barriers.

One can and should pay attention to European debates and approaches given that their integration challenges are warning signs, and reminders that we need to pay ongoing attention to social inclusion and cohesion to reduce the risks of replicating the Europe experience. And we should learn from Europe where appropriate (e.g., de-radicalization programs), just as Europe can learn from us (e.g., immigration selection). But we have to recognize that each country's approach will invariably reflect its particular situation, history and reality, and we need to focus on Canada's unique realities, which cannot be assimilated to the European ones.

Phil Ryan, in addition to noting this need to focus on Canada and the Canadian experience, characterizes many critics as suffering from what he labelled *multicultiphobia* in his book by the same name. Starting with what he considered the classical critiques of multiculturalism by Bissoondath, Bibby, Granatstein, and Gwyn[33] he systematically reviews their arguments and identifies these major fallacies:

---

[32] "State multiculturalism has failed, says David Cameron," BBC News, 11 February 2011.
"Angela Merkel: German multiculturalism has 'utterly failed'," *The Guardian*, 17 October 2010.
"Sarkozy joins multiculturalism attack," *Financial Times*, 10 February 2011.

[33] Bissoondath's *Selling Illusions*, Reginald Bibby's *Mosaic Madness: The Poverty and Potential of Life in Canada*, Richard Gwyn's *Nationalism without Walls: The Unbearable Lightness of Being Canadian*, and Jack Granatstein's *Who Killed Canadian History*.

- not understanding — or acknowledging — the multiculturalism policy framework and its relationship with the Constitutions and the full body of Canadian laws;

- a tendency to assume culture is monolithic;

- greater reliance on argumentation and anecdotes than on evidence; and,

- attributing responsibility for most ills of contemporary Canada to multiculturalism and cultural relativism.

For Ryan, the premise of these and similar critiques is that there is a "default Canadian" and that new Canadians are like "house guests," not full citizens. Moreover, critics assume and argue that multiculturalism inevitably divides society into hostile camps, impeding a common and shared civic identity and citizenship, without much more than anecdote to back these assertions up. For some critics, multiculturalism should have little or no place in the public sphere and be relegated only to the home or private sphere, rather than recognizing that many expressions of identity do and can exist in the framework of Canadian civic identity.

Ryan, along with Kymlicka, provides specific evidence that multiculturalism policies have been effective and contributed to integration. Examples include studies that show that multiculturalism strengthens mutual identification between native-born citizens and immigrants, provides an "integration orientation" combining ethnic and civic identities, improves educational outcomes, and generates a more inclusive political process.[34]

At times, many critics of multiculturalism appear nostalgic for a uniform, pre-multiculturalism past, arguing that Canada is an oasis of Western democracy that could be spoiled by the "coloured immigrant," forgetting or ignoring some of the undemocratic discrimination and inequalities that were part of that past.[35] Moreover, as Kymlicka puts it, contemporary "critics focus not on the justice or injustice of particular policies, but rather on the way that the general trend towards minority rights threatens to erode the sorts of civic virtues, identities, and practices that sustain a healthy democracy."[36]

What this eroding-citizenship critique seems to suggest is that multiculturalism is inherently divisive and destabilizing, and ultimately undemocratic: that it undermines democratic institutions and culture, which are defined as *essentially* European (primarily Anglo-Saxon), not just of European origin. This attempt to "ethnicize" democracy has been a common thread in much of Canadian history. As Doug Saunders notes, using the example of previous waves of Irish and Italian Catholics and East European Jews:

---

[34] Kymlicka, "The Current State of Multiculturalism in Canada" 7-11. Michael Adams cites similar examples in *Unlikely Utopia: The Surprising Triumph of Canadian Pluralism*.

[35] **Kamal** Dib and Ian Donaldson, "The Adams-Cohen Debate on Canada's Identity and Diversity" 145-149.

[36] Kymlicka, "The New Debate on Minority Rights" 46.

> We see it over and over again when a new group of immigrants arrives
> who are members of a religious minority, usually poor and ill-accustomed
> to the language and folkways of their new country and the workings of its
> economy. In response to public alarm at the strange newcomers, writers
> and politicians offer the same set of frightened, frightening ideas: *They are*
> *different from previous groups. They do not want to integrate. Their religion compels*
> *them to impose their values on us. The reproduction rates will swamp us. They're*
> *disloyal and capable of violence.*[37]

Specific — and legitimate — concerns about poor treatment of women, ethnic voting blocks, and diaspora politics are often matched — less legitimately — with a general perception that some ethnic communities are inherently less disposed to democracy. And while some members of ethnic groups, both new and old, may remain more loyal to their group or faith than their country of residence or citizenship, it is far from clear, at least for Canada, that this is true for anything more than a small minority of immigrants. The most recent target of these accusations are, of course, Muslim Canadians.[38]

In other words, the fact that our democratic institutions and culture are primarily derived from British institutions and practise is conflated with identification with British ethnicity, which ignores the many waves of immigrants from Europe and elsewhere that have become part of Canada's democratic culture and fabric.

Moreover, recognition of this historical reality does not exclude cognizance of the unique aspects of Canadian democracy, such as the original accommodation with First Nations and French Canada and subsequent political and judicial accommodations. Nor does it preclude recognition of how earlier waves of European immigration also shaped and continue to shape our democratic culture or further evolution based on the contributions of more recent immigrant communities.[39] Multiculturalism is part of that evolution and arguably is a unique Canadian reality and democratic innovation.

Michael Adams notes that multiculturalism may in fact be our national project:

> It is the effort to live in a country of peace and prosperity, with laws that
> are just, people who are humane, and where citizens of all backgrounds

---

[37] Doug Saunders, *The Myth of the Muslim Tide* 136.

[38] E.g., Steyn's *Lights Out: Islam, Free Speech And The Twilight Of The West*, "I believe Western culture -- rule of law, universal suffrage, etc. -- is preferable to Arab culture: that's why there are millions of Muslims in Scandinavia, and four Scandinavians in Syria." Similarly, Mansur: "The culture of Muslim immigrants grounded on the religious belief stands in opposition to liberal values, foremost being the freedom of conscience and the freedom of speech. It makes a mockery of multicultural piety that all cultures are of equal merit." Ibid. p. 137

[39] For an in-depth examination of the extent of British influence during a formative time in Canadian identity, see C.P. Champion, *The Strange Demise of British Canada: The Liberals and Canadian Nationalism 1964-68.*

encounter equal opportunities when they set out to realize their potential, contribute to their communities, participate in the Canadian economy, and engage the Canadian political system.[40]

One of the strongest statements in citizenship ceremony speeches is that "In Canada we are all responsible for writing the pages of our country's history," speaking to the ongoing contribution of immigrants to Canada's development — but a contribution built on the existing foundation of laws, values, and culture.[41]

Even one of the strongest critics of multiculturalism, Gilles Paquet, is forced to concede that:

> The more timid and gradualist Canadian way is not necessarily an inferior strategy [compared to Australia], since it fits the Canadian ethos. However, it entails a complex and somewhat erratic process of social learning, where progress comes most of the time by fits and starts, locally, and by trial and error, rather than as a result of broadly debated revolutionary transformation. This often means that social learning is fractured and slower ....

> However frustrating and ineffective the Canadian way may appear by radical standards, it is not only efficient ... but.... may even constitute a truly attractive strategy for polyethnic, multicultural, and plural societies in general ...."[42]

In dealing with the increased diversity and the "somewhat erratic process" of this social learning, the question arises: how do we respectfully discuss and debate what form of multiculturalism we want, what accommodations are or are not reasonable and what represents an appropriate balance between different rights?

One approach is what the Aga Khan refers to as a "cosmopolitan ethic:"

> This is an elegant way of stating the need to engage in a conversation with another citizen whose background, loyalties, religion, and ethnicity may be completely different from yours. This kind of discourse requires considerable effort, continuing education, and thoughtful sensitivity. But it is the only way in which we can discern the difference between personal beliefs and public engagement.[43]

---

[40] Adams, *Unlikely Utopia* 149.

[41] Speaking notes for Chris Alexander, Canada's Citizenship and Immigration Minister at a special citizenship ceremony during Citizenship Week 2014, 16 October 2014.

[42] Gilles Paquet, *Deep Cultural Diversity: A Governance Challenge* 123-4.

[43] Adrienne Clarkson, *Belonging: The Paradox of Citizenship* 85.

Ryan takes this one step further with some "thou shall nots" for both supporters and opponents of multiculturalism. Critics, in particular, should avoid the "the knee-jerk yelp of 'relativism'; the fondness for once-upon-a-time narratives; the likening of multiculturalism's defenders to 'cult' members [and] …. the indulgence in untested and dogmatic interpretations." Similarly, supporters of multiculturalism need to avoid tarring all questioning of multiculturalism policies and practices as being "an expression of latent or open racism" or being "rooted in xenophobia."[44]

In making these points, Ryan notes the need for the "willingness to dialogue," practicing the "cosmopolitan ethic," given that far too much commentary lies in talking past one another rather than engaging. And in this dialogue, recognize the uniqueness of Canada. While international comparisons are helpful, and we must guard against complacency. There are limits to what we can learn from the experience of countries — particularly European ones — with different histories, political dynamics and policies.

---

[44] Phil Ryan, *Multicultiphobia* 210-11.

CANADA DOES WELL COMPARED TO OTHER COUNTRIES

How well does Canada compare to other countries? One of the most comprehensive comparisons has been carried out by the OECD using 2008-9 data from member states. The table below highlights some significant indicators for both "new world"and "old world" immigration countries.[45]

TABLE 2: INTERNATIONAL IMMIGRANT INTEGRATION COMPARISONS - SELECT COUNTRIES AND INDICATORS - OECD - 2008-9							
	Canada	Australia	USA	UK	France	Germany	Netherlands
Social - Education							
PISA G2 compared to native born	1%	19%	8%	-3%	-26%	-23%	-16%
Post-Secondary 15-64 foreign-born	52.1%	38.1%	34.3%	47.3%	24.3%	18.9%	26.2%
Economic							
Household poverty rates	22.9%	20.2%	31.2%	19%	21.1%	13.8%	24%
Unemployment 15-34 G2 compared to native born	-1.9%	-1.5%	-0.6%	2%	5.5%	3.7%	6%
Public Sector Employment 15-34 G2 compared to native born	-0.3%	-3.8%	-3.9%	-0.2%	-5.7%	-12.2%	-5.9%
Home Ownership	68%	70%	52%	48%	47%	39%	45%
Political							
Foreign-born all ages	19.6%	26.5%	12.5%	11.3%	11.6%	12.9%	11.1%
Naturalization 15 or older	75%	69%	49%	43%	56%	34%	70%

Not surprisingly, immigration-based countries like Canada, Australia and the U.S.A., which select immigrants largely on the basis of labour market needs (with a focus on skilled labour) do better than countries who have tended to have less active immigrant selection policies, and whose

---

[45] *Settling In: OECD Indicators of Immigrant Integration 2012.* Although the report is from 2012, most of the data are from 2008 and 2009 with the exception of the naturalization rate which refers to 2005-6 and the percentage of foreign born residents (2009-10). G2 refers to second-generation immigrants.
I have also used this report for naturalization data rather than the more detailed OECD study (*Naturalisation: A Passport for the Better Integration of Immigrants?*) as the former naturalization data for Canada is more consistent with Statistics Canada and CIC operational data. The cumulative (all immigrants) Canadian naturalization rate was 85.6 percent from the NHS; the most recent naturalization rate data, as discussed in the next chapter, is significantly lower.

minority populations reflect post-colonial immigration (France, UK) and/or a guest-worker approach (Germany), generally for unskilled labour.[46]

This difference is particularly evident in each country with respect to education, second-generation unemployment rates, and public sector employment. However, European countries have lower household poverty rates, which may reflect a stronger safety net. The UK does relatively well compared to other European countries for all indicators save the naturalization rate.

In addition, I have used general attitudes towards Muslims as an indicator of how recent immigrants are perceived, recognizing that polling and timing varies among non-EU countries. For Canada, 24 percent have a favourable opinion of Muslims, 54 percent unfavourable (for Quebec, 16 percent and 69 percent respectively).[47]

For comparison purposes, I have also used the Anti-Defamation League index of antisemitic attitudes, where Canada scored 14 percent, representing the percentage of adults in this country who answered "probably true" to a majority of the eleven anti-Semitic stereotypes tested.[48]

I have used Australia and the United States as immigration-based comparator countries, and the UK, France, Germany and the Netherlands as "old world" comparator countries. These country profiles provide a brief overview of the major characteristics of each country, and some of the key similarities and differences.

Australia: Of all countries, Australia is most similar to Canada. Immigration and citizenship-based selection, integration and multiculturalism policies mean that Canada and Australia tend to learn from each other's policies and program. Both countries have significant Aboriginal populations, but Canada has two founding cultures, the British and the French, unlike Australia with its British founding culture. While Australia does not have a multiculturalism act, it has decreed a series of multiculturalism policy statements since 1989.

Like Canada, Australia has considerable diversity among the foreign-born population. The top five countries of birth of the foreign-born represented are the UK (5.4 percent of total population), New Zealand (2.4 percent), China (1.7 percent), India (1.5%), and Vietnam (0.9%).[49]

---

[46] The USA is a more complex mix because it has both elements of uncontrolled migration from Mexico as well as more selective immigration from other countries.

[47] Angus-Reid, "Canadians view non-Christian religions with uncertainty, dislike," October 2013.

[48] Anti-Defamation League, *Global 100: An Index of Antisemitism*. While there are legitimate concerns regarding some of the methodology of this survey (see Michael Kaplan's "Some Question Methodology in ADL Study of Global Anti-Semitism," *The Forward*), this nevertheless provides a reasonable sense of the relative degrees of antisemitic attitudes among countries.

[49] Australian Bureau of Statistics, "State And Territory Composition Of Country Of Birth," 2011 Census.

About three percent are Aboriginal people, and like Canada, with similar social and economic challenges.[50]

Second-generation immigrants outclass the educational performance of the native-born to a greater extent in Australia than any other country. Post-secondary levels are significantly lower than Canada but higher than the USA and Europe save for the UK. Poverty rates are 1.7 times greater for immigrant households compared to native-born households. Unemployment rates for second-generation younger workers (15-34) are lower than for the native-born. The share of public sector second-generation employment for the same age cohort is less than that of the native born, which is comparable to the US.

Some 12 percent have favourable attitudes towards Muslims, 48 percent unfavourable, with 35 percent neutral.[51]

Australia's score on the ADL antisemitism index is 14 percent, the same as Canada.

As in Canada, immigrants live in the major cities. Over 60 percent of residents in the suburbs of Australia's largest cities (Sydney and Melbourne) are foreign-born, and over 75 percent speak a language other than English at home. There are also some concentrations of particular ethnic and cultural communities.[52]

While there is a lively debate within Australia between critics and supporters of multiculturalism and related policies, and ongoing efforts by Australian governments to curb arrival by boat of illegal immigration, both major parties are strongly supportive of immigration, citizenship and multiculturalism.

United States: Although also an immigration-based country like Canada and Australia, the legacy of slavery and the large Hispanic population are two defining characteristics of the American approach to diversity. The American metaphor of the melting pot is based on assimilation to American values and culture, although in practice there is also strong identification with one's ethnic origin and there are many ethnic neighbourhoods.

The main origins of the 12.9 percent of American residents who are foreign-born are: Mexico and Asia (3.8 percent each of total population), other Latin American (3.0%), Europe (1.5 percent). Other origins account for 0.9%.[53] Some 12.9 percent are Black and one percent are Amerindian.[54]

---

[50] Australian Bureau of Statistics, "Estimates of Aboriginal and Torres Strait Islander Australians, June 2011."

[51] Andrew Markus, *Mapping Social Cohesion 2014: National Report* 45.

[52] Ibid. 12.

[53] United States Census Bureau, "Foreign-Born Population by Sex, Age, and World Region of Birth: 2012," and "Population by Sex, Age, Nativity, and U.S. Citizenship Status: 2012."

[54] CIA World Fact Book, United States, 2007 data.

Second-generation immigrants have better educational outcomes compared to the native-born. Post-secondary education is lower than in Canada, Australia and the UK. Household poverty rates are, at 31 percent, higher than in other countries, reflecting a weaker social safety net. The second-generation unemployment rate is lower than for the native-born while public sector second-generation employment is less than the native-born. Compared to Canada and Australia, the US has a lower naturalization rate, reflecting the larger number of lower-income immigrants and the relatively high cost of citizenship.

Affirmative action programs were introduced in the 1960s to address some of the barriers and discrimination faced by minority groups, equivalent to Canadian employment equity and related initiatives, although subject to more controversy, particularly when goals have been translated as quotas.

Some 27 percent of Americans hold favourable attitudes towards Muslims compared to 45 percent who hold unfavourable attitudes. The remainder answered "neutral" or "don't know."[55]

The United States ADL antisemitism index score is 9 percent, lower than Canada.

Despite the melting pot metaphor, many communities followed the common settlement patterns of concentrating in ethnic enclaves, and there are historically African-American neighbourhoods which also tend to have high poverty levels. However, this pattern has declined since 1980, with the largest minorities living in neighbourhoods that are at least one-third white. Many African Americans are moving towards suburbs and more integrated communities, reflecting this broader trend towards greater neighbourhood racial integration.[56]

US debates on immigration and multiculturalism are shaped to a great extent by the large Latino population and the related concerns regarding illegal immigration (the current population of undocumented immigrants is estimated at 11 million) and whether or not to regularize their status, and provide a pathway to citizenship. The US, along with Canada, is one of the few Western countries providing automatic citizenship at birth. Political debates over immigration and citizenship are highly polarized, with the Democrats and Republicans generally at opposite ends of the debate.

United Kingdom: Notwithstanding its similarity to France and, to a lessor extent, the Netherlands, in its legacy of empire and colonies, the UK is significantly different, and is more similar to 'new world' countries in its greater diversity of immigrant source-countries. Of the 11.3 percent of the foreign-born population, the top five countries represented are India (1.2 percent of the total population), Poland (1.1 percent), Pakistan (0.8 percent), Ireland (0.6 percent) and Germany (0.5 percent).[57]

---

[55] Arab American Institute, "American Attitudes Toward Arabs and Muslims."

[56] William H. Frey, "Glimpses of a Ghetto-Free Future," *The New Republic*, 26 November 2014.

[57] UK Office for National Statistics, "Population By Country of Birth and Nationality tables January 2013 to December 2013."

Outcomes are also closer to immigration-based countries. Second-generation educational outcomes are largely similar to the native-born and post-secondary levels are high. Second-generation unemployment rates are slightly higher than for the native-born but public sector second-generation employment is virtually identical between immigrants and native-born. Naturalization rates are low, however.

Some 64 percent have favourable attitudes towards Muslims compared to 26 percent who do not.[58]

The United Kingdom's antisemitism index score is 8 percent, lower than Canada's.

About half of the foreign-born in the UK are in London (split roughly evenly between inner and outer London) and the Southeast, with pockets of Pakistani and Bangladeshi origin inhabitants.[59] Recent studies based on the UK 2011 Census suggest that segregation has decreased within most local authority districts for all ethnic minority groups and that the most ethnically diverse neighbourhoods are in districts that have seen a decrease in segregation for the majority of ethnic minority groups. Moreover, rural areas and towns are becoming more diverse,[60] and surveys show that an overwhelmingly large percentage of ethnic minorities have "striking support for mixing and integrating: with positive feelings about the cultures of both origin and destination countries."[61]

UK public opinion on immigration and multiculturalism has become increasingly polarized. Along with Chancellor Merkel, Prime Minister Cameron pronounced multiculturalism dead in 2011 and the government has stated that its current focus is on "community cohesion."

A series of major terrorist attacks have stoked fears of Muslims, notwithstanding the overall favourable attitude noted above. Debates over immigration are linked to debates over European integration, accentuated by increased immigration from new members of the EU. A new right-wing party, the UK Independence Party, has risen and gained support over these concerns, forcing the other parties, particularly the Conservative Party, to harden their positions.[62]

---

[58] Pew Research, "5 facts about the Muslim population in Europe."

[59] The Migration Observatory, _Migrants in the UK: An Overview_. See also John Iceland, _Residential Segregation: A Transatlantic Analysis_, which uses the _dissimilarity index_ to measure the _evenness_ of the distribution of people across neighbourhoods in a city or metropolitan area. The index ranges from zero to 100, with higher numbers indicating more segregation. Dissimilarity scores over 60 are high in absolute terms, those from 30 to 60 are moderate, and those below 30 are low.

[60] Gemma Catney quoted in "Neighbourhood ethnic segregation: has it decreased?" _The Guardian_, 27 February 2013.

[61] Anthony Heath, "Has multiculturalism failed in the UK? Not really," _The Guardian_, 10 August 2012.

[62] "Immigration and politics: The melting pot," _The Economist_, 25 October 2014. In the May 2015 general elections, UKIP won 11.6 percent of the popular vote, up 9.5 percent from the 2011 elections but given the vagaries of the first-past-the-post system, UKIP obtained only 1 seat.

France: While immigration from within Europe accounts for some 45 percent of all immigrants (first and subsequent generations), French immigration reflects the country's history as a former colonial power, with almost 30 percent of immigrants and their descendants coming from the Maghreb (mainly Algeria and Morocco) and over 10 percent from subsaharan Africa.[63] 10.5 percent of France's population are foreign-born, with an additional 9.2 percent being second-generation (one or both parents).

The French integration policy is based on the underlying republican belief that "all citizens are equal", making it difficult to establish anti-discriminatory measure such as affirmative action or equal opportunity programs. France only collects statistics related to immigration but does not collect statistics on ethnic origin, religion or visible minorities, making accurate assessments of how different communities are doing more difficult.

Moreover, given France's republican history, it has adopted a particularly strict definition of secularism that not only stresses the neutrality of the state but is inflexible with respect to accommodating individual expressions of faith (e.g., hijab, kippa, or food requirements). This approach is reflected in France's unitary government structure and the historic assimilationist approach to regional minorities such as Bretons and Corsicans.

France has a relatively poor integration record, whether with respect to educational, achievement, second-generation unemployment rates, or second-generation public sector employment.

These challenges are particularly acute for France's Muslim population (7.5 percent of the population), many of whom live in *les banlieues*, the low-income areas in the outskirts of major cities.[64] These areas are characterized by high unemployment rates (double those of France as a whole),[65] high youth crime, high levels of policing compared to other urban settings,[66] and low educational attainment. Although France does not formally collect ethnic origin or religion statistics, between one-third and one-half of prisoners are estimated to be Muslim.[67]

---

[63] 2008 statistics from INSEE, "Immigrés et descendants d'immigrés en France, édition 2012," particularly the study "Les descendants d'immigrés plus nombreux que les immigrés : une position française originale en Europe."

[64] Pew Research, "5 facts about the Muslim population in Europe."

[65] Bernard Salanié, "The Riots in France:An Economist's View," 11 June 11 2006. Available at: http://riotsfrance.ssrc.org/Salanie/.

[66] Franck Poupeau, "French sociology under fire: a preliminary diagnosis of the November 2005 'urban riots'," 11 June 2006). Available at: http://riotsfrance.ssrc.org/Poupeau/.

[67] Graeme Hamilton, "France's problem: up to half its prisoners are Muslim and the jails are a hotbed for radicalization," *National Post*, 9 January 2015.

France has an active anti-immigrant and anti-Muslim party in the *Front national*. Overall, some 57 percent of French adults polled believe that France should admit fewer immigrants.[68] However (at least prior to the Paris killings), overall 72 percent of the French have a favourable view of Muslims, compared to 27 percent who do not.[69]

France's score on the ADL antisemitism index is 37 percent, one of the highest in Western Europe.

As France does not collect employment equity statistics for the public sector, the proportion of visible minority employees in that work force is unknown.

Germany: Unlike many other European countries whose colonial past played a significant role in sources of immigrants, immigration to Germany was largely driven by labour market needs. Out of Germany's population of 82 million, some 20 percent have an immigrant background: major source countries include Turkey (3.7 percent of the population), Poland (1.9 percent), Russia (1.5 percent) and Italy (0.9 percent).[70] Some 4 million Muslims live in Germany. Immigration was a greater feature of the former West Germany than the East, due to West Germany's much more dynamic economy.

The original German model was based on guest workers (*Gastarbeiter*), the temporary foreign workers needed for Germany's economic recovery in the 1950s and 60s. The expectation was that these workers would return to their country of origin. However, ongoing labour needs and better prospects than in their home countries caused most of these workers to stay and settle in Germany, with the result that the country is now home to a large second-generation population.

Over the past 15 years, Germany has recognized that it is a country of long-term immigration, not just guest workers, and has responded to this reality with new immigration legislation. Integration measures include language and culture courses, including targeting specific groups (e.g., youth, women). There has also been focus on pre-school age children given comparatively poor results compared to those of German origin. Like Canada, Germany as a federal state faces the challenge of coordinating national objectives across the länder (provinces).[71] Along with these reforms, Germany made it somewhat easier for long-term immigrants and their children to acquire German citizenship; when these changes were made, some 3.6 million immigrants qualified for citizenship.

However, while immigrant poverty rates are significantly lower than in other countries, likely reflecting stronger social safety programs, German immigrant education outcomes and

---

[68] Pew Research, "A Fragile Rebound for EU Image on Eve of European Parliament Elections."

[69] Pew Research, "5 facts about the Muslim population in Europe."

[70] Migrationsbericht des Bundesamtes für Migration und Flüchtlinge im Auftrag der Bundesregierung. Migrationsbericht 2012. (Migration report of the Federal Office for Migration and Refugees commissioned by the federal government. Migration Report 2012).

[71] Petra Bendel, *Coordinating immigrant integration in Germany Mainstreaming at the federal and local levels*.

unemployment rates reflect the general European pattern of being worse for immigrants than the native-born. Public sector second-generation immigrant employment and overall naturalization rates are significantly lower than those of other European countries.

Only about two-thirds of German immigrants are urbanized, mainly in the Rhine-Ruhr and Frankfurt/Main regions, followed by Munich, Hamburg, Stuttgart and the Leipzig-Halle and Bremen/Oldenburg regions. Overall, German cities have low-to-moderate levels of segregation measured by the dissimilarity index, as seen in Düsseldorf (30 percent) and Frankfurt (18 percent), with Munich having a significant foreign-born population (12 percent).[72]

While there are no major anti-immigrant and anti-Muslim parties in Germany, there is considerable opposition to Muslim immigrants, particularly in former East Germany, as as recent demonstrations organized by PEGIDA have shown.[73] Chanceller Angela Merkel, despite her 2011 remarks declaring multiculturalism dead, has in practice made major efforts to integrate the Muslim population, address racism, Islamophobia and antisemitism, and counter the language and rhetoric of PEGIDA. Overall, some 44 percent of German adults believe that Germany should admit fewer immigrants.[74] However, 58 percent have a favourable view of Muslims, compared to 33 percent who do not.[75]

Germany's score on the ADL antisemitism index is 27 percent.

Netherlands: The Netherlands have a total population of almost 17 million people, 79 percent of whom are of Dutch ethnic origin. The composition of its minority population reflects its colonial history. 2.1 percent of the total population is Surinamese, 0.9 percent is Dutch Caribbean, and 2.2 percent is Indonesian. Other major ethnic origins include Turkish and Kurdish (2.4 percent) and Moroccan and Berber (2.2 percent). People of German ethnic origin account for 2.2 percent.[76]

As in Germany, many of these immigrants originally arrived as guest workers in the 1960s, but stayed for the opportunities and over time settled with their families.

As Dutch society was originally based on vertically-organized "pillars," with separate public institutions for Catholics and Protestants, there was less emphasis on integration through

---

[72] Iceland, *Residential Segregation: A Transatlantic Analysis.*

[73] Timothy Garton Ash, "Germany's anti-Islamic movement Pegida is a vampire we must slay," *The Guardian,* 18 January 2015. Pegida stands for Patriotische Europäer gegen die Islamisierung des Abendlandes or Patriotic Europeans Against the Islamisation of the West German.

[74] Pew Research, A Fragile Rebound for EU Image on Eve of European Parliament Elections, 2014.

[75] Pew Research, 5 facts about the Muslim population in Europe.

[76] Netherlands Centraal Bureau voor de Statistiek. Bevolking; generatie, geslacht, leeftijd en herkomstgroepering, 1 januari 2014 (population; generation, gender, age and ethnic background, January 1, 2014).

common institutions. This, combined with settlement patterns and the economic challenges facing minority communities, resulted in low-income enclaves.

Over time, this changed given ongoing integration issues and poorer economic and social outcomes. In 2013, immigrants needed to pass an exam measuring their level of integration that tests Dutch language skills and knowledge of Dutch society within three to five years of entering the country.[77]

While slightly better than France and Germany, education outcomes are poor for the second-generation, both in terms of pre- and post-secondary education. Second-generation unemployment rates are significantly higher, and public sector second-generation employment significantly lower, than for the native-born. Naturalization, however, compares favourably to Canada and Australia.

Using the dissimilarity index, Antwerp has high levels of segregation (70 percent with respect to North Africans and Bosnians), Rotterdam moderate (50 percent with respect to Turks and 44 percent with respect to Moroccans) and Amsterdam also moderate (42 percent with respect to Turks, 41 percent with respect to Moroccans and 33 percent with respect to Surinamese).[78]

Public concerns about immigration and immigrant integration, largely with respect to Muslims, have increased, particularly after the killing of Theo van Gogh by an Islamic-inspired extremist in 2004. 54 percent oppose non-EU immigration to meet labour shortages whereas only 41 percent support it.[79] Moreover, 53 percent of Dutch voters had a negative view of Dutch integration politics over the last 10 years, 74 percent of Dutch voters say immigrants should conform to Dutch society and values and 83% support a ban on burqas in public spaces.[80]

The Netherland's score on the ADL antisemitism index is 5 percent, one of the lowest in the world.

Concerns regarding Dutch multiculturalism and immigrant integration predate the rise of Geert Wilders and the PVV (Party for Freedom), most notably from politicians Pym Fortuyn (assassinated in 2002) and Ayaan Hirsi Ali (who later emigrated to the US following her loss of Dutch citizenship in 2006). However, the ongoing influence of Wilders in Dutch society and politics that has continued to reinforce the shift in political discourse and policy against immigrants and their children.

Like Germany and the UK, in 2011 the Netherlands formally declared it was abandoning the pillar-based multiculturalism that encouraged segregation in favour of integration around the

---

[77] Wikipedia, Integration law for immigrants to the Netherlands.

[78] Iceland, "Residential Segregation: A Transatlantic Analysis."

[79] European Commission, *Awareness of Home Affairs Report*, 2012, given not covered in Pew Research study cited above.

[80] Maurice de Hond poll published by the centre-right newspaper *Trouw* on 19 June 2011. This poll was sponsored by Geert Wilders anti-Muslim and anti-immigrant party, the PVV.

"values of the Dutch people," along with more practical measures such as increased Dutch language training requirements, measures against force marriages, and removal of residents who fail the Dutch integration test.

CANADIANS ARE SUPPORTIVE OF IMMIGRATION

Beyond the academic debates and the international comparisons, what does public opinion research tell us about how this counter-narrative — multiculturalism as separation, not integration — has been received? How comfortable are Canadians with ongoing immigration? How comfortable are Canadians with encouraging newcomers to take up citizenship? And how comfortable are Canadians with the integration and accommodation model of multiculturalism?

Canada, in sharp contrast to other countries, has no party opposed to immigration and multiculturalism. While there are sharp debates over immigration, citizenship, refugee and multiculturalism policies and practices, there is general consensus on the fundamentals: Canada is an immigration-based country that encourages full integration into and participation in Canadian society.

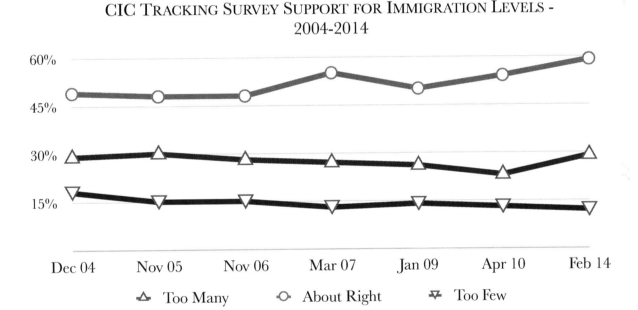

CIC TRACKING SURVEY SUPPORT FOR IMMIGRATION LEVELS - 2004-2014

CIC's annual tracking survey consistently confirms between 50 and 60 percent of the population is in favour of the current levels of immigration, with close to one-third thinking levels are too high.[81] There does appear to be an overall trend towards towards slightly greater support for current levels. The difference between 2010 and 2014 could reflect a mix of ongoing public debates over immigration and related issues (e.g., radicalization, accommodation issues), as well as some of the Government's messaging on citizenship and immigration fraud and refugee reform.

However, other surveys show different results. The 2015 Ekos survey shows that 46.3 percent believe Canada accepts too many immigrants, with 41.2 percent believing too many immigrants are visible minorities, showing a significant increase from the early 2000s.[82]

The 2007 and 2010 CIC tracking surveys included questions on citizenship confirming the general welcoming approach but consistent with overall Government messaging regarding the responsibilities of citizenship and the obligation to learn about Canada.[83]

In the 2014 tracking survey, Quebec has the highest level of support for current levels and the lowest number of those thinking that immigration levels are too high, recognizing the demographic and economic pressures facing Quebec. Yet at the same time, and understandably so, Québécois remain concerned about their linguistic, cultural and historical identity and how to preserve it. This has generated ongoing debates over accommodation and integration, most recently with respect to the proposed Quebec values charter of 2013.

There was no significant difference in support between rural and urban areas.

In 2010 and 2014, some groups that were more likely to believe the immigration levels are too high were resident of Ontario (and Alberta in 2014), those 45 years of age and older, and those with less educational attainment.[84]

---

[81] It should be noted that most respondents do not know current levels of immigration (see "Canadians in the dark about immigration numbers: survey," Ottawa Citizen, 27 August 2014), and that when informed of current levels (some 250,000 per year), the number of citizens thinking that Canada is accepting too many immigrants increases by ten percent. This chart is derived from the *CIC Annual Tracking Survey — Winter 2010 Final Report* and the *2013 - 2014 Citizenship and Immigration Canada Annual Tracking Survey - Methodology Report*. The level of detail in the most recent tracking survey compares poorly to earlier surveys, both the 2010 and *CIC Annual Tracking Survey — Summer 2007* are more comprehensive in their questions regarding citizenship and immigration, with some probing of attitudes towards multiculturalism.

[82] *Tolerance Under Pressure?*, Ekos, 12 March 2015. But the "Focus Canada – Spring 2015 Canadian public opinion about immigration and multiculturalism" confirms general public support for immigration (57 percent disagree that there is too much immigration to Canada versus 38 percent who agree).

[83] Other useful sources of public opinion on immigration, among other issues, include the Environics Institute's *Focus Canada 2012* which confirms 60 percent support for current levels of immigration, with 80 percent believing immigration beneficial to the economy. Both measures have been roughly stable for the last 10 years.

[84] *CIC Annual Tracking Survey — Winter 2010 Final Report*.
2013 - 2014 Citizenship and Immigration Canada Annual Tracking Survey - Methodology Report.

CIC TRACKING SURVEY REGIONAL SUPPORT FOR IMMIGRATION LEVELS 2014

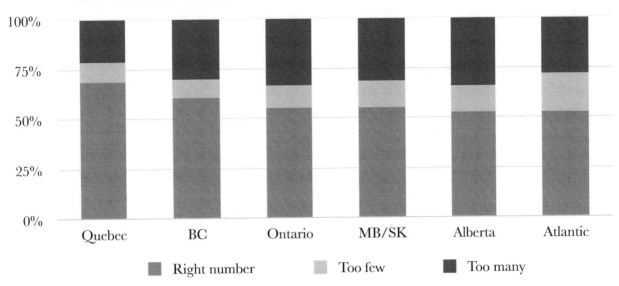

Ethnic origin support for current levels is not surprisingly higher from more recent immigrant groups, particularly African and Middle Eastern, which also have the greatest support for higher levels of immigration. Aboriginal Peoples, not surprisingly given their history, and Americans are most likely to believe that immigration levels are too high.

CIC TRACKING SURVEY ETHNIC ORIGIN SUPPORT FOR IMMIGRATION LEVELS 2014

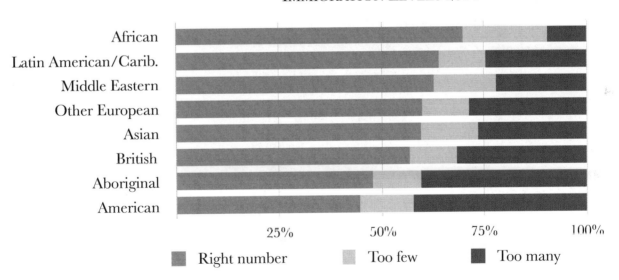

Compared to other countries, immigration is less controversial in Canada, identified by only 15 percent of Canadians as one of the top three political issues. In contrast, 43 percent in the UK, 32 percent in Australia, 22 percent in Germany and 21 percent in France do place immigration among the top three concerns. Surprisingly, given press coverage, the US figure was comparable to Canada (16 percent), but that may reflect the 2013 timing of the survey.[85]

When it comes to the responsibilities and behaviours of citizenship, 89 percent of Canadians believe that foreign-born Canadians are just as likely to be good citizens as those born in Canada, with 81 percent believing that permanent residents are just as likely to be good citizens.[86] Moreover, both Canadian-born and foreign-born Canadians believe that Canadian citizenship has the right balance between rights and responsibilities, although slightly more Canadian-born believe that citizenship gives too many rights and not enough responsibilities.[87]

TABLE 3: INSTITUTE FOR CANADIAN CITIZENSHIP: BALANCE BETWEEN RIGHTS AND RESPONSIBILITIES - ENVIRONICS 2012

	Born in Canada	Born Elsewhere
Too many rights/not enough responsibilities	22%	19%
Balance is about right	64%	70%
Too many responsibilities/not enough rights	10%	8%

There are virtually no differences between Canadian-born and foreign-born with respect to agreement to abide by Canadian values (70 and 68 percent respectively) and mandatory voluntary service (34 percent support). Slightly more of the foreign-born than Canadian-born favour mandatory voting (58 compared to 52 percent).

Multiculturalism remains iconic, regularly being identified by Canadians as one of the top ten list of accomplishments that makes one proud to be Canadian.[88] Moreover, Canadians overwhelmingly view themselves as welcoming of minority groups and believe that Canada's diversity is a strength.[89] But Canadians clearly view multiculturalism in an integrative sense, with an expectation that new arrivals will adopt Canadian values and attitudes.[90]

---

[85] "Britain is most concerned about immigration control," Ipsos-MORI.

[86] *Canadians on Citizenship*. Institute for Canadian Citizenship (Environics) 2012.

[87] Ibid. This survey predates the 2014 changes to the *Citizenship Act* but reflects *Discover Canada* and the changes to the citizenship test.

[88] E.g., "Harper gov't poll for Cda's 150th birthday cites Liberal, NDP icons" *CTV*, 15 June 2014 (multiculturalism placed sixth) and *Focus Canada 2012* (multiculturalism placed third during the period 1994-2012). This general high level of support is largely within an integration rather than accommodation framework, although English Canada is generally more open to accommodation compared to Quebec ("Quebecers say they're too accommodating, other Canadians disagree," Angus Reid, 16 September 2013).

[89] "On the Verge of Canada Day, Four in Five (81%) Canadians Believe Compatriots Should Show More Patriotism" Ipsos-Reid, 30 June 2014.

[90] "CBC News Poll on Discrimination" had 73 percent agreeing with the statement that: "Immigrants should make their best effort to assimilate to Canadian values and culture." November 2014.

FEELINGS TOWARDS RELIGIOUS GROUPS - ANGUS-REID
2015

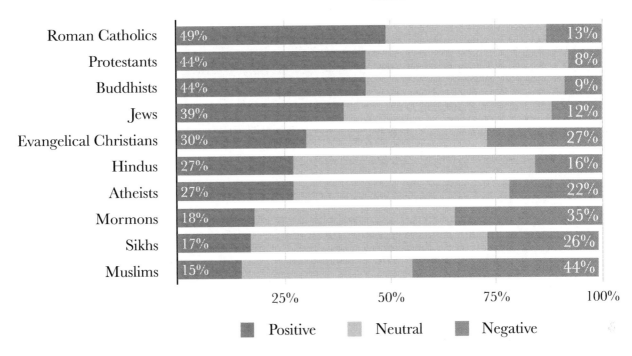

And while many Canadians are uncomfortable with some religious minorities, particularly Mormons, Sikhs and Muslims, they are reasonably accepting of religious symbols and clothing (with the exception of the Kirpan and the Niqab). There is greater resistance in Quebec and among those over the age of 55, but the same general pattern remains.[91]

Taken together, this general high support for immigration, a relatively open pathway to citizenship and pride in Canada's diversity and multiculturalism make it no surprise that the differences between Canadian political parties over immigration issues tend not to take the existentialist and essentialist form common in many other countries.

---

[91] *Religion and faith in Canada today: strong belief, ambivalence and rejection define our views*, April 2015. *Most Canadians view Muslim community as a "partner", not "problem" in fight against radicalization*, 26 November 2014. Both surveys by the Angus Reid Institute.

The Conservative Re-Emphasis on Integration

The Conservative Government has been somewhat influenced by this counter-narrative against multiculturalism in its emphasis on British and French historic symbols, the monarchy, and Canadian values (or liberal democratic values), and its shift towards the language of responsibilities, not just rights.[92] Its recognition of the historical roots of Canadian democracy should not be controversial. However, how these roots are portrayed, the relative neglect of social history and the omission of the equality provisions of the Charter are more debatable.

In many ways, the Conservative Government's much vaunted recent resetting of Canadian multiculturalism (and citizenship) was more about restoring and re-emphasizing integration than a wholesale abandonment of the framework. It recognized that integration challenges were no longer just between the "mainstream" and visible minorities, that faith communities were part of the integration challenge, and that racism and discrimination strategies needed to be targeted to individual communities.

One could disagree with some of the specific initiatives (e.g., an almost exclusive focus on antisemitism with minimal to no attention to other groups, the general downplaying of equality issues, the distinction made between single and dual national Canadian citizens in the 2014 *Citizenship Act* revisions, and some of its less-than-inclusive language). However, the general emphasis on integration, and the explicit broadening of multiculturalism to include inter-ethnic and inter-faith relations, were appropriate for and necessary to the continuing evolution of Canada's diversity.[93]

All this has to be taken in context. Canada has no anti-immigrant political parties and all parties actively compete for ethnic community votes. A significant part of the Conservative government's success was driven by the relentless political outreach by Minister for Multiculturalism (and Economic Social Development) Jason Kenney, where his messaging resonated positively with segments of the various communities. While there are significant differences between political parties in terms of immigration, citizenship and multiculturalism, they are all enmeshed in a country that that relies on immigration for its continued economic growth and responds to the diversity of opinion within and among immigrant groups.[94]

---

[92] The core four values listed in most speeches are: freedom, democracy, human rights and the rule of law.

[93] See my earlier book on the policy changes that describes the extent of the policy shift, *Policy Arrogance or Innocent Bias: Resetting Citizenship and Multiculturalism*. It is worth noting that the Mulroney Conservative government introduced the *Employment Equity Act* 1986, the *Canadian Multiculturalism Act* 1988, in sharp contrast to the current Conservative government.

[94] It is unclear how many of the extensive immigration, refugee and citizenship changes implemented by the Conservative government would be fundamentally undone by a different incoming government or whether it would be more in the nature of minor adjustments and corrections.

CONCLUSION

Canada is unique in its embrace of diversity policies as a unifying force. The country was built on the arrival of immigrants and their interaction with native peoples starting four centuries ago. Canada may have been lucky, a country built by immigrants and their descendants who joined the native peoples starting four centuries ago, with a combination of geography, history, immigration and settlement patterns that enabled the development of an inclusive approach. But Canada's current approach also reflects conscious policy choices to facilitate integration while accommodating difference.

While Canada has — and always has had — ethnic neighbourhoods, these are generally not combined with concentrations of poverty and unemployment as seen in Europe and in some Black communities in the US. Canada has been relatively successful at creating common spaces (e.g., marriage, workplace, school, community, clubs, etc.) for all citizens.[95]

From an integration perspective, the more people from different origins mix together in common spaces, the better, and the lower the risk of suspicion and conflict. Of course, some segments of communities, particularly more fundamentalist strains in faith communities, will 'opt-out' of this wider participation and integration. However, as long as this remains a relatively small percentage, this is part of the reality of diversity but not a major issue.

In practice, Canada's multiculturalism policy continues to aim for the integration, not the assimilation, of religious and visible minorities, all within the framework of the *Charter* and Canadian laws. Social inclusion and cohesion is fostered through constantly building common spaces and paths to voluntary integration. Separation and divisiveness are discouraged, common public institutions are favoured, differences are respected, and inclusion of all Canadians — whatever their skin colour, style of dress, customs, and religion — is encouraged.

Overall, as the above international comparisons make clear, Canada continues to do well in relation to other countries in its approach to integrating newcomers and encouraging them to take up citizenship and participate in Canadian society.

Multiculturalism is the Canadian response to some of the challenges of large-scale immigration and social transformation. Research has shown that social integration is a complex process that cannot be hastily imposed on individuals or groups. While debate and discussion over the pace and nature of change can be polarizing and divisive, it is also part of the democratic process.

The Canadian approach of public dialogue and royal commissions, although neglected by the current government, has served the country well over the past decades in providing a framework for open-but-respectful discussion. Given the sometimes fractious nature of such discussion, and the range of sensitivities involved, finding a way to tackle dialogue and discussion on citizenship and multiculturalism will always be challenging. The 2008 Bouchard-Taylor

---

[95] An illustration of the common and open spaces concept can be found in Kamal Dib, Ian Donaldson and Brittany Turcotte, "Integration and Identity in Canada: The Importance of Multicultural Common Spaces."

hearings on reasonable accommodation in Quebec provide a cautionary tale of the risks involved in discussing these issues, but it is better to have these struggles in the open, where they can provoke a wider debate, than sweep them under the rug.

Through such dialogue, and given its history as an immigration-based country, Canadians have been more supportive of large-scale immigration and a relatively easy pathway to citizenship, and are generally welcoming of increased diversity and multiculturalism compared to Europeans and others. This success reflects in part the recognition and in many cases celebration of the various ethnic and religious identities of Canadians, and the encouragement of and participation in these celebrations by a wide range of communities.

One need only compare the European experience with guest workers with Canada's immigrant-to-citizen approach to realize why so many in Europe look to Canada as a model to be emulated. We can also compare the challenges, in Europe, of reconciling strong national monocultures with minorities' need for recognition with the less defined and more fluid approach to Canadian identity that, to revert to the language of the *Bi and Bi Report*, means "unity in diversity." Some 45 years later this framework remains valid, allowing for diversity within a common constitutional and legal framework, one reinforced by core common norms and values.

Along with federal and provincial legislative human rights frameworks aiming at economic, social, racial and gender equality, successive Liberal and Conservative governments have emphasized the facilitation of citizenship and accommodation of diversity as a means of promoting integration within the context of Canadian laws and values (although the current Conservative government has shifted this approach by making citizenship more difficult to obtain and downplaying the equality element of multiculturalism).

As noted earlier, while some common norms are fixed (e.g., democracy, rule of law, respect for human rights, respect for others), their precise definition can vary. Other values are less fixed but evolve along with society (e.g., the long history of women's rights, the more recent struggles over gay marriage and LGBT rights, acceptance of religious 'headgear'). This dynamic process of integration and accommodation, while while sometimes uncomfortable, nevertheless ensures that Canadian society is inclusive even as it finds and defines the appropriate balances.

The next chapters of the book, the national and provincial overviews, will review in detail how well Canadian immigration, citizenship and multiculturalism is working in terms of economic, social and political outcomes, from both overall and community perspectives. This evidence provides background to a number of ongoing policy issues and challenges where attention will be required for Canada to continue to integrate successfully newcomers and their children, reducing the risk of social fragmentation and alienation.

Some of the major issues that underpin discussion of Canadian multiculturalism and the risks to social inclusion and cohesion include:

Settlement patterns: While Canada's immigrants do not settle in ethnic enclaves to the extent that they do in most other countries, there are pockets, physical and virtual of concentrated communities. These may make integration into common spaces more challenging in the future. Combined with the overall fragmentation of interests and media, and ongoing globalization, identities will likely continue to become more varied and complex. While historically, communities have always had an understandable tendency to live in the same areas, it is unclear whether subsequent generations will choose to remain in their ethnic neighbourhoods or not. Workplaces, however, as long as they remain largely integrated, will attenuate some of these isolating settlement trends.

Integration and accommodation balance: Canadian multiculturalism has always been built around a balance between integration and accommodation. The definition of what constitutes "reasonable accommodation" continues to evolve along with Canadian values. It has always needed to be understood in the context of Canadian law, and the balance between competing rights. Most issues revolve around religious accommodation and the degree to which religious obligations, as defined by the individual, are compatible with her or his other fundamental rights and freedoms, as well as with the rights and freedoms of others. Whether it is better to continue the current *ad hoc* approach or shift to a more prescriptive or Cartesian one that specifies what is and is not legitimate accommodation will remain a subject of public debate and discussion.

Racism and discrimination: Visible minorities, particularly first-generation immigrants, have significantly poorer economic outcomes than both other ethnic communities and the "mainstream." The experience varies by community, but the overall pattern is clear. Second-generation outcomes show smaller gaps, and by the third-generation, the gaps have largely disappeared for most communities. But blind C.V. tests confirm bias in hiring processes. Fears of increased antisemitism have been the focus of the federal government, with relatively little attention paid to anti-Muslim attitudes (Islamophobia), or traditional colour-based racism and discrimination. Given Canada's increasing diversity, ongoing attention to how communities are doing is needed.

Radicalization: The extreme case of dual loyalties is radicalization, when an individual's loyalty shifts to a foreign extremist entity (and commits violence in Canada or abroad as a result) or takes on an extreme fundamentalism incompatible with Canadian rights and values. Violent extremism is more clear cut, but non-violent extremism is also largely incompatible with the overall aims of multiculturalism: integration, acceptance and respect for others.

Diaspora politics and dual loyalties: Canada has a remarkably open policy towards dual nationalities, and has a relatively low-key debate about whether dual loyalties to Canada and the 'homeland' are problematic (except in the case of Islamic-inspired extremism). The interest of ethnic Canadians in events of their country of origin or ancestry is largely accepted, although governments often pick and choose which diaspora issues to support or not as part of "shopping for votes." But this fragmentation of interests makes it more challenging to find policies and priorities that address broader foreign and domestic issues, and and the challenge will only increase as newer communities become more established and politically active.

"Harder to get and easier to lose" citizenship: The 2014 *Citizenship Act* revisions emphasized citizenship as "place" by improving the integrity of the citizenship acquisition process and tightening the related requirements. These changes should reduce the number of "citizens of convenience" and the incidence of citizenship fraud. Yet in an era of ongoing globalization, where many of the most in-demand immigrants view citizenship more instrumentally, this tightening of citizenship requirements may adversely affect our ability to attract highly skilled immigrants, making us less competitive relative to other countries. The net effect of these changes will be a further reduction in the naturalization rate, already in decline, given that they fall disproportionately on the less educated, and a number of visible minority groups, making it harder for members of these communities to become full Canadians with political rights. This results in a larger disenfranchised population.

Political and public service representation: Ideally, public institutions, political parties and legislature members should be representative of the populations they serve. The federal public service and a number of provincial governments have made progress in this regard, but this progress is uneven across the full range of government services, including education, healthcare, and police. Similarly, political representation remains inadequate with respect to both women and visible minorities. Parliamentary representation of women has largely plateaued at 25 percent. However, all political parties actively court ethnic communities (increasingly running candidates from these communities) and can be characterized as pro-immigration, although significant policy differences remain. There is limited information on judicial appointments but studies show serious gaps for female and visible-minority representation on the bench.

Multiculturalism policy and program changes: The 2010 changes to the multiculturalism program included three new objectives: increasing emphasis on integration between ethnic and faith communities (not just between visible minorities, taken as a group, and the "mainstream"); shifting emphasis from employment equity in the public service to improving the ability of public institutions to serve the needs of a diverse population; and,actively engaging in international discussions on diversity. From a program perspective, this has not made much of a difference given the small size of the multiculturalism grants and contribution program (less than $10 million, with frequent lapses). In addition, the policy focus continues to become diluted within Citizenship and Immigration Canada. What has made a greater impact is the somewhat harsher, less inclusive language recently used by Ministers to describe citizenship and multiculturalism, and the clearer targeting by political parties of specific communities aligned with their electoral interests.

Media and public debate: Invariably, specific issues provoke media commentary and public debate, whether those issues are to do with reasonable accommodation (like requests related to gender) or with radicalization and extremism. How these debates are treated in the media and political leaders matters. By and large, with the exception of Sun Media and some outlets in Quebec, most media and political commentary has been much more respectful than in Europe and the US.[96] However, language and tone remain important, and given that there will always be — and should always be — debate over what multiculturalism should and should not allow, attention to how issues are presented and discussed is still needed. Extreme "political correctness" is not required, but sensitivity is.

Hopefully, both the evidence presented in subsequent chapters, and the policy and reflections on the above issues in Chapter 12, will be helpful to policy-makers and others interested in the ongoing health of multiculturalism in Canada, and the identification of what further research, analysis and policy work is required.

But before begining the national and provincial overviews, let us close this chapter with Adrienne Clarkson's reminder of what integration means, and how it is built into the Canadian model of immigration, citizenship and multiculturalism:

> Immigrants are future citizens, and we recognize them as citizens in the making. As Aristotle said in Physics, "With respect to what is eternal, there is no difference between *being possible* and *being*." New citizens take on the same responsibilities as existing citizens: obeying laws, paying taxes, voting. And once a new citizen is adopted into the family of fellow citizens, he must accept the good with the bad, both past and present, in order to contribute to and help shape the future. Canada is the land of our ancestors, as it says in our national anthem, and we are each and every one of us adopted by those ancestors. Newcomers are not invited to this country to spend a few years working, only to depart like migrants.[97]

With this overview, let us turn to what the data tells us about how well multiculturalism is working in Canada.

---

[96] Most commentary by Ezra Levant provides the example that proves the rule. The Conservative Government's penchant for bumper sticker names of legislation (e.g., *Zero Tolerance for Barbaric Cultural Practices Act*) is another example of what should be avoided.

[97] Clarkson 181.

Chapter 3 — Canada: A National Perspective

This chapter provides an overview in of Canada's demographics in terms of both ethnic and religious diversity, considering how these are linked to economic and social outcomes as well as political integration indicators. It is organized accordingly.

Employment equity information is embedded in the economic (for the federally regulated sectors) and political (for the public service) sections.

While subsequent chapters contain detailed analysis for each province, this national overview provides some comparative views. Each province is different in its level of diversity and my goal here is to highlight similarities and differences, emphasizing that the expressions of Canadian diversity are themselves diverse, and that we need to understand its regional dimensions.

Similarly, diversity varies at the municipal level, and this chapter will highlight the different forms diversity takes in Canada's major cities. Provincial chapters will provide further detail on a wider range of Canadian cities.

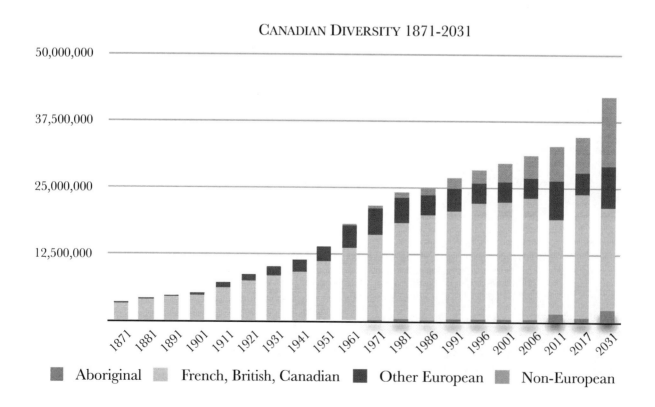

CANADIAN DIVERSITY 1871-2031

The above chart shows the ongoing evolution of Canadian diversity from Confederation to the present, with 2017 and 2031 projections included.[98] For much of Canada's history, traditional European immigration has dominated, with a significant number of those whose families have been in Canada for a number of generations identifying themselves as Canadians.

Starting in the 1960s with more open colour-blind immigration policies, immigration growth shifted to those coming from non-European countries, largely visible minorities.

Longer-term projections estimate that Canada's population will grow to over 50 million by 2063 (medium-growth scenario), driven largely by immigration, with most growth occurring in Ontario and the Western provinces, especially Alberta (immigration rates in Quebec and Atlantic Canada are in relative decline). Canada's population would also continue to age, with the number of seniors increasing to 25 percent compared to 15 percent at present.[99]

---

[98] _Annual Report on the Operation of the Canadian Multiculturalism Act 2010-2011_ updated with 2011 NHS data and 2031 projections. There is an anomaly between the 2006 Census and NHS shares for French, British and Canadian, and Other European. The 2017 projections understated Aboriginal Peoples (the 2011 NHS placed greater effort on Aboriginal Peoples compared to the Census.

[99] "Population Projections for Canada (2013 to 2063), Provinces and Territories (2013 to 2038)," _Statistics Canada._

A HISTORY OF AN IMMIGRATION-BASED COUNTRY

Significant, non-aboriginal immigration occurred over almost two centuries. There was a slow but progressive settlement by the French of Quebec and Acadia, and smaller numbers of American and European entrepreneurs, along with British military personnel, also arrived during this period. It all culminated with the influx of 46–50,000 British Loyalists refugees fleeing the American Revolution. Most were moving from the Mid-Atlantic States into what are now Southern Ontario, the Eastern Townships of Quebec, New Brunswick, and Nova Scotia (some 2,000 Black Loyalists settled in this last province).[100] A second wave of 30,000 Americans settled in Ontario between the late 1780s and 1812 with promises of land. Scottish Highlanders fleeing land clearances also immigrated to Canada during this period.[101]

After the War of 1812, immigrants from Britain and Ireland were encouraged to settle in Canada, including British army regulars who had served in the war. The colonial governors of Canada, worried about another American invasion attempt and seeking to counter the French-speaking influence of Quebec, rushed to promote rural settlement, primarily by immigrants from Britain and in the area of Upper Canada (present-day Ontario). Irish immigration increased further as a result of the Irish Potato Famine between 1846 and 1849.

The Dominion Lands Act of 1872 offered ownership of 160 acres of land free to any man over 18 or any woman heading a household, provided they lived on the plot and improved it.[102]

Post-Confederation, the completion of the Canadian Pacific Railroad (CPR) and the overcoming of the Métis rebellion opened up the West for settlement. The initial targets were immigrants from Britain, Eastern Canada and the U.S.

In the early 20th Century, prior to World War I, settlement of the West accelerated, with significant immigration from Ukraine and other Eastern European countries.

This was also the time of immigration restrictions and wartime internment.

Chinese immigration was curtailed through the 1885 Head-Tax, which was initially set at $50, rising to $500 in 1903 before eventually being abolished in 1923, when the *Chinese Immigration Act of 1923* virtually stopped all Chinese immigration. Sikh immigration largely ended with the 1908 "continuous journey" clause that barred immigration from countries where a direct, non-stop shipping service was not available. When technological developments made a continuous journey possible from India, the government responded by imposing a $200 head tax and pressuring steamship companies not to provide direct service to Canada.

During World War I, internment camps were set up given concerns over dual loyalty among immigrants from the Austro-Hungarian Empire, primarily of Ukrainian origin.

---

[100] Lawrence Hill's, <u>The Book of Negroes</u>, captures the harshness of their experience in Nova Scotia.

[101] For this summary history and the regional immigration histories, I have relied heavily on the following books: Valerie Knowles, *Strangers at our Gates: Canadian Immigration and Immigration Policy*; Peter Li, *Destination Canada: Immigration Debate and Issues*; and, Ninette Kelley and Michael Trbilcock, *The Making of the Mosaic: A History of Canadian Immigration Policy*. For settlement service history, see Robert Vineberg, *Responding to Immigrant Settlement Needs: The Canadian Experience*.

[102] 160 acres is a quarter section of a square mile, or the equivalent of 0.65 km^2.

Immigration declined during World War I, grew modestly in the 1920s and then declined again during the Great Depression, with a reversion to preference for British immigrants and restrictions on non-European and non-white immigration. Jewish refugees from the impending war in Europe were refused ("none is too many"), and the M.S. St. Louis, a ship carrying over 900 refugees, was refused entry to Cuba, the US and Canada.

During World War II, the familiar pattern of wartime registration and internment affected Japanese, Italian and German Canadians, with Japanese Canadians suffering the most.[103] Following the war, immigration increased from a wide variety of European countries, including some 50,000 displaced person refugees, setting the stage for a multicultural Canada.

The "continuous journey" clause was repealed in 1947 and the Chinese Immigration (Exclusion) Act of 1923 was finally repealed in 1948, although other formal and informal barriers largely prevented Indian and Chinese immigration until barriers to non-European immigration were removed in the 1960s.

Canada established distinct Canadian citizenship in 1947 (previously inhabitants had been British subjects) based upon birthright citizenship (*jus soli*) and naturalization. Gender and wedlock discrimination was removed in 1977.

Racial restrictions ended in 1962, under the Conservatives, and the more objective and consistent point system was introduced in 1967, under the Liberals. In many ways, like other policies and programs in the 1960s, this change reflected a conscious and bipartisan choice that Canada should become a more open and inclusive society. The shared assumption was that immigrants would arrive, integrate, become citizens and participate in Canadian society. Moreover, while there was always an effort to match skill levels to the needs of the economy, these were relatively relaxed given the overall demand for a larger workforce.

For Liberal governments, an open immigration policy was part of reaffirming a distinctly Canadian identity, with reduced emphasis on historic connections to Britain, best exemplified by the adoption of the new Canadian flag in 1965. Conservative governments also maintained an open immigration policy, although the Harper government has strengthened the relative emphasis on economic immigration.

In contrast to many European countries, with their guest-worker approach and former colonies driving immigration, or the US with its Southern border generating Latino immigration, Canada set the stage for its greater diversity through a mixture of luck (its geography and history) and planning (the conscious decision to be open to all).

Canada's immigration since the 1970s has overwhelmingly been of visible minorities from the developing world.

Since the late 1980s, Canada has accepted some 225,000 to 275,000 immigrants annually. Canada also has one of the world's highest naturalization rates compared to other immigrant-receiving countries.

---

[103] Joy Kogawa's novel *Obasan* brings to life this shameful episode in Canada's history.

DIVERSITY WITHIN DIVERSITY — CANADA'S DEMOGRAPHICS

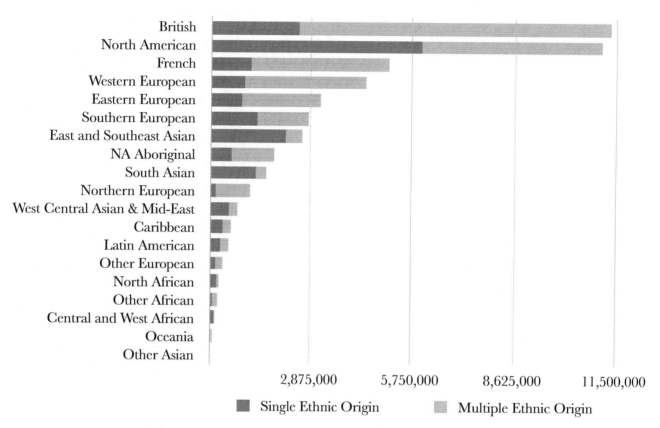

CANADA: ETHNIC ORIGINS 2011

The above chart shows the overall ethnic origins reported by Canadians, including both single and multiple origins. The traditional European communities continue to be predominant. North American is largely composed of those identifying themselves as Canadian.

More recent communities from Asia and the Mid-East form an increasing aspect of Canadian diversity. Caribbean includes both long standing Black communities as well as more recent immigration.

Other European includes those who identify themselves as Jewish (83 percent) as well as small percentages who identify themselves as Roma, Basque or Slav.

African ethnic origins reflect recent immigration. Oceania is largely Australian and New Zealand origin.

Given current trends in new immigrants (permanent residents), grouped by ethnic origin, the chart below makes clear how the face of Canada has changed over the last 25 years, becoming more Asian, Mid-Eastern, African and Latin American.

CANADA: ANNUAL AVERAGE IMMIGRANT INTAKE BY
REGION - 1988-2013

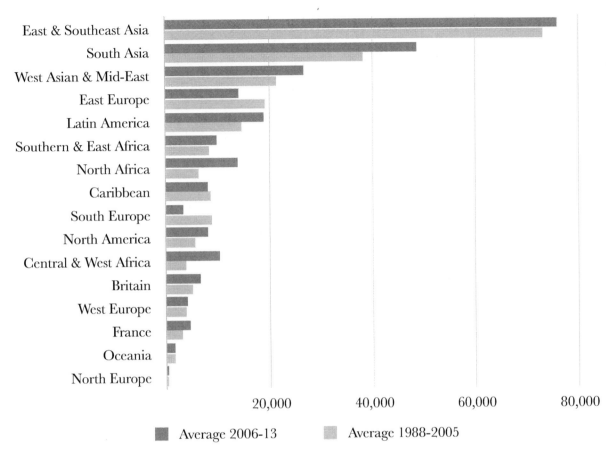

Looking at immigration by religious groups over the most recent ten year period, Christians are still the largest group (41.9 percent), followed closely by religious minorities (36.2 percent) and those with no religious affiliation (21.9 percent).

A more detailed listing of the top 50 ethnic origins in Canada can be found in Appendix D.

CANADA: IMMIGRATION BY RELIGIOUS AFFILIATION 2001-2011

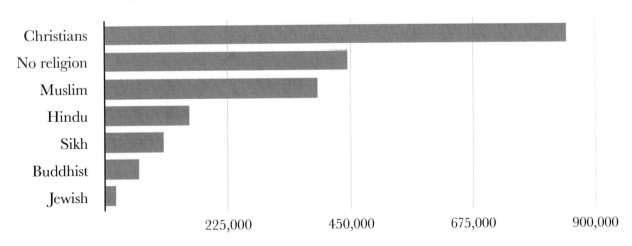

Who is "Canadian?" — Multiple Ethnic Origins

Since Canada is a country of immigrants, many of whom have been here for generations, it is not surprising that a large number of Canadians report multiple ethnic origins — about 42 percent overall. The rate varies by community, however. European communities have the highest level of multiple-origin members (around 80 percent), and Asian communities have the least (less than 10 percent).

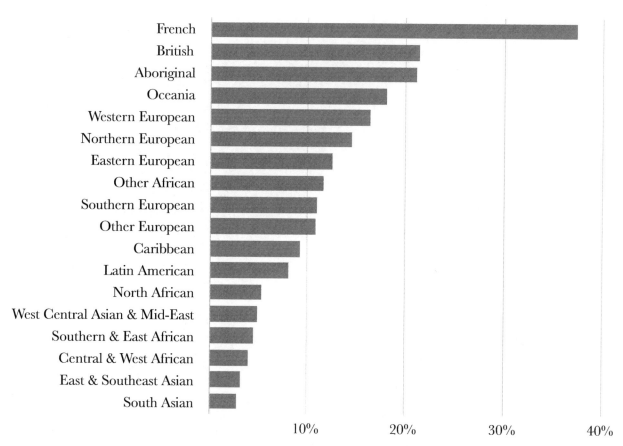

PERCENTAGE ETHNIC ORIGIN IDENTIFYING
THEMSELVES AS HAVING CANADIAN ANCESTRY 2011

As the following generation chart shows, the longer a community is in Canada, the higher the percentage of those reporting multiple origins. There are some exceptions, particularly Aboriginal Peoples and "Canadians" who report higher first- and second-generation rates than third-generation or higher. This suggests that many of the concerns about immigrant integration overly focus on first- and second-generation issues, neglecting to realize that by the third-generation or later, as Lawrence Hill asks, "who among us is not all mixed up?

Mixed unions, as defined by visible minority/non-visible minority couples and couples of two different visible minorities, continue to increase. In 2001, mixed unions represented 4.6 percent of all couples, with Japanese, Latin American and Black most likely to be in a mixed union and South Asian and Chinese least likely. Not surprisingly, most mixed unions occur in our cities. The five cities with the largest number of mixed unions are Vancouver (9.6 percent), Toronto (8.2

percent), Victoria (7.2 percent), Ottawa (7.2 percent) and Calgary (7.0 percent).[104] Montreal has a relatively low share of mixed unions (5.2 percent). So over time, the percentage of those who are "mixed up" will continue to increase, with individual identities becoming more complex and diverse.

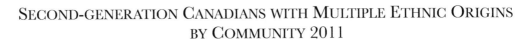

SECOND-GENERATION CANADIANS WITH MULTIPLE ETHNIC ORIGINS BY COMMUNITY 2011

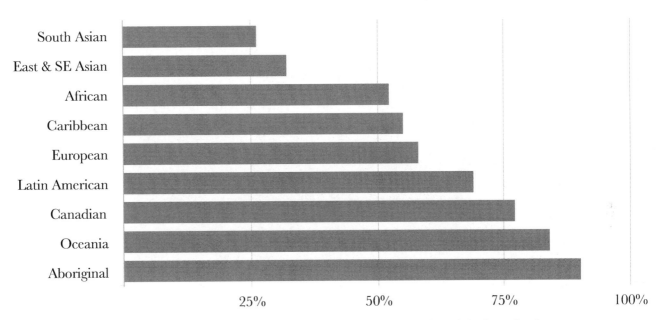

The relatively high percentage of people who are of French ethnic origin but also have Canadian ancestry reflects France's original founding role, and that the term "Canadien" connotes both French and Canadian origins. Reflecting this, 43.1 percent of those identifying themselves as Canadian/Canadien live in Quebec compared to only 27.6 percent in Ontario.

CANADIAN ETHNIC ORIGIN BY GENERATION 2011

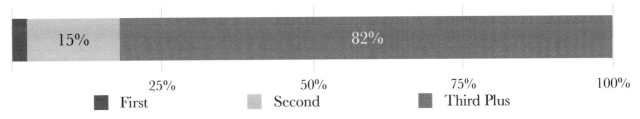

Over 80 percent of those identifying themselves as having Canadian ancestry are third-generation or more. Less than three percent are first-generation. Of those who identify themselves as *only* having Canadian ancestry, 96 percent are third-generation or more, and the

---

[104] "Mixed unions in Canada," *Statistics Canada*.

balance are second-generation. Less than four percent identify with their regional identity (Acadien and Québécois primarily).[105]

If one looks at at second-generation immigrants with multiple origins, one finds that relatively few South Asians and East and Southeast Asians report multiple ethnic origins.

Those of European ethnic origin similarly are third-generation or more, while more recent immigrants tend to be more equally divided among first and second-generations.

Not surprisingly, these trends show up in those groups that have been in Canada longest, particularly French, British and Aboriginal.

While many multiple origins reflect mixed unions from within the same general category (e.g., North Europeans marrying South Europeans), there are an increasing number of mixed unions between visible minorities and non-visible minorities, as well as between different visible minority communities. In general, religion is a more important factor than place of birth or language spoken.[106]

---

[105] The "Canadian Ethnic Origin by Generation" chart refers to those identifying their ethnic origin as Canadian, either either partly or solely, including the very small number (less than five percent) who identify with their regional identity (e.g., Acadian, Québécois).

[106] "Mixed Unions in Canada."

Wide Range of Diversity within Provinces and Cities

PROVINCIAL DIVERSITY 2011

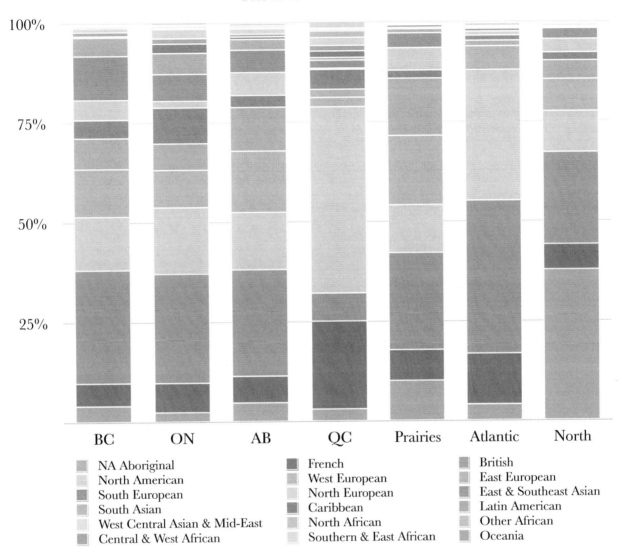

NA Aboriginal	French	British
North American	West European	East European
South European	North European	East & Southeast Asian
South Asian	Caribbean	Latin American
West Central Asian & Mid-East	North African	Other African
Central & West African	Southern & East African	Oceania

Taking a look at provincial diversity, we find a wide range of diversity levels:

- British and Ontario are the most diverse;
- Atlantic Canada is the least diverse;
- Quebec is less diverse than Alberta;
- Manitoba and Saskatchewan are characterized by a large
- First Nations and Métis population; and,
- the North is unique in its majority-Inuit-and-other-aboriginal population.

Cities show a similar pattern, with diversity reflecting where economic growth is strongest. The shift to the West can be seen in Calgary's higher lever of diversity than Montreal. Edmonton follows close behind.

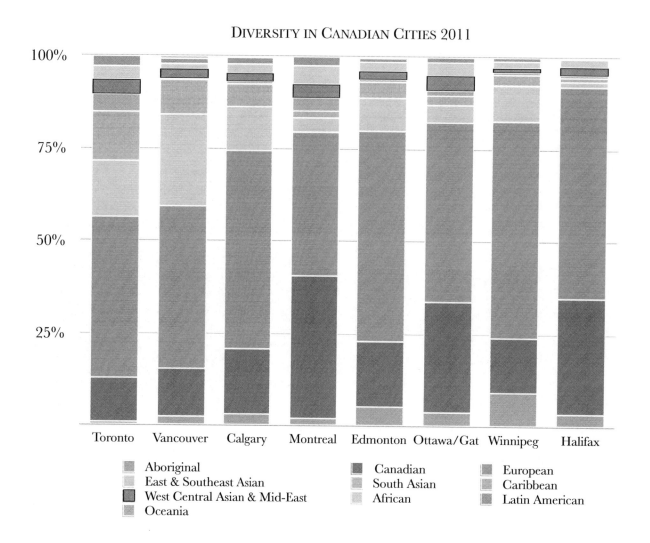

DIVERSITY IN CANADIAN CITIES 2011

Increase in Religious Diversity

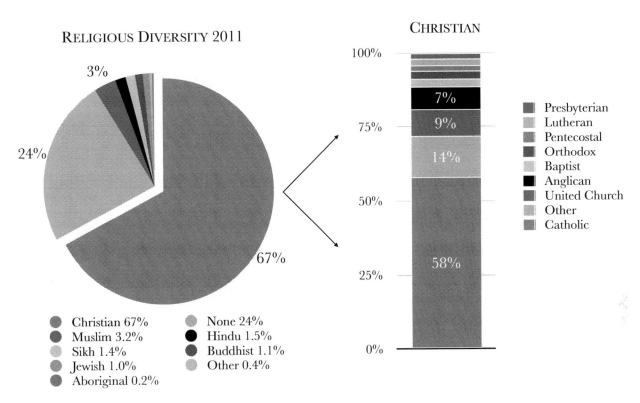

RELIGIOUS DIVERSITY 2011

3%

24%

67%

- Christian 67%
- Muslim 3.2%
- Sikh 1.4%
- Jewish 1.0%
- Aboriginal 0.2%
- None 24%
- Hindu 1.5%
- Buddhist 1.1%
- Other 0.4%

CHRISTIAN

100%
75%
50%
25%
0%

7%
9%
14%
58%

- Presbyterian
- Lutheran
- Pentecostal
- Orthodox
- Baptist
- Anglican
- United Church
- Other
- Catholic

Not surprisingly, most residents of Canada identify themselves as Christian. Roughly 60 percent of Christians identify as Catholic and 25 percent as one of the various Protestant denominations.

About a quarter do not identify with any religious affiliation.

Muslims form the largest religious minority, followed by Hindus, Sikhs, Buddhists, and Jews. Very few practice (or at least identify themselves as practising) aboriginal spirituality (about 65,000).

The religious affiliations of visible minorities vary according to the minority as seen in the following chart, with South Asians being the most religiously diverse.

CANADA: RELIGIONS OF VISIBLE MINORITIES 2011

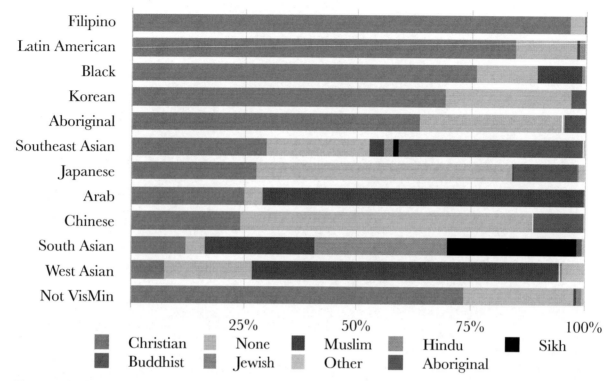

The results from a generational perspective are not surprising. Members of religions that have more recently come to the fore are largely first-generation immigrants. Canadian Jews are split evenly among the generations. In contrast, Christians, followers of aboriginal spirituality, and those with no religious affiliation are more likely to have a longer familial history in Canada -- two-thirds or more are third-generation.

FIRST-GENERATION CANADIANS PERCENTAGE BY RELIGION 2011

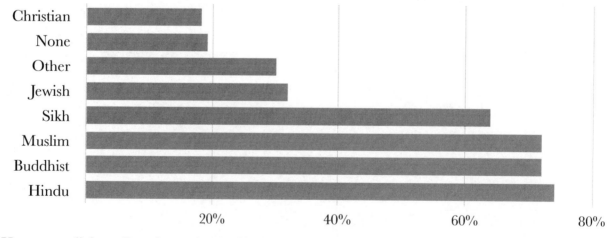

However, religious diversity varies significantly from province-to- province and city-to-city, and in its variation follows a similar pattern to ethnic diversity. British Columbia is particularly notable for the high number identifying "none" as their religion, reflecting in part its large Asian population but also many European-origin residents. Quebec, in contrast, is overwhelmingly

Christian. Minority religions form a relatively high share of the population in British Columbia and Ontario, as would be expected.

RELIGIOUS MINORITIES IN THE PROVINCES 2011

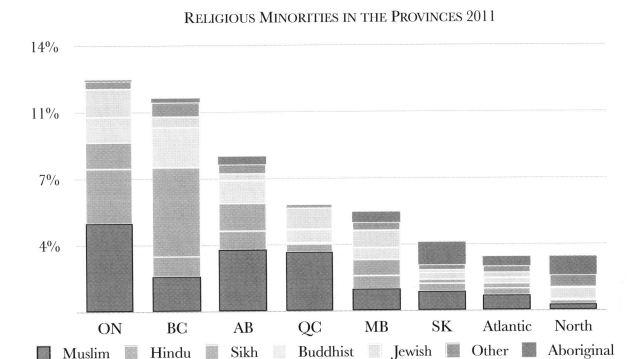

Cities reflect these overall patterns, and it is noteworthy that Calgary has more religious diversity than Montreal, with the latter having a higher number of Muslims.

RELIGIOUS MINORITIES IN MAJOR CITIES 2011 (CMAs)

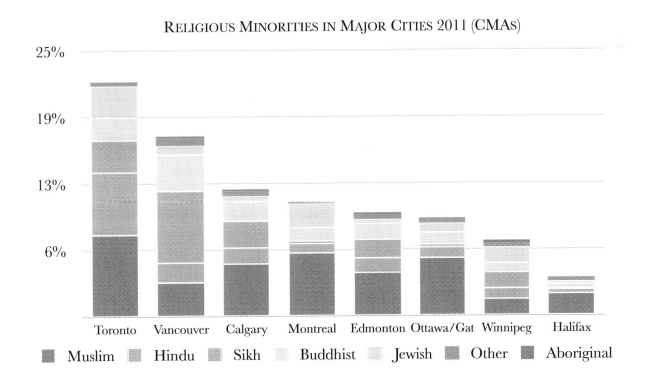

THE PERSISTENCE OF ECONOMIC DIFFERENCES

Most immigrants come to Canada for economic reasons, to better their lives and provide more opportunities for their children. As then-Minister for Citizenship and Immigration Jason Kenney said:

> ...people choose to immigrate to Canada not because they want to live a seminar in diversity, not because they have particular grievances related to their country of origin. They come here for opportunity. They come here with the expectation that if they work hard, they'll be able to have a higher standard of living, and pass on their future to their kids, significantly more prosperous than what they should have had back home.[107]

While there is strong political consensus that immigration strengthens the economy, there are contrary voices arguing that large-scale immigration and the change in source countries from Europe have resulted in a net drain to Canada. For example, Grady and Grubel have argued that the net cost to Canada is about $6,000 per immigrant for more recent cohorts of immigrants (1987-2004), based upon their lower incomes and higher fiscal transfers. This forms the basis of their rationale for dramatic reductions in the number of immigrants, particularly with respect to visible minority immigrants given their relatively poor economic outcomes..[108]

Mohsen Javdani and Krishna Pendakur focus on earlier, more established immigrant cohorts (1970-2004). They make different calculations of property tax paid, use the Canadian-born as their comparator rather than "all Canadian residents" (which includes immigrants) and note the need to account for public goods, such as defence spending, that are not directly linked to immigration levels (unlike education and healthcare for example). They also identify errors in Grady and Grubel's calculations and show a much lower fiscal transfer of $500 per immigrant.[109]

However, both series of studies agree that more recent cohorts are not doing as well. The same is true of more recent research, notably studies by Corak, Pendakur and Pendakur, and Block and Galabuzi, which focus on some of the barriers faced by visible minorities and other communities of recent immigrants.[110]

There are different measures of economic success. For the purpose of this analysis, I will mainly focus on unemployment rates, low-income cut-off (LICO) prevalence (families spending

---

[107] Quoted in Susan Delacourt, *Shopping for Votes: How Politicians Choose Us and How We Choose Them* 234-5.

[108] Herbert Grubel and Patrick Grady, "Fiscal Transfers to Immigrants in Canada: Responding to Critics and a Revised Estimate."

[109] Mohsen Javdani and Krishna Pendakur, "Fiscal Transfers to Immigrants in Canada" and "Fiscal Effects of Immigrants in Canada."

[110] Miles Corak, "Immigration in the Long Run: The Education and Earnings Mobility of Second-Generation Canadians"; Krishna and Ravi Pendakur, "Colour By Numbers: Minority Earnings in Canada 1996-2006;" and, Sheila Block and Grace-Edward Galabuzi, "Canada's Colour Coded Labour Market: The Gap For Racialized Workers."

20 percentage points more than the average family on food, shelter and clothing) and full-time employment median income from the point of ethnic origin, visible minorities, and religion.

CANADA: VISIBLE MINORITY UNEMPLOYMENT AND LICO PREVALENCE COMPARED TO NON-VISIBLE MINORITY 2011

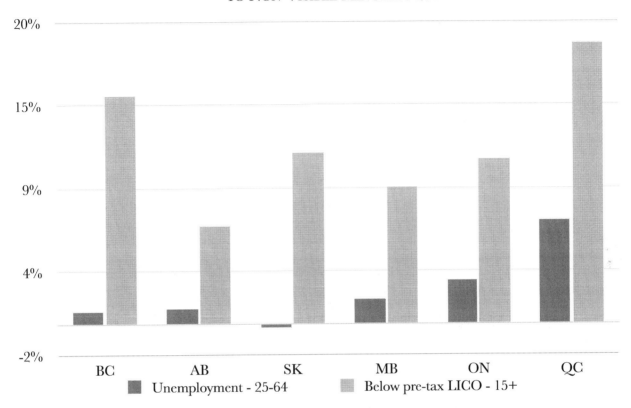

Comparing the larger provinces in terms of the relative economic success between visible minorities and non-visible minorities focussing on unemployment and LICO provides an initial sense of the disparities. The following chart shows that in all provinces except Saskatchewan, unemployment rates are higher for visible minorities. The gap is particularly large in Quebec, where the unemployment rate for visible minorities is almost 7 percent higher than for non-visible minorities.[111]

Similarly, LICO prevalence is generally between two to three times higher for visible minorities, with only Alberta faring somewhat better.

By way of comparison, unemployment rates for Aboriginal people are generally higher across the country, while LICO prevalence is generally lower.

At the national level, for simplicity's sake, I will focus on two areas: the contrast between first and second generations (to measure how well the children of immigrants are doing in relation to

_____

[111] I have not included Atlantic Canada and the North given the relatively small numbers of visible minorities. However, the high prevalence of below pre-tax LICO in Atlantic Canada is comparable to Quebec. In the North, visible minorities have markedly lower unemployment rates, unlike the high unemployment rates of Aboriginal peoples.

their parents) and the difference in outcomes between men and women. The main emphasis will be on working-age adults, defined as those between 25 and 64.

I will also look at visible minority seniors, given that this view captures those who were not born and educated in Canada, and who often have weaker language skills. To partially address some of the issues raised by Grubel and Grady, I will also examine government transfers and taxes paid as percentage of income for seniors, recognizing that this does not measure consumption of public services such as healthcare.

Most visible minorities reflect recent waves of immigration hence the low number of second-generation individuals (between 10 to 20 percent). Larger second-generation groups include: Chinese (92,230), South Asian (83,420), Black (74,875) and Filipino (24,520). Numbers for immigrants of the third-generation or higher are extremely low, as the chart below illustrates. This is true even for visible minorities with a longer history of immigration such as Southeast Asian and Black (about five percent, compared to one or two percent for others). Only Japanese Canadians have a relative balance between the generations.

CANADA: VISIBLE MINORITY 25-64 BY GENERATION 2011

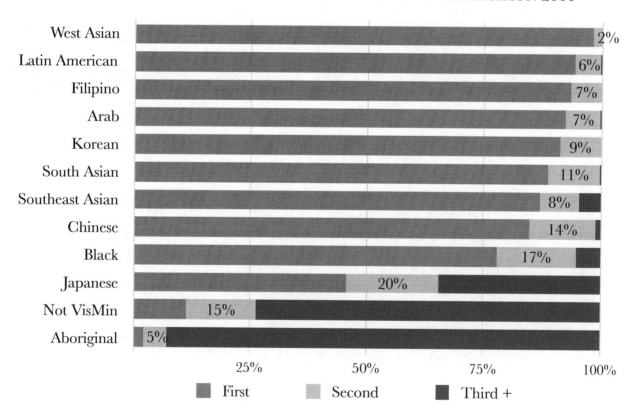

For the purpose of overall assessment of how well the various communities are doing, I will focus on the second-generation, members of which have all benefitted from Canadian education, are fluent in English or French and have Canadian "cultural fluency."

Strong Workforce Participation but Weaker Employment

Canada has a workforce of close to fifteen million working-age adults (ages 25 to 64). Close to three million are visible minorities.

Starting with participation in the workforce (willingness to work), second-generation participation rates are greater for all communities compared to non-visible minorities, save for West Asian Canadians. First-generation participation rates are more mixed, depending on the community.

CANADA: PARTICIPATION RATE 2011 DIFFERENCES BY
GENERATION COMPARED TO NON-VISIBLE MINORITY 25-64

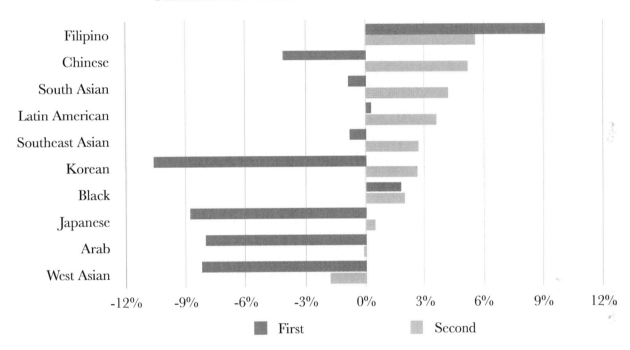

Non-visible minority participation rates for the most part show little variation between generations, with the exception of Aboriginal people, West Europeans and South Europeans. This is not surprising, since these groups have either always resided in Canada (Aboriginal people) or reflect earlier waves of immigration (Europeans).

CANADA: PARTICIPATION RATE 2011 BY GENERATION FOR
ABORIGINAL, CANADIAN AND EUROPEAN ORIGINS 25-64

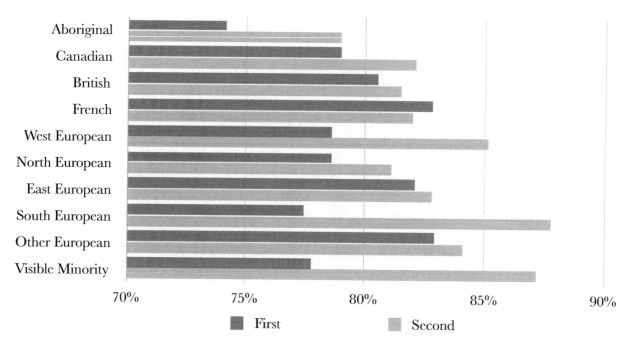

The next chart compares visible minority unemployment rates to the non-visible minority unemployment rate, separated out by first and second-generation working-age adults (25-64). As noted above, the number of second-generation immigrants in this category is relatively small for visible minority groups other than Japanese Canadians.[112]

CANADA: UNEMPLOYMENT RATE DIFFERENCES 2011 BY
GENERATION COMPARED TO NON-VISIBLE MINORITY 25-64

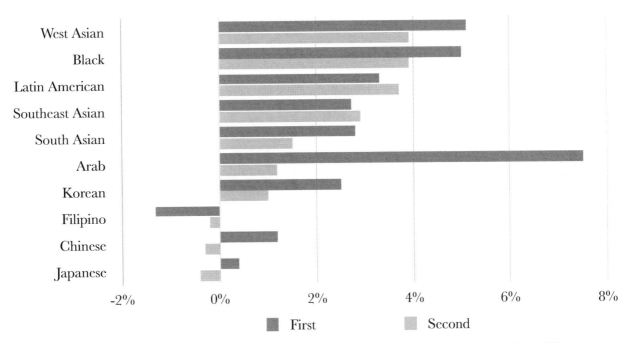

While a difference of two to four percent may not appear significant, compared to differences of six percent or more with respect to youth (15-24) and younger workers (24-29), the numbers affected are significant. Looking at the overall Canadian picture in 2011, some 5.9 percent, or 720,000 non-visible minorities are unemployed, compared to 8.3 percent or 235,000 for visible minorities. If, however, the visible minority rate was the same (5.9 percent), this would mean almost 70,000 fewer unemployed, a reduction of almost 30 percent. Or conversely, if the non-visible minority rate was 8.3 percent as is the case for visible minorities, almost 300,000 more unemployed would result, more than 30 percent higher than the current level.

In general, however, and as expected, the second-generation has slightly lower unemployment than the first-generation. The exception is Arab Canadians, who show nearly a five percent decrease in unemployment between these generations. But for virtually all visible minority groups, unemployment is higher than for non-visible minorities, save for second-generation

---

[112] Only Black and Japanese Canadians have more than 10,000 third-generation in the workforce. Compared to non-visible minorities, the unemployment rate for third-generation Black Canadians is 4.2 percent higher, and for third-generation Japanese Canadians, it is 1.7 percent lower.

Chinese, Japanese and Filipinos, with only first-generation Filipinos having even less unemployment than non-visible minorities.[113]

With unemployment, a similar picture of improving outcomes for the second-generation emerges for those in the workforce.

Looking at those of European ethnic origin, the gaps between generations are minimal, with the exception of East and South European. There is also a significant improvement in unemployment rates for second-generation Aboriginal people.[114]

CANADA: UNEMPLOYMENT RATE 2011 BY GENERATION FOR NON-VISIBLE MINORITY MEN AND WOMEN 25-64

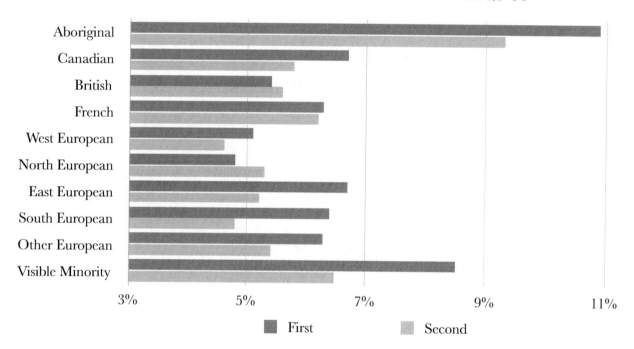

---

[113] Some studies show that, not surprisingly, newcomers were harder hit by the 2008 recession with more pushed into self-employment as a result compared to more established residents. Maya Roy, Navjeet Sidhu and Beth Wilson, "The Economy And Resilience of Newcomers (EARN): Exploring Newcomer Entrepreneurship."

[114] Aboriginal people second-generation outcomes are not that meaningful. The vast majority of Aboriginal people (93.0 percent) identify as third-generation or higher, 5.7 percent as second-generation and 1.4 percent as first-generation. However, we have included this information to be consistent.

Let us shift from generations to gender, starting with visible minorities. As Table 4 shows, first-generation participation gender gaps are significant for both visible minorities and non-visible minorities (12 percent), with gaps greatest for Arab, South Asian, West Asian and Japanese immigrants.

There is no significant difference in gender participation rates between visible minorities and Aboriginal people and those of Canadian and European ethnic origin for the first-generation. However, second-generation visible minorities generally have a smaller gender gap than those of European origin.

The picture changes dramatically for the second-generation. Participation differences are generally smaller, with West Asian, Black, Southeast Asian, South Asian and Filipino women having higher participation rates than men. Gender differences are minimal with respect to those of European origin.

With respect to unemployment, starting with visible minorities, the gender gap has largely disappeared for most. The exceptions are the Black, Korean and Southeast Asian communities, in which more women than men participate in the workforce, and the West Asian community, where the opposite is true.

There is a smaller difference between male and female visible minorities and non-visible minorities for the second-generation, but there remains a persistent difference of more than two percent for West Asian, Black, Latin American and South Asian.

CANADA: UNEMPLOYMENT RATE 2011 COMPARED TO CHRISTIANS 25-64

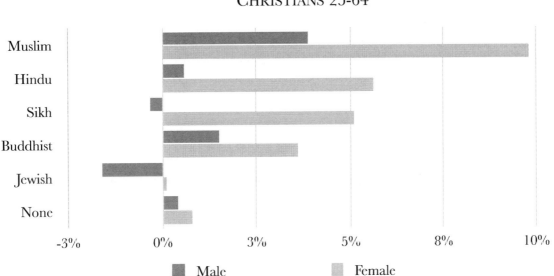

Looking at religion, while all minority religions have higher unemployment rates than Christians (Jewish males and females are the exception, but the difference for the latter is statistically insignificant), the gender gaps for minority religions are relatively high for Muslims, Sikhs and Hindus (after comparing women and men within each ethnic group with Christian

TABLE 4: WOMEN 25-64 IN THE ECONOMY COMPARED TO MEN BY GENERATION 2011				
	Participation Rate		Unemployment Rate	
	First	Second	First	Second
Visible Minority				
Arab	-18.5%	-2.2%	4.4%	0.0%
Black	-9.7%	2.9%	0.9%	-2.2%
Chinese	-9.3%	-0.1%	1.5%	0.1%
Filipino	-3.1%	0.6%	-0.1%	-0.7%
Japanese	-15.3%	-7.5%	4.3%	0.0%
Korean	-11.9%	-1.8%	1.2%	-4.2%
Latin American	-14.0%	-3.0%	1.7%	-0.3%
Not VisMin	-12.0%	-9.1%	0.6%	-0.7%
South Asian	-17.4%	0.6%	4.6%	-1.5%
Southeast Asian	-13.0%	2.1%	1.2%	-2.1%
West Asian	-16.5%	6.8%	3.9%	3.5%
Non-Visible Minority				
Aboriginal	-10.5%	-7.7%	-3.7%	-1.1%
Canadian	-14.0%	-8.7%	1.0%	-1.0%
British	-10.8%	-8.1%	-0.3%	-0.6%
French	-9.1%	-7.5%	0.3%	-1.1%
West European	-13.8%	-9.2%	0.9%	0.0%
North European	-11.7%	-8.7%	0.1%	-1.1%
East European	-10.5%	-7.7%	1.5%	-1.1%
South European	-13.3%	-6.1%	0.5%	-0.3%
Other European	-10.8%	-9.3%	1.0%	1.3%

women and men).[115] This pattern largely repeats itself in all provinces, with the largest differences in Quebec.

Correlating visible minority groups with religion for second-generation adults aged 25-34, table 5 shows unemployment rates by religion within each visible minority group and vice versa. It appears that the visible minority group is a more important factor than religion: there is generally a greater variation between visible minority groups than between religious groups. Black and West Asian Canadian Christians have have higher unemployment rates that other Christians, with West Asian Muslims having the highest unemployment rate for this generation and age cohort.

For members aged 25-34 of all generations (but especially the first), the variations are larger. This reflects some of the integration challenges of first-generation immigrants.[116]

TABLE 5: CANADA: UNEMPLOYMENT RATES 2011 BY RELIGION AND VISIBLE MINORITY SECOND GENERATION 25-34

	Christian	None	Muslim	Buddhist	Hindu	Sikh	Jewish
South Asian	8.0%	7.5%	7.7%	8.3%	6.6%	6.8%	
Chinese	5.4%	4.9%		5.9%			
Black	9.9%	9.7%	7.6%				
Filipino	5.1%	4.8%					
Latin American	8.1%	11.8%					
Arab	7.9%	7.6%	7.0%				
Southeast Asian	5.9%	7.6%		9.7%			
West Asian	10.4%	0.0%	20.3%				
Korean	7.3%	7.3%					
Japanese	6.5%	4.0%		0.0%			
Not VisMin	5.8%	6.6%	6.7%	7.8%			7.8%

[115] As previously noted, the very small percentage practicing Aboriginal spirituality (less than five percent of the Aboriginal population) makes this view less relevant than Aboriginal ethnic origin. But both men and women practicing Aboriginal spirituality have a significantly higher unemployment rate compared to Christians (17.3% for men and 11.3% for women). I have also not included "other" given the small numbers (under 60,000 for both genders), with a 2.5 percent gap for males and 3.3 percent for females.

[116] This table only includes data of religious affiliation within each visible minority group with a minimum of one percent of each visible minority group who follow a particular religion.

Persistent Income Differences

Looking at income, both in terms of pre-tax LICO prevalence for individuals and median income, a similar pattern emerges in that some communities are doing better than others. Among visible minorities, Chinese and Japanese Canadians are doing relatively the best in terms of median income, with Korean Canadians doing the worst.

From a low-income cut-off (LICO) perspective, the picture is somewhat varied. For some communities, there is a relatively direct correlation between there being a large number of working-age adults (25-64) below LICO, and a tendency towards lower incomes. This is particularly true for Korean, West Asian and Arab Canadians. In other cases (such as that of Filipino, Southeast Asian [no comma] and South Asian Canadians), the number below LICO is lower than median income would suggest. This likely reflects, in part, higher participation rates. For virtually all groups, second-generation LICO prevalence is between 30 to 50 percent lower than it is for the first-generation.

CANADA: LOW-INCOME CUT-OFF PREVALENCE FULL-TIME
EMPLOYED 25-64 - 2011

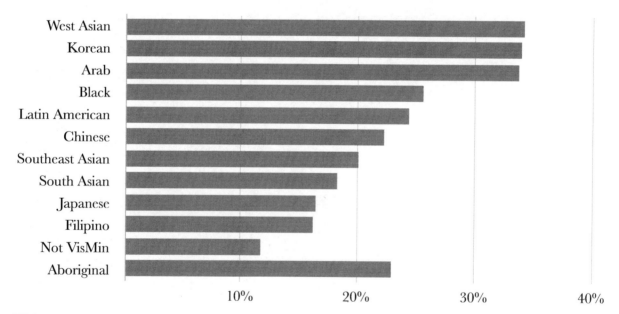

This pattern is generally reflected across the country. However, some variations stand-out. Quebec shows a high concentration of immigrants below LICO, especially in its South Asian, Chinese, Black, Latin American and West Asian population (over 30 percent compared to 13 percent for non-visible minorities). Even Japanese Canadians are doing relatively poorly in Quebec. Atlantic Canada is also doing poorly, but its visible minority population is small. Predictably, Alberta does better than all the other provinces that also have large minority populations.

For Aboriginal people, below-LICO prevalence is highest in British Columbia, Saskatchewan and Manitoba, all of which have rates over 25 percent.

CANADA: MEDIAN INCOME FULL-TIME EMPLOYED 25-64 - 2011

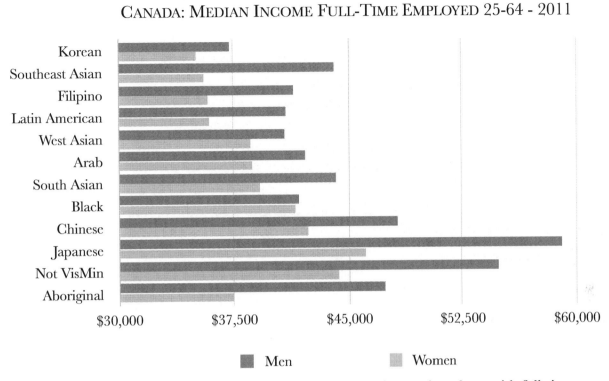

With respect to median income at the national level, I have focussed on those with full-time employment, who comprise 86.8 of all employed (for both visible minorities and others). Some groups are, however, somewhat more likely to have lower rates of full-time employment (Korean, West Asian and Japanese at 83.2, 82.9 and 81.6 percent respectively).

From a gender perspective, women are more likely to have part-time employment for both non-visible minorities (55.8 percent) and visible minorities (55.1 percent). But some interesting group differences emerge. Part-time rates for Arab and West Asian women are significantly higher, at 66.8 and 63.4 percent respectively. In contrast, Filipino men are more likely to have part-time employment (57.0 percent). Women with part-time employment, whether or not they are visible minorities or not, have higher median incomes than men with part-time employment, , which may reflect a combination of the workplace and/or hours of work. The difference is greater for visible minority women, who make 114.4 percent of visible minority male median incomes, than it is for those who are not visible minorities, who make 104.6 percent of the income of their male counterparts.

For those with full-time employment, the gap between visible minority and non-visible minority shrinks for the second-generation, particularly for women. For Japanese and Chinese Canadians, the gap essentially disappears. For most others, a significant gap remains (particularly for Black and Latin American Canadians). Japanese, Chinese, and Korean Canadian women enjoy higher median incomes than non-visible minority women, with South Asian women virtually equal with this group.

MEDIAN INCOME OF SECOND-GENERATION CANADIANS
25-64 - 2011

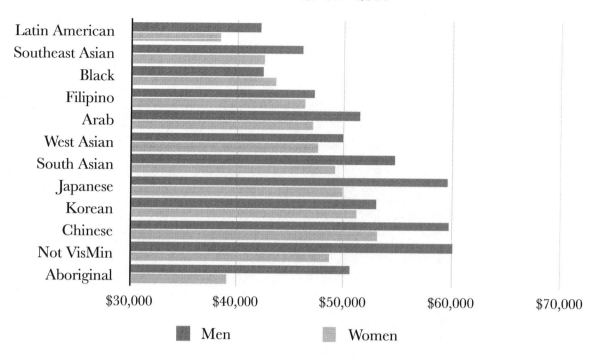

Regionally, more visible minority groups have significantly lower median incomes ($10,000 difference or more) in Alberta, Saskatchewan and Ontario (mainly South Asian, Filipino, Latin American, Southeast Asian, West Asian and Korean). Japanese Canadians have higher median incomes in most provinces and Arab Canadians have higher median income in Manitoba compared to other provinces.

However, if we only look at the younger cohort of the university-educated second-generation between 25 and 34 years old, some 204,000 people (about one-third of this group), the gaps shrink further for men.[117] West Asian, Arab, Japanese, South Asian and Chinese Canadian men have incomes higher or equal to men who are not visible minorities. Latin American, Southeast Asian, Black, Filipino and Korean Canadian men have lower median incomes. Filipino, South Asian, Chinese and Korean women have higher median incomes than women who are not visible minorities, while the median incomes of those in other groups are lower.

The gaps are particularly large for Black and Latin American men (83.4 and 83.7 percent of non-visible minority male median incomes). For women, West Asian Canadian women have the largest gap (88.0 percent of non-visible minority women median income).

While the income picture for this age group is reasonably good overall, it needs to be considered in conjunction with unemployment rates, which are higher. On the whole, visible minorities aged 25-34 have an unemployment rate of 7.2 percent, one percent higher than non-

---

[117] The percentage of second-generation residents aged 25-34 ranges from 52.6 percent of all Black second-generation to 67.5 percent of Southeast Asian second-generation, with only Japanese Canadians outside of this range at 42.5 percent. In terms of university education, this ranges from 25 percent for Latin Americans to two-thirds of Chinese Canadians.

CANADA: MEDIAN INCOME FULL-TIME EMPLOYED SECOND-GENERATION 25-34 UNIVERSITY-EDUCATED 2011

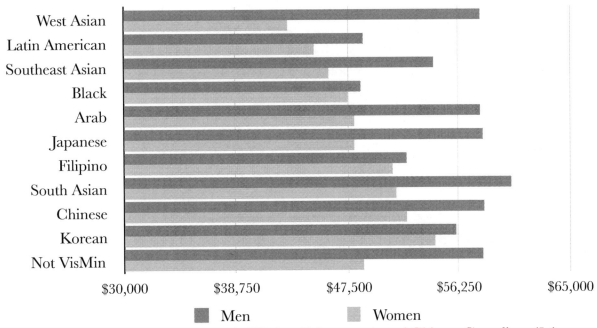

visible minorities. Japanese (4.9 percent), Filipino (5.0 percent) and Chinese Canadians (5.1 percent) have the lowest unemployment rates. West Asian (10.0 percent), Black (9.8 percent) and Latin American Canadians have unemployment rates over 50 percent greater than non-visible minorities.

CANADA: MEDIAN INCOME FULL-TIME EMPLOYED SECOND-GENERATION 25-34 POST-SECONDARY 2011

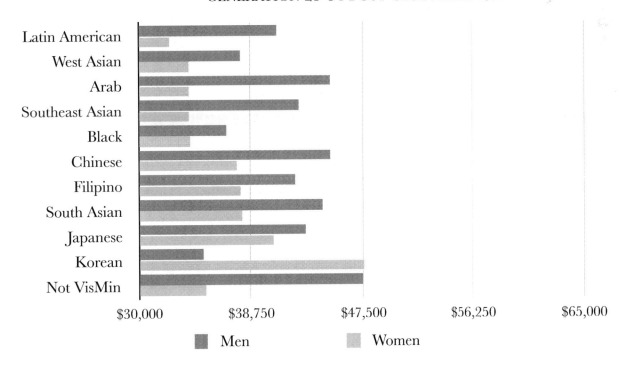

If we take a look at second-generation immigrants 25-34 with post-secondary education (community colleges, CEGEPs or non-university degree), we find that a different pattern of larger and more frequent median-income gaps emerges. Latin American, West Asian, Arab, Southeast Asian and Black Canadian women all have lower median incomes, with Chinese, Filipino, South Asian and Japanese Canadian women having higher median incomes. All male, visible minority groups have lower median incomes than males who are not visible minorities, though Korean and Black Canadian men fare particularly poorly (making 74.0 and 77.8 percent respectively of the median income of males who are not visible minorities).

Given that second-generation visible minorities benefit from Canadian education, language skills and cultural familiarity, the persistence of these income and employment gaps may reflect in part ongoing barriers and discrimination.

The most convincing example of discrimination is the blind C.V. test in which researchers submit identical C.Vs (controlling for education and experience) to employers, but with different names. The results were striking: Canadians with foreign-sounding names were 40% less likely to be called back for a job interview than those with identical resumes and non-foreign-sounding (English) names. In the words of Professor Oreopoulis, who conducted the study:

> Unfortunately, the study shows an applicant's name matters considerably more than his or her additional education, multiple language skills and extracurricular activities.[118]

Furthermore, in a follow-up study looking at why hiring managers might be biased against applications from candidates with ethnic-sounding names, Oreopoulos found that hiring managers assume that someone with an ethnic-sounding name must be a new immigrant, rather than, for instance, a second-generation Canadian candidate with the requisite education and "social and communications skills to be successful in the job." Examples of hiring manager comments in this study include:

> "I personally am guilty of gravitating toward Anglo names on résumés, and I believe that it's a very human condition – [a result of]resistance to change."

> "... It's difficult to imagine hiring someone with a long first name, as it might be impractical in terms of answering the phone and saying it. People with easy-to-use shorter names are easier to hire and work with."

> "I'm down to about seven seconds to vet a résumé ... I do realize how unfair the whole process is."

Without company policies that remove the names of candidates to avoid such bias, it is unlikely that many visible minorities will be given a fair opportunity to compete for positions, Oreopoulos concludes.[119]

---

[118] "Right résumé, wrong name." *The Globe and Mail.* 20 May 2009.

[119] "How an ethnic-sounding name may affect the job hunt." *The Globe and Mail.* 17 November 2011.

One example of corporate leadership to recognize — and address — these biases is the recent Royal Bank of Canada and Ernst Young study, _Outsmarting our brains: Overcoming hidden biases to harness diversity's true potential_, which suggests leaders and managers ask themselves the following questions to reduce bias in hiring and other related management decisions:

- _Do I typically hire the same type of person, or personality type?_

- _When I say a candidate is not the right fit, what do I mean?_

- _What does my slate of candidates look like? Do I speak up if it is not sufficiently diverse?_

- _Which of my past hires were successful, and what can I learn from those choices that didn't work out as well?_

- _Who do I like to assign to work on project teams? Who do I tap for the lead role? Do I have the same go-to people all or most of the time?_

- _Who do I take to important client or cross-team meetings?_

- _Who do I encourage to lead or speak out at meetings? Am I creating opportunities for those less extroverted to demonstrate their capabilities equally to clients or other colleagues?_

- _How do I identify candidates for promotion and succession?_

The report goes on to summarize research showing that:

> … leaders who identify and confront their hidden biases are better at managing multiple viewpoints and perspectives, improving connections with clients and delivering bottom-line results. And while it may not be easy, it's important for leaders to raise their awareness, challenge their thinking and develop truly inclusive leadership behaviours in order to set the course for others and drive change.[120]

---

[120] Royal Bank and Ernst & Young, _Outsmarting our brains: Overcoming hidden biases to harness diversity's true potential_.

Seniors are Struggling

In Canada, there are approximately 4.5 million seniors, only about 10 percent of whom are a visible minority.

In general, more visible minority seniors are in the low-income category compared to non-visible minorities. Exceptions are South Asian, Japanese and Filipino visible minority seniors. For the most part, gender differences are relatively small, except for West Asian, Southeast Asian, South Asian and Filipino Canadians, as shown in the chart below (which ranks groups by their number of low-income female seniors).

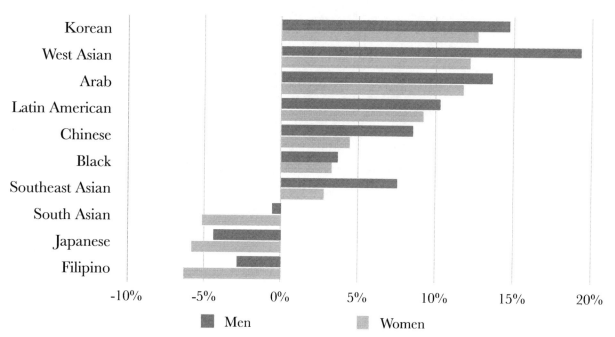

CANADA: VISIBLE MINORITY SENIORS PRE-TAX LICO PREVALENCE COMPARED TO NON-VISIBLE MINORITY 2011

A broader set of economic indicators for seniors can be seen in Table 6, which compares LICO percentages with percentage of income from government transfers and income tax paid, again contrasting seniors who are visible minorities with those who are not. There is no consistent and direct correlation between LICO and the amount of government transfers, although female seniors are more dependent on government transfers generally. Low income does correlate to lower percentage of income taxes given the nature of the tax system, with a more pronounced effect for women seniors.

Appendix P complements Table 6 by providing the raw rather than relative numbers along with median income.

Gender differences are more significant for those of European ethnic origin (between six and 10 percent) than visible minorities (between two and six percent), with the difference greatest for Black, Latin American and Japanese Canadian seniors.

Lower incomes for seniors may reflect a combination of reduced Canada Pension Plan benefits for women (due to fewer years of contribution given child-rearing or other work absences) and the fact that some immigrants may not qualify for the Old Age Security benefit (not having spent a sufficient amount of time in Canada, the minimum being 10 years after the age of 18).

CANADA: ABORIGINAL, CANADIAN, EUROPEAN ETHNIC ORIGIN SENIORS PRE-TAX LICO PREVALENCE BY GENDER 2011

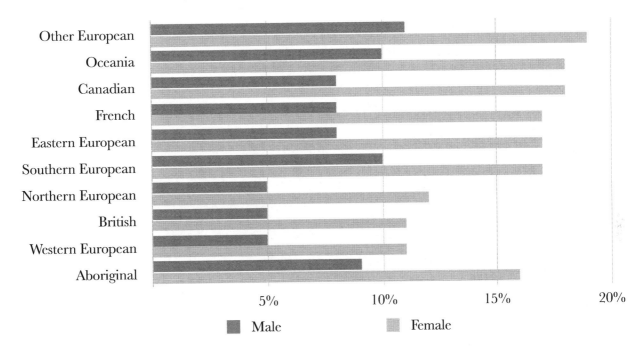

TABLE 6: CANADIAN SENIORS: ECONOMIC INDICATORS COMPARED TO NON-VISIBLE MINORITIES 2011					
	Below pre-tax LICO		Government Income Share of Total		Income Taxes Paid	
	Men	Women	Men	Women	Men	Women
Korean	14.7%	12.7%	9.1%	6.4%	-3.3%	-3.2%
West Asian	19.3%	12.2%	5.5%	16.3%	-0.8%	-5.0%
Arab	13.6%	11.8%	3.3%	12.5%	-0.4%	-3.3%
Latin American	10.3%	9.2%	9.2%	16.0%	-1.0%	-5.0%
Chinese	8.5%	4.4%	7.8%	7.9%	-2.2%	-3.6%
Black	3.7%	3.3%	6.0%	5.0%	-1.2%	-2.5%
Southeast Asian	7.5%	2.8%	12.5%	18.6%	-3.1%	-5.3%
South Asian	-0.6%	-5.2%	2.1%	10.1%	-0.6%	-3.4%
Japanese	-4.4%	-5.8%	-4.0%	-5.8%	-0.2%	-0.4%
Filipino	-2.8%	-6.3%	7.0%	2.4%	-3.1%	-2.3%

Banks, Telecoms and Transport — The Federally Regulated Private Sector

Of the 772,000 employees in the federally regulated private sector (FRS), those working in banking, communications and transportation account for 92 percent (these three main components employ approximately the same proportion of workers). The FRS includes 516 companies, 444 of which are in the major sectors.[121]

Employment equity in Canada targets four designated groups, namely women, Aboriginal Peoples, persons with disabilities and visible minorities.

There are five measures to test the state of employment equity for each group: representation, hiring, promotion, separation, and salaries. Representation (stock) and hirings (flow) are compared to the labour market availability of the targeted groups.

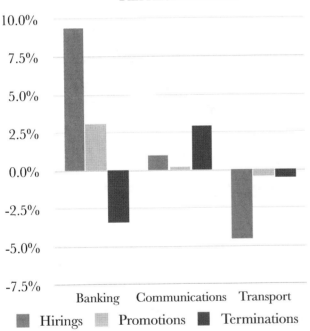

FRS VISIBLE MINORITY 2012 STAFFING COMPARED TO LMA & REPRESENTATION

Representation: Overall representation is below labour market availability (LMA 2011) for women (40.9 percent compared to a LMA of 48.2 percent) and Aboriginal Peoples (2.0 percent compared to a LMA of 3.5 percent).

However, for visible minorities, representation is greater (18.6 percent, compared to a LMA of 17.8 percent).

Hirings, Promotions and Terminations: Not surprisingly given their heavy retail presence, the banking and communications sector hiring and promotions are greater than both labour market availability and representation.[122] Reaching more customers means in part having representatives that reflect customer demographics.

There is no data available in published reports to explain the relative differences between promotions and terminations in the banking and communications sectors.

While the spirit of employment equity aims to have an employed workforce that mirrors society, this strong performance more likely reflects the need for representatives to reflect diverse customer demographics.

---

[121] All data is from the Labour Canada's *Employment Equity Act: Annual Report 2013*. I have not analyzed in detail the "other" group of industries that are federally-regulated given the diverse nature of this group. However, this group does relatively better with respect to Aboriginal Peoples, above LMA, likely given that many companies are resource industries, located in remote locations.

[122]   Promotions are compared to total promotions or to non-EE inside the sector and not to general LMA.

In contrast, while the transportation sector has consumer-oriented companies (e.g., airlines, bus and rail companies), most of the sector serves business and industry, which means a lower business imperative for diversity (except for Aboriginal people in some resource-based sectors such as mining).

FRS 2012 OCCUPATIONAL GROUPS COMPARED TO 2011 LMA

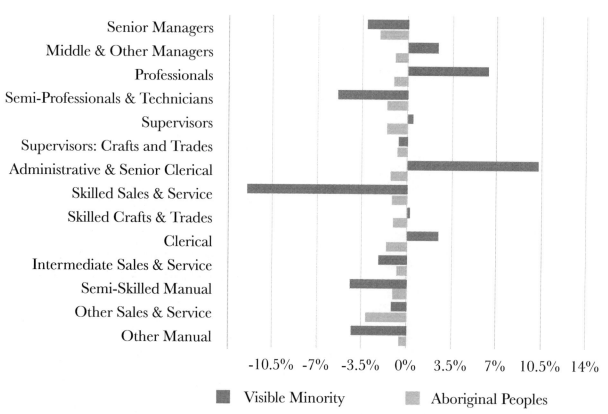

Occupations: With respect to occupational categories, visible minorities are doing relatively better than women. Aboriginal Peoples are relatively close to their labour market availability.

All three groups are somewhat under-represented, with women particularly subject to major variations between occupational groups. Women are proportionately under-represented among professionals and semi-professionals, skilled sales and service and other related personnel, and other manual workers.

Visible minorities, in contrast, tend to be slightly over-represented in some occupational groups (e.g., middle managers, professionals, clerical personnel), though there are some exceptions (e.g., senior managers, technicians, skilled sales and service). But the overall picture is positive, as the variations, with some exceptions, are within five percent of availability.

Salaries: As to salary levels, there are significant differences between Aboriginal Peoples and non-Aboriginals, and between women and men. Male and female Aboriginal people, and women as a whole, are disproportionately concentrated in the lower salary levels.

FRS INCOME DISTRIBUTION COMPARED TO MEN 2012

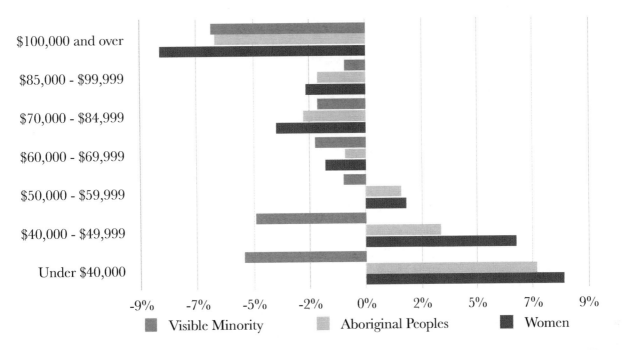

Visible Minority   Aboriginal Peoples   Women

Visible minorities, on the other hand, are more evenly spread across occupational groups. From a salary perspective, however, they are under-represented at both the lowest and highest salary bands. ends of salary bands.

Overall, the federally regulated sector has a higher percentage of low-salary (under $40,000) employees than the federal public service, at close to 20 percent.

While there is limited information regarding non-federally regulated industries, corporate boards have major representation gaps with respect to women and visible minorities. A recent study showed that for companies on the FP 500 index (which includes the larger federally regulated sector companies), just 17.1 percent of directors are women, and only 2 percent are visible minorities.[123]

---

[123] "Women gain on corporate boards but visible minority representation dips," *The Globe and Mail,* 19 November 2014.

SOCIAL

I have focussed on two social indicators. First, as a measure of human capital development, education. Second, as a measure of social inclusion and cohesion, I have focussed on three aspects: hate crimes and perceived discrimination, public institution diversity (healthcare, social services and education) and the degree to which ethnic enclaves exist in Canada.

Strong Educational Achievement

Whether one looks at ethnic origin, visible minorities or religion, more recent communities, reflecting the nature of market demand for skilled workers, tend to be well-educated. In all cases, these groups are better-educated than people who are not visible minorities and, in many cases, those of European ethnic origin.

CANADA: VISIBLE MINORITY LEVELS OF EDUCATION 25-64 - 2011

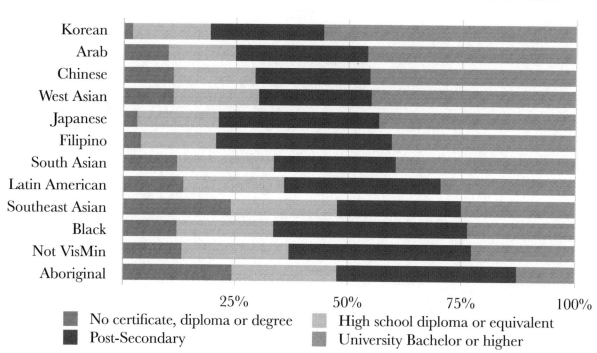

Most visible minorities, particularly those of Asian and Arab origin, are better educated than those who are not visible minorities, particularly those of Asian and Arab origin. Levels of education for Latin American, Southeast Asian and Black Canadians are lower, but still comparable. Black Canadians are more likely to have completed community college, an apprenticeship or other equivalent experience than members of other communities. Overall, 38.1 percent of visible minorities are university-educated compared to 23.0 percent of non-visible minorities.

An ethnic origin perspective shows the variation of education levels among different European origins, with those of Canadian or Aboriginal ethnic origin having the lowest levels of post-secondary and university education. This is partly a reflection of the fact that visible minorities tend to be younger, on average, than Canadians of European origin. Moreover, European-origin

94

Canadians may have a relative preference towards vocational training compared to visible minorities who may prefer university education.

The "Other European" origin is largely Jewish, accounting for the high level of university diplomas as shown in the Education Level by Religion chart below.

And yet these higher levels of education for visible minorities, as seen in the earlier section, are not reflected in lower unemployment rates or higher median incomes.

CANADA 2011 ABORIGINAL, CANADIAN AND EUROPEAN EDUCATION LEVELS 25-64

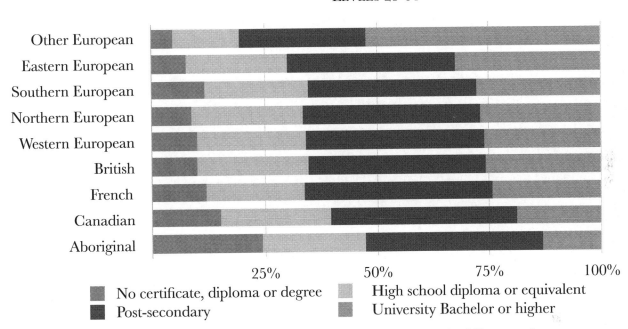

- No certificate, diploma or degree
- Post-secondary
- High school diploma or equivalent
- University Bachelor or higher

Looking at religion, and using university education as the benchmark, differences between groups are greater than differences between men and women of the same group, which are generally less than one percent, save for Muslims (still minimal at two percent higher for men) and Aboriginal people (four percent higher for women). There are slighter more female Christians than male Christians with a university diploma (1.4). The same is true for those without a religious affiliation (1.7 percent).

Another education indicator is the OECD's Programme for International Student Assessment (PISA), which compares the academic performance of fifteen year olds across OECD member countries and some select non-member countries or regions.

While Canada's math, literacy and science scores generally compare well to other OECD countries, Canada is somewhat stronger in equity aspects.[124] This is particularly true of the most diverse Canadian provinces (British Columbia, Alberta, Ontario and Quebec) and is no small achievement given the range of religions and ethnicities represented in Canada's student body.

---

[124] OECD, *PISA 2012 Results in Focus* and Council of Ministers of Education Canada, *Measuring Up: Canadian Results of the OECD PISA Study 2012*. It should be noted that despite the general above average score, Canadian math and science scores have been declining, both with respect to some European countries and some regions in Asia.

CANADA: RELIGION AND LEVELS OF EDUCATION 25-64 - 2011

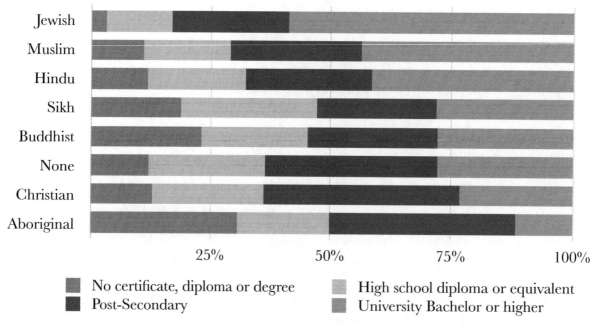

Compared to other immigration-based countries (Australia, New Zealand, USA), and European countries with significant minority populations (France, Germany, UK), Canada has stronger educational outcomes, both overall as well with respect to equity aspects.[125]

---

[125] Among comparator countries, there is not, however, a statistically significant difference with Canada compared to Australia and Germany.

Hate Crimes, Prejudice and Discrimination Remain an Issue

Canada, like a number of other countries, has been collecting information on police-reported hate crimes.[126] A police-reported hate crime involves a higher burden of proof than reporting hate crimes to organizations such as B'nai Brith which collect their own community statistics and who play an important role in raising awareness of the need to report hate crimes.[127]

Most hate crimes (69 percent) involve only mischief, but 31 percent involve violence of some kind. Both the accused and the victims tend to be young (57 percent under 25). Unsurprisingly, most such crimes occur in our major cities.

For the last four years, the number and type of hate crimes has been largely stable (about 1400 per year).

The following charts show hate crimes by ethnic origin and religion. For ethnic origin, the rate is relatively low at less than 300 per million hate crimes against Blacks, the group with the highest rate.

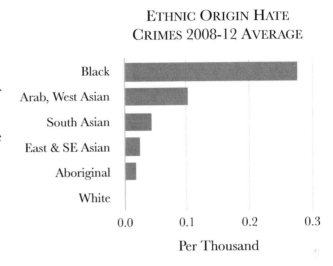

ETHNIC ORIGIN HATE CRIMES 2008-12 AVERAGE

Per Thousand

For religion, the high rate of incidents against Canadian Jews (close to 700 per million) reflects several factors: a heightened awareness within the community of antisemitism and the risk of hate crimes, the activities of B'nai Brith and other organizations to encourage reporting, and the well-established nature of the Jewish community, which increases the willingness of its members to report incidents to the police.

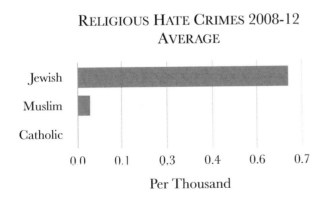

RELIGIOUS HATE CRIMES 2008-12 AVERAGE

Per Thousand

Canadian Muslims are a newer, less well-established and more diverse community, and given the ongoing media attention on Islamic-inspired extremism, members of this community may be more wary of reporting hate crimes. Some anti-Muslim hate crimes may be captured under ethnic origin (Arab and West Asian).

Some 13 percent of all hate crimes were motivated by sexual orientation.

Although on a lower level than hate crimes, the

---

[126] "Police-reported hate crime in Canada, 2012," *Statistics Canada* and earlier 2008-11 reports. In 2013, the number of hate crimes fell by 17 percent, reflecting a 30 percent decline in non-violent hate crimes, although these increased for some groups, with the most notable decline with respect to Canadian Jews ("Police-reported hate crime in Canada, 2013").

[127] "2014 Audit of Antisemitic Incidents," *B'nai Brith*. The National Council of Canadian Muslims recently launched a similar initiative to report on anti-Muslim incidents. "NCCM Launches National Hate Crimes Awareness Project," *NCCM*, 9 June 2015.

2010 CIC Tracking Survey showed that significant numbers of visible minority Canadians had encountered discrimination, as shown in the following chart:[128]

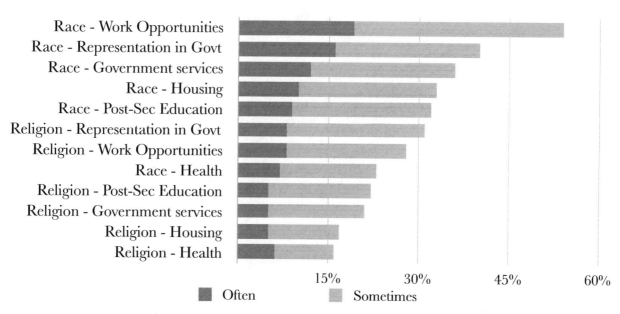

PERCEIVED DISCRIMINATION BY PLACE AND TYPE
CIC TRACKING SURVEY - EKOS 2010

Perceived discrimination appears to be a greater problem when it comes to race than it is for religion, particularly in the workplace — and, worryingly, in the government (with respect to both representation and access to services).

Lastly, we should pause here to recognize that the persistence of bias and prejudice reflects, in part, the hard-wired tendency of our brains to categorize and make generalizations. As noted earlier, the impact on employment and advancement opportunities is real. This emphasizes the importance of actively working to overcome these tendencies.

As one recent survey of recent psychological and neuroscience put it:

> The upshot of all of this research is that in order to rid the world of prejudice, we can't simply snuff out overt, conscious, full-throated racism. Nor can we fundamentally remake the human brain, with its rapid-fire associations and its categorizing, essentializing, and groupish tendencies. Instead, the key lies in shifting people's behaviour, even as we also make them aware of how cultural assumptions merge with natural cognitive processes to create biases they may not know they have.[129]

---

[128] "CIC Annual Tracking Survey — Winter 2010 Final Report," Ekos, April 2010. Subsequent tracking surveys or equivalent government public opinion research have not asked these questions to my knowledge and perusal of studies publicly available.

[129] Chris Mooney, "The Science of Why Cops Shoot Young Black Men," *Mother Jones*, 1 December 2014.

Anyone who takes the Implicit Association Test (IAT), measuring automatic preferences, will quickly realize, as I did, just how deeply ingrained these preferences are, no matter how unbiased and open one thinks one may be.[130]

In other words, we have initially to learn how to shift out of automatic "fast thinking," to use Daniel Kahneman's phrase, to more deliberative "slow thinking," pending training to shift from categorizing and essentialist tendencies toward new, less biased, patterns of thought.[131]

---

[130] For the rational, deliberative self-assessment of bias and prejudice, see Harvard University's Project Implicit website and then contrast one's self-assessment with the IAT results.

[131] Daniel Kahneman, *Thinking, Fast and Slow*.

Representative Public Institutions — Strengths and Weaknesses

Healthcare and education are two of the public services Canadians interact with most. While healthcare and social services are generally only used in times of need, education is critical to the integration process for immigrants and their children.

TABLE 7: TABLE PROVINCIAL PUBLIC INSTITUTION VISIBLE MINORITY EMPLOYEES 2011						
	LMA	Other		Education		
		Healthcare	Social Services	Schools	Colleges	Universities
British Columbia	23.2%	26.3%	22.8%	14.6%	21.6%	27.5%
Alberta	13.1%	21.8%	20.4%	9.2%	13.4%	24.0%
Ontario	21.6%	24.2%	25.5%	13.5%	17.9%	26.8%
Quebec	7.9%	10.4%	12.4%	5.9%	7.0%	16.1%

Even in healthcare and social services, however, visible-minority representation helps to increase sensitivity to the needs of, and issues faced by, members of this group. It may also help reduce cultural or other barriers. A diverse workforce that more or less mirrors social demographics helps all employees develop a greater appreciation for the varying needs, habits and concerns of individuals in an increasingly diverse public.

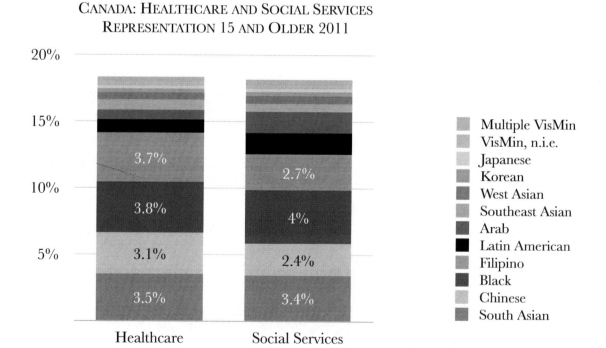

CANADA: HEALTHCARE AND SOCIAL SERVICES
REPRESENTATION 15 AND OLDER 2011

Representation in both healthcare and social services more closely reflects the overall diversity of Canada. Out of the 1.65 million people employed in healthcare, visible minority employees form 18.3 percent. In social services, out of 440,000 employees, 17.9 percent are visible minorities. Again, regional variations reflect the overall pattern, with British Columbia, Alberta and Ontario having the largest share of visible minority employees, and Quebec having a lower share (as shown in Table 7).

TABLE 8: CANADA: REPRESENTATION BY VISIBLE MINORITY IN HEALTHCARE AND SOCIAL				
	Healthcare		Social Services	
	Men	Women	Men	Women
South Asian	4.4%	3.3%	3.3%	3.4%
Chinese	4.6%	2.8%	3.2%	2.2%
Black	3.6%	3.9%	4.7%	3.8%
Filipino	3.5%	3.8%	1.6%	2.9%
Latin American	1.1%	0.9%	1.6%	1.6%
Arab	1.6%	0.5%	1.2%	1.6%
Southeast Asian	1.0%	0.7%	0.7%	0.5%
West Asian	0.7%	0.4%	0.6%	0.6%
Korean	0.5%	0.2%	0.3%	0.3%
Japanese	0.3%	0.2%	0.2%	0.2%
VisMin n.i.e.	0.3%	0.3%	0.3%	0.3%
Multiple Visible Minority	0.5%	0.4%	0.3%	0.4%
Not Visible Minority	77.9%	82.6%	81.9%	82.1%

75 percent or more of immigrants working in healthcare and social services are first-generation (the remainder are mostly second-generation). Japanese Canadians employed in these sectors are the exception: close to 40 percent are third-generation.

Healthcare median incomes show a number of visible minorities doing relatively better than non-visible minorities in some occupations. Groups with a larger share of the professionals (compared to support staff) in doctor's offices include South Asian, Chinese, Arab and Southeast Asian Canadians. There is a similar pattern in dental offices (with a higher proportion of Chinese, Southeast Asian, Korean and Japanese Canadians in professional positions) and hospitals (where South Asian, Chinese, West Asian, Korean and Japanese Canadians dominate).

From a gender perspective, only about 19 percent of healthcare workers, and 12 percent of social service employees, are male. Visible minorities as a group have a slightly higher share of male employees in healthcare (21 percent compared to 18 percent for non-visible minorities), but gender representation in social services is almost identical to that of other Canadians.

There are significantly more Chinese, Arab, West Asian and Korean Canadian men in healthcare in proportion to women compared to the male-female breakdown for non-visible minorities. The gender gap is particularly high for Arab Canadians (42 percent of Arab healthcare workers are male). For social services, Filipino Canadians have the lowest proportion of male workers (7 percent) compared to a 12 percent of non-visible minority males. Most other visible minority group males form between 10 to 17 percent of social service employees.

CANADA: EDUCATION REPRESENTATION 15 AND OLDER 2011

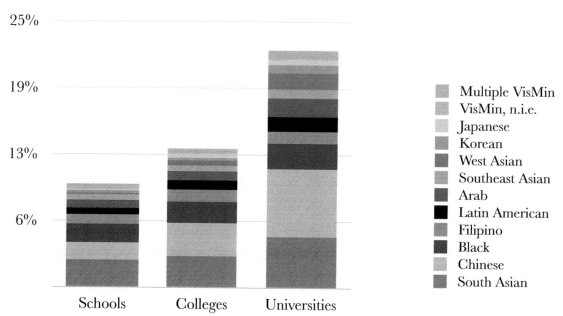

Legend:
- Multiple VisMin
- VisMin, n.i.e.
- Japanese
- Korean
- West Asian
- Southeast Asian
- Arab
- Latin American
- Filipino
- Black
- Chinese
- South Asian

Schools   Colleges   Universities

Turning to education, the higher the level of education, the greater the diversity. This trend applies across Canada. There are over 850,000 people employed in elementary and high schools, 110,000 in community colleges and CEGEPS, and 300,000 in universities, of which visible minorities comprise 9.8 percent, 13.0 percent and 22.3 percent respectively.

The same pattern presents itself with the most diverse provinces having the greatest visible minority representation. Once again, Quebec has significantly lower representation for all three levels of education.

Universities in all provinces, given the specialized nature of requirements and the international nature of competition for academic posts, have an over-representation of visible minorities relative to the population as a whole.

Overall, the same generational pattern repeats itself with all visible minority groups being over 75 percent first-generation, save Japanese (53 percent) and Southeast Asian (69 percent) Canadians.

In elementary and secondary schools, all visible minority groups have a disproportionate share of support positions and/or lower seniority based upon median income data (ten percent difference or more) compared to non-visible minorities. Chinese and Japanese Canadians are the exception (eight percent lower and eight percent higher respectively). For community colleges, this pattern of lower median incomes applies to all groups, with Japanese Canadians having the least difference (six percent lower). And despite the overall good representation numbers in universities, median income data suggests visible minorities hold a disproportionate share of junior and support staff positions.

From a gender perspective, women comprise a majority of employees at all three levels: elementary and secondary schools (73.6 percent), community colleges and CEGEPs (57.9 percent) and universities (54.1 percent).

For schools, Black, Filipino and Southeast Asian males are over-represented compared to non-visible minorities, with more than a five percent difference. For colleges, Latin American and Arab men are over-represented, and again, there is the greatest gender gap in favour of men among Arab Canadians. The inverse is true of Korean and Japanese Canadians — in their cases, women outnumber men in college employment by over ten percent. Arab, Southeast Asian, and Arab men are over-represented among university employees by more than ten percent. Table 9 details the composition of visible minorities in the education sector.

TABLE 9: CANADA: REPRESENTATION BY VISIBLE MINORITY IN EDUCATION 2011

Level	Schools		Colleges		Universities	
	Men	Women	Men	Women	Men	Women
South Asian	2.3%	2.6%	2.9%	2.8%	5.4%	4.3%
Chinese	1.9%	1.6%	3.3%	3.0%	6.7%	6.1%
Black	2.2%	1.6%	2.2%	1.9%	2.7%	2.2%
Filipino	1.1%	0.8%	1.1%	1.2%	0.8%	1.3%
Latin American	0.6%	0.5%	1.0%	0.8%	1.5%	1.4%
Arab	0.9%	0.8%	1.1%	0.7%	2.6%	1.2%
Southeast Asian	0.6%	0.3%	0.5%	0.5%	1.0%	0.7%
West Asian	0.2%	0.2%	0.5%	0.5%	2.1%	1.2%
Korean	0.2%	0.2%	0.2%	0.3%	0.9%	0.6%
Japanese	0.2%	0.2%	0.2%	0.3%	0.4%	0.5%
VisMin n.i.e.	0.2%	0.2%	0.2%	0.2%	0.2%	0.3%
Multiple Visible Minority	0.3%	0.2%	0.4%	0.3%	0.5%	0.6%
Not Visible Minority	89.1%	90.6%	86.3%	87.5%	75.3%	79.7%

Urban and Rural Divides and Increased Ethnic Enclaves

The urban-rural divide represents yet another dimension of diversity. Urban areas in the most populated provinces are more diverse, and have more ridings with high numbers of visible minorities, than rural areas.

That Canada is a country of immigrants is made clear by the following chart, which illustrates the diversity of the population in the 338 ridings of the 2015 electoral map according to three rubrics: the percentage whose ethnic origin is of a non-founding group (one other than Aboriginal, French, English, or "Canadian), the percentage that is a visible minority, and the percentage that identifies with a religion other than Christianity.

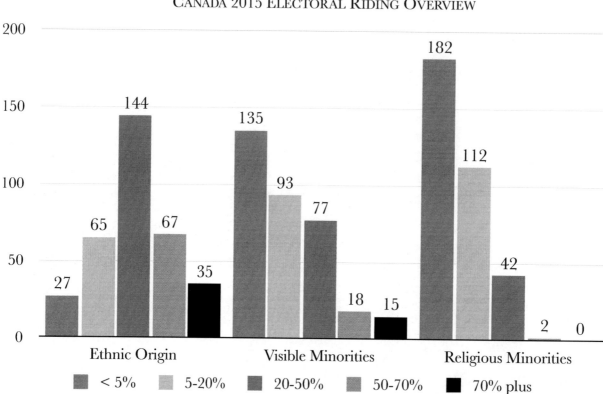

CANADA 2015 ELECTORAL RIDING OVERVIEW

The historic ethnic diversity, from earlier waves of immigration, is reflected in all provinces, but much less so in Quebec and Atlantic Canada. This trend is even more pronounced with respect to visible minorities and religion.

Only about 30 percent of ridings have more than 80 percent of citizens identifying themselves as from the "founding groups."

The large earlier waves of immigration from Europe are reflected, particularly the settling of the West, where East Europeans, such as Ukrainians, played a large role, along with post-World War II immigration from Western and Southern Europe.

In contrast to more recent waves of immigration, in which some groups have tended to form concentrated communities, descendants from the earlier waves are more dispersed in their settlement patterns, with only Italian Canadians having more than 20 percent in four ridings.[132]

Other larger European communities typically have concentrations in the 10-20 percent range, which is true of German Canadians in 10 ridings,[133] Ukrainian Canadians in two,[134] and Portuguese Canadians in one.[135]

One sees how growth has eluded Quebec and Atlantic Canada, which have much higher relative shares of the "founding groups."

Subsequent waves of immigration are reflected in the chart above through the lens of visible minority.

While two-thirds of ridings are largely "white," the remaining third have significant visible minority communities; and 33 ridings, or 10 percent of the total, are "majority visible minority."

Religious minorities, however, dominate in relatively few ridings. Only two ridings have a majority of religious minorities (Brampton East and Surrey Newton, both with large Sikh populations), and only 42 ridings have significant populations (between 20 and 50 percent) of religious minorities. Appendix O lists these ridings and their respective composition of religious minorities.

Only in three of the 42 ridings with a significant population of religious minorities does a single minority religion dominate (which is to say, constitute over 20 percent of the total population in the riding, while also being twice as large as the next largest religious minority).[136] .

Looking at the provincial breakdown (2011 ridings) illustrates further the regional differences in Canada. The 2011 electoral map had 214 ridings (69 percent of the total) with visible minority populations under 20 percent. Of these, 127 ridings (41 percent) had visible minority populations of less than five percent. These ridings were primarily in rural and Atlantic Canada.[137]

---

[132] Vaughan—Woodbridge, King—Vaughan, Saint-Léonard—Saint-Michel, Honoré-Mercier.

[133] Humboldt—Warman—Martensville—Rosetown, Portage—Lisgar, Provencher, Medicine Hat, Cypress Hills—Grasslands, Kitchener—Conestoga, Battlefords—Lloydminster, Moose Jaw--Lake Centre—Lanigan, Regina—Lewvan, Regina—Wascana.

[134] Yorkton—Melville, Kildonan—St. Paul.

[135] Davenport.

[136] British Columbia ridings of Surrey Newton, Fleetwood—Port Kells, Surrey Centre, with large Sikh populations.

[137] Riding data taken from Statistics Canada NHS 2011 Profile. Classification used adapted from Dan Hiebert, _Exploring Minority Enclave Areas in Montréal, Toronto, and Vancouver_, who in turn adapted the methodology used by Poulson, Johnston and Forrest (2001) and adapted for Canada by Walks and Bourne (2006).

FEDERAL RIDINGS (2011) PERCENTAGE VISIBLE MINORITIES

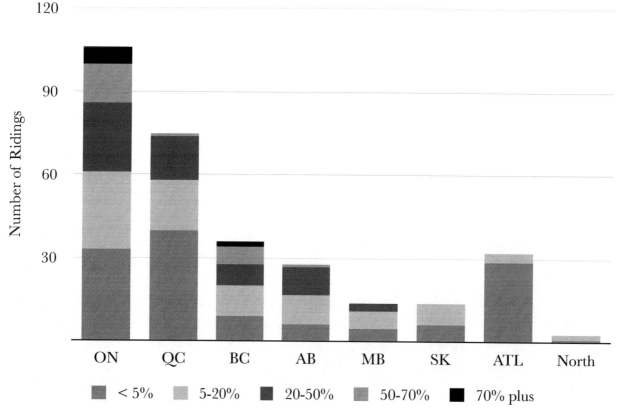

Moreover, Atlantic Canada and Saskatchewan have no ridings with more than 20 percent visible minorities and, in the case of Atlantic Canada, only only three ridings in Nova Scotia (all in Halifax) have visible minority populations above five percent.

Not surprisingly, British Columbia and Ontario have the largest number of ridings with over 50 percent visible minority populations (8 and 20 respectively), with Alberta and Quebec having one such riding each.

Of the 8 ridings with more than 70 percent visible minorities, four of these have dominant visible minorities (defined as one community having more than twice as many as the second largest community). Three of these are largely Chinese Canadian (two in British Columbia, the other in Ontario), the other is largely South Asian in Ontario.

Taking a broad perspective, we find that there is a pattern of community concentration without there being monolithic ethnic enclaves at the riding level. Concentration in neighbourhoods is tempered with the dispersion of visible minorities *across* neighbourhoods. Appendix M lists the 30 most diverse ridings (2011 elections) and their largest communities.

The change in riding boundaries for the 2015 election means that 30 new ridings are being added. Most if not all of the additions are in the ethnically diverse and visible-minority-rich suburban areas of British Columbia, Alberta, and Ontario.

The following chart compares 2011 and 2015 ridings and reveals a small but significant shift towards ridings with a greater percentage of visible minorities. Ridings with greater concentration (more than 50 percent visible minority) have increased slightly from 29 to 33, but equally significantly, there has been a greater *dispersion* of visible minorities. There are 18 more ridings in 2015 with visible minority populations between 20 and 50 percent.

CANADA: 2011-2015 RIDING COMPARISON PERCENTAGE VISIBLE MINORITIES

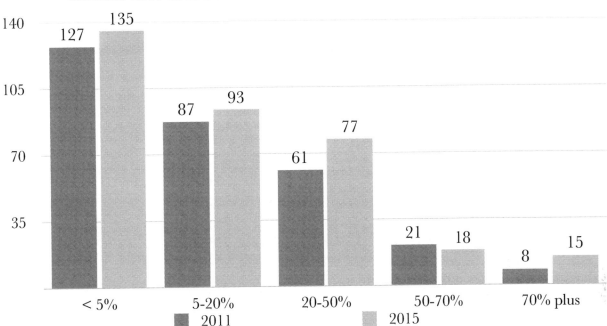

More detailed studies on ethnic enclaves and neighbourhoods that have looked at the census tract level (which breaks regions up into segments with an average population of above 5,000 people) confirm this general pattern of ethnic neighbourhood concentration and dispersion.[138] Dan Hiebert looked at 2006 Census data from 2,400 census tracts in Montreal, Toronto and Vancouver, finding that: [139]

- Recent immigrants tended to settle in their ethnic neighbourhoods more than second-generation immigrants;

- Enclaves (defined as areas where more than 70 percent of the population is a visible minority) tend to have higher unemployment rates, slightly greater dependence on government transfers, with a greater incidence of low income. However, the percentage of inhabitants with a university education is similar to the general population;

- Most are mixed minority enclaves, with considerable diversity among visible minorities, particularly in Toronto;

- Members of minority religions represent more than half of enclave residents;

---

[138] Statistics Canada definition of Census Tracts (CTs): "Small, relatively stable geographic areas that usually have a population between 2,500 and 8,000 persons. They are located in census metropolitan areas and in census agglomerations that had a core population of 50,000 or more in the previous census."

[139] Dan Hiebert, *Exploring Minority Enclave Areas in Montréal, Toronto, and Vancouver*, March 2009. Updated with findings presented to the 2015 Canadian Metropolis Conference.

- The contrast between Montreal, where enclave census tracts correlate with poverty, and Toronto and Vancouver, where the socioeconomic profile is more complex, is particularly sharp;

- Enclaves of very high ethnocultural concentration and very high poverty rates tend to be in mid-town locations, with residents mainly recent first-generation immigrants. The diversity of such enclaves — South Asian Canadians in Montreal, Black Canadians in Toronto, and Chinese Canadians in Vancouver — "demonstrate that there is not a single visible minority group that faces the greatest degree of socio-economic exclusion across all parts of Canada";

- The proportion of visible minorities in Toronto enclaves (both mixed visible minority or majority visible minority) has grown from 17 percent in 1996 to 44 percent in 2011, with Vancouver showing similar growth, but much less in Montreal, where enclaves correlate with poverty;

- Most enclaves have a dominant group but many are also characterized by hyper-diversity;

- Montreal enclaves are more diverse than average, Vancouver enclaves less diverse than average (reflecting its large Chinese Canadian and Indo-Canadian populations), and Toronto is representative of the average; and,

- Enclaves appear to conform more to the super-diversity view than the parallel lives view.

The next section will focus on the political implications of the concentration and dispersion just discussed.

POLITICAL AND PUBLIC SERVICE UNDER-REPRESENTATION

Political integration starts with citizenship: having the fundamental right to vote, along with the responsibility to participate in political discussion and debate when exercising that right.

Declining Citizenship

The chart below shows the citizenship of foreign-born residents in Canada, breaking it down by those who have Canadian citizenship only, those with dual citizenship and those who are not Canadian citizens. The last group includes those who are not yet eligible for citizenship (having lived in Canada for less than four years) and those who have chosen not to take up Canadian citizenship.[140]

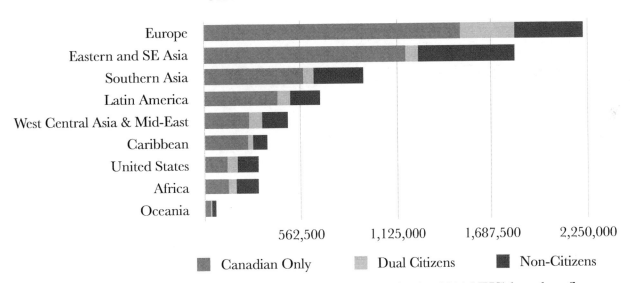

CITIZENSHIP FOREIGN-BORN CANADIAN RESIDENTS 2011

Canada's oft-cited high rate of naturalization (85.6 percent in the 2011 NHS) largely reflects earlier waves of immigration and citizenship. The naturalization rate was over 90 percent up until 1991-2000, but fell to 77 percent in 2001-5 and 38 percent in 2006-7. It is unclear whether Canada's current naturalization rate remains the highest among immigration-based countries.[141]

Citizenship and Immigration Canada operational statistics confirm this downward trend. For the years 1989-2008, accounting for some two-thirds of foreign-born Canadians, CIC operational statistics show a cumulative citizenship uptake of 71 percent (some 3.2 million new citizens). This reflects a shift from a high naturalization rate of between 75-80 percent until 2003, to a significantly lower one in subsequent years, as depicted in the chart below. This drop holds

---

[140] Out of the 6,775,800 foreign-born (20.6% of the population), 6,042,200 million were eligible for citizenship (89% of the foreign born). 5,175,100 have taken up citizenship (85.6% naturalization rate), and 867,100 chose not to take up citizenship.

[141] Australia: 74.0% of the country's foreign-born population were naturalized in 2011. United States naturalization rate among foreign-born population was 43.7% in 2010 according to their respective censuses. "Obtaining Canadian citizenship," *Statistics Canada*.

true whether we consider the six years after an immigrant's arrival ("since landing") or the entire period of their residency in Canada.[142]

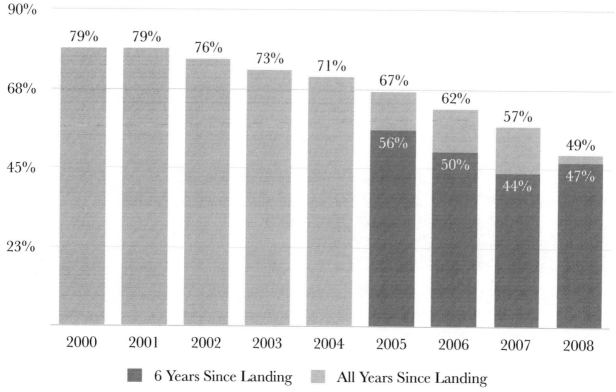

CITIZENSHIP TAKE-UP RATES BY PERMANENT RESIDENCY ARRIVAL YEAR 2000-2008 - 2014 DATA

■ 6 Years Since Landing   ▨ All Years Since Landing

Some of this decrease dates back to previous governments, but the Conservative government has made a number of policy and program changes to correct what it perceived as an imbalance towards facilitation and a lack of program integrity, changes that "[make] citizenship harder to get and easier to lose."[143]

The introduction, in 2010, of a more comprehensive citizenship guide (*Discover Canada*, which is also written in more sophisticated language) and a harder citizenship test, coupled with an increase in the percentage required to pass (up to 75 percent from the previous 60) had resulted in the pass rate declining from an average of 96.3 percent between 2005-9 to 82.7 percent between 2010-13 (within the target range of 80-85 percent set by the Minister), as shown in the chart above. Visible minority communities were disproportionately affected, which likely reflects

[142] The more time spent in Canada, the greater the percentage of those taking up citizenship (e.g., a permanent resident of 2008 has six years of residency, one of 2007 has seven years and one of 2006 has eight years and so on. Hence looking at citizenship take-up six years after landing provides a more consistent basis for assessing trends (between 75-80 percent of those who take up citizenship do so within 6 years of permanent residency, with modest further increases in subsequent years).

[143] Meaningfulness is defined in this context as having greater knowledge about Canadian history, society and legal and constitutional framework than in previous knowledge tests, demonstrated basic competence in one of Canada's official languages, and physical presence during the residency qualification period.

a mix of lower education levels, less testing experience from school and weaker language ability.[144]

However, CIC documents show that the average pass rate declined to 70-75 percent in 2012, below the target range, prompting considerable activity to change test questions and administration to ensure more applicants passed the test. These changes implemented in 2014 resulted in an increase in the overall pass rate to 90.3 percent, with smaller differences between visible and non-visible minorities. Some visible minority groups showed greater relative improvements than others.

PERCENTAGE DECLINE IN CITIZENSHIP TEST PASS RATES BY COUNTRY OF BIRTH - 2010-13 AND 2014 COMPARED TO 2005-9

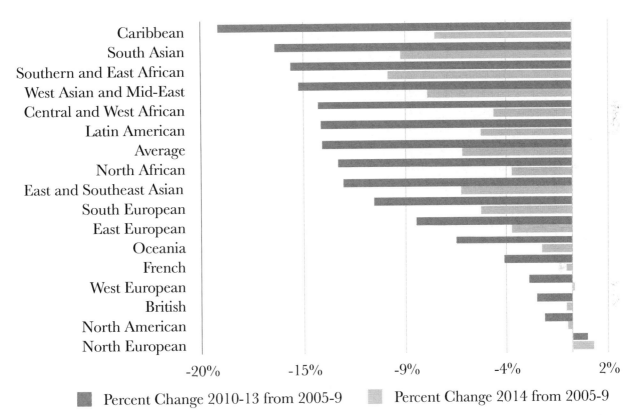

Language assessment was made more rigorous in 2011, and measures to reduce fraud (largely related to residency) were also introduced.

_____

[144] During the roll-out of the test changes, Statistics Canada analyzed the results and found that education was the main variable. A further more detailed internal CIC study, Citizenship Test Results - Multivariate Regression Analysis, confirmed that education level was largely determinant. This data is from CIC operational statistics, 2004-2013.

Moreover, citizenship judges applied a more rigorous approach to their language and knowledge assessment. Judge refusals increased by almost 200 percent between the 2004-9 and 2010-13 periods.[145]

In addition, increased emphasis on reducing fraud and misrepresentation, the introduction of a residency questionnaire and other measures meant longer processing times and delays in obtaining citizenship.

The major cause of this decline, however, is probably the chronic issue of under-management and under-funding of the citizenship program, which resulted in periodic backlogs under both Liberal and Conservative governments.

PERMANENT RESIDENTS, CITIZENSHIP APPLICATIONS, NEW CITIZENS -
OPERATIONAL DATA 2004 TO 2014

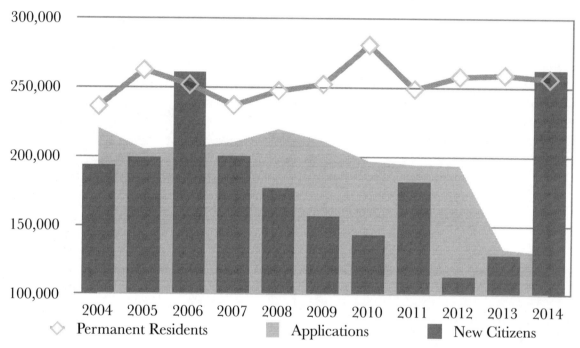

The more recent backlog generated between 2008 and 2013 resulted from a combination of the policy changes mentioned above, and was exacerbated by program review cutbacks. The chart above compares Canada's number of permanent residents (relatively stable but a more complex program to manage), citizenship applications (which measure demand for citizenship

---

[145] CIC Operational Statistics. Refusals based on a lack of knowledge almost tripled from a 2004-9 annual average of 1,869 to an average of 5,442 during 2010-13. Refusals based on language showed a similar increase from an annual average of 690 during 2004-9 to 2,061 during 2010-13. Refusals based on residency showed a slight decline (861 to 845 annual average).

and which show a steady decline and then a major one in 2013 and 2014), and the number of new citizens (which fell dramatically after 2008).[146]

To address this decline and backlog, the government (belatedly) injected an additional $44 million over two years in Budget 2013, which resulted in over 260,000 people becoming citizens in 2014. It also made a number of changes to the *Citizenship Act* to streamline processing in the future.

No explanation has been provided by CIC at the time of writing (July 2015) to explain the dramatic drop in the number of citizenship applications in 2013 and 2014.[147] Possible explanations include: methodological changes (e.g., only counting completed applications, given the authority in the new *Citizenship Act* to return incomplete applications), operational reasons (giving priority to addressing the backlog rather than entering applications into the computer system), or a more fundamental change in the behaviour of permanent residents in terms of the desirability of citizenship, their ability to pay the 2014 increase in fees, or in their perception of their chances to become citizens.

Other longer-term factors that may account for part of this decrease in citizenship applications and acquisition include a more instrumental view of citizenship given transnational identities and greater mobility, emigration to seek better opportunities, and a decreased perception of the value of Canadian citizenship compared to permanent residency. Ironically, the shift towards more highly-skilled and educated immigrants means that there is greater mobility for new arrivals than there was for the less-skilled immigrants of the past.

Canada's formerly-high naturalization rate reflected, on the one hand, the desire of immigrants to become citizens (for reasons of belonging as well as instrumental ones) and, on the other, what was arguably an overly-easy naturalization process that incorporated limited measures against fraud and misrepresentation.

More recent changes include increases to application fees for citizenship (quintupling to $530) and the associated changes to the *Citizenship Act* (2014). These will likely further reduce naturalization rates given the combination of lengthened residency requirements and expansion of knowledge and language testing to older applicants (extension to younger applicants will likely have minimal impact given that they will have spent a minimum of four years in Canadian schools).

---

[146] CIC operational statistics *Clients by Current Citizenship and by PR Landing Year (in Persons) 1989-2008* comparing citizenship, permanent residency records and take-up of citizenship. Yet during this period of declines in naturalization (2003-8), there was only a gradual decline in the number of applications, from 220,000 in 2008 to 194,000 in 2012 (11.8 percent), before the dramatic decline to approximately 130,000 applications in both 2013 and 2014 (over 30 percent). For the backlog, see CIC Press Release "Archived - Citizenship and Immigration Minister Joe Volpe Announces New Measures to Improve the Citizenship Application Process," 18 April 2005.

[147] In response to an ATIP request, CIC indicated (10 July 2015) that it had no records pertaining to the reasons for this drop.

From Citizenship to Voting

Becoming a citizen provides the right to vote, but how many exercise this right? And how significant a role do visible minorities play in the electoral and governmental processes?

The data suggests that there is not much difference between Canadian-born and established immigrants (defined as those who immigrated to Canada before 2001) in this regard, with voting rates in the 2011 federal election of 67.1 and 66.3 percent respectively. However, for more recent immigrants, the voting rate falls to 51.1 percent. There are no major differences in voting participation between men and women in all three categories.[148]

A more detailed view of voting by country of birth shows minor variations. Those of European birth vote slightly more than the Canadian-born (with the exception of Eastern Europeans), as do those born in Southern Asia. Voting participation is lower in communities from developing countries, and the largest gender difference exists among those born in Africa, followed by those born in Southeast Asia.

CITIZEN VOTING RATES BY COUNTRY OF BIRTH COMPARED TO CANADIAN-BORN 2011

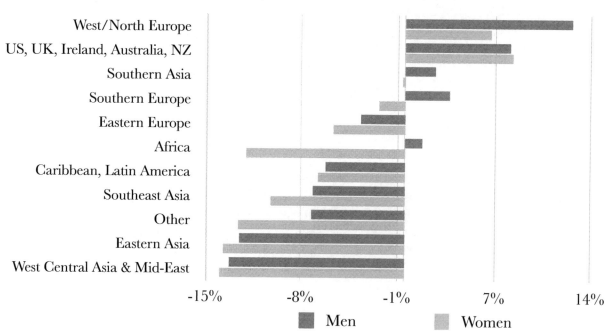

Similarly, the greatest differences in voting between established and more recent immigrants occurs with respect to those from countries with weaker democratic traditions, particularly Africa (27.2 percent), Eastern Europe (21.1 percent), and West Central Asia and the Mid-East (17.4 percent).

---

[148] "Factors Associated with Voting," *Statistics Canada*, February 2012. This study uses the May 2011 Labour Force Survey which added a question on voting. This self-declaration results in slightly higher voting numbers compared to actual election day results.

A number of factors may explain this, "including the lack of democratic traditions in some regions of the world, the lack of trust in institutions or differences in political culture (Bevelander and Pendakur 2007 and 2009)."[149]

---

[149] Ibid. As established immigrants tend to be older, the normal pattern of older citizens voting may also be a factor.

Political Party "Competition" for Ethnic Votes

All federal parties compete for ethnic votes. Community concentrations in specific ridings influence candidate selection and election results. The transformation of the Reform Party to the Canadian Alliance to the Conservative Party, culminating in extensive outreach of Minister for Multiculturalism Jason Kenney, reinforces just how mainstream ethnic communities are.[150]

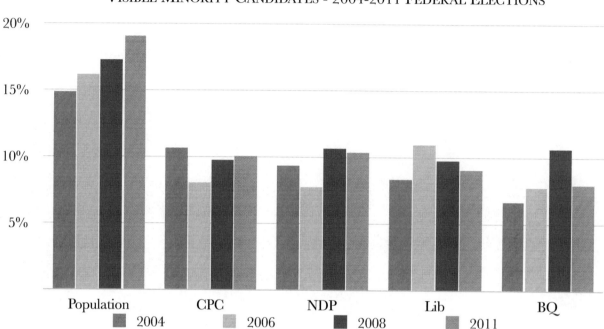

VISIBLE MINORITY CANDIDATES - 2004-2011 FEDERAL ELECTIONS

And while most "shopping for votes" strategies are targeted to pocket book issues, some are more narrowly focussed on community-specific interests. The Conservative government implemented a historical recognition program to commemorate the experience of communities affected by immigration restrictions (e.g., Chinese Canadian, Indo-Canadian and Jewish) and wartime internment (e.g., Ukrainian and Italian Canadian).[151]

All Canadian governments have made diaspora politics part of foreign policy, whether with respect to responding to natural disasters (e.g., Haiti earthquake and Philippines typhoon) or to taking sides in international disputes (e.g., Mid-East, Ukraine, Sri Lanka). The difference is one of degree: the current government is making more one-sided choices in above international disputes than previous governments in its response to diaspora concerns. Sensitivity to such concerns is part and parcel of citizen participation and engagement.

However, notwithstanding this responsiveness and overall positive story, under-representation remains an issue. The chart below shows the number of visible minority candidates running in

---

[150] One of the better profiles can be found in "The inside story of Jason Kenney's campaign to win over ethnic votes," *Macleans*, 2 February 2013.

[151] The short-lived Liberal government under Paul Martin had also planned a smaller scale historical recognition program.

competitive ridings for the past four elections, a number that has remained mostly flat for the major parties despite the increase in our population's diversity since 2004.[152]

While it is beyond the scope of this section to detail voting patterns among immigrants, studies suggest that established immigrants (e.g., Italian, Greek, Portuguese and older South Asians) are more likely to vote for the Conservatives, while those who have been here between six and ten years favour the NDP, and more recent immigrants favour the Liberals.[153]

FEDERAL REPRESENTATION - 2011 ELECTION

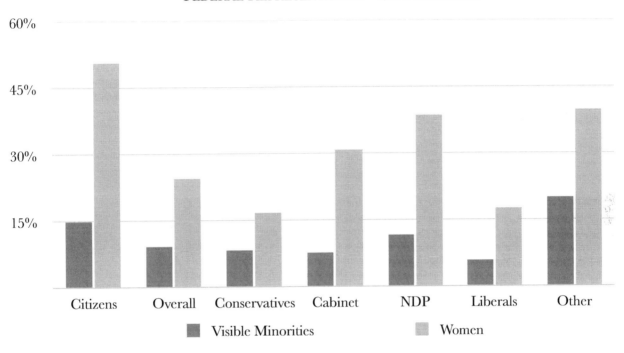

---

[152] Numbers taken from Jerome Black's "Racial Diversity in the 2011 Federal Election: Visible Minority Candidates and MPs." Competitive ridings are defined "as those where the party in the immediately previous election, either won or, if they lost, did so by a margin of 10% or less."

[153] "Who Really One the Ethnic Vote in the May Election," *Pundits Guide*, 2011. See also Stuart Soroka et al, "Capturing change (and stability) in the 2011 campaign," *Policy Options*. June 2011. The latter argues that there was a relatively small shift of ethnic voters to the Conservatives compared to 2008 at the macro level. Others disagree, looking at ridings with large numbers of immigrant voters. Taylor, Triadafilopoulos and Cochrane argue, in their analysis of the Greater Toronto Area election results, that the Conservatives made major gains compared to the Liberals in "On the Backs of Immigrants? Conservative Politics and New Canadian Voters," CPSA 2012. Tom Flanagan discusses the new fourth sister of Canadian politics, immigrants and ethnic communities in "The Emerging Conservative Coalition" in the same issue of *Policy Options*. CBC summarizes the Conservative and other party approaches, including micro-targeting, in "Ethnic riding targeting key to Conservatives' 2011 victory," 23 October 2012.

Further studies of interest include Inder Marwah, Triadafilos Triadafilopoulos, and Stephen White, "Immigration, Citizenship, and Canada's New Conservative Party" in David Rayside's *Conservatism in Canada*, and Erin Tolley, "Partisan players or political pawns? Immigrants, minorities and conservatives in Canada," revised version of a paper presented at the annual meeting of the Atlantic Provinces Political Science Association. Charlottetown, PEI.

Taking a closer look at the most recent federal election, visible minorities and women continue to be underrepresented at the federal level, though there was some modest improvement in the 2011 election. The federal Cabinet, however, includes a higher percentage of women than the Conservative caucus, reflecting a conscious decision by the Prime Minister to give the government a more inclusive face. Visible minority Cabinet members are all junior ministers (multiculturalism, seniors and sport).

Ethnic diversity is higher than the visible minority presence, of course, given that many MPs come from a range of European backgrounds (e.g., Southern and Eastern European).[154]

Looking at the 30 ridings with more than 50 percent visible minorities, mainly in British Columbia and Ontario, the gender balance in these ridings is slightly better than the overall pattern in the House of Commons (30 percent compared to 24.7 percent). Representation of visible minorities is much higher (40 percent compared to 9.4 percent, but still significantly less than the percentage of visible minorities in these ridings).

Examples of visible minority MPs include Brampton-area MPs Parm Gill and Bal Gosal, Richmond MP Alice Wong, Surrey MP Jasbir Sandhu, and Scarborough MP Rathika Sitsabaiesan.[155]

Typically, as shown in Appendix M, successful visible minority MPs come from the dominant community in the riding.

This is, of course, the mirror image of what occurs in ridings with less than 20 percent visible minorities, where candidates reflect the European background that predominates in their riding.

Just as Prime Minister Harper has used Cabinet appointments to be more inclusive of women, he has used Senate appointments to be more inclusive of visible minorities. 13.6 percent of his 59 Senate appointees have been visible minorities, all born outside of Canada.[156]

---

[154] Public Policy Forum, "Edging Towards Diversity: A Statistical Breakdown of Canada's 41st Parliament, with Comparisons to the 40th Parliament," compared to NHS 2011 population figures. I have used the total number of visible minorities who are also Canadian citizens (78.3 percent of all visible minorities) as the benchmark for representation ("Immigration and Ethnocultural Diversity in Canada," "Obtaining Canadian citizenship" and relevant NHS data tables).

[155] An example where targeting support from particular communities goes too far is when messaging is exclusively targeted towards a community and only in a community language. See "Federal Liberals cultivate Mandarin powerhouse in GTA," *The Globe and Mail,* 18 August 2014.

[156] Tolley, Ibid.

Under-Representation in Judicial Appointments

On the other hand, with respect to judicial appointments, the Government's record is less inclusive.

Women comprise only 30 percent of judicial appointments since 2006 compared to 37 percent of all lawyers who are women.[157] There are no reliable statistics for visible minorities and Aboriginal Peoples but recent studies show 0.5 percent and 1 percent respectively.[158]

Yet the availability of potential visible minority judges is higher, as seen in the following table for the largest provinces:[159]

TABLE 10: NUMBER OF VISIBLE MINORITY LAWYERS 25-64 2011					
	Canada	BC	Alberta	Ontario	Quebec
Total Number	78,020	11,180	8,505	32,690	18,450
Number of VisMin	10,190	1,815	1,110	5,620	1,295
Percentage VisMin	13.1%	16.2%	13.1%	17.2%	7.0%

Ontario reports on the number of visible minority judicial appointments (along with other employment equity groups).[160] British Columbia initiated reporting on visible minority appointments starting in 2014.[161]

However, the Government presents a more representative and inclusive face with respect to citizenship judges, who have largely a symbolic role following the 2014 changes to the *Citizenship Act*.

Out of 31 citizenship judges, 15 (48 percent) are women. 7 (22 percent) are a visible minority, which exceeds the proportion of Canadian residents who are visible minorities (19.1 percent).[162]

---

[157] Lee-Anne Goodman, "Harper Conservatives Rapped Over Appointing Women Judges," *Canadian Press*. 27 June 2014. See also Canadian Parliament "Order Paper Q-1088 3 December 2013 for 2006-12 Appointment Numbers by Gender" and "Of 100 new federally appointed judges 98 are white, Globe finds," *The Globe and Mail*, 17 April 2012.

[158] The Office of the Commissioner for Federal Judicial Affairs only tracks the appointment of women, not visible minorities. Particularly helpful articles were "How do we get more diversity on the bench when there's no transparency in the appointments process?" by Stephen Lautens and "Tories chastised for lack of racial diversity in judicial appointments," Globe and Mail, 10 April 2014. Both rely heavily on the research of Rosemary Cairns Way, "Deliberate Disregard: Judicial Appointments Under the Harper Government."

[159] The Quebec numbers also include notaries, about 15 percent of the total.

[160] *Ontario Judicial Appointments Committee Annual Report 2012*.

[161] *British Columbia Judicial Council Annual Report 2013*.

[162] Data from the CIC website, "Profiles of citizenship judges," 27 September 2014.

Consistent Under-Representation in the Provinces

With respect to the provinces, a similar picture emerges. I will first look at female representation as a sort of control group. Overall, women make up 25.4 percent of elected provincial representatives (British Columbia and Ontario have the best representation of female MLAs at over 35 percent, with Alberta following closely at 33 percent).[163]

PROVINCIAL POLITICAL REPRESENTATION OF WOMEN 2014 (PRINCE EDWARD ISLAND AND ALBERTA 2015)

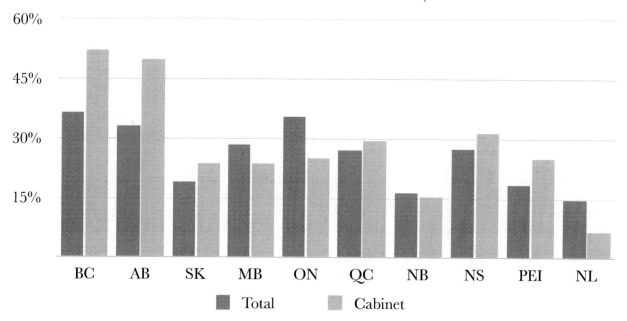

Similarly to the federal government, some provincial governments have higher Cabinet representation of women to compensate for the number of women government representatives elected. British Columbia and Alberta Cabinets have gender parity.

But some provincial cabinets, such as Manitoba, Ontario and Newfoundland, under-represent women compared to the overall legislature count.

Visible minorities, in turn, are underrepresented both generally and in the Cabinet in all provinces except Nova Scotia (given Halifax Cabinet representation). It is unsurprising that the other Atlantic provinces, with their small visible minority populations, lack visible minority representation. However, Saskatchewan has a legislature empty of any visible minority members despite a visible minority population of 6.3 percent.

---

[163] Provincial data is taken from a mix of the analysis by the organization Equal Voice ("Equal Voice: Elected Women by the Numbers June 2014") for women, verified by the Parliament of Canada "Party Leader and Standings website," provincial legislature websites, supplemented by party websites and representative biographies as needed. While figures on women representatives are readily available, no compilations of visible minority representatives exist. A mixture of names and photos was used to compile these statistics. All provincial data is from September 2014 except for Alberta and Prince Edward Island which reflects their 2015 election results (May 29 data). Population taken from 2011 NHS.

Ontario, as the second-most diverse province, has the highest visible minority representation in both its legislature and cabinet. But it nevertheless falls 10 percent short of parity with the percentage of visible minorities in its population.

The following chart shows the respective levels of under-representation of visible minorities. Apart from Nova Scotia, visible minorities are under-represented in all other provinces (visible minority MLAs in Halifax, two of whom are in Cabinet, account for Nova Scotia's uniqueness):

PROVINCIAL REPRESENTATION OF VISIBLE MINORITIES COMPARED TO NUMBER OF VISIBLE MINORITY CITIZENS 2014 (PRINCE EDWARD ISLAND AND ALBERTA 2015)

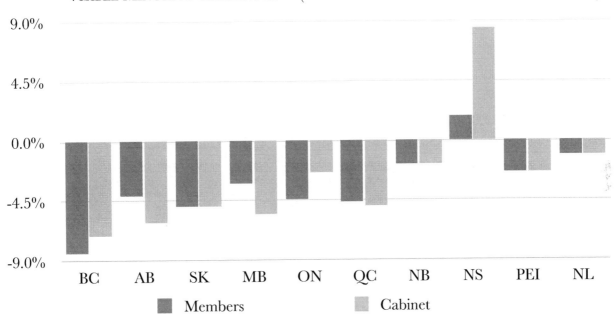

Public Service Representation Depends on the Benchmark

One of the hallmarks of a successful multicultural society is the degree to which national institutions, both public and private, reflect the various communities that form that society.

While information about individual communities is limited, national data is available on employment equity groups (Aboriginal Peoples, persons with disability, visible minorities and women) for Canada's core public administration and some of its larger employers.[164]

In previous years, employment equity reports for the public service were more comprehensive. For example, in the 2006-08 report, detailed breakdowns were available for members of designated groups by gender and age distribution within each occupational group.[165]

Additionally, most provinces also do report on employment equity groups for *their* core public services, but some do so more consistently than others. My chapters on each of the provinces will include include their employment equity reports where available. Alberta, Newfoundland and Labrador and Prince Edward Island do not report on employment equity for their public services. New Brunswick reports only on employment equity for women.

I have used more recent EE data (2012-13) than the 2011 NHS demographic data. I have used men, women and Aboriginal Peoples as comparator groups for visible minorities.[166] While the number of applicants and hirings are compared to labour market availability (LMA) given that these are open to the public, promotions and separations are compared to representation within the public service rather than the overall workforce given that these are internal to the public service.

One note on the LMA number I have used: my figure is for the number of visible minorities who are also Canadian citizens (15.0 percent), not the Federally Regulated Sector LMA of 17.8 percent nor the general visible minority population number (19.1 percent). This presents the most

---

[164] Core public administration is defined by those departments and agencies for which Treasury Board is the employer. Separate employers (e.g., CFIA, CRA), the Canadian Forces, RCMP and CSIS are not included in the CPA employment numbers but file separate employment equity reports. CSIS, RCMP and the Canadian Forces reports are available from the Library of Parliament. RCMP appears to be focused more on gender issues ("Gender-Based Assessment"). Press articles have highlighted the challenges facing the Canadian Forces ("Military missing employment equity recruiting targets," CBC News, 2 August 2012). CRA's report can be found at *Employment Equity at the Canada Revenue Agency: Annual Report 2012-2013*, and shows that CRA representation at 20.4 percent, with 23.2 percent of promotions.

[165] Treasury Board, *Employment Equity in the Public Service of Canada 2006–2007 and 2007–2008*. For 2011 LMA, I have used the number of visible minorities who are also Canadian citizens. For women and Aboriginal Peoples, I have used LMA for the federally-regulated sectors.

[166] Although persons with disabilities is one of the employment equity groups, I have not used this as a comparator group given that the issues are more particular to that particular group.

positive picture of employment equity numbers; shifting to one of the other benchmarks would change the picture significantly.[167]

Federal Public Service

My analysis focusses on the consolidated data on the core public administration, which consisted of some 188,000 federal public servants as of 31 March 2013.

FEDERAL PUBLIC SERVICE EMPLOYMENT EQUITY 2012-13

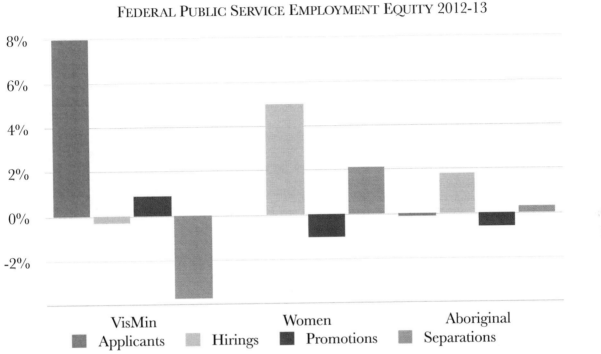

As the *Annual Report to Parliament: Employment Equity in the Public Service of Canada 2012–13* indicates, the overall numbers are encouraging, albeit based on old 2006 LMA estimates (I have put 2011 LMA numbers in parentheses):[168]

> Despite a reduction of the CPA workforce resulting from the implementation of Budget 2012, three of the four designated groups continued to show progress with respect to their representation. Aboriginal Peoples continued to increase their

---

[167] Preference is given in the following order (Public Service Employment Act 39. (1):

(a) a person who is in receipt of a pension by reason of war service, within the meaning of the schedule;

(b) a veteran or a survivor of a veteran, within the meaning of the schedule; and

(c) a Canadian citizen, within the meaning of the Citizenship Act, in any case where a person who is not a Canadian citizen is also a candidate. The preference in hiring in order is veterans, followed by Canadian citizens.

[168] Charts are based on the statistical tables attached to the *Annual Report*. One of the weaknesses of the *Annual Report* is that it does not present data separating out men who are neither visible minority nor aboriginal as a "control group" for comparison purposes. 2006 LMA for Aboriginal Peoples was three percent, for persons with disabilities four percent.

representation to 5.0 per cent in 2012–13, and persons with disabilities to 5.8 per cent. Members of a visible minority group increased their representation to 12.6 per cent, surpassing their labour market availability estimate of 12.4 per cent (2011 LMA 15.0 percent). For the third consecutive year, the representation of women decreased marginally, from 54.6 per cent to 54.2 per cent; however, women still surpass their labour market availability of 52.3 per cent (2011 LMA 47.9 percent).

However, the increase in labour market availability from the 2011 NHS for visible minorities, in particular, changes that part of the picture.[169]

For the federally regulated sectors, I have included Aboriginal Peoples and women as comparators when appropriate.

Hiring: More visible minority applicants are applying for government positions than 2011 labour market availability but slightly fewer are being hired. This may reflect natural attrition, and the implementation of federal Budget 2012 reductions. Hiring of aboriginal people, however, remains above the LMA. It is odd, then (and goes unexplained in government reports) why the number of appointments of visible minorities should decrease relative to LMA when the number of applicants is comparatively high.[170]

Promotions: The report shows that visible minorities are being promoted at a higher rate than expected given their level of representation in the public service, and in comparison to other groups. Recent studies by the Public Service Commission indicate that "men who are members of visible minorities have greater chances of promotion than their comparison group [while] women who are members of visible minorities have fewer chances of promotion than their comparison group. The promotion odds ratio for men who are members of visible minorities is 1.10; the ratio for women is 0.94."[171]

Moreover, there are ongoing perception issues regarding the application of the merit principle and fairness for both male and female

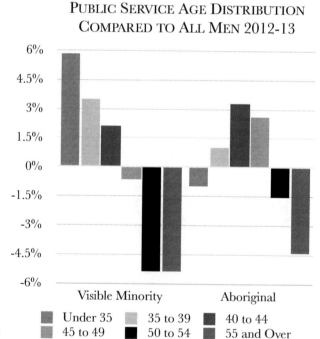

PUBLIC SERVICE AGE DISTRIBUTION COMPARED TO ALL MEN 2012-13

- Under 35
- 35 to 39
- 40 to 44
- 45 to 49
- 50 to 54
- 55 and Over

---

[169] Given TBS has as of writing (June 2015) not issued a revised public service LMA for 2011, I have used the number of visible minorities who are also Canadian citizens as the measure (15.0%). This presents the data in a more favourable light than compared to the general visible minority population (19.1 percent).

[170] *Appointments to the Public Service by Employment Equity Designated Group for 2012-2013 – Statistical Update*, Public Service Commission (PSC).

[171] "Study on Members of Employment Equity Groups: Chances of Promotion," PSC.

visible minorities.[172]

Separations: Visible minorities have few separations relative to their current representation in the public service.

Age distribution: This shows younger visible minority employees composing a larger-than-expected share of the public service at 58.2 percent (with women and Aboriginal people, in contrast, split almost equally between the under-44 and over-45 age groups). This should, over time, result in greater representation for visible minorities, as these young employees move up the ranks.[173]

Aboriginal Peoples show a less marked trend of younger public servants.

The age distribution curve for women is largely flat, except for a small dip in those over 55.

Occupations: But what about the occupations of the different groups? Are there any patterns of interest?

PUBLIC SERVICE OCCUPATIONAL GROUPS COMPARED TO
REPRESENTATION 2012-13

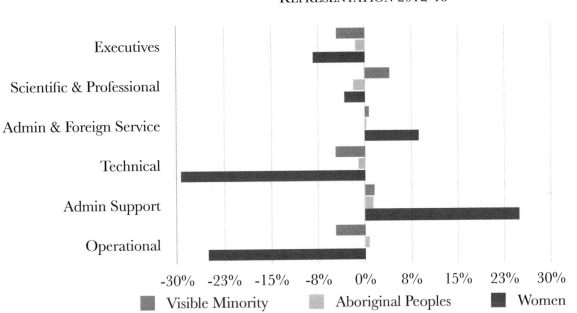

All three groups are under-represented in the executive category. Visible minorities are strong in the scientific and professional category, and under-represented in the technical and operational categories.

Aboriginal Peoples are under-represented in the scientific and professional category.

---

[172] "Study on Members of Employment Equity Groups: Perceptions of Merit and Fairness in Staffing Activities," PSC.

[173] As the PSC and TBS reports do not break out men by aboriginal people or visible minority, I have used the aggregate "men" category as our benchmark.

The greatest variation, however, is with respect to women. They are dramatically underrepresented in technical and operational categories, but vastly over-represented in administration.

Salaries: Another perspective is to consider the distribution of salary scales, comparing men with other groups. These salary scales largely correspond to the different occupational groups.

PUBLIC SERVICE INCOME DISTRIBUTION COMPARED TO MEN
2012-13

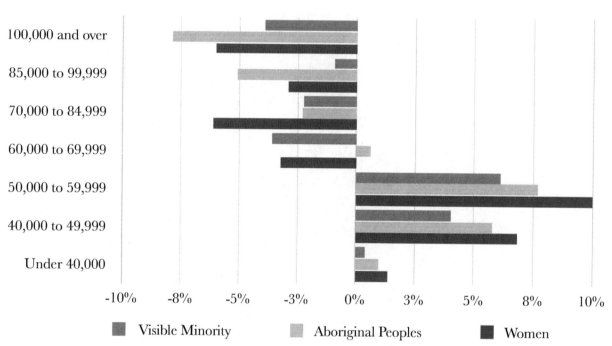

All employment equity groups are over-represented in lower and middle-scales, and under-represented in the higher scales (particularly Aboriginal Peoples). In the case of visible minorities, this is likely a result of the low average age mentioned above (younger employees are naturally more likely to be in junior positions). Analysts and scientists probably account for the relatively large number of visible minorities earning $70,000-100,000.

Visible minority salaries, are closer, in most cases, to male salaries. This could be partly due to the fact that the group "men" includes male visible minorities. However, it also includes Aboriginal men — so other factors, particularly representation in certain occupational groups, are likely determinant.

Another view is provided by NHS representation data that allows us to compare the federal public service (413,000 employees) with the provinces and territories (351,000) and municipalities

(424,000).[174] Visible minority representation in federal government is slightly higher (14 percent) than other levels of government (11 percent). One should note, however, that provincial and municipal governments have a larger proportion of services to rural and less-populated areas that are less diverse. The national numbers are somewhat skewed by the lower diversity in Quebec and the Atlantic provinces.

TABLE 11: VISIBLE MINORITY FEDERAL PUBLIC SERVANTS COMPARED TO LMA 2011				
	LMA VisMin Citizens	Federal	Provincial	Municipal
National	15.0%	14.1%	11.3%	11.0%
British Columbia	21.4%	22.4%	15.2%	14.8%
Alberta	14.4%	13.4%	15.6%	11.5%
Ontario	20.3%	19.0%	20.4%	14.9%
Quebec	8.6%	8.4%	6.0%	4.8%

The more diverse the province, the greater the representation of visible minorities in provincial and municipal governments. British Columbia (15.2 percent provincial, 14.8 percent municipal), Alberta (15.6 percent provincial, 11.5 percent municipal) and Ontario (20.4 percent provincial, 14.9 percent municipal) have the greatest representation. Quebec, despite having an only slightly smaller visible minority population than Alberta, has dramatically lower representation in the provincial (6.0 percent) and municipal (4.8 percent) governments.

From a generational point of view, it is not surprising that the vast majority of visible minority government employees are first-generation, generally over 75 percent, reflecting the visible minority workforce as a whole. Japanese Canadians are an exception, with the majority being third generation. The opposite is true of those who are not visible minorities, over three-quarters of whom are third generation or more for all levels of government. There is a slight relative increase of second-generation visible minority employees at the municipal level compared to other levels. This level also generally has greater representation of third-generation visible minority employees (although numbers of third-generation are small).

This data also provides a breakdown of the generic "visible minority" category. Larger and more established visible minority groups are more represented (e.g., South Asian, Chinese and Black) compared to smaller and more recent immigrant communities.

Median incomes vary. Groups that have lower median incomes (difference of 10 percent or more compared to non-visible minorities), meaning a greater portion of employees in support or other lower income occupations, include: Black, Filipino and Southeast Asian (federal

[174] For federal public administration, NHS data includes all public servants save "defence services," a broader population than contained in the TBS and PSC employment equity reports which only cover the core public administration mentioned earlier. This larger group includes separate employers (Schedule V) such as CRA, CFIA, CSIS, NRC, Parks Canada among others. This data, however, only provides information on representation, with no data on hirings, promotions, separations and salaries.

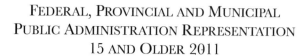

FEDERAL, PROVINCIAL AND MUNICIPAL
PUBLIC ADMINISTRATION REPRESENTATION
15 AND OLDER 2011

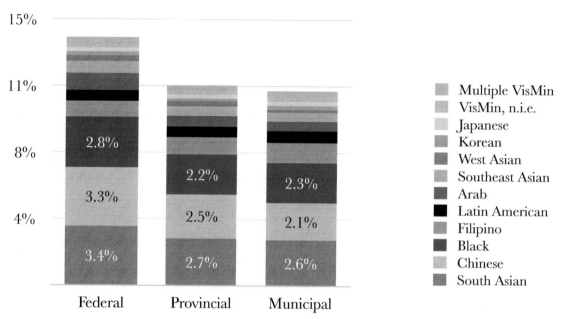

government); Black, Latin American and Arab (provincial); and Latin American, Arab and Korean (local).

From a gender perspective, more women than men are public servants at both the federal (53.3 percent) and provincial (57.5 percent) levels. However, the pattern is reversed at the municipal level, where men comprise 55.4 percent (which include traditionally male-dominated tasks like garbage collection, snow removal, etc.).

Some visible minority communities show a different pattern of gender representation, varying by five percent or more from those who are not visible minorities. Communities with an over-representation of men at the federal level include South Asian, Arab, West Asian and Korean. At the provincial level, Filipino women are over-represented and Arab and West Asian women under-represented compared to non-visible minorities. Only the Arab community has more male (57 percent) than female employees. At the municipal level, Black, Filipino, Latin American and Korean women are over-represented.

Canadian Forces and RCMP Record "Dismal", but CSIS Different

The Canadian Forces, as distinct from the civilian public servants at the Department of National Defence, report employment equity separately. Like the RCMP (discussed below) the Forces face particular challenges when it comes to being representative of the population, although Aboriginal people are to some extent an exception (likely reflecting a mix of recruitment efforts and the nature of employment opportunities).

TABLE 12: CANADIAN FORCES, RCMP AND CSIS REPRESENTATION 2012-13					
	Canadian Forces		**RCMP**		**CSIS**
	Members	Officers	Non-commissioned officers	Commissioned Officers	Staff
VisMin	4.0%	6.0%	8.8%	3.3%	14.3%
Women	13.2%	16.8%	21.0%	12.4%	49.5%
Aboriginal	2.5%	1.4%	7.9%	6.7%	2.1%

Women are vastly under-represented, with a more than 30 percent gap between their percentage share of the general population and that among Force officers and members. Visible minorities are similarly under-represented, although more visible minority officers are being promoted.

CANADIAN FORCES COMPARED TO LMA AND
REPRESENTATION 2012-13

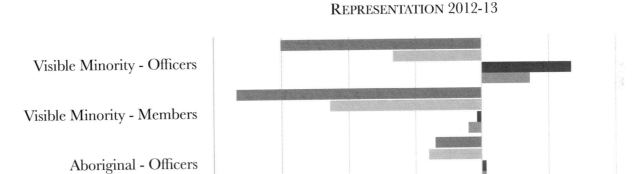

Given the uniqueness of military service, more modest representation goals have been set (11.8 percent for visible minorities, 25.1 percent for women; only for Aboriginal people is the goal of

3.4 percent in line with the overall population).[175] Moreover, the Forces are seeking to reduce these targets further (8.2 percent for visible minorities, 17.6 percent for women, and 2.6 percent for Aboriginal people) to depict more positively the significant representation gap.[176]

RCMP COMPARED TO LMA AND REPRESENTATION 2012-13

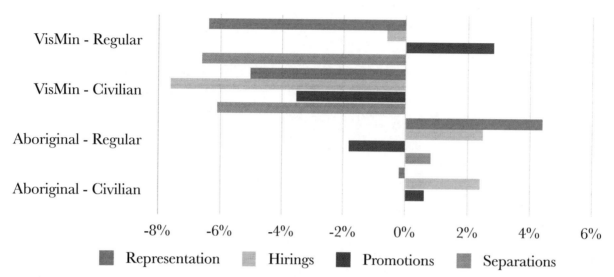

The RCMP provides data separately for regular (wearing the uniform) and civilian members. Compared to the general labour market availability, the RCMP does reasonably well with respect to Aboriginal people but faces significant challenges in visible minority representation among both regular and civilian members. Women, not captured in the chart below, are even less well

---

[175] The Canadian Forces report notes: "The unique nature of employment in the CAF and the related challenges in developing a workforce analysis methodology that can be used to establish appropriate LMA estimates is the subject of a current CAF research project. As the CAF moves forward with this project, ongoing consultations with external EE stakeholders in the Labour Program at Employment and Social Development Canada (ESDC) and at the Canadian Human Rights Commission (CHRC) will continue." *Canadian Armed Forces Employment Equity Report 2012-13*, Ottawa: Dept. of National Defence, October 2013. I have used the number of visible minorities who are Canadian citizens for LMA (15.0 percent).

[176] "Overall interest in military careers low for Black, Latin-American and Filipino Canadians," *National Post*, 31 December 2014. The Ipsos Reid 2014 survey cited in this article highlights the recruitment challenges among these minority groups given their career preferences elsewhere.

represented among regular members, with representation and hiring at roughly half of the general labour market availability.[177]

The numbers are better for non-commissioned officers than the officer ranks, as shown in the table below, suggesting that over time, as RCMP regular members move up the ranks, better representation should be achieved. And while under-representation in rural Canada may not be a concern, it is a crucial issue in urban Canada given the high levels of diversity and the types of issues (e.g., radicalization) being addressed by the RCMP in those areas.

CSIS, on the other hand, is strong in its representation of visible minorities and women. This is in part a reflection of its external orientation: international expertise and languages are required, and, moreover, intelligence work takes analytical and other similar skills (making it similar to policy work in other government departments where visible minorities and women are reasonable well represented). In sharp contrast to the almost excusatory language of the RCMP and Canadian Forces, the CSIS Annual Report states:

> At CSIS we believe that the diversity of our employees and having a workforce that is reflective of the Canadian population is a source of our strength.[178]

CSIS COMPARED TO LMA AND REPRESENTATION 2012-13

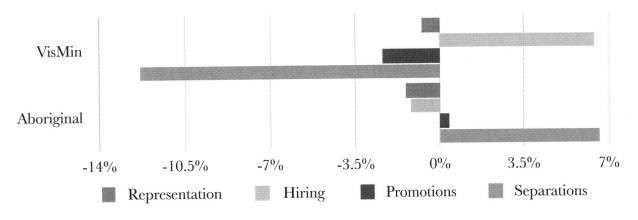

[177] RCMP data comes from *RCMP (Members) Employment Equity Report Fiscal Year 2012-2013*, September 2013. The RCMP uses an internally developed separate measure for labour market availability for regular members (2011 general LMA in brackets): women 20.1% (48.2%), aboriginal 4.0% (3.5%), visible minorities 6% (17.8%). No detailed methodology is provided (beyond "percentage of the workforce that is 18 years of age or older, has a Canadian secondary school diploma or equivalent, and is a Canadian citizen") and the gaps are particularly large. I have used the general LMA, recognizing that it overstates the actual labour market availability for regular members but illustrates the gap between a police force that is seen as being representative of the population and the current reality. Using the RCMP's internal regular member LMA, the negative portrait above turns positive.

[178] *CSIS Annual Report to the Treasury Board on the Employment Equity Program, 2012-13* 1. For the LMA, I have used the same approach as for the Canadian Forces and RCMP: the number of visible minorities who are also Canadian citizens.

The numbers largely support that claim, with the rate of hiring for visible minorities above LMA. However, only 7.6 percent of executives are visible minorities, all of whom are at the most junior EX-1 or Director level (women are more reasonably represented, making up about 30 percent of employees at most of the five EX levels). Like those in the core public administration, visible minority employees tend to be more represented in younger age cohorts and among professionals, semi-professionals and technical personnel.

Limited Data Regarding Other Police Forces

There is no authoritative source of information about employment equity in Canadian police forces. Moreover, many major police forces (e.g., OPP, Toronto, Calgary, Vancouver, Montreal) do not publicly report on the diversity of their workforce, although many do mention employment equity or diversity in their recruitment sections and feature a reasonably diverse workforce in their reports, websites and other publications.[179]

Police member union boards are overwhelmingly white and male in our major cities, rarely including more than one female or visible minority member in their membership.[180]

POLICE RESOURCES COMPARED TO 2011 LMA - 2013

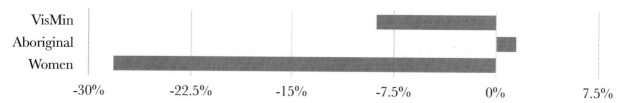

The Statistics Canada report *Police Resources in Canada, 2012* provides an overall snapshot on the diversity within police forces in Canada. Interestingly, representation of visible minorities is higher (at 11 percent) among experienced officers than it is among recent recruits (at four percent). The report does not offer an explanation for this difference (possibilities include self-reporting preferences or challenges in hiring and retaining).[181]

---

[179] For the Toronto, Montreal, Vancouver and Calgary, I contacted the police forces by phone and email. Urban-based forces tend to emphasize diversity more given the communities they serve. Sûreté du Québec is one of the rare police forces that reports on employment equity: 2013 statistics are 8.3 percent visible minority, 0.8 percent Aboriginal people and 21.4 percent women.

[180] Bob Ramsay, "Debate over police powers missing key voices: women and minorities," *The Globe and Mail*, 31 December 2014.

[181] "Police Resources in Canada, 2012," *Statistics Canada*. It should be noted that this report may understate diversity given that some police forces (e.g., Calgary and likely other Alberta police forces) do not collect employment equity data.

The following table provides information related to employment equity in the police forces of Toronto, Vancouver and Montreal.[182]

	Toronto		Vancouver		Montreal	
TABLE 13: MUNICIPAL POLICE FORCES 2013 AND 2014 DATA						
	Women	VisMin	Women	VisMin	Women	VisMin
Representation	29%	23%	24.4%	n/a	31%	6.7%
Promotions	5%	1%	n/a	n/a	22%	3.3%
Hirings	16%	31%	50% (est)	n/a	20%	100%
Separations	29%	9%	n/a	n/a	n/a	n/a

[182] Toronto data from Diversity and Inclusion Unit (email 16 February, current data), Vancouver Police Media Relations Unit (email 4 March 2015, current data), Montreal from Media Relations Unit (email 19 February, 2013 data). Montreal also reports on non-visible minority ethnic origins such as Italian Canadians and other European origins (4.1 percent).

OVERALL OBSERVATIONS — A MIXED PICTURE

Standing back, what does the above survey say about Canadian multiculturalism and society today, from the demographic, social, economic and political perspectives?

Some key observations emerge:

1. Canada's diversity continues to evolve and become more complex and varied, with over 250 ethnicities, an ever-larger and growing visible minority population, and increased religious diversity. The broad categories of "visible minority" and "ethnic origin," while useful for macro-level comparisons, fail to capture the degree of diversity contained /within/ these categories: in terms of religion, country of origin, time of immigration to Canada, or individual values and perspectives.

2. MTV (Montreal, Toronto, Vancouver) has been replaced by TVC (Toronto, Vancouver, Calgary), and Alberta (in a reflection of its greater economic growth) has displaced Quebec as Canada's third-most-diverse province. Moreover, diversity continues to expand outwards from the largest cities and their suburbs to more medium-sized cities.

3. Educational outcomes at the post-secondary level for most visible minority groups are significantly stronger than they are for those who are not visible minorities. In most groups, the difference in education level between men and women is minor. Canada continues to do a good job of integrating new Canadians in primary and secondary education.

4. Reported hate crimes and perceived discrimination remain an issue.

5. Representation of visible minorities in the public institutions that Canadians interact with the most — healthcare, social services and education (particularly higher education) — is close to representation in the general population in the larger provinces.

6. While there are areas of ethnic group concentration (if we look at the federal riding level, where 33 ridings in 2015 were composed of more than 50 percent visible minorities), most ridings have a mix of communities, some larger than others. Typically — but not universally — visible minority MPs elected in the 2011 election tended to represent ridings with large populations of their group.

7. Economic differences — whether measured by LICO prevalence, unemployment rates, and median income — between visible minorities and those of Canadian or European origin persist, even if workforce participation rates are stronger. This is also the case for most second-generation immigrants who have been schooled in Canada. However, some second-generation visible minority women are doing better than women who are not visible minorities. Moreover, university-educated second second-generation visible minorities aged 25 to 34 show many groups are in many cases doing as well or better than those that are not visible minority. Visible minority seniors, particularly women, have higher levels of relative poverty than non-visible minorities.

8. The Canadian model of immigration leading to citizenship is at risk given declining naturalization rates (at an average of 61 percent from landing years 2004-8), which have been exacerbated by policy changes that make citizenship "harder to get and easier to lose."

9. Visible minorities (along with women) make up a disproportionately low share of our federal and provincial political representatives, with the number of visible minority candidates

relatively stable at ten percent among all major parties since 2004. However, Canada has no anti-immigration party and all parties are competing for the ethnic vote. Visible minorities (and women) are seriously under-represented in judicial appointments.

10. Core public service employment of visible minorities is roughly in line with labour market availability at the federal level, with the exception of a few departments and agencies (e.g., Canadian Forces, RCMP). The larger provincial governments also have reasonable representation, with the exception of Quebec.

Chapter 4 — British Columbia: Or Should it be Asian Columbia?

British Columbia, Canada's third largest province with a population of 4.3 million, is also the second most-diverse province after Ontario. Asian Canadians form the largest visible minority groups, and have close economic and social ties to Asian countries and communities.

IMMIGRATION HISTORY

Prior to the completion of the Canadian Pacific Railway (CPR), non-native settlement in British Columbia was primarily motivated by the fur trade. Most inhabitants were French-Canadian and Métis employees, their British administrators, or Hawaiian and Iroquois peoples. With the Gold Rush of 1857, the population expanded, with most immigrants coming from California (mainly Chinese, American or European origin). Chinese immigrants formed up to one-third of the population of many mining towns.

The construction of the CPR generated a further wave of Chinese immigration, with some 10,000 railways workers coming mainly from mainland China. Completion of the CPR in 1885 and the Grand Trunk railway in 1913 led to expanded immigration and settlement, mainly by Europeans (most from Germany and Scandinavia).

In the early 1900s, restrictions on Chinese and Indian immigration increased, given fears of large-scale non-white immigration (the 1907 anti-Asian riots of Vancouver being one example). The Chinese Head Tax, first introduced following the construction of the CPR, was increased in 1900 and 1903 (some 45,000 Chinese immigrants paid the tax). In 2006, the Harper government made a formal apology to Chinese Canadians and provided *ex gratia* payments to survivors.

The first wave of Sikh immigration took place between 1904-08. About 5,000 immigrants arrived, most to work in lumber mills. In 1908, the "continuous journey" clause was implemented to prevent further immigration, which led to the 1914 voyage of the *Komagata Maru* in an unsuccessful effort to challenge this measure. Japanese immigration was also severely restricted.

Following World War I, British Columbia's population increased by almost 170,000 from a mix of domestic and international migration, bringing British Columbia's population to almost 700,000 on the eve of the Depression.[183]

During World War II, about 20,000 Japanese Canadians (many employed in the salmon fishery), two-thirds of whom were Canadian citizens, were removed from their homes in the lower mainland and dispersed to ghost towns in the BC interior. Their property was confiscated, and a number were eventually sent back to Japan. The last controls were removed in 1949 and the Mulroney government signed a redress agreement with the Japanese Canadian community in 1988.

Most immigration following World War II was European, as it was in the rest of Canada. In addition, restrictions on Chinese and Indian immigration were also removed.

The removal of ethnic and racial preferences in the late 60s provided the basis for British Columbia's growing diversity and becoming more of an Asian centre. Chinese immigration grew rapidly, particularly from Hong Kong given the 1997 transfer agreement, but increasingly from mainland China.

Today, British Columbia is one of Canada's most diverse provinces, with diversity concentrated in Vancouver and the lower mainland.[184]

---

[183] Separate statistics for British Columbia were not collected until 1929. In 1929-30, British Columbia accounted for some 13 percent of immigrants to the West.

[184] Same general sources as per Canadian immigration history, along with British Columbia (*Canadian Encyclopedia*), "Immigration to Canada" (*Canadian Museum of History*) and various sites for redress references.

DEMOGRAPHICS

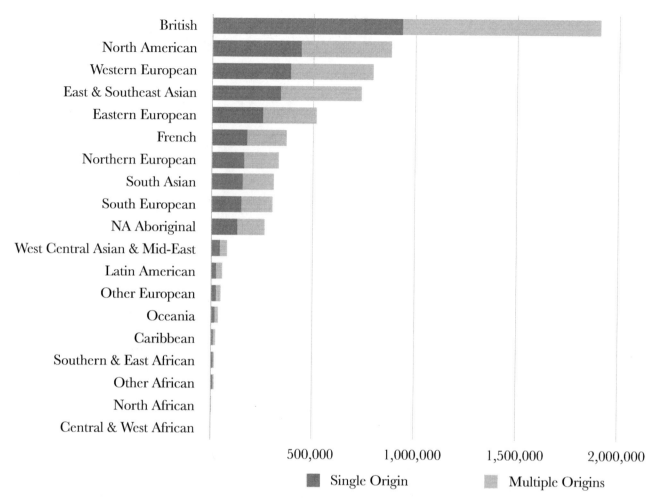

BRITISH COLUMBIA: ETHNIC ORIGINS 2011

The above chart shows the ethnic origins reported by British Columbians, including whether these origins are single or multiple.

While traditional European communities predominate, British Columbia has the highest relative share of Asian Canadians, with the Chinese, East Asian, Filipino communities the most significant.

This trend of heavy Asian (and Indian) immigration is expected to continue, with 70 percent of immigrants in recent years originating from these areas.

Appendix E lists the top 50 ethnic origins in British Columbia. This provides greater detail in terms of countries of origin than the more broad brush strokes depict above.

Overall, 50.8 percent of British Columbia residents report multiple ethnic origins, slightly higher than the national average.

BRITISH COLUMBIA ANNUAL AVERAGE IMMIGRANT INTAKE BY REGION 1988-2013

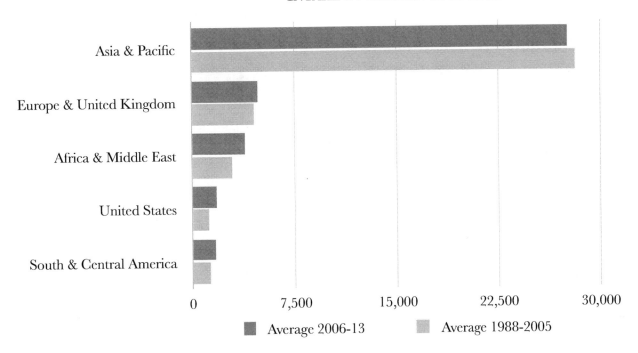

British Columbia's Cities

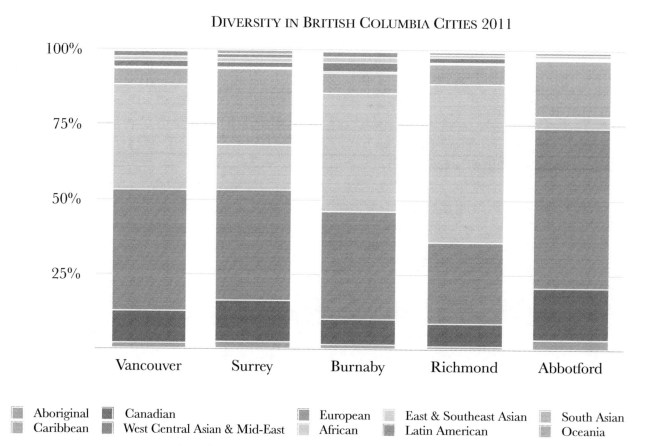

DIVERSITY IN BRITISH COLUMBIA CITIES 2011

| | Aboriginal | | Canadian | | European | | East & Southeast Asian | | South Asian |
| | Caribbean | | West Central Asian & Mid-East | | African | | Latin American | | Oceania |

Vancouver and the lower mainland have characteristically large Asian-origin communities. East and Southeast Asian communities (Chinese, Filipino, Korean and Japanese) predominate, as do South Asian (Sikh and Hindu).

Vancouver is the most mixed, but surrounding communities are also diverse. Burnaby and Richmond are heavily East and South Asian and Surrey has a large South Asian (mainly Sikh) population. Abbotsford is the least diverse, but still houses a large South Asian community.

Appendix E lists the top 20 ethnic origins in the major cities of British Columbia.

Religious Diversity

BRITISH COLUMBIA: RELIGIOUS DIVERSITY 2011

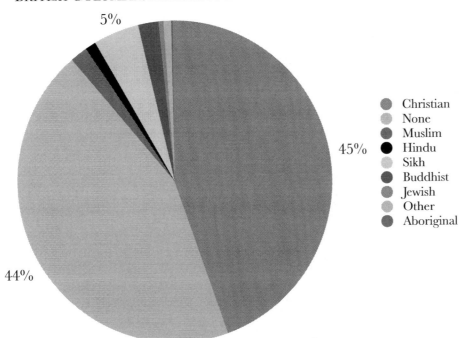

Legend:
- Christian
- None
- Muslim
- Hindu
- Sikh
- Buddhist
- Jewish
- Other
- Aboriginal

45%

44%

5%

Of all the provinces, British Columbia has the highest number of residents who identify as having "No religious affiliation." Identifying as such is most common among Chinese and Japanese British Columbians (66.1 and 64.5 percent of whom, respectively, report no religious affiliation) and those who are not visible minorities (47.6 percent, a much higher percentage than elsewhere in Canada).

In contrast, while Chinese Canadians in Ontario are similar to those in British Columbia in terms of the high number with no religious affiliation, only 24.3 percent of non-visible minorities in Ontario have no religious affiliation.

Sikh Canadians (who make up 63 percent of the South Asian community in British Columbia) are the largest religious minority, followed by Buddhists, Muslims, Hindus and Jews. Very few practice (or at least identify themselves as practising) Aboriginal spirituality despite an Aboriginal population of about 267,000.

This high proportion of residents without a religious affiliation is remarkably constant throughout the major cities. This is due to their large Chinese Canadian populations and the high number of non-visible minorities who are not religious. Two exceptions are Surrey and Abbotsford, with their large Sikh populations.

RELIGIOUS MINORITIES IN BRITISH COLUMBIA CITIES 2011

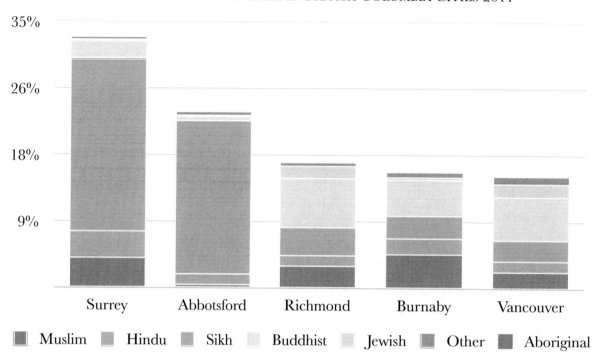

ECONOMIC

While Filipino and Japanese Canadians have unemployment rates lower than, and Chinese Canadians comparable to, that of non-visible minorities, all other groups have higher unemployment rates. In most cases, the gap is greater than two percent. Arab and West Asian Canadian unemployment rates are particularly high.

BRITISH COLUMBIA: 2011 VISIBLE MINORITY UNEMPLOYMENT RATE 25-64

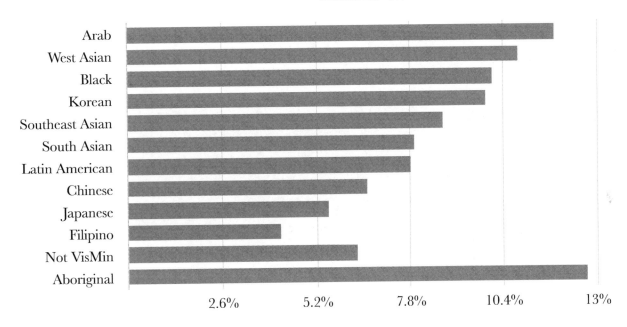

BRITISH COLUMBIA: 2011 LOW-INCOME CUT-OFF PREVALENCE FULL-TIME EMPLOYED 25-64

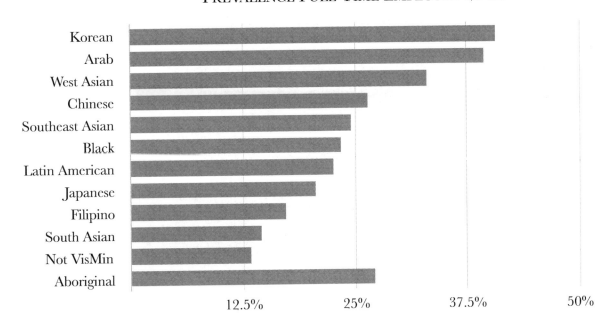

Similarly, pre-tax low-income cut-off (LICO) prevalence shows variation among different groups of visible minorities. The chart below, ranked by LICO prevalence among men, illustrates this. South Asian and Filipino Canadians have comparable rates to non-visible minorities, but all other groups have significantly higher rates, with Southeast Asian, Chinese, West Asian, Arab and Korean Canadians being twice as likely — or more — to fall under LICO. Overall, LICO prevalence among visible minorities is 23 percent, compared to 13 percent for non-visible minorities.

Looking at median incomes for all generations, ranked by women, there is considerable variation. On the low end, Korean Canadians in BC have median incomes at 68.0 percent of non-visible minorities. On the high end, Japanese Canadians are at 93.3 percent. The majority of visible minorities have median incomes of between 75 and 85 percent of the median for British Columbians who are not visible minorities.

BRITISH COLUMBIA: 2011 MEDIAN INCOME FULL-TIME EMPLOYED 25-64

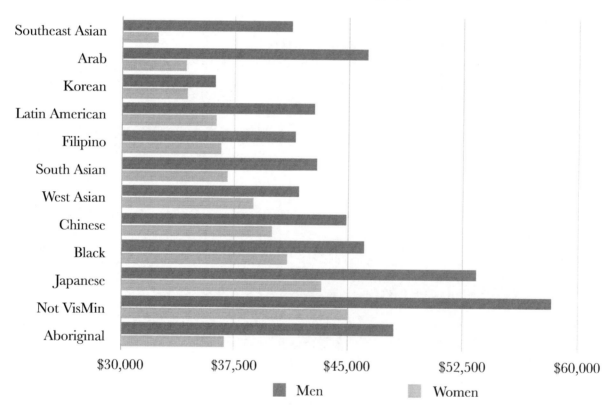

However, a different picture emerges with respect to the second-generation, ranked this time by women. Second-generation South Asian and Korean Canadian have median incomes comparable to non-visible minorities (within five percent), and Chinese, Arab and Japanese Canadians exceed the median for non-visible minorities.

Overall, the median incomes of visible minority women are 97.9 percent of what they are for women who are not visible minorities, while for men, the difference is greater: the median is 88.2 percent of that for non-visible minority men.

BRITISH COLUMBIA: 2011 MEDIAN INCOME SECOND-GENERATION 25-64

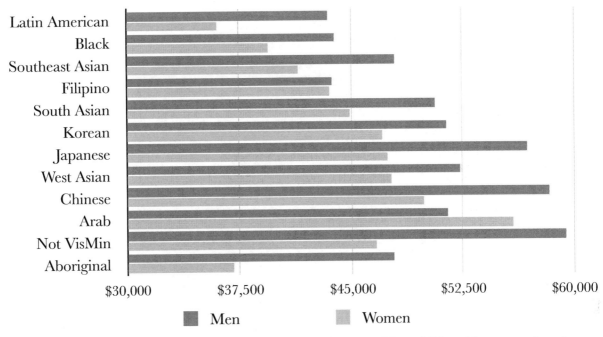

Looking at second-generation immigrants who are between 25 and 34 and have a university educated (just under 32,000 BC residents), we see that most visible minority men have median incomes nearly equal to or greater than those of non-visible minorities. The exceptions are Arab, Latin American and West Asian Canadian men. The same is true for visible minority women, with the exceptions being Southeast Asian, Arab, and Black Canadian women.

BRITISH COLUMBIA: 2011 MEDIAN INCOME FULL-TIME EMPLOYED SECOND-GENERATION 25-34 UNIVERSITY-EDUCATED

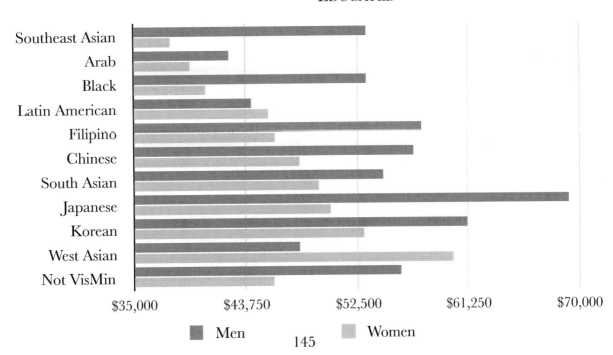

SOCIAL

BRITISH COLUMBIA: 2011 VISIBLE MINORITY LEVELS OF EDUCATION
25-64

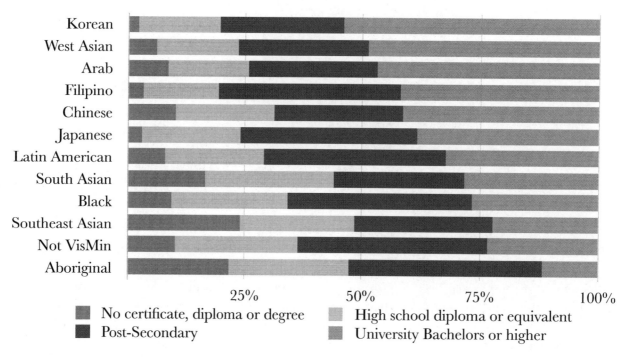

In terms of education, British Columbia follows the national pattern. Between 50 and 60 percent of Asian and Mid-Eastern British Columbians are university educated, and all groups (except Southeast Asians) have a greater proportion of university-educated members than the portion of the population that is not a visible minority. Filipino, Japanese, Latin American and Black Canadians are more likely than others to have an education in the trades or something equivalent.

Overall, 37.4 percent of visible minorities are university-educated, compared to 23.4 percent of non-visible minorities.

Only Southeast Asian Canadians have a high proportion (almost 25 percent) without any diploma.

In terms of how well government services represent the population they serve, the overall numbers indicate that British Columbia is doing reasonably well.

For healthcare and social services, which people generally encounter in their time of greatest need or vulnerability, representation is in line with British Columbia's population: 26.3 and 22.8 percent respectively, compared to labour market availability of 25.8 percent. And while many visible minorities are in support or junior positions (as discussed in the chapter on Canada), there are also many visible minority professionals (e.g., doctors, dentists). Not surprisingly, the largest groups in British Columbia (South Asian, Chinese and Filipino) are well represented in these sectors.

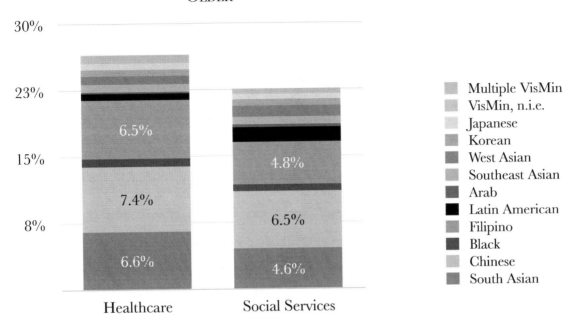

BRITISH COLUMBIA: 2011 HEALTHCARE AND
SOCIAL SERVICES REPRESENTATION 15 AND
OLDER

When it comes to education, staff at primary and secondary schools (whether in urban or rural areas) are less representative than those at community colleges and universities (which are located in urban areas). Universities are the most diverse. This reflects the more specialized qualifications required of employees, which brings into play the strong educational achievements of many visible-minority communities outlined above. Once again, South Asian and Chinese Canadians are well represented in the education sector.

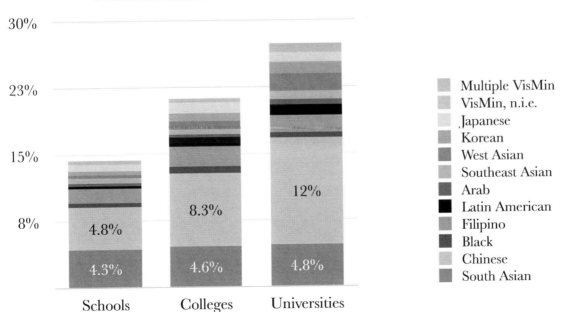

BRITISH COLUMBIA: 2011 EDUCATION
REPRESENTATION 15 AND OLDER

POLITICAL

BRITISH COLUMBIA: 2015 FEDERAL RIDINGS
PERCENTAGE VISIBLE MINORITIES

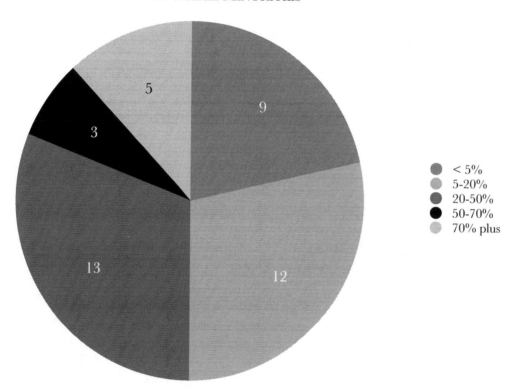

Legend:
- < 5%
- 5-20%
- 20-50%
- 50-70%
- 70% plus

British Columbia and Ontario both have the largest number of ridings that are dominated by single- or mixed-ethnicity enclaves.

Five ridings have more than 70 percent visible minorities and an additional three have between 50 and 70 percent. Religious minorities, on the other hand, make up more than 20 percent of the population in only three ridings: Surrey-Newton (44.3 percent Sikh), Surrey Centre (23.7 percent Sikh) and Fleetwood-Port Kells (19.6 percent Sikh).

Table 14 below details the ethnic mix in those federal ridings where visible minorities make up more than 50% of the total population.

	S. Asian	Chinese	Black	Filipino	Latin	Arab	SE Asian
TABLE 14 - BRITISH COLUMBIA FEDERAL RIDINGS OVER 50 PERCENT VISMIN							
Riding with over 70 % VisMin							
Vancouver South	18.2%	39.6%	1.0%	9.9%	2.0%	0.3%	4.0%
Surrey — Newton	59.0%	2.8%	1.3%	3.9%	1.1%	0.5%	1.2%
Vancouver Kingsway	6.9%	38.1%	0.8%	13.0%	1.3%	0.2%	6.1%
Steveston — Richmond East	10.5%	42.8%	0.6%	7.6%	0.8%	0.6%	1.2%
Richmond Centre	4.7%	51.4%	0.7%	5.8%	0.9%	0.5%	1.1%
Ridings with 50-70 % VisMin							
Burnaby South	8.3%	34.1%	1.3%	6.1%	1.8%	0.8%	2.0%
Fleetwood — Port Kells	27.1%	11.1%	1.3%	9.3%	1.1%	0.7%	4.5%
Surrey Centre	33.2%	4.8%	1.9%	8.1%	1.9%	1.5%	4.9%

In terms of representation in the British Columbia legislature, the the fact that the larger ethnic communities are concentrated in certain ridings contributes to the under-representation of visible minorities.

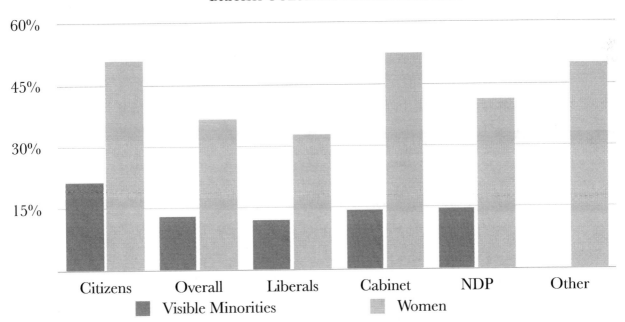

BRITISH COLUMBIA LEGISLATURE 2014

Overall representation of visible minorities is about half of what it should be given the province's visible minority population, with no significant differences between the two major parties. Representation of women, while below the population, is nevertheless stronger than at the federal level. Notably, British Columbia has the only Cabinet with gender equality (11 out of 21), with visible minority cabinet representation at 14.3 percent (three out of six caucus members).

British Columbia publishes a comprehensive employment equity report covering its core public service of some 39,000 employees.[185] Overall, women and Aboriginal Peoples are represented near labour market availability levels, with women over-represented in terms of their share of the overall population. Representation of women at senior levels is strong (45.5 percent), whereas visible minorities only comprise 6.1 percent of senior managers.

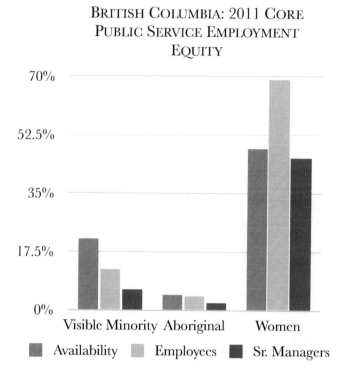

BRITISH COLUMBIA: 2011 CORE PUBLIC SERVICE EMPLOYMENT EQUITY

Looking at NHS public administration statistics for federal public servants located in British Columbia, visible minorities comprise 19.5 percent compared to 23.2 percent labour market

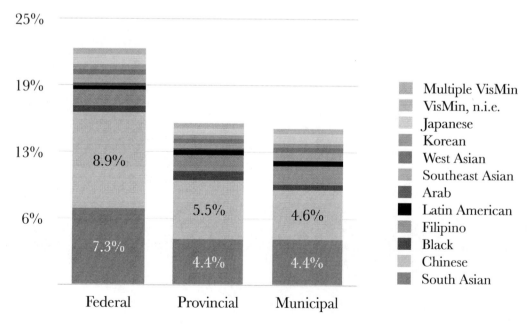

BRITISH COLUMBIA: 2011 PUBLIC ADMINISTRATION REPRESENTATION 15 AND OLDER

availability. Provincial and municipal visible minority representation is lower (at 15.2 and 14.8 percent respectively), due in part to the fact that these levels of government provide many services in rural BC.

As expected, to the extent that visible minorities are represented, South Asian and Chinese Canadians are the dominant groups.

Chapter 5 — Alberta: The New Face of Diversity

Alberta, until the recent fall in oil prices, has been the main driver of economic growth in Canada. As a result, the flow of immigrants to the province has increased, and Alberta has become Canada's third most diverse province. It has a growing population of 3.6 million, and offers stronger economic outcomes for most visible minorities than other regions.

EARLY IMMIGRATION AND SETTLEMENT

Mass immigration to the Prairie provinces followed the enacting of the *Dominion Lands Act* in 1872, which provided free land to settlers with the completion of the CPR ensuring direct transportation to the West. While the ethnicities considered most "desirable" were British, Belgian, American, Dutch, German, Finn, and Scandinavian, these groups were not the most productive farmers.

Immigration took off after 1896 under Minister for the Interior Clifford Sifton. He promoted large-scale immigration from Eastern Europe, stating that "a stalwart peasant in a sheep-skin coat, born on the soil, whose forefathers have been farmers for ten generations, with a stout wife and a half dozen children, is a good quality." This shift settled rural Western Canada and resulted in increased numbers of Ukrainian, Hungarian and Mennonite immigrants, populations that are still reflected in the province's ethnic composition today.

Extensive advertising and international immigration agencies helped encourage some three million immigrants to came to Canada between 1896 and 1914, many of them settling in the West. Some of the migration was internal, with French and Chinese settlers moving to the West. Other immigrant groups included people from Iceland and Romania. There was also considerable immigration from the United States, given high land costs and over-development in the American West. The American, Dutch, German, Finnish and Scandinavian settlers that arrived during this period proved prosperous, and had the advantage of being considered ethnically desirable — similar to British immigrants, and accustomed to democratic institutions. Alberta's population grew to 400,000 by 1911.

The West also became a refuge for persecuted groups, including American Blacks (most of whom resettled elsewhere in Canada), Doukhobors, Jews, Mennonites and Mormons.[186]

Following World War I, immigration slowly opened up, but with clear priority given to British immigrants. The British government subsidized emigration in response to some of its post-war

---

[186] Same general sources as per Canadian immigration history, along with Erica Gagnon, "Settling the West: Immigration to the Prairies from 1867 to 1914," Howard Palmer and Tamara Jeppson, "Peoples of Alberta: Portraits of Cultural Diversity" and Jim Frideres, "Four Strong Winds: Immigration Without Direction in Alberta" along with relevant *Canadian Encyclopedia* entries.

social and economic problems. However, despite these efforts, British immigration only accounted for about a quarter of immigrants during the 1920s. Due to these low numbers, and relatively limited immigration from the United States and Scandinavia (and, to a lesser extent, Western Europe), immigration from "non-preferred" countries in Central and Eastern Europe was reopened for agriculture workers and domestics, due also to pressure from the Canadian Pacific Railway. More Ukrainian, Hungarian, Romanians and Mennonites were joined by Poles and Russians among others. Given settlement patterns, rural ethnic enclaves were common. Immigration largely ended with the arrival of the Great Depression.

The 1920s saw a further increase of 100,000 in Alberta's population from a mix of domestic and international migration, bringing its population to over 730,000 on the eve of the Depression.[187]

Particular groups that settled in Alberta (in addition to the general patterns of Eastern European immigrants dating from the Sifton years) included Mormons, the Dutch, Danes, Norwegians and Swedes. Many of the Americans who settled in Alberta were former Canadians or Europeans. While some Blacks wanted to settle in Alberta, Black immigration was highly restricted.

---

[187] Frideres, Ibid.

DEMOGRAPHICS

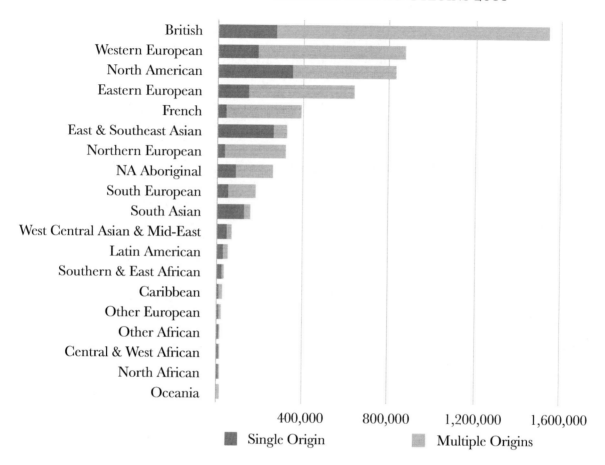

ALBERTA: ETHNIC ORIGINS 2011

The above chart shows the overall ethnic origins reported by Albertans, including both single and multiple origins.

The traditional European communities continue to be predominant, but Alberta (like Saskatchewan and Manitoba) has a relatively large Eastern European population, composed primarily of Ukrainian and Polish Canadians.

More recent communities from Asia and the Mid-East form an increasingly important part of Alberta's diversity. Recent immigration trends reinforce this tendency, with some 70 percent of recent immigrants originating from Asia.

Appendix F lists the top 50 ethnic origins in Alberta.

Overall, 51.6 percent of Alberta residents report multiple ethnic origins.

ALBERTA: ANNUAL AVERAGE IMMIGRANT INTAKE BY REGION 1988-2013

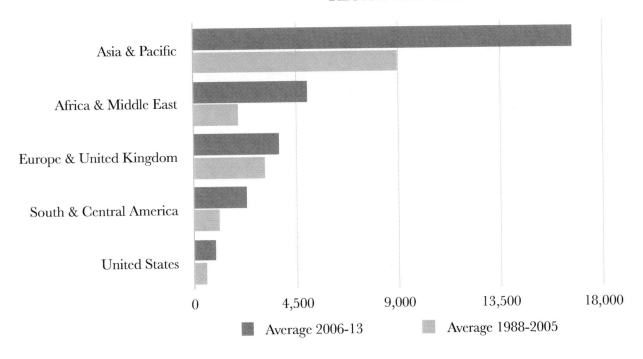

Religious Diversity

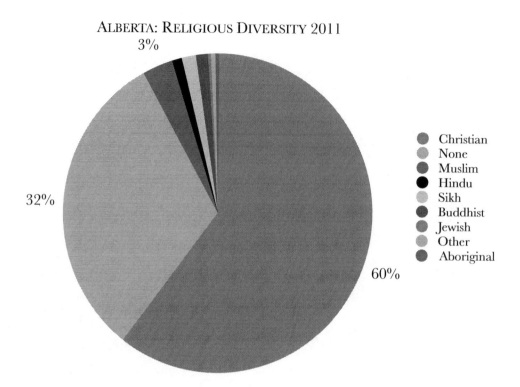

ALBERTA: RELIGIOUS DIVERSITY 2011

3%

32%

60%

Christian
None
Muslim
Hindu
Sikh
Buddhist
Jewish
Other
Aboriginal

Not surprisingly given majority European origins, most Albertans identify themselves as Christian (these numbers are roughly in line with the average in English Canada as a whole).

Muslim Canadians form the largest religious minority in Alberta (the first mosque in Canada was established in Edmonton in 1938), followed by Sikhs, Buddhists, Hindus, those who practice Aboriginal spirituality and Jews.

Some visible minority groups have greater religious diversity than others. South Asian religious affiliations include Sikh (33 percent), Muslim (28 percent) and Hindu (23 percent). 18 percent of Blacks are Muslim. The vast majority of West Asians (76 percent) and Arabs (83 percent) are Muslim.

Alberta's Cities

Calgary and Edmonton have grown to become the third- and fifth-most diverse cities in Canada, with significant East and Southeast Asian, and South Asian populations. Calgary is slightly more diverse with larger Asian communities. Edmonton has a larger aboriginal community. Red Deer and Lethbridge are more rural and overall less diverse, with Asian and Aboriginal communities being the larger communities.

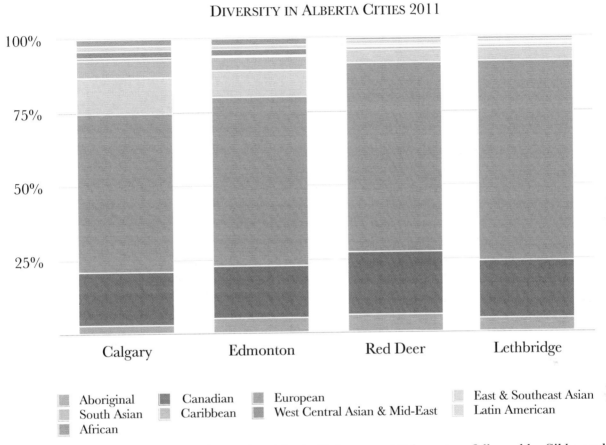

DIVERSITY IN ALBERTA CITIES 2011

Muslims form the largest religious minorities in Calgary and Edmonton, followed by Sikhs and Buddhists. There are few religious minorities in Red Deer and Lethbridge, reflecting lower levels of ethnic diversity.

Appendix F lists the top 20 ethnic origins in the major cities of Alberta.

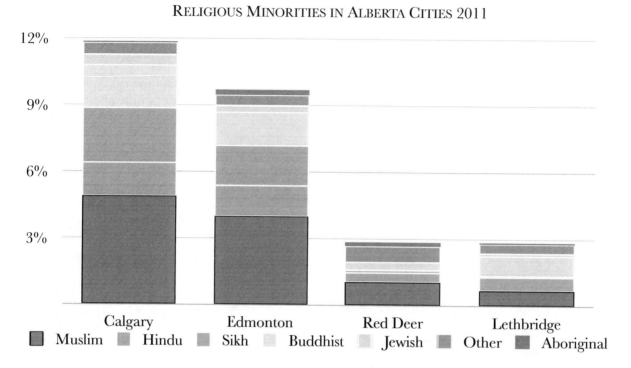

RELIGIOUS MINORITIES IN ALBERTA CITIES 2011

ECONOMIC

As expected, visible minorities in Alberta have some of the lowest unemployment rates in Canada, at 5.5 percent. This is lower than the national average of 8.3 percent, and is only 0.7 percent higher than the unemployment rate for Albertans who are not visible minorities.

ALBERTA: 2011 VISIBLE MINORITY UNEMPLOYMENT RATE 25-64

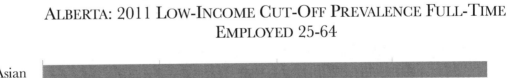

As in British Columbia, Filipino and Japanese Canadians have lower unemployment rates than non-visible minorities, and Chinese Canadians have comparable rates. Rates for South and Southeast Asian groups are only slightly higher (less than one percent). Unemployment rates for

ALBERTA: 2011 LOW-INCOME CUT-OFF PREVALENCE FULL-TIME EMPLOYED 25-64

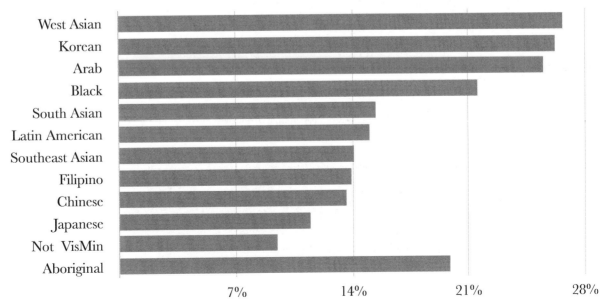

Black, Arab and West Asian residents surpass that of non-visible minorities by two percent or more.

Similarly, while pre-tax low-income cut-off (LICO) prevalence of visible minorities is lower than the Canadian average (16 percent compared to 22 percent), there is variation among different groups of visible minorities. However, all groups have higher LICO prevalence than non-visible minorities, with only Japanese Canadians having roughly comparative rates (12 percent compared to 10 percent). The chart below, ranked by LICO prevalence among men, illustrates this. Black, Arab, Korean and West Asian Canadians all have LICO rates more than double that of non-visible minorities.

ALBERTA: 2011 MEDIAN INCOME FULL-TIME EMPLOYED 25-64

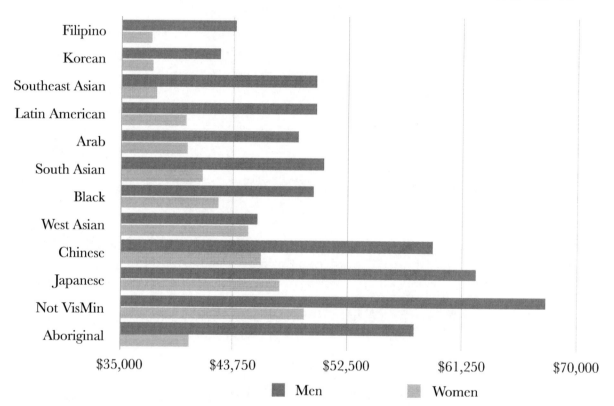

Looking at median incomes for all generations, Alberta also does better than the rest of Canada, with the highest median incomes in the country after the North: the average for Albertans who are not visible minorities is $58,418, compared to the Canadian average of $49,712. For visible minorities, Alberta median incomes are $45,233, compared to the Canadian average of $41,127.

However, there remains considerable variation between visible minority groups (see chart below, ranked again by incomes for women). On the low end, Korean and Filipino Canadian men have median incomes at 63.2 and 64.9 percent of the non-visible minority median, respectively. On the high end, Japanese and Chinese Canadian men are at 92.1 and 87.3 percent, respectively. The majority of visible minorities fall between 75 and 85 percent of the median income for other Alberta residents.

ALBERTA: 2011 MEDIAN INCOME SECOND-GENERATION 25-64

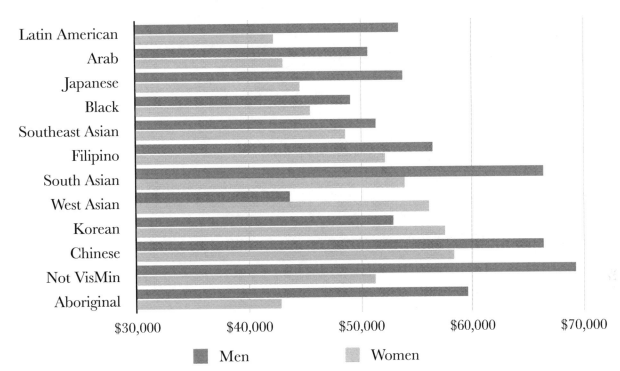

A different picture emerges with respect to the second generation (see chart below, ranked by women's median income). Second-generation South Asian, Chinese, West Asian, Filipino and Korean Canadian women all have median incomes greater than non-visible minority women. Latin American and Arab women have the lowest median incomes, at 82.5 and 84.1 percent of non-visible minority median incomes respectively. For men, the picture is less positive, with only South Asian (96.0 percent) and Chinese (95.8 percent) Canadians approaching non-visible minorities. Black (70.9 percent), Arab (73.1 percent) and Southeast Asian (74.2 percent) men have the lowest median incomes.

Overall, the median income for visible minority women is slightly greater (by 2.6 percent) than it is for other women. The difference for men is greater: median incomes of visible minority men are 86.6 percent of the median income for other Albertans.

Looking at university educated, second-generation immigrants between 25 and 34 (under 23,000 people in Alberta), some interesting variations come up. Japanese men and women have the lowest median incomes, in sharp contrast to elsewhere in the country. Latin American, West Asian, Arab, South Asian and Chinese Canadian men have incomes equal to or greater than the provincial average for non-visible minorities, as do Korean, Filipino and Chinese Canadian women. There are not sufficient numbers of West Asian women for median income data for this cohort.

ALBERTA: 2011 MEDIAN INCOME FULL-TIME EMPLOYED
SECOND-GENERATION 25-34 UNIVERSITY EDUCATED

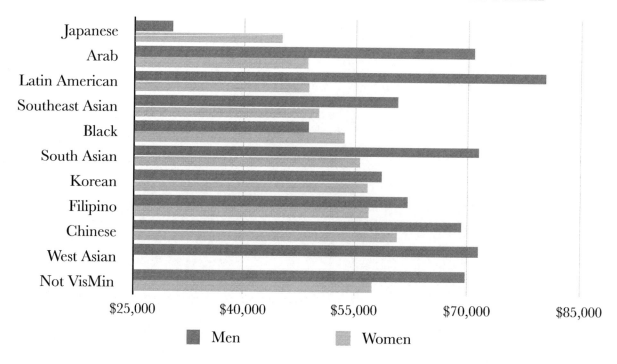

SOCIAL

ALBERTA: 2011 VISIBLE MINORITY LEVELS OF EDUCATION 25-64

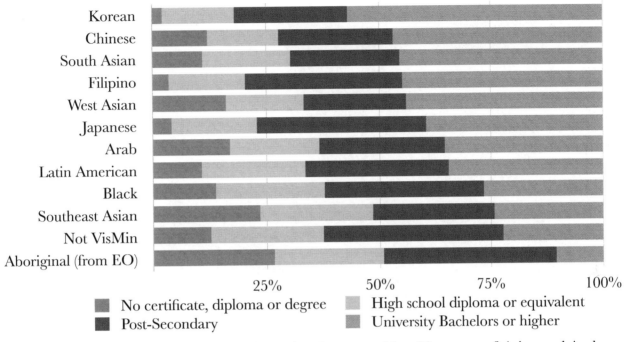

▮ No certificate, diploma or degree		▮ High school diploma or equivalent	
▮ Post-Secondary		▮ University Bachelors or higher	

In terms of education, Alberta follows the national pattern: 50 to 60 percent of Asian and Arab Albertans are university educated. All visible minority groups have a greater proportion of university-educated members than do non-visible minorities. Trades education or equivalent is stronger for Filipino, Japanese, Latin American and Black Canadians. More West Asian and Arab Canadians are without a diploma than members of other groups, at 15 to almost 25 percent. Overall, 40.6 percent of visible minorities are university educated, compared to 22.1 percent of non-visible minorities.

In terms of how well government services represent the population they serve, the overall numbers indicate that Alberta is doing reasonably well, notwithstanding the absence of any active employment equity policies.

For healthcare and social services, which people tend to encounter at their times of greatest need and vulnerability, representation of visible minorities is greater than Alberta's labour market availability of 17.3 percent: at 21.8 percent for healthcare and 20.4 percent for social services. While many visible minorities are in support or junior positions (as discussed in the chapter on Canada), median income data suggests that there are also many visible minority professionals in Alberta, particularly of Arab, South Asian, Chinese, or West Asian descent.

When it comes to education, staff at primary and secondary schools (whether in urban or rural areas) are less representative than those at community colleges and universities (which are located in urban areas). Universities are the most diverse. This reflects the more specialized qualifications required of employees, which brings into play the strong educational achievements of many visible-minority communities outlined above.

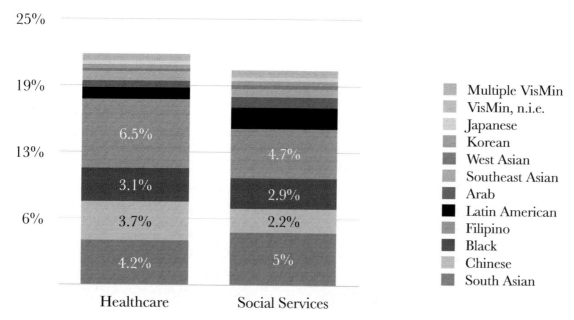

ALBERTA: 2011 HEALTHCARE AND SOCIAL
SERVICES REPRESENTATION 15 AND OLDER

Visible minorities are underrepresented in primary and secondary schools (at 9.2 percent of staff) and community colleges (13.4 percent) in Alberta. They are overrepresented in universities, where they make up 24 percent of employees. Once again, South Asian and Chinese Canadians are well-represented in the education sector. Based on median income data, visible minorities working in the education sector are predominantly in junior or support positions, with the exception of South Asian and Japanese Canadians in community colleges.

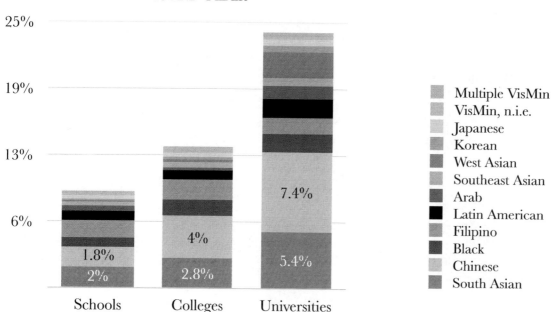

ALBERTA: 2011 EDUCATION REPRESENTATION
15 AND OLDER

POLITICAL

ALBERTA: 2015 FEDERAL RIDINGS VISIBLE MINORITY CONCENTRATION

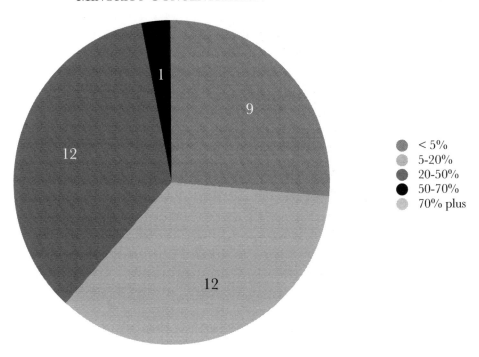

- < 5%
- 5-20%
- 20-50%
- 50-70%
- 70% plus

While only one Alberta riding — Calgary Skyview — has over 50 percent visible minorities (South Asian 34.1 percent, Filipino 7.8 percent), 12 ridings have significant visible minority populations. The visible minority population in three of these ridings exceeds 40 percent of the

ALBERTA LEGISLATURE 2015

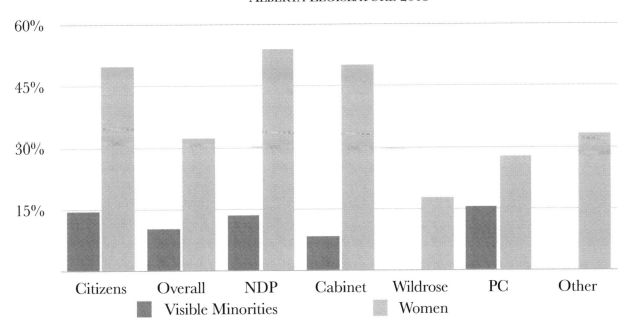

total: Calgary Forest Lawn (47.6 percent), Edmonton Mill Woods (42.4 percent) and Calgary Nose Hill (40.3 percent).

In terms of representation in the 2015 Alberta legislature, visible minorities are under-represented overall, including (though to a slightly lesser degree) in the government benches. The election of an NDP government resulted in a dramatic increase in female MLAs, with Alberta now having the third-highest percentage of female MLAs of all the provinces (after British Columbia and Ontario). Alberta also joins British Columbia in having gender parity in Cabinet. Compared to the previous government, visible minority representation declined slightly in the legislature (from 12.6 to 10.3 percent) and the Cabinet (from 12.0 to 8.3 percent).

While Alberta does not track employment equity data for its 29,000 provincial government employees, the National Household Survey indicates that overall, visible minorities are slightly underrepresented in all three levels.[188] Visible minorities comprise 13.4 percent of federal public servants located in Alberta, falling short of their 17.3 percent labour market availability (the federal *Employment Equity in the Public Service of Canada* report, which considers only core public administration, shows 11.3 percent representation). Provincial representation is slightly higher (15.6 percent) and municipal visible minority representation is lower (11.5 percent), the latter likely reflecting the provision of services in rural areas.

ALBERTA: 2011 FEDERAL, PROVINCIAL AND
MUNICIPAL PUBLIC ADMINISTRATION
REPRESENTATION 15 AND OLDER

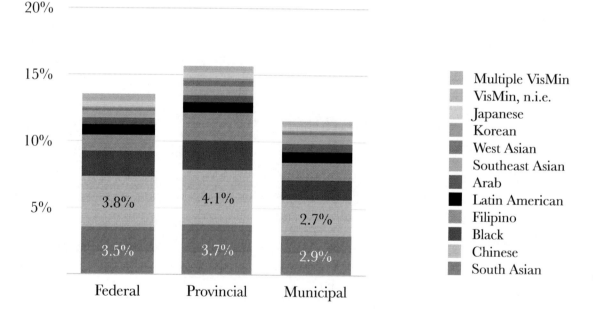

As expected, representation reflects the population of visible minorities, with South Asian and Chinese Canadians predominant in all three levels, and Black and Filipino Canadians making a stronger showing in the provincial government.

---

[188] Government of Alberta, <u>About Us: Careers with the Government of Alberta</u>.

Chapter 6 — Saskatchewan: Steady Growth

Saskatchewan has benefitted from strong economic growth as a result of its strong resource base, with immigration almost quadrupling over the past eight years compared to earlier periods. Saskatchewan's population is about one million.

However, like Alberta, Saskatchewan has been affected by the recent drop in oil prices.

EARLY IMMIGRATION AND SETTLEMENT

Like all Prairie provinces, early immigration to Saskatchewan exploded under the policies introduced by Minister of Interior Sifton.[189]

Saskatchewan's population increased from 20,000 in 1880 to 258,000 in 1906 to 492,000 by 1911. While about half of these new arrivals were Canadian-born, the rest were a diverse group, and often formed farm bloc settlements dominated by a single ethnicity. Examples of significant groups include the British (English, Welsh and Scottish), Americans, Hungarians, Romanians, Belgians, Austrians, Germans, Scandinavians, Ukrainians and and members of religious sects like the Mennonites, Doukhabours and Hutterites. Immigrants from Francophone countries were joined by Francophone migration from Quebec, Manitoba and the U.S., creating some 32 distinct Francophone settlements.

These bloc settlements, like current patterns of immigrant settlement, eased settlers' adjustment to their new harsh environment. This also helped these groups to maintain their language and culture, often to the discomfort of early Canadian-born and British-origin settlers.

Agriculture, primarily the growing of wheat, exploded from some 1,500 farms and 70,000 acres in 1886 to 56,000 farms and 3.3 million acres in just 20 years.

Saskatchewan became a province in 1905. Immigration was put on hold during World War I, with about half of the 8,000 Ukrainian and other former citizens of the Austro-Hungarian empire being interned during the war coming from Saskatchewan. German immigrants were also targets of persecution.

By the 1920s, Saskatchewan had about twice as many immigrants of non-British origin than of British origin.

---

[189] Same general sources as per Canadian immigration history, along with Michael Cottrell, "History of Saskatchewan," Alan Anderson, "Ethnic Bloc Settlements," and Joseph Garcea, "Settlement and Integration in Saskatchewan."

The 1920s saw another 150,000 immigrants arrive in Saskatchewan, bringing its population to over 900,000 on the eve of the Depression.

DEMOGRAPHICS

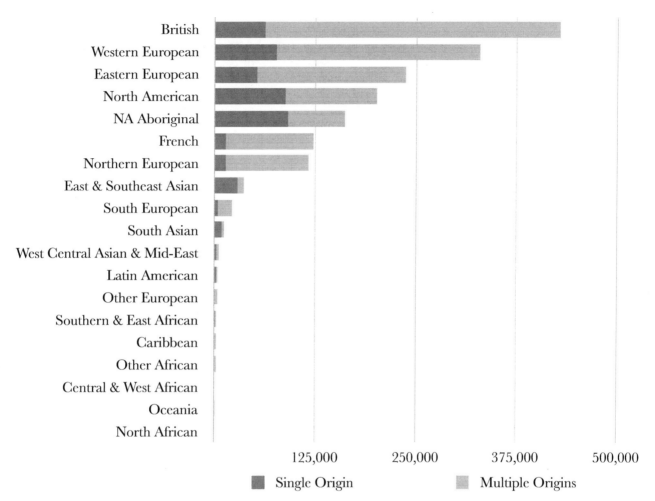

SASKATCHEWAN: ETHNIC ORIGINS 2011

This shows the overall ethnic origins reported by residents of Saskatchewan, including both single and multiple origins.

While the traditional European communities continue to be predominant, Eastern European communities (composed mostly of Ukrainian and Polish Canadians) are particularly significant, as they are in Alberta and Manitoba. Visible minorities currently form a relatively small share of the population, at 6.3 percent.

But as in Manitoba, the relatively high aboriginal presence (15.6 percent) distinguishes Saskatchewan from most provinces. More recent communities from Asia and the Mid-East are relatively smaller than in the larger provinces.

Immigration trends show close to 70 percent of recent immigrants coming from Asia, with over 10,000 immigrants of all origins per year over the last few years.

Appendix G lists the top 20 ethnic origins in Saskatchewan.

Overall, 55.3 percent report multiple ethnic origins, higher than the national average.

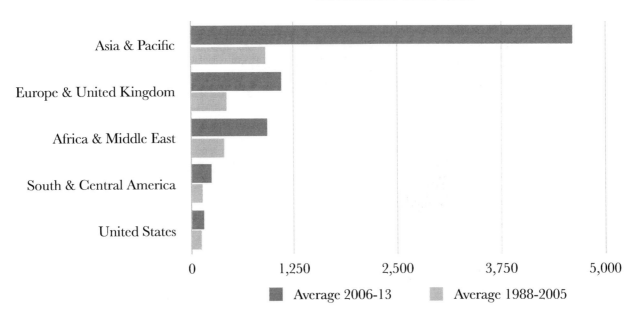

SASKATCHEWAN: ANNUAL AVERAGE IMMIGRANT INTAKE
BY REGION 1988-2013

Religious Diversity

SASKATCHEWAN: RELIGIOUS DIVERSITY 2011

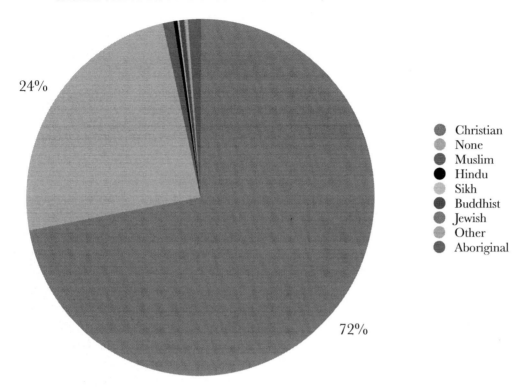

Saskatchewan has a proportion of residents declaring "No religious affiliation" similar to the national average. Its percentage of Christians is slightly higher, and it is home to relatively few people of other faiths.

Given the high aboriginal population, traditional aboriginal spirituality is the second-most followed religion, followed by Islam, Buddhism, Hinduism, Sikhism and Judaism. However, the percentage of residents practicing Aboriginal spirituality remains small (at 1.2 percent) compared to the province's Aboriginal population (15.6 percent of the total population).

Saskatchewan's Cities

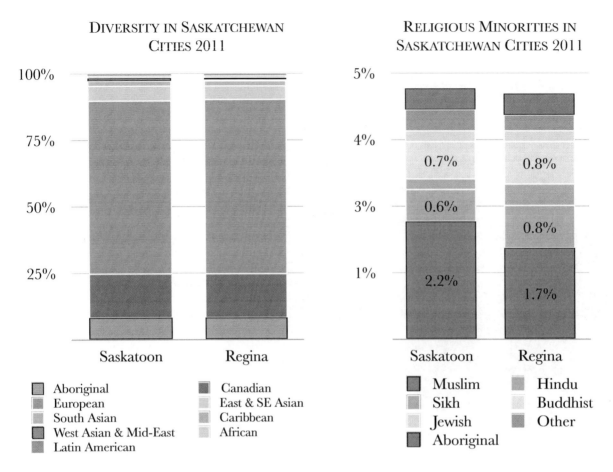

DIVERSITY IN SASKATCHEWAN CITIES 2011

Aboriginal
European
South Asian
West Asian & Mid-East
Latin American

Canadian
East & SE Asian
Caribbean
African

RELIGIOUS MINORITIES IN SASKATCHEWAN CITIES 2011

Muslim
Sikh
Jewish
Aboriginal

Hindu
Buddhist
Other

Non-European and non-aboriginal ethnic origins form 10.2 percent of the population in Saskatoon and 9.7 percent in Regina. Aboriginal people make up 8.2 percent of Saskatoon's population, and 8.3 percent of Regina's.

There are no major differences between the two major cities of Saskatoon and Regina in terms of either ethnic origin or religious diversity. Both are characterized, as in Manitoba, by relatively large aboriginal populations, and relatively small ethnic minority communities. Of the ethnic minorities who are present, the largest groups are East and Southeast, and South Asian immigrants. Muslims have the largest minority-religion population.

Appendix G lists the top 20 ethnic origins in Saskatoon and Regina.

ECONOMIC

Reflecting strong economic growth and the lowest unemployment rate in Canada, relatively few Saskatchewan visible minorities are unemployed, 4.6 percent compared to the national average of 8.3 percent, and only 0.7 percent more than non-visible minorities.

SASKATCHEWAN: 2011 VISIBLE MINORITY UNEMPLOYMENT RATE
25-64

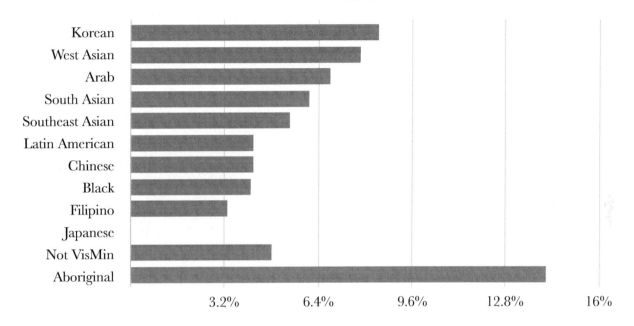

SASKATCHEWAN: 2011 LOW-INCOME CUT-OFF PREVALENCE
FULL-TIME EMPLOYED 25-64

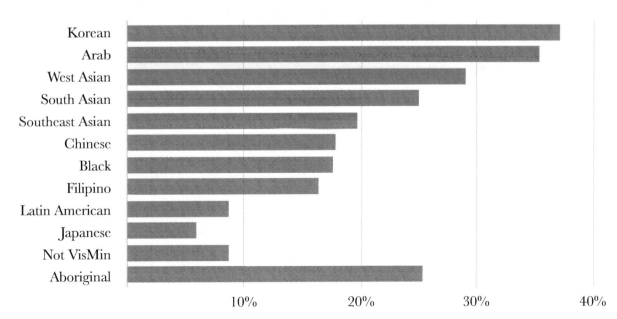

Black, Chinese, Filipino, Japanese and Latin American communities in Saskatchewan have lower unemployment rates than non-visible minorities. Korean, Arab and West Asian unemployment rates are, however, higher than the rate for non-visible minorities by two percent or more.

Pre-tax low-income cut-off (LICO) prevalence for visible minorities is double that of non-visible minorities (20 compared to 9 percent, slightly lower than the Canadian average of 22 percent for visible minorities), and there is a similar variation among different groups of visible minorities as there is on the national level. However, no visible minority group has lower LICO prevalence than non-visible minorities, with only Japanese Canadians and Latin Americans having the same LICO prevalence as non-visible minorities. The chart below, ranked by LICO prevalence among men, illustrates this. Black, Chinese, Southeast Asian, South Asian, West Asian, Arab and Korean men in Saskatchewan all have LICO rates more than more than double that of men who are not visible minorities.

Looking at median incomes for all generations, ranked by women, Saskatchewan's median income is $49,539 for non-visible minorities, compared to the Canadian average of $49,712. For visible minorities, Saskatchewan median income is $39,187, compared to the Canadian average of $41,127.

SASKATCHEWAN: 2011 MEDIAN INCOME FULL-TIME EMPLOYED 25-64

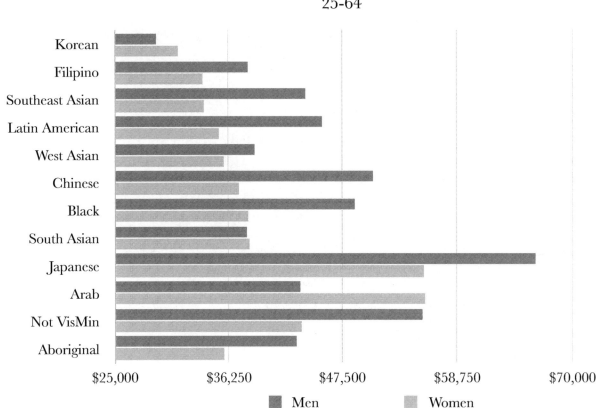

There is also considerable variation in the second generation (ranked by incomes for women). On the low end, Latin American and Arab Canadian men in Saskatchewan have median incomes at 44.9 and 65.5 percent of that for non-visible minority men, respectively. On the high end, Chinese and Southeast Asian Canadian men in Saskatchewan sit at 110.3 and 102.3 percent of the non-visible minority median, respectively. Filipino men approach parity at 95.5 percent. Chinese, Black, Latin American and Filipino female residents have higher median incomes than women who are not visible minorities — by a large margin, in the case of Black women in Saskatchewan (113.2 percent). South Asian and Southeast Asian women have lower median incomes (90.3 and 84.3 percent respectively). There is no data for West Asian, Korean and Japanese residents (male and female) or Arab Canadian women, due to the small size of these populations in Saskatchewan.

SASKATCHEWAN: 2011 MEDIAN INCOME SECOND-GENERATION 25-64

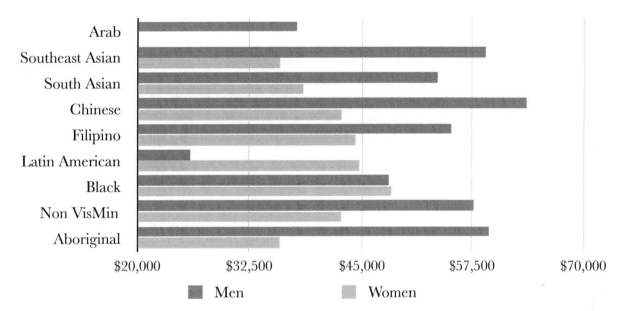

SOCIAL

SASKATCHEWAN: 2011 VISIBLE MINORITY LEVELS OF EDUCATION
25-64

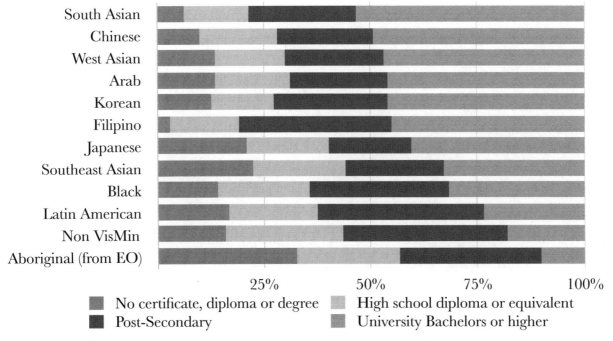

In terms of education, Saskatchewan follows the national pattern. Between 50 and 60 percent of Asian and Arab residents are university educated. All visible minority groups have a higher proportion of university-educated members than do those who are not visible minorities. Education in the trades (or equivalent) is more common among Filipino, Latin American and Black Canadians in Saskatchewan. Overall, 43.4 percent of visible minorities are university educated (the second highest after Atlantic Canada), compared to 18.0 percent of non-visible minorities (the lowest in Canada).

In terms of the extent to which government services represent the population they serve, the numbers indicate that Saskatchewan is doing reasonably well.

For healthcare and social services, which people tend to access in times of need or vulnerability, visible minority representation is greater than their Saskatchewan labour market availability of 6.3 percent, at 7.8 percent in healthcare and 5.9 percent in social services. While many visible minorities are in support or junior positions, as discussed in the chapter on Canada, median income data suggests that there are also many visible minority professionals (e.g., doctors, dentists) in Saskatchewan, particularly in the Arab, South Asian, Chinese, Southeast Asian and Black communities.

When it comes to education, staff at primary and secondary schools (whether in urban or rural areas) are less representative than those at community colleges and universities (which are located in urban areas). Universities are the most diverse. This reflects the more specialized qualifications required of employees, which brings into play the strong educational achievements of many visible-minority communities.

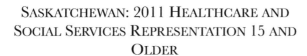

SASKATCHEWAN: 2011 HEALTHCARE AND
SOCIAL SERVICES REPRESENTATION 15 AND
OLDER

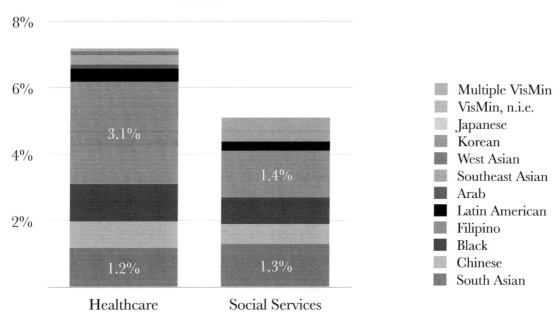

Visible minorities are underrepresented in primary and secondary schools (at 3.1 percent of staff) and community colleges (3.4 percent), but over-represented at universities (16.3 percent of staff). Again, South Asian and Chinese Canadians are well represented at universities; Southeast Asians slightly less so. Based on median income data, visible minorities in the education sector are concentrated in junior or support positions, with the exception of Chinese and Black Canadians in elementary and secondary schools.

SASKATCHEWAN: 2011 EDUCATION
REPRESENTATION 15 AND OLDER

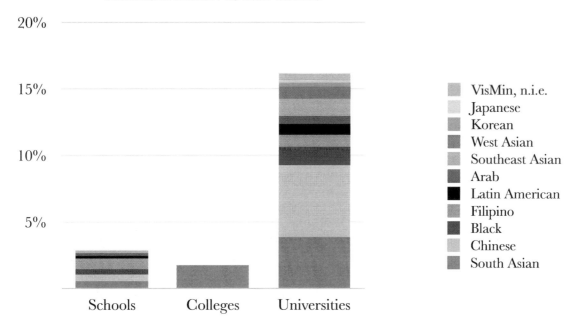

POLITICAL

SASKATCHEWAN: 2015 FEDERAL RIDINGS VISIBLE MINORITY CONCENTRATION

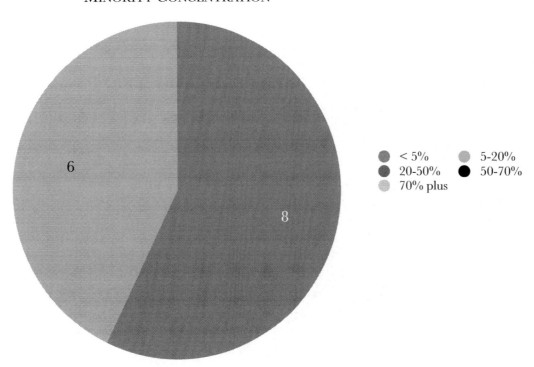

- ● < 5%
- ● 20-50%
- ● 70% plus
- ● 5-20%
- ● 50-70%

No ridings in Saskatchewan have significant numbers of visible minorities. The most diverse riding, Saskatoon West, has a visible-minority population of only 15.0 percent, with the largest group being Filipino Canadians, at 5.5 percent.

SASKATCHEWAN LEGISLATURE 2014

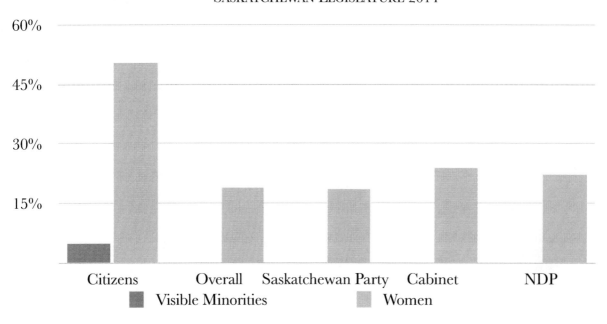

- ■ Visible Minorities
- ■ Women

In terms of representation in the Saskatchewan legislature, it is unsurprising given the small proportion of visible minorities in the population (6.3 percent) that there are no visible-minority representatives. Women are also underrepresented, making up only 19 percent of government representatives: 23.8 percent of the cabinet, and 18.4 of the caucus.

Saskatchewan provides monthly updates on its progress with meeting employment equity goals for its 15,000 employees. These show that visible minorities, Aboriginal people and women are all under-represented.[190]

The National Household Survey, however, indicates that while visible minorities are under-represented at all three levels. Federal visible minority public servants located in Saskatchewan comprise 4.0 percent of that workforce, compared to 6.3 percent labour market availability (the federal *Employment Equity in the Public Service of Canada* report, which considers core public administration, shows a representation of 5.8 percent). Representation among provincial government employees is only slightly lower (at 5.5 percent), and municipal representation is the same as that in the federal government (4.0 percent).

As expected, the composition of those visible minorities who are in government reflects the population, with South Asian, Chinese and Filipino Canadians predominating at all three levels.

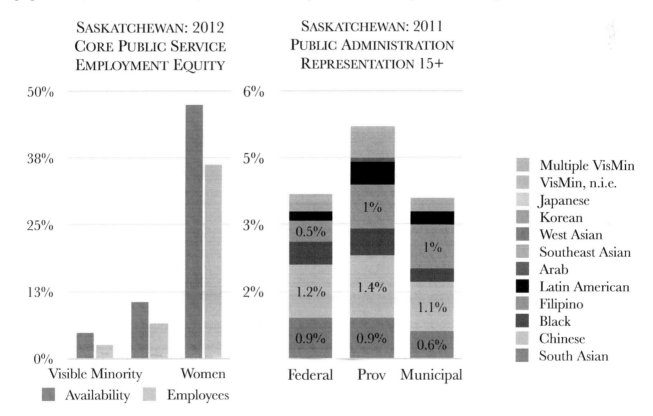

SASKATCHEWAN: 2012 CORE PUBLIC SERVICE EMPLOYMENT EQUITY

SASKATCHEWAN: 2011 PUBLIC ADMINISTRATION REPRESENTATION 15+

Chapter 7 — Manitoba: Quiet Success

Manitoba, the original business and immigration hub of the West, was always more diverse than the other Prairie provinces — until the oil and gas sector fuelled growth in Alberta. Immigration has more than doubled over the past eight years. Manitoba's population is about 1.2 million.

EARLY IMMIGRATION AND SETTLEMENT

As it did in all the Prairie provinces, early immigration to Manitoba exploded under the policies introduced by Minister of Interior Sifton.

Manitoba's population increased from 66,000 in 1881 to 461,000 by 1911, at which time Winnipeg had 140,000 residents. 30,000 new farms were established each year between 1896 and 1922.[191]

While 50 percent of Manitoba's population spoke French in 1870 (reflecting its large numbers of Métis people and settlers from Quebec and other French-speaking areas), the proportion declined to a mere 7.3 percent by 1911 due to an influx of non-French-speaking settlers. Efforts to increase settlement from Quebec met with only modest success, as many French Canadians chose instead to emigrate to the US.

Métis fears over their rights, land and survival as a distinct people led to two rebellions. The first, in 1869, was resolved by negotiation, and resulted in the creation of Manitoba in 1870. A significant number of Métis moved to Saskatchewan at the time. A perceived failure of the province of Manitoba to live up to its earlier commitments, and encroachment on Métis lands, led to the North-West Rebellion of 1885. This rebellion was resolved by force, and ended with the execution of Métis leader Louis Riel.

Between 1876 and 1881 (prior to the completion of the Canadian Pacific Railway), 40,000 immigrants, mainly British Ontarians, were drawn West by the prospect of wheat farming made more profitable by new machinery and milling processes. Mennonites and Icelandic immigrants also arrived in the 1870s, the former settling around Steinbach and Winkler, the latter near Gimli and Hecla. Immigration then slowed until the late 1890s.

---

[191] Same general sources as per Canadian immigration history, along with "Immigration and Settlement: 1870-1919" *Manitobia*, "Manitoba" *Historica Canada*, Morris Deveson, "The History of Agriculture in Manitoba (1812-2007)," "Manitoba" *Jewish Virtual Library*, Tom Carter and Benjamin Amoyaw, "Manitoba: The Struggle to Attract and Retain Immigrants."

Like elsewhere in the Prairies, settlers arrived in large numbers in the period between 1894 and the outbreak of the First World War, including large numbers from Eastern Europe (particularly Ukraine, Russia and Poland). Manitoba's population increased to 461,000 by 1911. By 1914, the province was home to some 30,000 Ukrainian settlers. Winnipeg became a centre for Eastern European Jewish immigrants, with some 17,000 living in the city by 1921.

Given this influx, there were concerns about Ukrainian and Doukhobor immigrants outnumbering British and American settlers.

The 1920s saw many more immigrants arrive in Manitoba. However, given that Manitoba immigration statistics included Alberta and Saskatchewan until 1929, the exact number of the 166,000 arrivals who stayed in Manitoba is not published (but we do know that it was the majority).[192] Manitoba's population increased to over 700,000 on the eve of the Depression.

---

[192] For example, in 1929 and 1930 when Western provincial immigration is broken down, Manitoba accounts for 52 percent of Western settlers.

DEMOGRAPHICS

This shows the overall ethnic origins reported by Manitobans, including both single and multiple origins. While the traditional European communities continue to be predominant, Eastern European communities (largely Ukrainian and Polish Canadians) are significant, as they are in Alberta and Saskatchewan.

MANITOBA: ETHNIC ORIGINS 2011

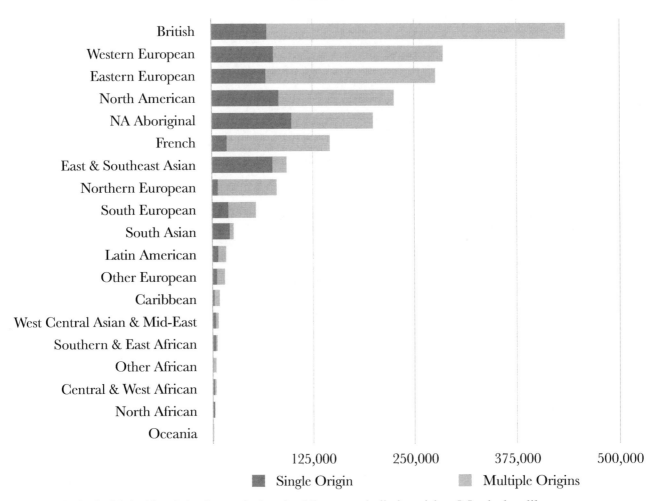

Its relatively high Aboriginal population (at 17 percent) distinguishes Manitoba, like Saskatchewan, from most other provinces. Communities of more recent immigrants from Asia and the Mid-East are smaller than in the larger provinces.

However, recent immigration trends show over 60 percent of recent immigrants coming from Asia, gradually changing the mix in Manitoba.

Appendix H lists the top 20 ethnic origins in Manitoba.

Overall, 51.1 percent of Manitoba residents report multiple ethnic origins.

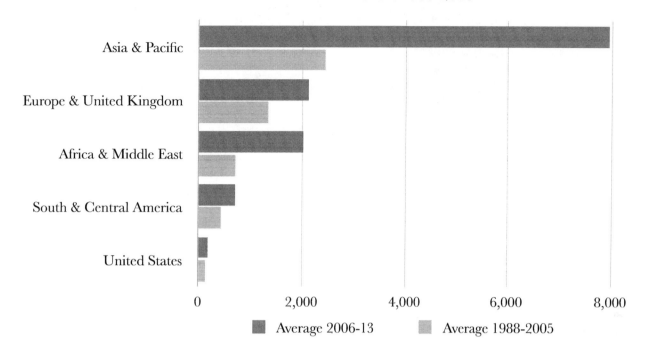

MANITOBA: ANNUAL AVERAGE IMMIGRANT INTAKE BY
REGION 1988-2013

Religious Diversity

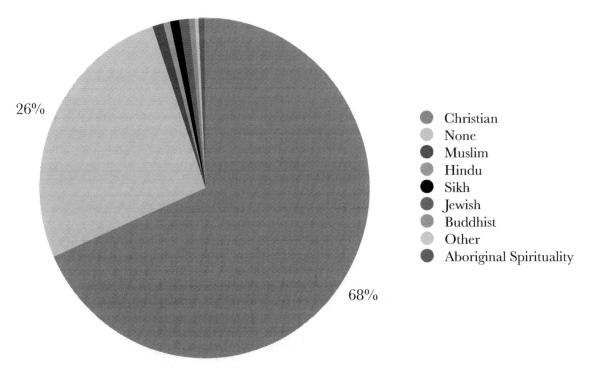

MANITOBA: RELIGIOUS DIVERSITY 2011

- Christian
- None
- Muslim
- Hindu
- Sikh
- Jewish
- Buddhist
- Other
- Aboriginal Spirituality

Not surprisingly, most Manitobans identify themselves as Christian. About a quarter do not identify a religious affiliation, which is similar to the national average.

Muslim Canadians form the largest religious minority, but are a relatively small community (at about 1 percent). They are followed in size by those identifying with Judaism, Sikhism, Hinduism, Aboriginal Spirituality (ranking near the bottom of religious minorities despite Manitoba's large Aboriginal population) and Buddhism.

Manitoba's Cities

As in Saskatchewan, the relatively large Aboriginal population stands out in Manitoba's cities. The population with an Asian ethnic origin is also significant.

Appendix H lists the top 20 ethnic origins in Manitoba's two major cities.

Numbers of Christians and those without a religious affiliation track the national average. Those following aboriginal spirituality are smaller than the population would suggest, including in comparison to Saskatchewan. The mix of minority religions is diverse, with Muslim, Hindu, Sikh and Jewish populations roughly comparable in size in Winnipeg.

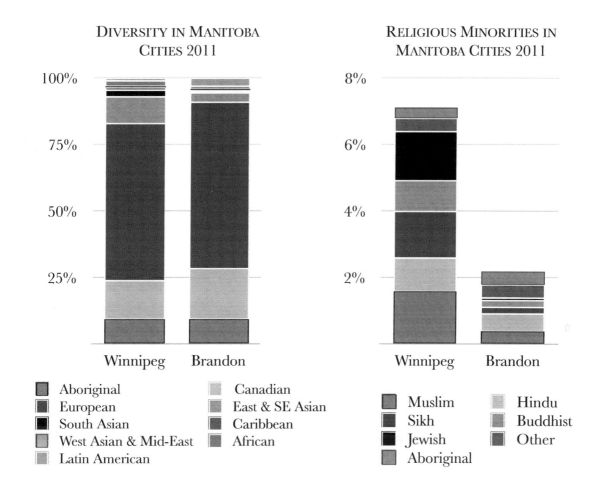

ECONOMIC

In contrast with booming Alberta and Saskatchewan, most visible minorities in Manitoba are less likely to be employed than their non-visible minority counterparts. The unemployment rate for visible minorities in Manitoba is 6.3 percent — lower than the national average of 8.3 percent, but 1.6 percent higher than that of non-visible minorities in the province.

MANITOBA: 2011 VISIBLE MINORITY UNEMPLOYMENT RATE 25-64

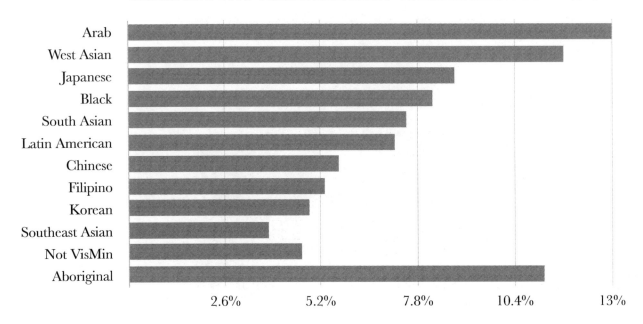

MANITOBA: 2011 LOW-INCOME CUT-OFF PREVALENCE FULL-TIME EMPLOYED 25-64

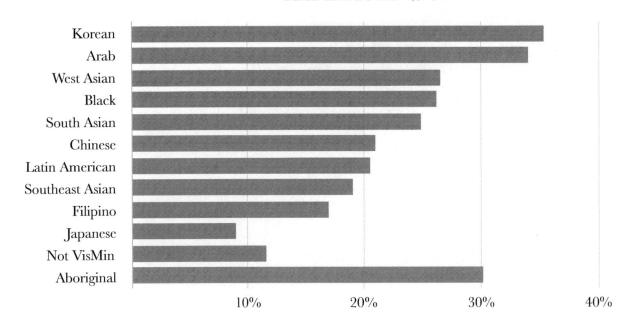

Southeast Asian Canadians have lower unemployment rates than non-visible minorities, with Chinese, Filipino and Korean Canadians having only marginally higher rates. However, Arab, West Asian, Japanese, Black, South Asian and Latin American Canadian unemployment rates are two percent or more greater than the rate for non-visible minorities.

Pre-tax low-income cut-off (LICO) prevalence for visible minorities, at 21 percent (slightly below the Canada-wide average of 22 percent), is almost double that of non-visible minorities, at 12 percent. Variation between visible-minority groups follows a pattern similar to that seen in Canada as a whole. However, all groups — except for Japanese Canadians — have higher LICO prevalence than non-visible minorities. The chart below, ranked by LICO prevalence among men, illustrates this. South Asian, West Asian, Black, Arab and Korean Canadians all have LICO rates more than twice that of non-visible minorities in Manitoba.

Looking at median incomes for all generations, ranked by women, Manitoba's median income is $45,851 for non-visible minorities (the Canadian average is $49,712). For visible minorities, the median is $36,769 (compared to the Canadian average of $41,127).

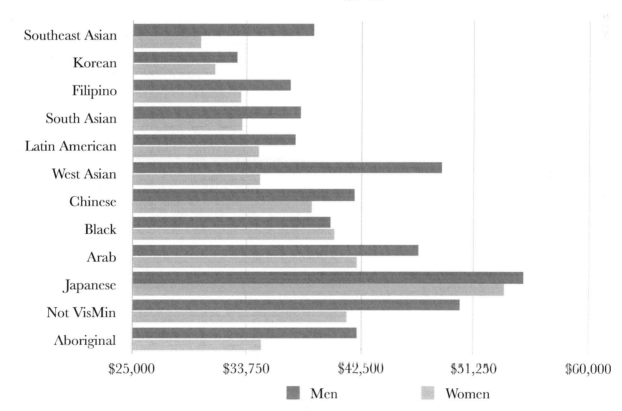

MANITOBA: 2011 MEDIAN INCOME FULL-TIME EMPLOYED 25-64

There is considerable variation in second-generation median incomes, ranked here by women. On the low end, the median incomes for men of Latin American and Southeast Asian ethnic origin sit at 42.6 and 58.6 percent of non-visible minority median income, respectively. In contrast, Korean, Chinese and Japanese Canadian men have median incomes at 133.9, 117.6 and 109.6 percent of the non-visible minority median, respectively. South Asian, Chinese and Japanese Canadian women all have higher median incomes than Manitoban women who are not visible minorities. Southeast Asian and Latin American women in the province have significantly lower median incomes, at 59.4 and 74.2 percent of the non-visible minority median, respectively. Because of the small size of their second-generation populations, there is no data for West Asian men and women in Manitoba, nor for Korean women.

MANITOBA: 2011 MEDIAN INCOME SECOND-GENERATION 25-64

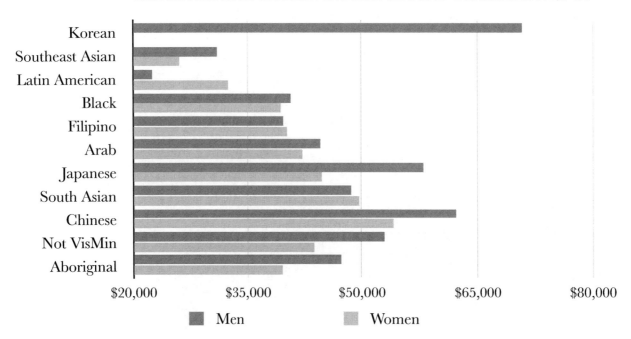

SOCIAL

MANITOBA: 2011 VISIBLE MINORITY LEVELS OF EDUCATION 25-64

Arab
Korean
South Asian
Chinese
West Asian
Japanese
Filipino
Black
Latin American
Southeast Asian
Not VisMin
Aboriginal (from EO)

25%   50%   75%   100%

■ No certificate, diploma or degree   ■ High school diploma or equivalent
■ Post-Secondary   ■ University Bachelors or higher

In terms of education, Manitoba follows the national pattern: Asian and Mid-Eastern residents have rates of university education between 50 and 60 percent. All visible minority groups have higher proportions of university-educated members than do non-visible minorities. Education in the trades or equivalent is more common for Filipino and Black Canadians in the province. Only among Southeast Asian Canadians is there a high proportion of individuals without a diploma, at 25 percent. Overall, 36.8 percent of visible minorities are university educated, compared to 20.5 percent among those who are not visible minorities.

In terms of the degree to which government services represent the population they serve, the overall numbers indicate that Manitoba is doing reasonably well.

When it comes to healthcare and social services, which people tend to access in times of need or vulnerability, visible minority representation exceeds the labour market availability of 13.2 percent in healthcare (at 17.3 percent) and falls just short of parity in social services (at 12.3 percent). While many visible minorities are in support or junior positions (as discussed in the chapter on Canada), there are also many visible minority professionals (e.g., doctors, dentists). Not surprisingly, the largest visible minority groups in Manitoba (those of South Asian, Chinese, Black or Filipino ethnic origin) are well represented in these sectors.

MANITOBA: 2011 HEALTHCARE AND SOCIAL
SERVICES REPRESENTATION 15 AND OLDER

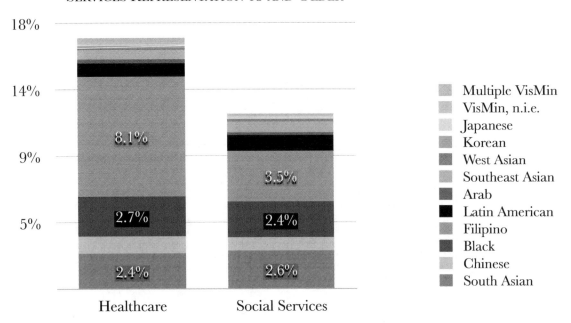

When it comes to education, staff at primary and secondary schools (whether in urban or rural areas) are less representative of visible minorities than those at community colleges and universities (which are located in urban areas). Universities are the most diverse. This reflects the more specialized qualifications required of employees, which brings into play the strong educational achievements, outlined above, of many visible-minority communities. Apart from primary and elementary schools, the four largest visible-minority groups mentioned above are well represented in the education sector.

MANITOBA: 2011 EDUCATION
REPRESENTATION 15 AND OLDER

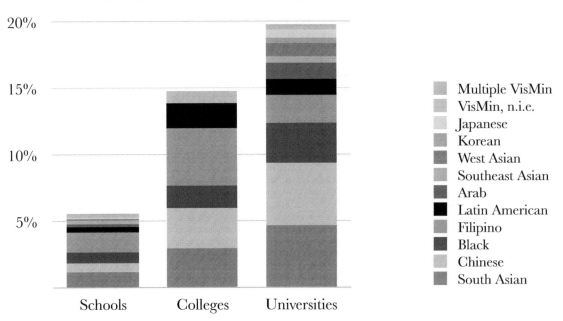

POLITICAL

MANITOBA: 2015 FEDERAL RIDINGS VISIBLE MINORITY CONCENTRATION

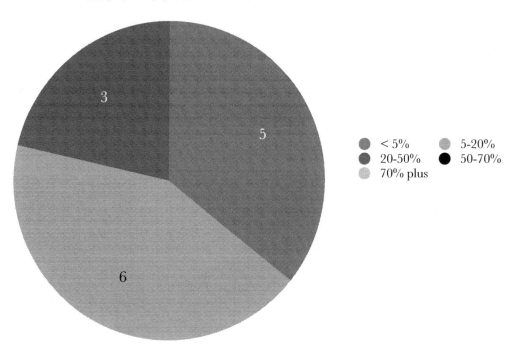

- ● < 5%
- ● 20-50%
- ● 70% plus
- ● 5-20%
- ● 50-70%

MANITOBA LEGISLATURE 2014

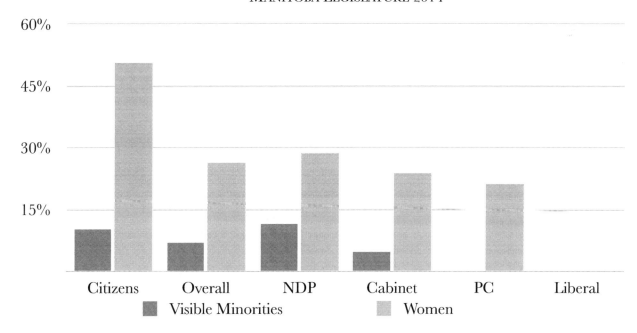

■ Visible Minorities ■ Women

While it is more diverse than Saskatchewan, Manitoba has only three ridings (of 14) where visible minorities make up more than 20 percent of the total population. These are Winnipeg North (42.6 percent visible minorities, of whom 28.6 percent are Filipino), Winnipeg Centre (35.8 percent visible minorities, 20 percent Filipino) and Winnipeg South (25.8 percent visible minorities, composed of a more diverse mix of South Asian, Chinese, Black and Filipino Canadian residents).

In terms of Manitoba's legislature, while visible minorities and women *are* underrepresented, the gap for visible minorities is small: the Government caucus is about one percent away from proportionate representation of visible minorities, and the Cabinet less than six percent. The opposition, as one might predict given its rural support base, has no visible minority representatives.

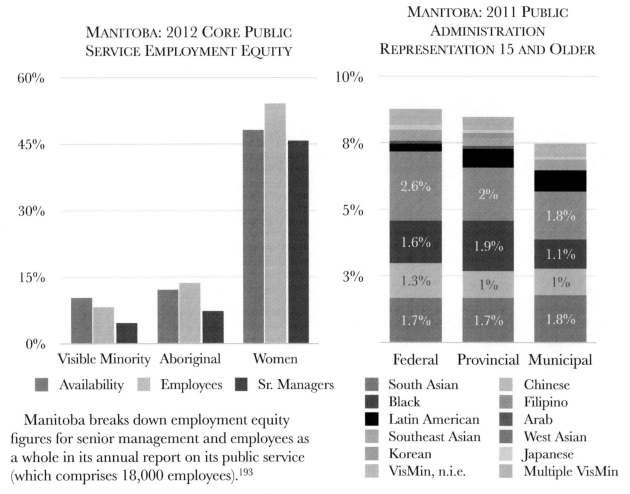

MANITOBA: 2012 CORE PUBLIC SERVICE EMPLOYMENT EQUITY

MANITOBA: 2011 PUBLIC ADMINISTRATION REPRESENTATION 15 AND OLDER

Manitoba breaks down employment equity figures for senior management and employees as a whole in its annual report on its public service (which comprises 18,000 employees).[193]

When we consider the National Household Survey's statistics on public administration, we find that visible minorities are underrepresented among federal public servants located in Manitoba. They make up 8.9 percent of this workforce, while labour market availability is 10.3 percent (the federal *Employment Equity in the Public Service of*

---

[193] Government of Manitoba, *Manitoba Civil Service Commission, Annual Report 2012-13*. Manitoba uses its own government benchmark to measure availability (8 percent compared to 10.3 percent, the percentage of Manitoba's population who are visible minority and Canadian citizens).

Canada report, which considers the core public administration, shows 9.0 percent representation). Representation of visible minorities is lower at the provincial and municipal levels (with visible minorities making up 8.6 percent of provincial employees and 7.7 percent of municipal employees), due in part to the fact that both offer many services in rural Manitoba.

To the extent that visible minorities are represented, we find as expected that these employees reflect the diversity in Manitoba's visible-minority population. The four largest visible minority groups — South Asian, Chinese, Black and Filipino ethnic origin — have similar representation in all three levels of government (at between one and two percent).

Chapter 8 — Ontario: Multiculturalism at Work

Ontario is Canada's largest province, home to almost 40 percent of its population (over 13 million people). It has been hit hard by by economic restructuring over the last ten years, leading to reduced manufacturing capacity and activity. Immigration to Ontario has declined from 59 percent of total immigration to Canada in 2001, to 40 percent in 2011. This reflects reduced economic opportunities, and policy changes (particularly the provincial nominee program) aimed at encouraging immigrants to settle outside of Toronto, Vancouver and Montreal. Immigration to Ontario has declined from an annual average of 121,000 before 2006, to 109,000 in more recent years.

EARLY IMMIGRATION AND SETTLEMENT

Large-scale European settlement of the province did not begin until the 1780s. There were scattered French settlements, especially around the Detroit/Windsor area, but the first major non-Aboriginal phase of immigration was that of the Loyalists, refugees from the American Revolution.

The Loyalists gave the province its Anglo-Saxon character, which was reinforced by waves of immigration from the United States in response to a shortage of good farmland. Following the War of 1812 and the Napoleonic Wars, British colonial officials no longer encouraged immigration from the United States given loyalty concerns. Instead, they encouraged immigration from the British Isles. As a consequence, two-thirds of immigrants during this period were from Britain.

Concerned about loyalty and security issues around Irish immigration to England, the British government instead tried to direct Irish immigration to Ontario. The Irish Potato Famine in the mid-1850s resulted in large numbers of Irish immigrants settling in Ontario and Quebec.

In 1851, 86 percent of Ontario's population was rural.

Beginning in the late 19th century there was localized immigration from Quebec into Eastern and Northeastern Ontario, creating a French-language fringe along the province's frontiers. Northern Ontario received some overseas immigration in the early 1900s.

Ontario was settled mostly by farmers, but in the mid-19th century, the population began shifting towards the cities. The mix of immigrants changed accordingly, towards greater numbers of unskilled and semi-skilled workers.

Although the main explosion in Canada's population in the Sifton years occurred in Western Canada, Ontario's population also grew greatly, from 2.2 million in 1901 to 3.4 million in 1931 (an increase of 55 percent). By the First World War, Ontario's population was predominantly urban..

It was not until after 1945 that immigration from continental Europe had a discernible impact in the main populated areas of the province. With the removal of racial criteria in 1962, the stage was set for Ontario to become the highly diverse province it is today.[194]

Large-scale movements of refugees occurred as part of the post-war boom. Particularly significant group arrivals included Hungarians in the 1950s, Czechs in the 1960s, Ugandans (mainly Ismailis) and Vietnamese "boat people" in the 1970s, Somalis in the 1980s and Sudanese in the 1990s.[195]

---

[194] Same general sources as per Canadian immigration history, along with "Ontario" *Historica Canada*.

[195] John Biles, "Integration and Inclusion in Ontario: The Sleeping Giant Stirs."

DEMOGRAPHICS

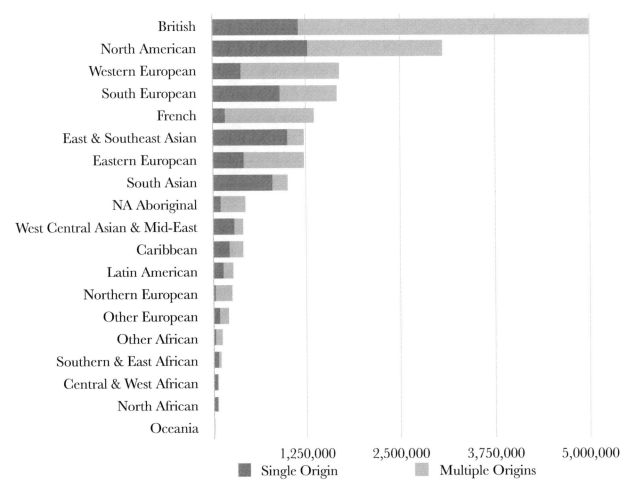

ONTARIO: ETHNIC ORIGINS 2011

The graphic above shows the ethnic origins reported by Ontarians, including both single and multiple origins.

As the largest province and (with British Columbia) the most diverse, Ontario features significant representation of a wide range of communities.

While traditional European communities are still predominant, three non-European ethnic origins are in the top ten largest groups: East and Southeast Asian (primarily Chinese and Filipino), South Asian (primarily East Indian, Sri Lankan and Parkistani), West Central Asian and Mid-Eastern (primarily Iranian and Lebanese).

Recent data shows 50 percent of immigrants coming from Asia, and nearly 25 percent from Africa and the Mid-East.

Appendix I lists the top 50 ethnic origins in Ontario.

Overall, 43.4 percent of Ontario residents report multiple ethnic origins.

ONTARIO: ANNUAL AVERAGE IMMIGRANT INTAKE BY REGION 1988-2013

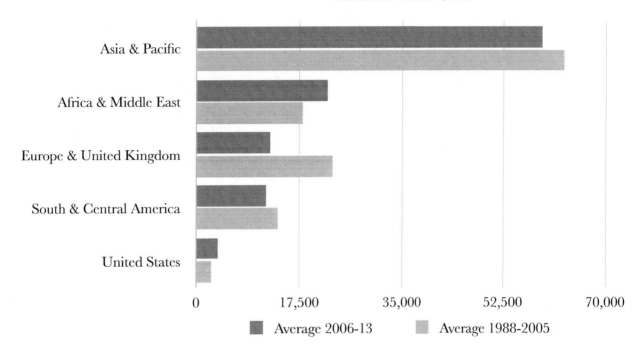

Religious Diversity

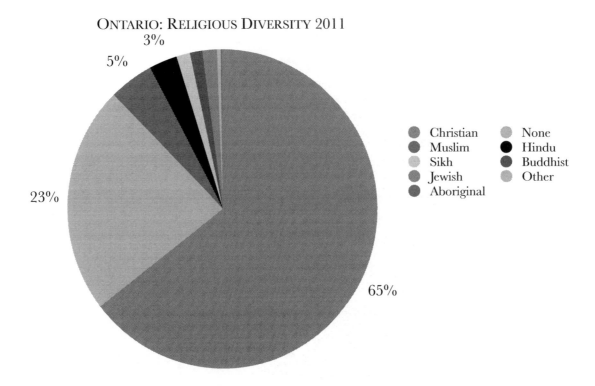

ONTARIO: RELIGIOUS DIVERSITY 2011

3%

5%

23%

65%

Christian   None
Muslim   Hindu
Sikh   Buddhist
Jewish   Other
Aboriginal

Most Ontarians identify themselves as Christian. As in most provinces, about a quarter do not identify any religious affiliation.

Muslim Canadians form the largest religious minority, followed by Hindus, Jews, Sikhs, and Buddhists. Very few Ontarians — only about 16,000 — practice, or at least identify themselves as practicing, Aboriginal spirituality.

Ontario's Cities

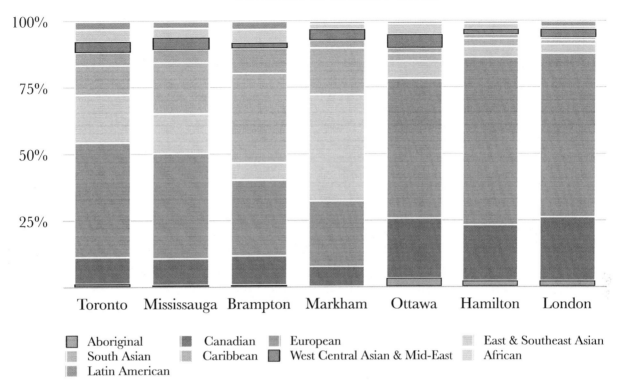

DIVERSITY IN ONTARIO CITIES

There is some variation between the Greater Toronto Area and Toronto itself, with more distinct settlement patterns in the major municipalities close to the city. Mississauga's population is relatively mixed. Brampton has a large South Asian (Sikh and East Indian) population, and Markham is heavily East and Southeast Asian (largely Chinese). In these three cities, visible minorities have become the visible majority.[196]

Other major cities in Ontario are less diverse by comparison, but remain more diverse than most other cities in Canada.

Appendix F lists the top 20 ethnic origins in the major cities of Ontario.

Turning to religion, most residents of Ontario cities identify themselves as Christian. Residents of Toronto and surrounding areas are less likely than average to be Christian, however.

The proportion of residents without a religious affiliation varies between cities. Brampton has relatively few (9.8 percent), reflecting its large Hindu and Sikh populations. Markham, with its large Chinese population, has relatively many (29.9 percent).

Muslims are present in all cities, and Toronto has a large Jewish population.

---

[196] Toronto, Mississauga, Brampton, Markham, Ottawa refer to the cities themselves, unlike Hamilton and London which refer to CMAs.

RELIGIOUS MINORITIES IN ONTARIO CITIES 2011

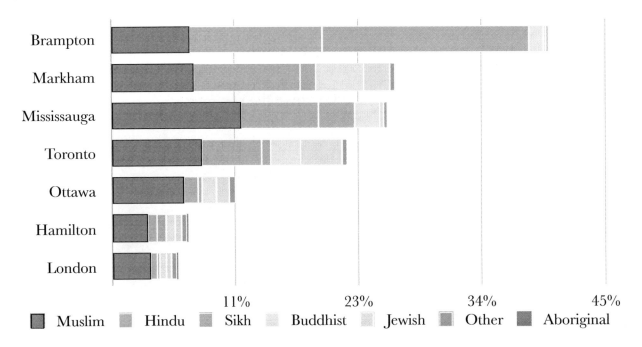

ECONOMIC

Although Ontario was hit hard by economic restructuring and the recession of 2008, the unemployment rate for non-visible minorities is still relatively low at 5.6 percent. 8.5 percent of visible minorities are unemployed, slightly higher than the national average of 8.3 percent, and almost three percent more than non-visible minorities.

ONTARIO: 2011 VISIBLE MINORITY UNEMPLOYMENT RATE 25-64

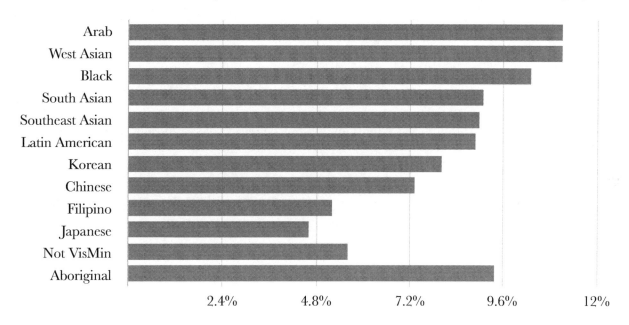

ONTARIO: 2011 LOW-INCOME CUT-OFF PREVALENCE FULL-TIME EMPLOYED 25-64

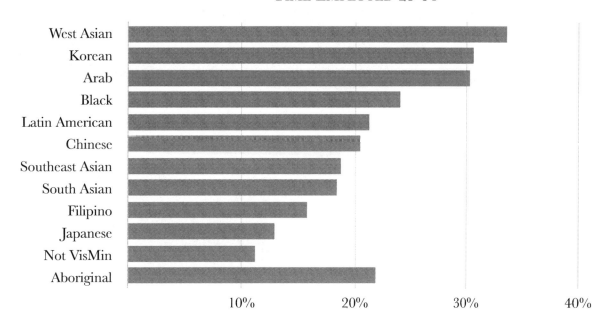

Only Filipino and Japanese Canadians in Ontario have lower unemployment rates than non-visible minorities. Unemployment rates are highest for Arab, West Asian and Black Canadians, about twice as high as for those who are not visible minorities.

Pre-tax low-income cut-off (LICO) prevalence for visible minorities in Ontario, at 21 percent, is slightly lower than the Canadian average of 22 percent — but nearly double the LICO prevalence of non-visible minorities (11 percent). Variation among different groups of visible minorities mirrors the national pattern: all visible minority groups have higher LICO prevalence than Ontarians who are not visible minorities, as illustrated in the chart below (ranked by LICO prevalence among men). Only Japanese Canadians come close to parity with non-visible minorities in this regard. Black, West Asian, Arab and Korean Ontarians all have LICO rates more than double that of non-visible minorities.

Looking at median incomes for all generations, ranked by women, Ontario's median income is $52,639 for non-visible minorities (the Canadian average is $49,712). The median income for Ontarians who *are* visible minorities is $43,007, while the Canadian average is $41,448.

There is considerable variation in median income for second-generation males (see chart below,

ONTARIO: 2011 MEDIAN INCOME FULL-TIME EMPLOYED 25-64

ranked by women). Lower medians include those of West Asian (63.8 percent of the non-visible minority median income), Latin American (73.7 percent) and Black (74.3 percent) Ontarians. Visible minority males with incomes near the median for those who are not visible minorities include Japanese (100.1 percent) and Chinese (98.2 percent) Ontarians.

ONTARIO: 2011 MEDIAN INCOME SECOND-GENERATION 24-64

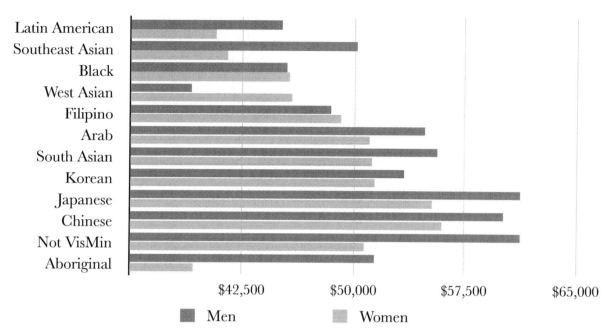

As elsewhere, second-generation visible minority women have median incomes largely comparable to non-visible minorities. Arab, South Asian, Korean, Japanese and Chinese women all have median incomes higher or equal to that of women who are not a visible minority. Latin American, Southeast Asian, Black and West Asian women in Ontario have lower median incomes, at between 80 and 90 percent of the non-visible minority median income.

ONTARIO: 2011 MEDIAN INCOME FULL-TIME EMPLOYED SECOND-GENERATION 25-34 UNIVERSITY EDUCATED

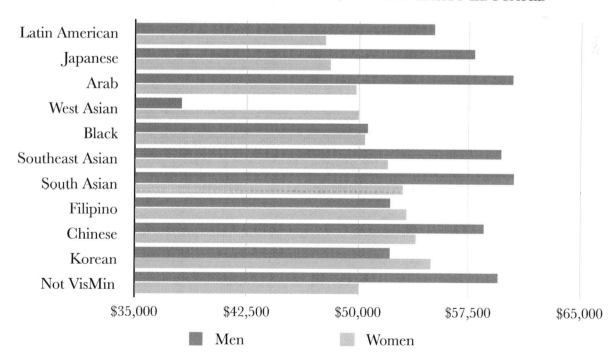

When it comes to second-generation, university-educated people between 25 and 34 (113,000 people in Ontario), Arab, Southeast Asian, South Asian, Chinese and Japanese Canadian men have median incomes equal to or greater than the median for non-visible minority men. West Asian men in this group have the lowest median incomes, at just 64.1 percent of the non-visible minority median. All groups of visible minority women in this cohort have median incomes equal to or greater than the non-visible minority median, with the exception of Latin American and Japanese Canadian women, who fall only slightly short.

SOCIAL

ONTARIO: 2011 VISIBLE MINORITY LEVELS OF EDUCATION 25-64

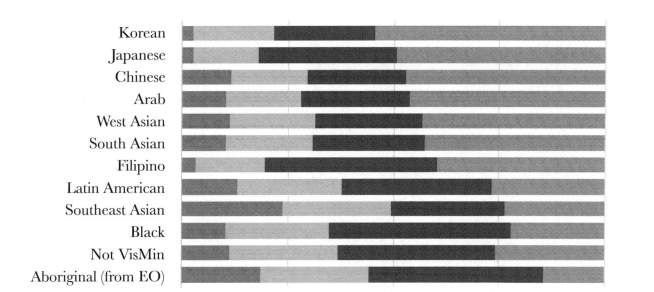

- No certificate, diploma or degree
- Post-Secondary
- High school diploma or equivalent
- University Bachelors or higher

In terms of education, Ontario follows the national pattern. Asian and Mid-Eastern residents have rates of university education between 50 and 60 percent. All groups except Latin American, Southeast Asian and Black Ontarians have a greater proportion of university-educated members than do non-visible minorities.

Trades education or equivalent is most common among Filipino, Latin American and Black Canadians in Ontario. Only Southeast Asian Canadians have a high proportion of people without any diploma, at almost 25 percent. Overall, 38.4 percent of visible minorities are university educated, compared to 25.7 percent of non-visible minorities (the highest percentage of university-educated non-visible minorities in Canada).

In terms of how well government services represent the population they serve, the overall numbers indicate that Ontario is doing reasonably well.

For healthcare and social services, which tend to serve people in times of need or vulnerability, visible minority representation is in line with Ontario's population. Visible minorities make up 24.2 percent of healthcare workers, and 25.5 percent of social service workers, very near their labour market availability of 24.4 percent. While many visible minorities are in support or junior positions, as described in the chapter on Canada, there are also many visible minority professionals (e.g., doctors, dentists). Unsurprisingly, the largest visible minority groups in Ontario (those of South Asian, Chinese, Black and Filipino ethnic origin) are well represented in these sectors.

When it comes to education, staff at primary and secondary schools (whether in urban or rural areas) are less representative than those at community colleges and universities (which are located in urban areas). Universities are the most diverse. This reflects the more specialized qualifications

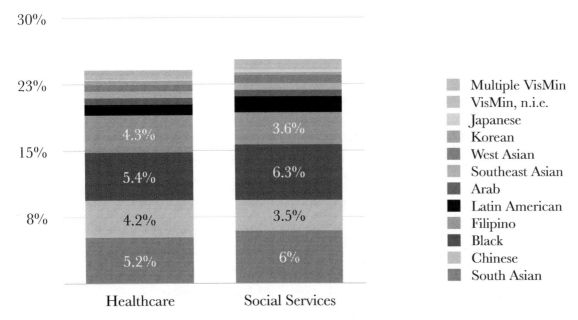

ONTARIO: 2011 HEALTHCARE AND SOCIAL
SERVICES REPRESENTATION 15 AND OLDER

required of employees, which brings into play the strong educational achievements of many visible-minority communities outlined above.

Visible minorities are underrepresented in primary and secondary schools (at 13.5 percent of staff) and community colleges (17.9 percent) in Ontario. They are slightly overrepresented in universities, where they make up 26.8 percent of employees. South Asian, Chinese and Black Canadians are well represented in the education sector.

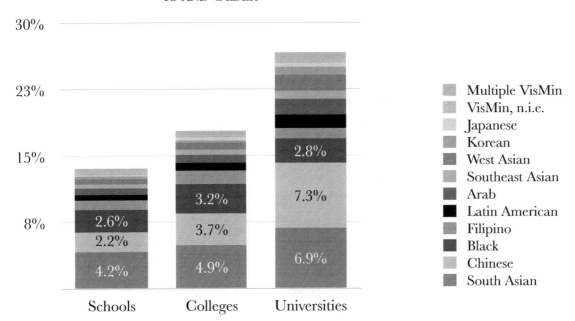

ONTARIO: 2011 EDUCATION REPRESENTATION
15 AND OLDER

POLITICAL

ONTARIO: 2015 FEDERAL RIDINGS VISIBLE MINORITY CONCENTRATION

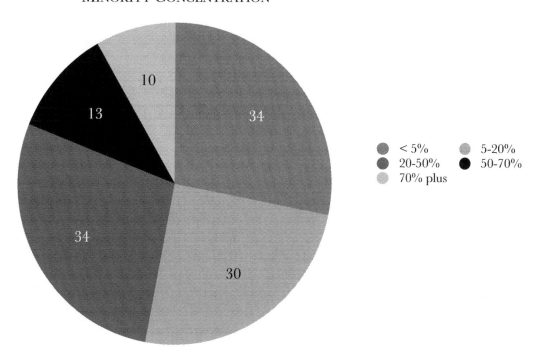

Ontario has ten ridings that are majority or mixed majority ethnic enclaves (which have populations composed of over 70 percent visible minorities), the largest number of any province. This is illustrated in table 15. The largest communities are of South Asian, Chinese, and Black Canadians, followed by Filipino Canadians.

TABLE 15 - ONTARIO RIDINGS WITH OVER 70 PERCENT VISIBLE MINORITIES							
	S. Asian	Chinese	Black	Filipino	Latin	Arab	SE Asian
Scarborough North	25.4%	43.7%	7.1%	6.7%	0.7%	0.7%	1.4%
Brampton East	60.3%	1.4%	12.5%	2.0%	1.6%	1.5%	2.2%
Markham — Thornhill	30.8%	35.2%	4.1%	3.0%	0.5%	1.0%	1.1%
Scarborough — Agincourt	15.1%	46.0%	5.3%	3.8%	0.6%	1.6%	1.0%
Markham — Unionville	10.9%	57.2%	1.9%	1.9%	0.4%	1.5%	0.7%
Mississauga — Malton	37.7%	6.1%	10.4%	6.9%	2.3%	2.3%	3.4%
Etobicoke North	30.1%	1.6%	21.2%	3.6%	4.3%	2.1%	2.0%
York West	16.0%	3.6%	22.4%	2.9%	9.1%	2.0%	8.6%
Brampton	33.5%	1.4%	20.8%	5.4%	2.2%	0.7%	1.5%
Scarborough — Rouge Park	31.0%	4.5%	14.4%	9.2%	1.4%	0.5%	1.6%

Moreover, an additional thirteen ridings have over 50 percent visible minorities, as shown in Table 16:

TABLE 16 - ONTARIO RIDINGS WITH 50 TO 70 PERCENT VISIBLE MINORITIES							
	S. Asian	Chinese	Black	Filipino	Latin	Arab	SE Asian
Scarborough — Guildwood	31.6%	5.6%	13.5%	7.6%	1.8%	0.5%	1.0%
Don Valley North	9.7%	31.9%	4.7%	4.2%	1.2%	2.0%	0.8%
Mississauga Centre	26.4%	11.6%	5.0%	6.6%	2.4%	6.4%	2.6%
Scarborough Centre	24.6%	9.1%	8.5%	10.9%	1.8%	1.8%	1.4%
Brampton North	37.1%	1.8%	10.6%	2.3%	2.2%	0.6%	1.5%
Willowdale	4.5%	22.9%	2.2%	4.9%	1.0%	1.7%	0.5%
Brampton South	36.0%	1.3%	11.7%	3.7%	1.7%	0.5%	1.6%
Mississauga — Erin Mills	23.5%	9.9%	6.5%	5.1%	1.9%	4.9%	1.6%
Don Valley East	16.4%	8.1%	9.1%	6.1%	2.4%	3.2%	1.0%
Richmond Hill	6.6%	27.6%	1.9%	2.2%	0.6%	1.7%	0.9%
York South — Weston	7.1%	2.4%	21.2%	4.7%	9.0%	0.5%	4.8%
Brampton Centre	26.1%	1.8%	12.1%	3.9%	3.3%	0.7%	1.5%
Scarborough Southwest	18.3%	6.3%	10.0%	8.4%	1.4%	0.8%	1.3%

Looking at religious minorities: only in four Ontario ridings do more than 20 percent of residents identify with a religious minority. These are Brampton East (33.8 percent Sikh, 19.5 percent Hindu), Thornhill (37.1 percent Jewish), Brampton North (20.3 percent Sikh) and Eglinton Lawrence (22.0 percent Jewish). An additional 21 ridings have religious minorities making up 10 and 20 percent of their populations.

ONTARIO LEGISLATURE 2014

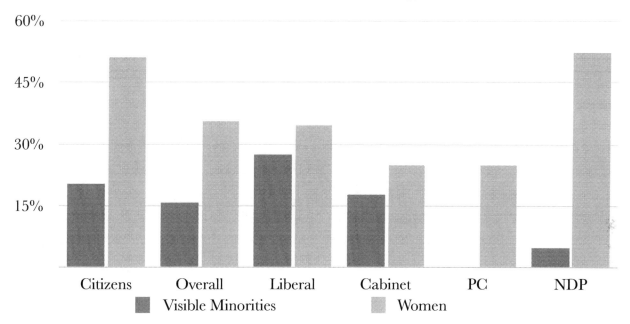

In terms of representation in the Ontario legislature, the dispersion of ethnic communities across more ridings results in greater representation of visible minorities than in similarly diverse British Columbia. Representation is at about 60 percent of what it should be given Ontario's visible minority population. Most visible minority MPPs are with the Liberal government, which has an urban base; the Progressive Conservative official opposition has no visible minority MPPs. Representation of women, while below population levels, is nevertheless stronger(at 35.5 percent) than it is federally (at 24.6 percent).

Ontario has an inclusion strategy, but relatively sparse reporting, for its 93,000 employees in the core public service.[197]

National Household Survey public administration statistics for federal public servants located in Ontario show visible minorities making up 19.0 percent of this workforce, compared to 20.3

[197] Government of Ontario, Inclusion Now! Ontario Public Service Inclusion Strategic Plan 2013 –2016 49. Employment figures from *Statistics Canada*, "Public sector employment, wages and salaries, by province and territory," 2011.

percent labour market availability (the federal *Employment Equity in the Public Service of Canada*

ONTARIO: 2011 PUBLIC ADMINISTRATION REPRESENTATION 15 AND OLDER

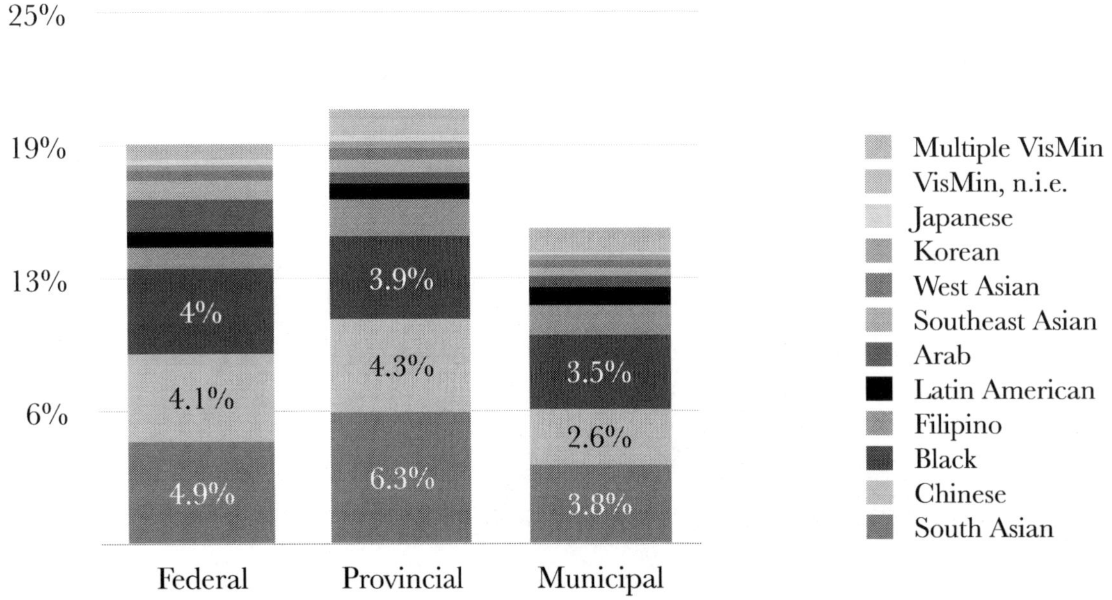
25%
19%
13%
6%
4%
4.1%
4.9%
3.9%
4.3%
6.3%
3.5%
2.6%
3.8%
Federal
Provincial
Municipal
Multiple VisMin
VisMin, n.i.e.
Japanese
Korean
West Asian
Southeast Asian
Arab
Latin American
Filipino
Black
Chinese
South Asian

report, which considers the core public administration, shows 16.4 percent representation).

Representation of visible minorities at the provincial level is slightly higher than LMA at 20.4 percent of the workforce. Representation at the municipal level is lower — at 14.9 percent — due to the provision of local services in rural Ontario.

As expected, representation reflects the population of visible minorities, with South Asian, Chinese and Black Canadians predominant.

ONTARIO: 2011 CORE PUBLIC SERVICE EMPLOYMENT EQUITY

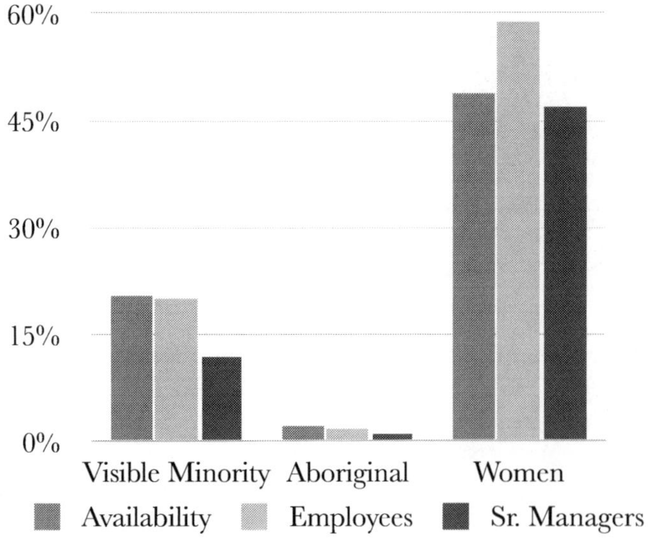
60%
45%
30%
15%
0%
Visible Minority
Aboriginal
Women
Availability
Employees
Sr. Managers

Chapter 9 — Quebec: Impact of a Complex Identity

Quebec, unique in being a minority culture within Canada and North America, has always had a more complex relationship with immigration and multiculturalism. While Quebec shares the Canadian model of encouraging immigration to meet demographic and economic challenges, sensitivities regarding the place of the French language and Quebec culture has meant a wider range of debates over values, identity and reasonable accommodation than elsewhere. Multiculturalism has often been viewed as a way to treat the Francophone minority as just another ethnic group.

As part of emphasizing the importance of Quebec's unique history and culture, interculturalism, rather than multiculturalism, is used to describe the Quebec model. The flexible nature of Canadian federalism has allowed Quebec considerable latitude in its immigration program and its approach to integration. The difference between multiculturalism and interculturalism is nonetheless a subtle one. Both fit within the framework of the Canadian constitution and Charter.

Given its uniqueness, and sensitivity regarding the minority status of Francophones in North America, Quebec has greater integration challenges than most parts of Canada, and a relative lack of immigrants outside greater Montreal.

EARLY IMMIGRATION AND SETTLEMENT HISTORY

Between 1608 and 1713, despite the success of its expansion on the continent, New France's population had only grown from several hundred to 15,000 inhabitants. In comparison, New England had a population of 400,000 in 1715 and more than 2 million in 1763, at which time New France's population had increased to almost 70,000 inhabitants.

After 1763, under the English regime, the remaining French-speaking population grew substantially, from less than 70,000 to some 100,000 in 1784, over 400,000 in 1825 and almost a million in 1860. By 1911 the French-speaking population in Quebec was about 2 million people.

At the end of the 18th century, people with British origins made up 12.5 percent of Quebec's population. Loyalists fleeing the American Revolution made up one of the first post-conquest waves of immigration. About 20 percent of them settled in Quebec.

Throughout the 19th century, Quebec attracted fewer immigrants than other provinces, while the source of immigration shifted to Britain, particularly Scotland and Ireland. About 20 percent of all Irish immigrants to Canada settled in Quebec. Up until 1866, the majority of Montreal's population was Anglophone.

Between 1840 and 1930, one million French-Canadians left Quebec, most of them seeking jobs in the manufacturing sector in New England.

Montreal, Quebec's main centre of immigration, was not very diverse by the end of the 19th century. Its population was 60.7 percent Francophone, and 33.7 percent Anglophone. This slowly began to change at the beginning of the 20th century. Predominantly Irish immigration was replaced by waves of East European Jews and Italians. The 1920s saw the arrival of immigrants from Eastern Europe. BY 1931, the Jewish community numbered 60,000 people, and Quebec was also home to some 25,000 Italians, 10,000 Portuguese and 1,000 Germans.

The Jewish population in Quebec grew from 1.5 percent of the total population in 1901 to 5.7 percent in 1941. The Italian population increased from only 0.5 percent in 1901 to 2.3 percent in 1941.[198]

In 1871 only 15 percent of Quebec residents lived in cities. The number doubled over the next two decades until, by 1921, 52 percent of residents lived in urban areas. This figure was above the Canadian average and comparable to settlement patterns in Ontario.

Quebec's overall population grew from 2.2 million in 1901 to 2.9 million in 1931, an increase of 74 percent.

After World War II, immigration of European groups to Quebec increased further.

Following the Quiet Revolution in the 1960s and subsequent efforts to reinforce Quebec's linguistic and cultural identity, Quebec was granted the power to select independent-class immigrants (economic) and determine financial and other criteria for family-class and assisted relative sponsorship (family reunification).[199]

Interculturalism

As noted earlier, given its history and its place as a minority Francophone culture in the Anglophone sea of North America, Quebec has always had particular sensitivities related to multiculturalism, integration, and diversity. Quebec even developed its own model of multiculturalism, *interculturalisme,* to express the uniqueness of its approach and a more explicit insistence that that newcomers should aspire to integrate themselves into Quebec national and cultural identity, not the more amorphous pan-Canadian identity.

Interculturalism was increasingly positioned in opposition to Canadian multiculturalism. There is a prevalent mythology in Quebec that Canadian multiculturalism was implemented by former Prime Minister Trudeau to diminish Quebec and Francophone Canada by rejecting biculturalism. While it is true that Trudeau rejected biculturalism and nationalism in favour of a focus on individual rights, both in the broader and language rights contexts, the prevailing myth meant that many Quebecers perceived multiculturalism policy as a diminishment of French Canadians from founding culture to just another ethnic community.

---

[198] Same general sources as per Canadian immigration history, along with "Quebec" *Historica Canada,* "Historic Overview Quebec Immigration" *Government of Quebec* and Annick Germain and Tuyet Trinh, "Immigration in Quebec: Profile and Players."

[199] "Forging Our Legacy: Canadian Citizenship and Immigration, 1900–1977, *CIC.* Penny Blacklumb, *Immigration: The Canada-Quebec Accord.*

This was not the first federal approach to be so characterized, but it was particularly ignorant of the role that Canadians of origins other than Aboriginal, French and English played in the development of the multiculturalism policy. In particular, Ukrainian Canadians viewed their contribution to the settling and development of the West as similar to that of French and British settlers elsewhere in Canada.

Quebec has a history of engaging in European-style debates, suspicion and distrust of newcomers, a reflection of its stronger identity and the minority status of Francophones in Canada and North America.

To help manage this debate and the related politics, the Charest government created the Bouchard-Taylor Commission in 2007. It was tasked with conducting hearings on issues related to diversity and accommodation across Quebec. The resulting 2008 report, *Fonder l'avenir: Le temps de la conciliation*, was intellectually sound, innovative and thoughtful, both within and outside the Quebec framework. However, the report's recommendations were unsuccessful in the sense that they were not implemented at the time. The Commission, Report, and follow-up debates passed largely without federal government comment, although officials followed the deliberations and debates closely.[200]

The report remains an importance reference document, and political figures and others have often returned to many of its recommendations in subsequent debates about accommodation.

In Quebec, the 2010 case of a niqab-wearing student who was expelled from French-language settlement classes after her demands for accommodation were considered disruptive to other students attracted widespread attention across Canada.[201] Soon after, the Charest government introduced Bill C-94 (*Un acte établissant des balises encadrant les demandes d'accommodement dans l'administration publique et dans certains établissements*), banning individuals from wearing the niqab when receiving public services. Then Intergovernmental Affairs Minister Josée Verner supported the move, while Minister Kenney, through a spokesperson, reaffirmed Quebec's jurisdiction.[202] Yet a few weeks later, when asked about Citizenship and Immigration Canada's procedures regarding women wearing the niqab, Minister Kenney stated a classic accommodation position, likely reflecting his views on religious freedom:[203]

> He instead confirmed that it was not a question of telling people how to
> dress, except when proper identification is needed. "In my department,
> when a woman arrives wearing a face covering, as part of an application
> for immigration or a visa, we insist that she show her face. ... In these

---

[200] Only Josée Verner, then-Minister of Intergovernmental Affairs, voiced her support for a proposed charter on laïcité, which would give priority to women's rights. See "A rights debate gone wrong," *The Globe and Mail*, 16 October 2009.

[201] "Une musulmane expulsée d'un cours à cause du niqab," *Cyberpresse*, 2 March 2010.

[202] "Feds offer limited support to Quebec in niqab uproar," *Montreal Gazette*, 5 March 2010.

[203] The original "house card" said nothing until it was pointed out that the Minister might be asked about how his department handles niqab-wearing women.

cases, generally, officials provide a female official to interact with the individual as often as possible."[204]

In 2011, the policy changed when the Minister announced that the niqab would not be allowed at citizenship ceremonies, since it prevented the citizenship judges from seeing if the potential citizen was speaking — or at least mouthing — the words when swearing the citizenship oath. Accommodation was no longer allowed. Kenney aligned himself with the Quebec approach — and Canadian public opinion.[205] Since then, the ban has been successfully challenged in federal court, and is under appeal at the time of writing.[206]

The Parti Québécois, in its 2013 Quebec Values Charter, prohibited "religious headgear" and symbols for all employees in the broader public sector (which includes healthcare and education) as part of its electoral strategy. There was lively debate regarding the wisdom and practicality of the proposed Charter, with a much more varied and balanced range of views than at the time of the Bouchard-Taylor Commission. In the end, the Parti québécois was defeated in the 2014 election, and the Liberal government of Premier Couillard introduced legislation in June 2015, similar to that created in 2010, that prevents the wearing of the niqab or burka when delivering or receiving government services.[207]

Beyond the ongoing political debates, what are the similarities and differences between Québécois *interculturalisme* and Canadian multiculturalism? As mentioned earlier, Gérard Bouchard captures the nuance as follows:

> In dual societies, therefore (or more precisely: in societies where ethnoculturality is addressed through the lens of a duality), a balance must be struck between the perpetuation and development of majority cultures, taking into account their ongoing history and founding myths, and the integration of minorities, taking into account their rights. The main challenge is to arbitrate between majorities and minorities in a spirit of conciliation, interaction and negotiation that respects ethnocultural diversity, while providing for the continuing cultural identity of founding

---

[204] "Le niqab des solitudes," *Le Devoir*, 20 March 2010.

[205] According to a 2010 Angus-Reid poll, 80 percent of Canadians outside of Quebec supported the Quebec niqab legislation ("Most Canadians Support Quebecs Veil Ban," Angus Reid, 29 March 2010). It's likely that a similar number would support the ban on the niqab at citizenship ceremonies. A contrary and thoughtful view from Professor Clifford Orwin notes that Canadian democracy and multiculturalism is a large tent and a broad-minded one ("No room at the inn for veiled women? Get real, Canada," *The Globe and Mail*, 23 August 2012). A more conventional view, also thoughtful, can be found in Dan Gardner's "The canvas of emotion," *The Ottawa Citizen*, 14 December 2011.

[206] "Niqab ban at citizenship ceremony struck down by court," *The Star*, 6 February 2015. The Government, in what appeared to be pre-election messaging, tabled the Oath of Citizenship Act in the dying days of the 41st Parliament (19 June 2015).

[207] "Proposed legislation would ban niqabs, burkas in Quebec's public sector," *Montreal Gazette*, 10 June 2015.

groups and their heritage. Respect for the fundamental values of host societies and the emergence of shared cultural expressions and practices, as part of the process of integration, also are at the heart of interculturalism. [208]

CIC officials worked with Bouchard to develop a series of tables that that compared multiculturalism and *interculturalisme*, showing greater commonality between the two than most than most political, academic and media commentary at the time would have suggested — especially given the Conservative government's explicit emphasis on the integrative aspects of multiculturalism made it closer to Bouchard's definition of *interculturalisme*. The more significant table reproduced below applies the high level paradigms and contrasts multiculturalism and *interculturalisme*:[209]

Table 10: Multiculturalism/Interculturalisme Comparison[210]

TABLE 17: INTERCULTURALISME AND MULTICULTURALISM COMPARISON

Element	Interculturalisme	Multiculturalism
Identity	Nation Québecois and aboriginal	Aboriginal, bilingual and diverse
Context	Minority within national (and continental) majority	National framework, regional application
Majority culture	Officially recognized and promoted	Implicit and assumed, but increased promotion and awareness of Canadian identity
Emphasis	Focus on interaction, bringing together, feeling of belonging and integration	Integration and accommodation dynamic, recent focus on commonalities
Language	Protection and promotion of French	Two official languages, English dominant language in North America
Values	Slightly more explicit formulation along Francophone lines	More case by case but within general societal and Charter values
Collective memory	Strong shared collective memory and narrative	Integration and accommodation dynamic within context of history, identity, and values

---

[208] Bouchard, Ibid.

[209] For more details on interculturalism and this work, see Griffith 71-78.

[210] Working Document, winter 2011, updated 2013.

DEMOGRAPHICS

The chart below shows the ethnic origins reported by Québécois, including both single and multiple origins.

The Ottawa River marks a sharp boundary line, in terms of diversity, between Ontario and Quebec. Quebec is much less diverse than neighbouring Ontario, and its new communities are much smaller.

The mix of communities is different. Quebec's East and Southeast Asian (primarily Chinese, Vietnamese and Filipino) populations are only marginally larger than its West and Central Asian, Mid-East (primarily Lebanese and other Arab), Caribbean (primarily Haitian) and North African (primarily Moroccan, Algerian and Egyptian) populations.

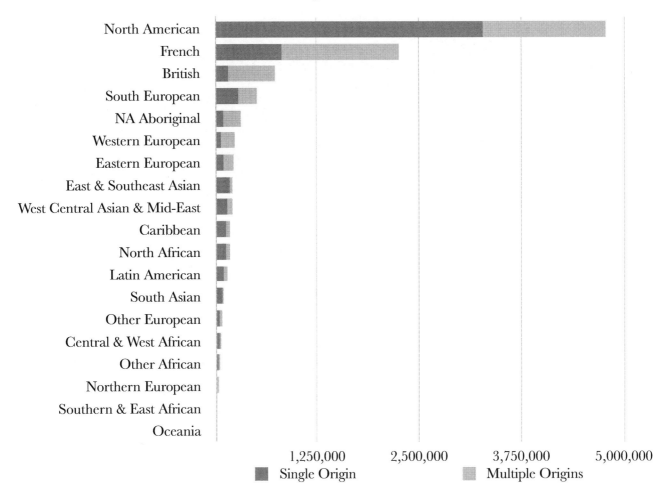

QUEBEC: ETHNIC ORIGINS 2011

Recent immigration trends are similarly unique, reflecting the priority given to French-speaking immigrants in the selection process. In contrast to other provinces, where immigrants from Asia and Pacific predominate (e.g., in Ontario, 54 percent are from Asia Pacific), immigrants from Africa and the Middle East constitute more than 40 percent of Quebec's immigrant population, followed by South and Central America and Europe and the United Kingdom (both at 20 percent).

QUEBEC: ANNUAL AVERAGE IMMIGRANT INTAKE BY REGION

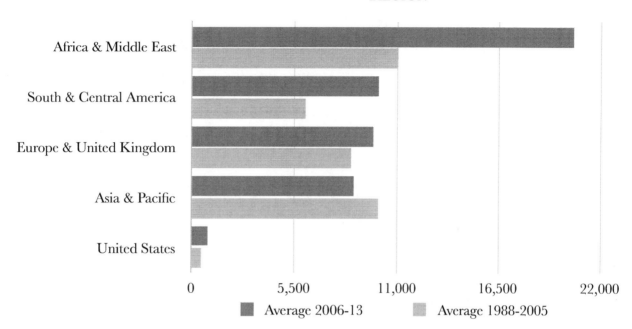

Appendix J lists the top 50 ethnic origins in Quebec.

Overall, 28.0 percent report multiple ethnic origins, the lowest percentage of any province (the Canadian average is 42.1 percent).

Religious Diversity

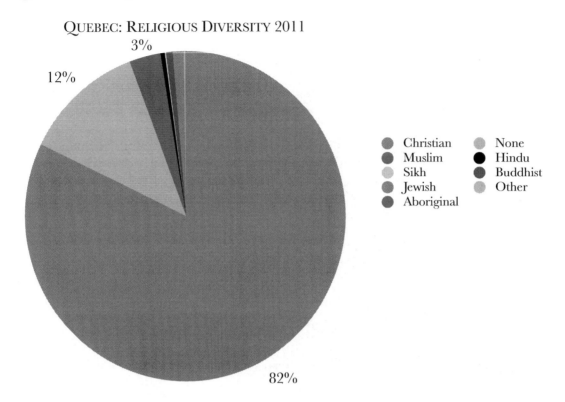

QUEBEC: RELIGIOUS DIVERSITY 2011

3%

12%

82%

Legend: Christian, Muslim, Sikh, Jewish, Aboriginal, None, Hindu, Buddhist, Other

Not surprisingly, most Québécois identify themselves as Christian. Also unsurprisingly, some 90 percent of Christians identify as Catholic, the highest number of any province outside Atlantic Canada. It is no wonder that removal of the Crucifix in the National Assembly is so controversial; despite Quebec being a largely secular society, the Church remains an important part of its identity.

About half as many Québécois as other Canadians have no religious affiliation.

Muslims form the largest religious minority, followed by Jews, Buddhists, Hindus and Sikhs. Only 2,000 people practice, or identify themselves as practising, Aboriginal spirituality.

Quebec's Cities

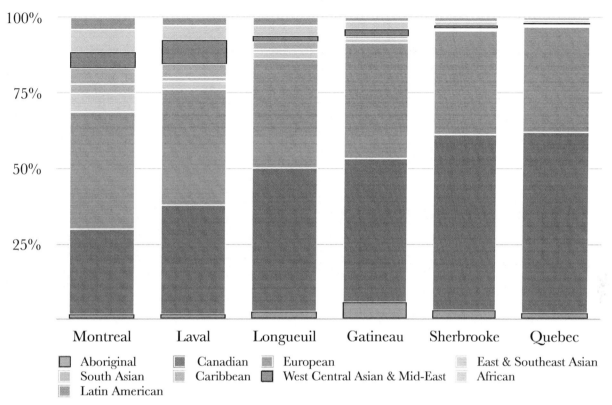

DIVERSITY IN QUEBEC CITIES 2011

In addition to lower diversity at the provincial level, the dispersion of visible minorities in the Montreal Census Metropolitan Areas (CMA) is significantly different than in the Toronto and Vancouver CMAs. Toronto and Vancouver have greater diversity in their suburbs than in their central cores. In contrast, the city of Montreal is more diverse than the major suburbs of Laval and Longueuil. Cheaper housing in Montreal than in the suburbs may play a role, particularly when combined with the greater disparity in economic outcomes between visible minorities and other residents. This is changing, however, with both Laval and Longueuil becoming more diverse.[211]

Quebec City (3.1 percent) and Sherbrooke (4.4 percent) are less diverse than Gatineau (8.9 percent visible minorities), itself less diverse than Ottawa (22.8 percent) just across the river.

Appendix J lists the top 20 ethnic origins in the major cities of Quebec.

Few people outside greater Montreal identify themselves with minority religions, a reflection of the concentration of Quebec's diversity in that city.

---

[211] Quebec and Sherbrooke are CMAs. Montreal, Laval, Longueuil, Gatineau are cities themselves.

RELIGIOUS MINORITIES IN QUEBEC CITIES 2011

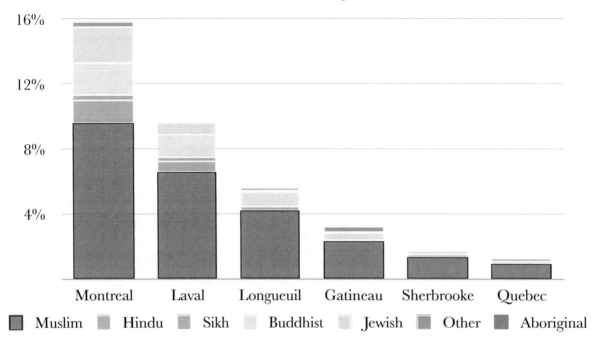

ECONOMIC

While Quebec's unemployment rate for residents who are not visible minorities is, at 5.6 percent, slightly better than the national rate (5.9 percent), the situation is different for visible minorities. Their overall unemployment rate is 12.4 percent — higher than the national rate of 8.3 percent, and more than twice as high than the rate for non-visible minorities in the province. Arab, West Asian, South Asian, Black and Latin Americans have unemployment rates more than twice that of non-visible minorities in Quebec, with no group having lower unemployment than non-visible minorities.

QUEBEC: 2011 VISIBLE MINORITY UNEMPLOYMENT RATE 25-64

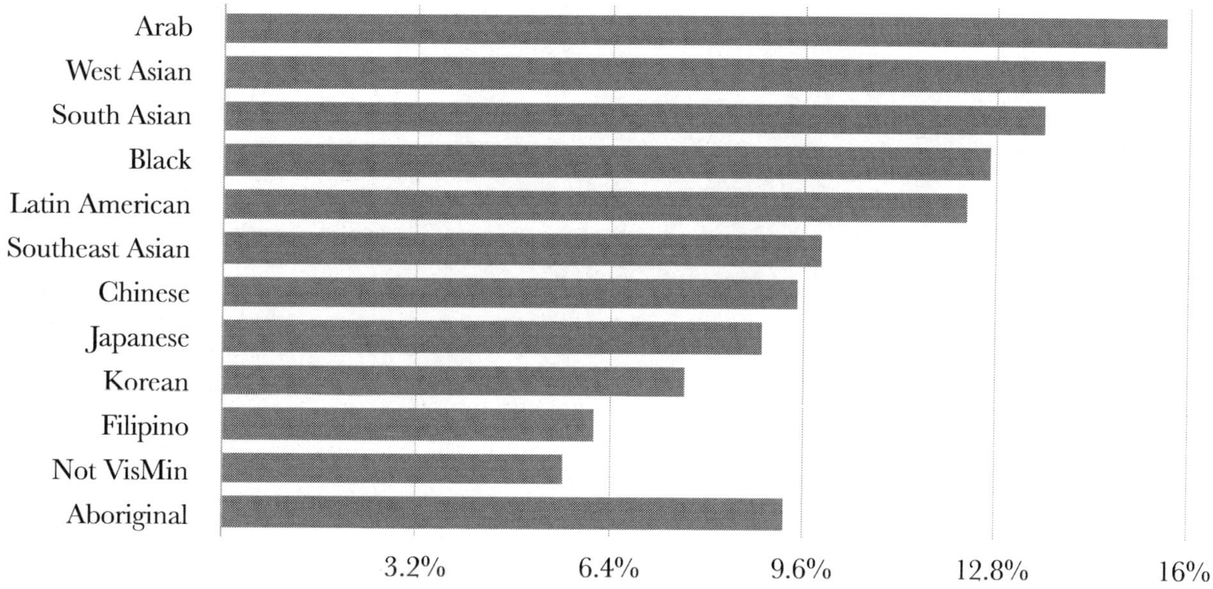

Pre-tax low-income cut-off (LICO) prevalence for visible minorities is double that of non-visible minorities (32 percent, compared to 13 percent; higher than the Canadian average for visible minorities of 22 percent). All visible minority groups have higher LICO prevalence than non-visible minorities. Rates for Arab and West Asian Canadians are particularly high as shown in the chart below.

QUEBEC: 2011 LOW-INCOME CUT-OFF PREVALENCE FULL-TIME EMPLOYED 25-64

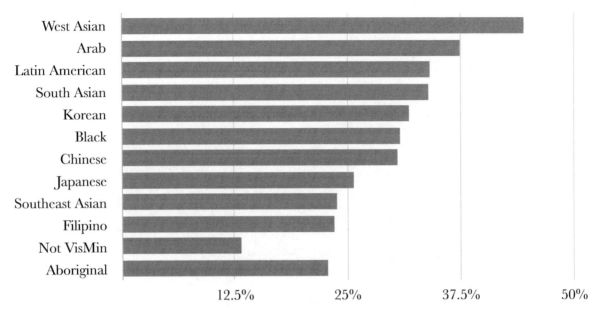

Looking at median incomes for all generations, ranked by women, Quebec's median income is $44,327 for non-visible minorities (lower than the Canadian average of $49,712). For visible minorities, the median income in Quebec is $35,071 (also lower than the Canadian average, $41,127).

QUEBEC: 2011 MEDIAN INCOME FULL-TIME EMPLOYED 25-64

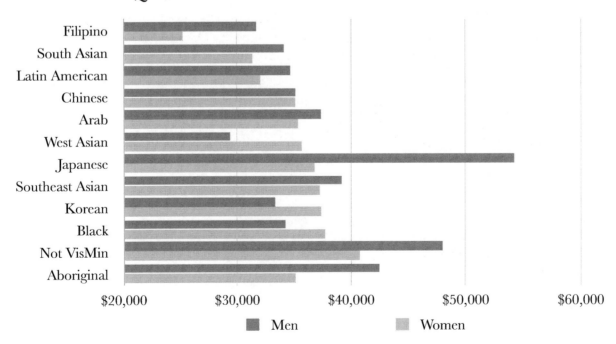

QUEBEC: 2011 MEDIAN INCOME SECOND-GENERATION 25-64

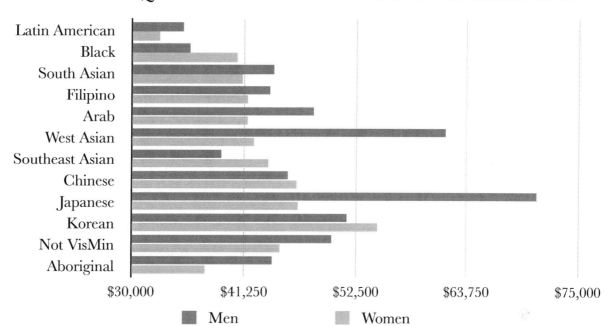

Men   Women

Second-generation immigrants, ranked here by median incomes for women, show considerable variation. Black and Latin American Canadian men have median incomes at 71.6 and 70.3 percent, respectively, of the non-visible minority median. Japanese, West Asian and Korean Canadian men are at 141.6 percent, 123.2 percent, and 103.2 percent, respectively. Chinese (121.8 percent), Korean (103.9 percent) and Japanese (103.8 percent) women all have higher median incomes than do women who are not visible minorities.

Latin American women in Quebec have a significantly lower median income than non-visible minority women, at 73.3 percent.

Looking at university-educated second-generation immigrants between 25 and 34 (a group of just over 25,000 people), only Korean, West Asian and South Asian men have median incomes higher than that of men who are not visible minorities. Arab, Filipino and Southeast Asian men come close to parity. Latin American and Black men have the lowest median incomes. Korean, Arab, Chinese, Japanese, Southeast Asian and Filipino women all have incomes equal to or greater than the median for women who are not a visible minority, while median incomes for Latin American and West Asian women are low.

QUEBEC: 2011 MEDIAN INCOME FULL-TIME EMPLOYED
SECOND-GENERATION 25-34 UNIVERSITY EDUCATED

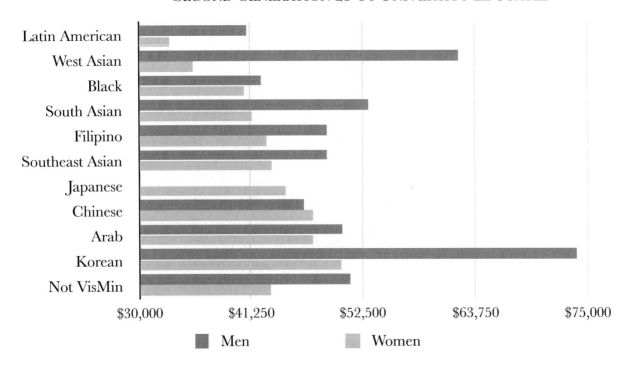

SOCIAL

QUEBEC: 2011 VISIBLE MINORITY LEVELS OF EDUCATION 25-64

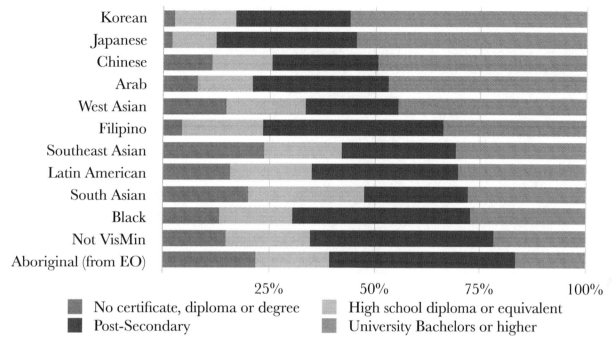

- ■ No certificate, diploma or degree
- ■ Post-Secondary
- ▨ High school diploma or equivalent
- ▨ University Bachelors or higher

In terms of education, Quebec follows the national pattern: Asian and Mid-Eastern groups have rates of university education between 50 and 60 percent. All groups but Southeast Asians have a greater proportion of university educated members than do non-visible minorities. Filipino and Black Canadians are more likely to have a trades education or equivalent, as are non-visible minorities and Aboriginal people. The highest numbers of people without a diploma are of Southeast Asian and South Asian ethnic origin, making up between 20 and 25 percent of these populations. Overall, 35.5 percent of visible minorities are university educated (the lowest rate in Canada), compared to 21.9 percent of non-visible minorities.

With respect to how well government services represent the population they serve, the numbers indicate that Quebec is doing reasonably well.

When it comes to healthcare and social services, which tend to serve people in times of need and vulnerability, employees are representative of Quebec's population. 10.4 percent of workers in healthcare, and 12.4 percent in social services, are visible minorities — slightly greater than the labour market availability of 9.8 percent. While many visible minorities are in support or junior positions (as discussed in the chapter on Canada), there are also many visible minority professionals (e.g., doctors, dentists), particularly of Arab, Southeast Asian and West Asian descent. Not surprisingly, Black, Latin American and Arab Canadians — as the largest visible minority ethnic origin groups in Quebec — are well represented in healthcare and social services.

When it comes to education, staff at primary and secondary schools (whether in urban or rural areas) are less representative than those at community colleges and universities (which are located in urban areas). Universities are the most diverse. This reflects the more specialized qualifications

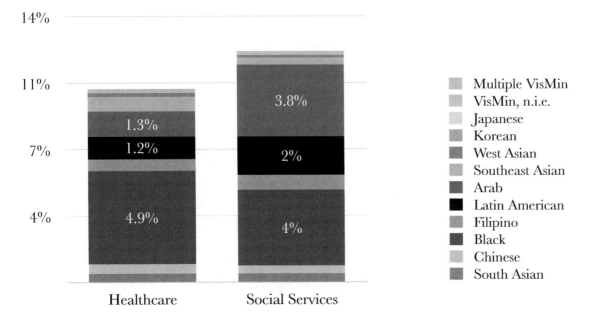

QUEBEC: 2011 HEALTHCARE AND SOCIAL
SERVICES REPRESENTATION 15 AND OLDER

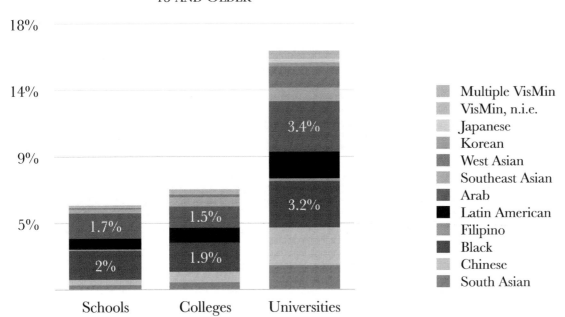

QUEBEC: 2011 EDUCATION REPRESENTATION
15 AND OLDER

required of employees, which brings into play the strong educational achievements of many visible-minority communities outlined above.

Visible minorities are underrepresented among staff at schools (5.9 percent) and community colleges (including CGEPs, 7.0 percent), which reflects the fact that many of these are located in less diverse areas of Quebec. Universities are the most diverse at 16.1 percent. Reflecting Quebec's visible minority population, Black, Latin American and Arab Canadians have the largest representation at all levels, although there are also significant numbers of South Asian, West Asian and Chinese Canadian employees in universities.

POLITICAL

QUEBEC: 2015 FEDERAL RIDINGS VISIBLE
MINORITY CONCENTRATION

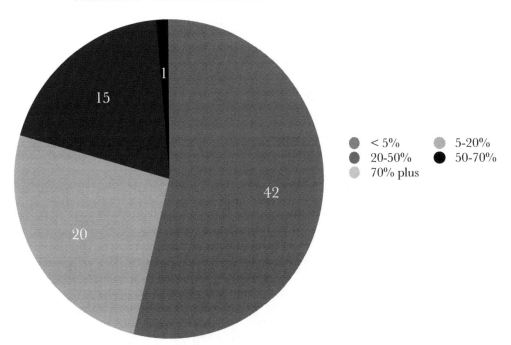

Legend: ● < 5%   ● 5-20%   ● 20-50%   ● 50-70%   ● 70% plus

Quebec has only one federal riding, located in Montreal, with a visible minority population above 50 percent: Saint-Laurent. 50.4 percent of its residents are visible minorities, with the major ethnic origin communities being Arab (15.0 percent), Chinese (8.3 percent) and Black (8.1 percent).

An additional three ridings have have visible minority populations between 40 and 50 percent: Saint-Léonard-Saint Michel (13.7 percent Black, 12.5 percent Arab and 8.5 percent Latin American), Papineau (11.2 percent South Asian, 8.7 percent Black, 6.7 percent Latin American and 6.7 percent Arab), and Bourassa (20.4 percent Black and 9.3 percent Arab).

From the perspective of religious diversity, Mount-Royal has a significant Jewish population (30.7 percent) and a number of other ridings, in addition to the three mentioned above, have significant minority religion populations: Pierrefonds-Dollard (Muslim - 9.1 percent and Jewish - 8.5 percent), Outremont (Jewish - 11.0 percent and Muslim - 9.5 percent) and Saint-Léonard — Saint-Michel (17.3 percent Muslim).

There are few visible minority representatives in the Quebec National Assembly, at only 4 percent of the total — less than half the proportion in the population, which is 11 percent. The concentration of visible minorities in Montreal, and the lack of significant diversity elsewhere in the province, largely account for this under-representation. Ironically, given its espousal of the Quebec Values Charter in the April 2014 election, the PQ has a higher percentage of its members from visible minorities than other parties. Women form 27. 2 percent of representatives, with no major differences between parties. Cabinet representation of visible minorities and women is slightly greater than caucus availability.

QUEBEC LEGISLATURE 2014

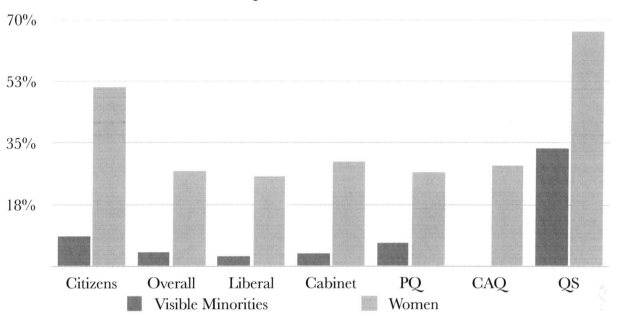

Quebec has 89,000 permanent employees in core public administration, and regularly publishes detailed information on employment equity. Unlike most such reports, however, it does not relate targets to labour market availability. [212]

Looking at National Household Survey public administration statistics for federal public servants located in Quebec, we find that visible minorities comprise 8.4 percent of the workforce — slightly lower than the 9.8 percent labour market availability (the federal *Employment Equity in the Public Service of Canada* report, which considers the core public administration, shows 9.1 percent representation).

QUEBEC: 2011 CORE PUBLIC SERVICE EMPLOYMENT EQUITY

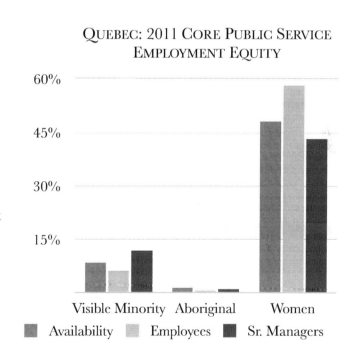

---

[212] Government of Quebec, <u>L'effectif de la fonction publique du Québec 2011-2012</u>. Note I have used federal LMA figures for Quebec as this report does not include LMA.

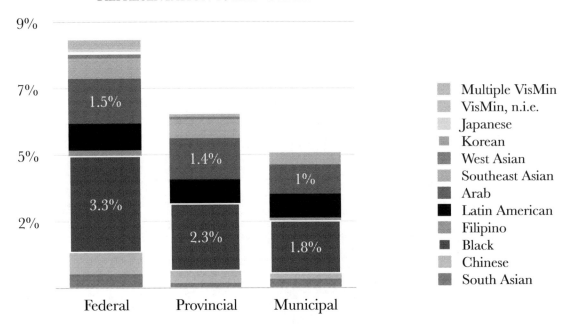

QUEBEC: FEDERAL, PROVINCIAL AND
MUNICIPAL PUBLIC ADMINISTRATION
REPRESENTATION 15 AND OLDER

Multiple VisMin
VisMin, n.i.e.
Japanese
Korean
West Asian
Southeast Asian
Arab
Latin American
Filipino
Black
Chinese
South Asian

Federal   Provincial   Municipal

Visible minority representation at levels other than federal is lower, with visible minorities making up 6.0 percent of provincial, and 4.8 of municipal, employees. This is partly due to the fact that these levels of government provide services in both urban and rural areas *outside* Montreal, where there is less diversity.

As expected, those visible minorities who do work in government are representative of the main ethnic groups within that category, with Black and Arab Canadians predominating.

As expected, representation reflects the population of visible minorities, with Black and Arab Canadians predominant.

Chapter 10 — Atlantic Canada: Immigrants Wanted, but Will They Come and Stay?

Atlantic Canada's provinces of New Brunswick, Nova Scotia, Newfoundland and Labrador and Prince Edward Island, were, along with Quebec, the earliest areas of European settlement. However, given greater economic opportunities elsewhere, Atlantic Canada has struggled to attract and retain immigrants. As a result, the area has comparatively little diversity, apart from Nova Scotia's historic Black community.

IMMIGRATION HISTORY

Atlantic Canada was the first region of Canada to be settled, first by the French (an area, Acadie, largely in what are now New Brunswick and Nova Scotia) and then by the British, including Loyalists fleeing the American Revolution. About 80 percent of the Loyalists who came to Canada settled in Atlantic Canada.

In 1750, there were some 10,000 Acadiens. Given British concerns regarding their loyalty during a war with France, some 6,000 were forcibly removed from the area and dispersed throughout the 13 American colonies. Many were refused, and sent back to Europe.[213]

While economic growth and immigration continued in the 19th century, it did so at a slower rate than in other areas of Canada. There were greater opportunities in Ontario in Quebec, and, following the construction of the Canadian Pacific Railway, in the Western provinces. Immigration from outside the British Isles was minimal, coming mainly from Germany, the Netherlands and Scandinavia.

New Brunswick: Despite the earlier Acadian expulsion, the population of French origin residents grew dramatically about a century after Confederation, from about 16 percent in 1871 to 24 percent in 1901 and 34 percent in 1931. Other important ethnic groups in New Brunswick in 1871 were the English (29 percent), Irish (35 percent) and Scottish (14 percent).[214]

---

[213] "The Acadians - Timeline," CBC News, Web, 15 February 2015.

[214] Same general sources as per Canadian immigration history, along with "New Brunswick," *Historica Canada* along with the chapters on the Atlantic provinces in *Integration and Inclusion of Newcomers and Minorities in Canada.*

From 1901 to 1931, New Brunswick's population grew from 331,000 to 408,000 — an increase of 23 percent.

Prince Edward Island: In spite of difficulties, primarily over land ownership, the population grew from just over 4,000 in 1798 to 62,000 around 1850. Although there was an influx of Loyalists after the American Revolution, the majority of the newcomers were from the British Isles. Several large groups were brought from Scotland in the late 1700s and early 1800s by landowners, and by 1850 the Irish represented a sizeable proportion of recent immigrants.[215]

From 1901 to 1931, PEI's population decreased from 103,000 to 88,000 — a drop of 15 percent.

Nova Scotia: Nova Scotia was the main province affected by the Acadian Expulsion, with more than 6,000 Acadian men, women and children rounded up and expelled from the region.

After the end of the French-British Seven Years War in 1763, Nova Scotia prospered, with settlers arriving from England, Ireland, Scotland and Germany. Loyalists, both white and black (some 3,000), as well as former black slaves, also arrived following the American Revolution. During the early part of the 19th century the colony grew as a fish exporting, lumbering and shipbuilding centre, and Halifax emerged as an important merchant hub and a base for British privateering captains.[216]

From 1901 to 1931, Nova Scotia's population grew from 460,000 to 513,000 — an increase of 12 percent.

Newfoundland and Labrador: Warfare between Britain and France, especially after 1793, resulted in the replacement of the traditional migratory fishery with greater settlement and a residential fishery. The majority of immigrants came from Southwestern England and Southern Ireland. On the West coast of the Island there are pockets of people of French descent (mostly Acadian) and some Scots whose ancestors were from Cape Breton, Nova Scotia.[217] Some 40,000 people lived in Newfoundland and Labrador by 1815.

From 1901 to 1935, Newfoundland and Labrador's population grew from 221,000 to 290,000 — an increase of 31 percent.[218]

---

[215] "Prince Edward Island," *Historica Canada*.

[216] "Nova Scotia," *Historica Canada*.

[217] "Newfoundland and Labrador," *Historica Canada* and "Voluntary Settlement: The Peopling of Newfoundland to 1820." *Newfoundland and Labrador Heritage*.

[218] "Historical Statistics of Newfoundland and Labrador Vol. I," Newfoundland and Labrador Statistics Agency, October 1970.

DEMOGRAPHICS

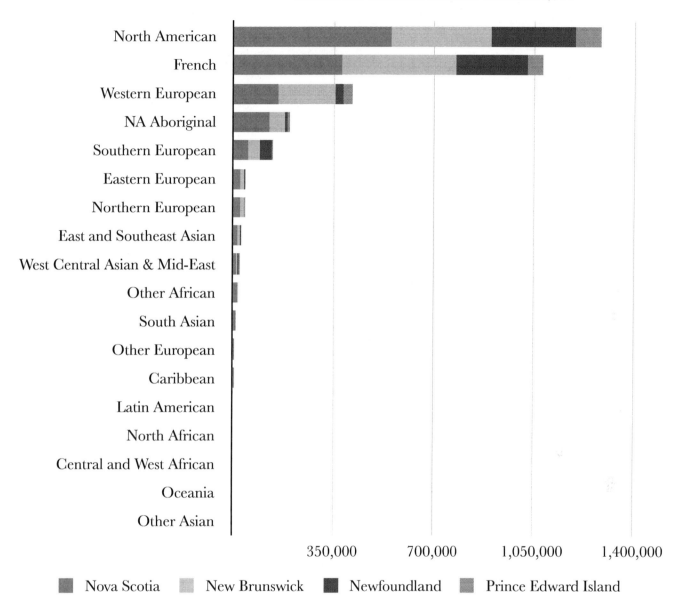

ATLANTIC CANADA: ETHNIC ORIGINS 2011

North American
French
Western European
NA Aboriginal
Southern European
Eastern European
Northern European
East and Southeast Asian
West Central Asian & Mid-East
Other African
South Asian
Other European
Caribbean
Latin American
North African
Central and West African
Oceania
Other Asian

350,000   700,000   1,050,000   1,400,000

■ Nova Scotia   ■ New Brunswick   ■ Newfoundland   ■ Prince Edward Island

The chart above shows the overall ethnic origins reported by residents of Atlantic Canada, including both single and multiple origins.

Atlantic Canada is much less diverse than the national average, with new communities making up only a tiny fraction of the province's population.

Nova Scotia, particularly Halifax, is more diverse than other Atlantic provinces, thanks in part to its historic Black community descended from the black Loyalists who came to Canada following the American Revolution.[219]

New Brunswick, with its large Francophone population, is the only officially bilingual province.

ATLANTIC CANADA: ANNUAL AVERAGE IMMIGRANT
INTAKE BY REGION 1988-2013

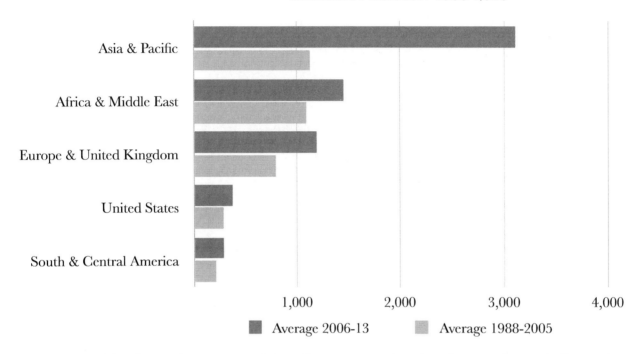

While the Atlantic provinces are much less diverse, recent immigration trends are similar to the rest of Canada in that most immigrants come from Asia and the Pacific, Africa and the Middle East, and South and Central America.

Appendix K lists the top 25 ethnic origins in Atlantic Canada.

Overall, 46.1 percent of Atlantic Canada residents report multiple ethnic origins.

---

[219] Lawrence Hill's *The Book of Negroes* provides a vivid picture of the harsh conditions and hostility faced in Nova Scotia.

Religious Diversity

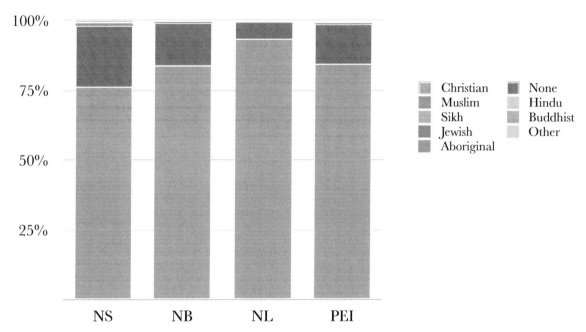

ATLANTIC CANADA: RELIGIOUS DIVERSITY 2011

Atlantic Canada is similar to Quebec in the large number who identify themselves as Christian, ranging from 76 percent in Nova Scotia to 93 percent in Newfoundland and Labrador, more than the national average of 67 percent.

Relatively few do not identify any religious affiliation.

Religious minorities form only about one percent of the population, except in Nova Scotia, where they make up two percent. There are small communities of Muslims, Buddhists, Hindus, Jews and Sikhs.

Atlantic Canada's Cities

Atlantic cities reflect an older, less diverse, Canada both in terms of ethnic origin and religion.

Halifax stands out among the Atlantic cities for its diversity (8.1 of its residents are not of European, Canadian, or Aboriginal origin), but is nonetheless homogenous compared to other cities across Canada. Aboriginal peoples make up a significant portion of minorities in Atlantic Canada.

DIVERSITY IN ATLANTIC CANADA CITIES 2011

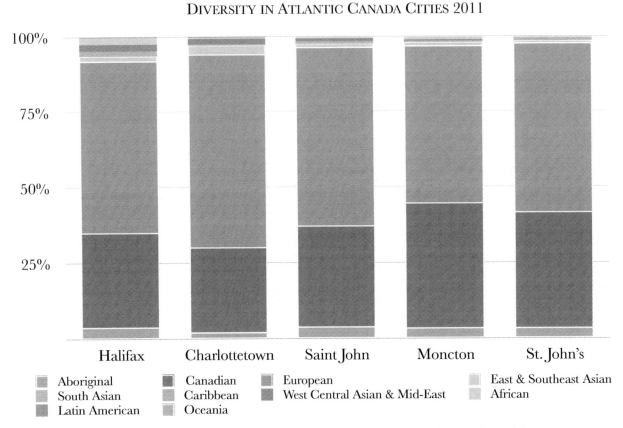

Moncton's relatively high francophone population distinguishes it from other cities.

Numbers of residents identifying themselves as practicing a minority religion are so small as to almost be rounding errors.

RELIGIOUS MINORITIES IN ATLANTIC CANADA CITIES 2011

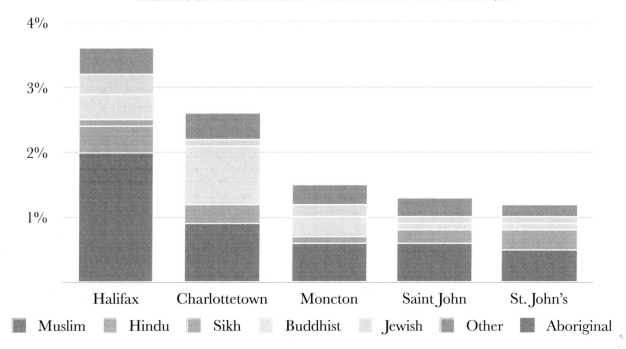

ECONOMIC

With respect to unemployment rates in Atlantic Canada, this section focuses only on visible minorities with a minimum population of 1,000 in any individual province, namely Black, Arab, Chinese, Filipino and South Asian visible minorities. It should be noted that the numbers are small even for these communities (the Black community in Nova Scotia has only 10,000 working-age adults 25-64). In PEI, there is only data for Chinese Canadians; in Newfoundland and Labrador, there is no data for Filipino Canadians.

ATLANTIC CANADA: 2011 VISIBLE MINORITY UNEMPLOYMENT RATE 25-64

Black · Arab · Chinese · Filipino · South Asian · Not VisMin · Aboriginal

Reflecting its weak economic growth, Atlantic Canada has higher rates of unemployment than other parts of the country, both for those who are and are not visible minorities (as illustrated in table 18).

TABLE 18: ATLANTIC CANADA UNEMPLOYMENT RATES					
	Nova Scotia	New Brunswick	Newfoundland	PEI	Canada
Not VisMin	8.0%	9.4%	13.5%	10.1%	5.9%
Visible Minority	10.7%	10.3%	8.5%	14.5%	8.3%

Pre-tax low-income cut-off (LICO) prevalence for all visible minorities (36.2 percent) is triple that of non-visible minorities (12.4 percent), and higher than the Canadian average for visible minorities of 22 percent. Variation among different groups of visible minorities is similar to the national pattern, but all these groups have higher LICO prevalence than do non-visible minorities. The communities with the least individuals falling under LICO — Japanese and Latin American Canadians — still have 50 percent greater LICO prevalence than residents who are not visible minorities. The chart below, ranked by LICO prevalence among men, illustrates this.

Chinese, West Asian, Arab and Korean all have LICO rates more than three times that of non-

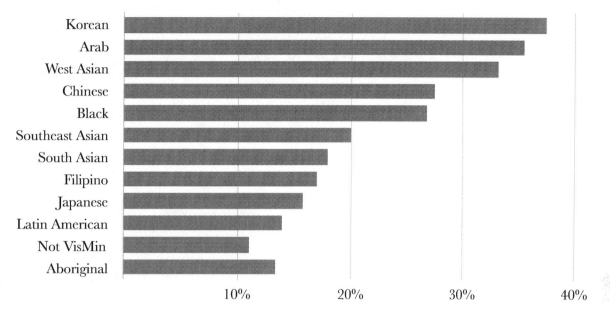

ATLANTIC CANADA: 2011 LOW-INCOME CUT-OFF PREVALENCE FULL-TIME EMPLOYED 25-64

visible minorities.

Only in Newfoundland and Labrador do visible minorities have a lower unemployment rate than other residents.

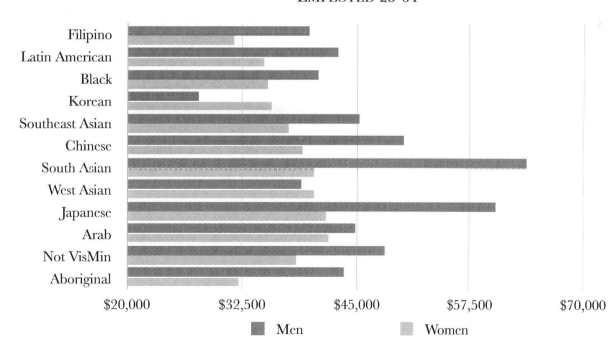

ATLANTIC CANADA: 2011 MEDIAN INCOME FULL-TIME EMPLOYED 25-64

Looking at median incomes for all generations, ranked by women, the median income in Atlantic Canada for those who are not visible minorities is $43,002 (lower than the Canadian median of $49,712). For visible minorities, the median income in Atlantic Canada is $40,146 (the Canadian median is $41,127), but some groups (Chinese, Japanese and South Asian men and women; Arab and West Asian women) are doing better than their non-visible minority counterparts.

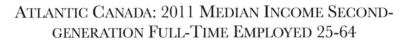

ATLANTIC CANADA: 2011 MEDIAN INCOME SECOND-GENERATION FULL-TIME EMPLOYED 25-64

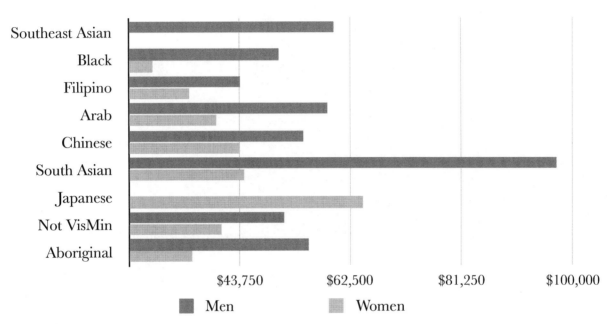

However, with respect to those second-generation immigrant communities in the region that are large enough for statistical analysis, Atlantic Canada is strikingly different from the rest of the country (see chart below, ranked by median incomes for women). Visible minority second-generation men are doing significantly better than other men in these provinces, and most visible minority women are doing as well or better than non-visible minority women (except for Black and Filipino Canadians).

This primarily reflects the fact that most visible minorities from these groups are professionals — especially doctors and others and healthcare — and so have higher-than-average incomes. Newfoundland and Labrador is the province with the greatest share of high-income visible minorities. Lower immigration to the Atlantic region is combined with a greater proportion of immigrants who are professionals (and who are employed in their professions), explaining why visible minorities with full-time employment are doing much better than other residents.

Given the small populations, there is no data for Southeast Asian Canadian women, Japanese Canadian men, and Korean and Latin American Canadian men and women.

SOCIAL

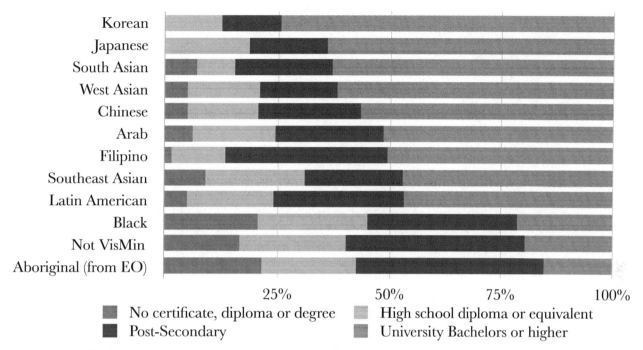

ATLANTIC CANADA: 2011 VISIBLE MINORITY LEVELS OF EDUCATION
2011 25-64

■ No certificate, diploma or degree   ■ High school diploma or equivalent
■ Post-Secondary   ■ University Bachelors or higher

In terms of education, the situation in Atlantic Canada is similar to that across the country. Between 50 and 60 percent of the area's Asian and Mid-Eastern population is university educated — an impressive 75 percent of Korean residents are university educated. All visible minority groups have higher rates of university education than do those who are not visible minorities, though Black Canadians exceed this last group only by a slim margin (at 21.4 percent, compared to 19.6 percent for non-visible minorities). Filipino and Black Atlantic Canadians are more likely to have an education in the trades or equivalent. Approximately 20 percent of Blacks in Atlantic Canada have no diploma. Overall, 44.4 percent of visible minorities are university educated, the highest rate in Canada, while only 19.6 percent of non-visible minorities are.

In terms of how well government services represent the population they serve, the lower numbers of visible minorities providing government services reflect the overall lower diversity in the region.

For healthcare and social services, which often serve people in times of need or vulnerability, the numbers are representative of Atlantic Canada's population. 3.3 percent of healthcare workers and 2.9 percent of social service workers are visible minorities, compared to the labour market availability of 2.9 percent. While many visible minorities are in support or junior positions (as discussed in the chapter on Canada), there are also many visible minority professionals (e.g., doctors, dentists). The largest visible minority groups are reasonably well represented in these sectors (Black and South Asian residents in both healthcare and social services; Chinese, Filipino and Arab residents in healthcare) though their numbers are still small.

ATLANTIC CANADA: 2011 HEALTHCARE AND
SOCIAL SERVICES REPRESENTATION 15 AND
OLDER

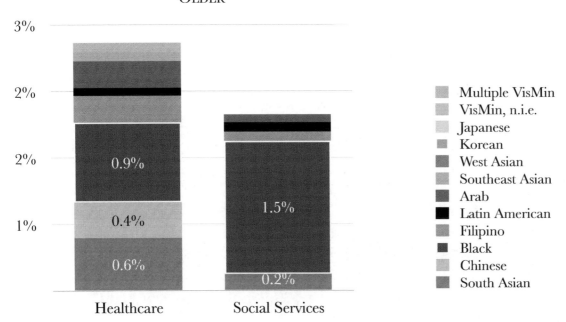

Atlantic Canada's lower diversity and rural nature is reflected in education, with small numbers of visible minorities in schools and community colleges. Universities, in line with the national pattern, are the most diverse, but visible minorities nonetheless make up only 9.7 percent of their

ATLANTIC CANADA: 2011 EDUCATION
REPRESENTATION 15 AND OLDER

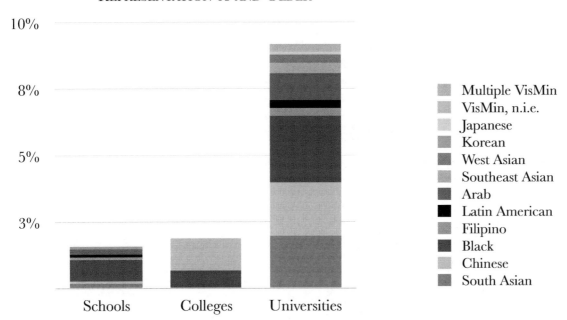

populations — while the numbers in other regions are between 15 and 25 percent. South Asian, Chinese, Black and Arab Canadians are relatively well represented in universities.

POLITICAL

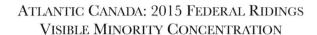

ATLANTIC CANADA: 2015 FEDERAL RIDINGS
VISIBLE MINORITY CONCENTRATION

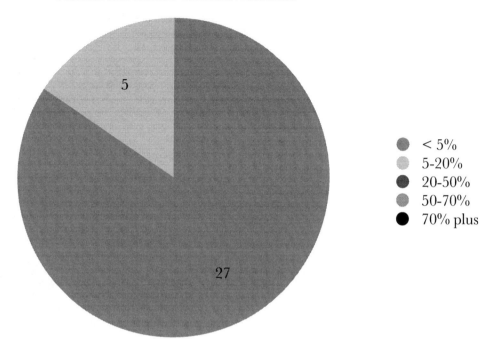

- ● < 5%
- ● 5-20%
- ● 20-50%
- ● 50-70%
- ● 70% plus

Only in five of Atlantic Canada's federal ridings do visible minorities make up between five and 20 percent of the population. These most diverse ridings are Halifax (13.4 percent visible minorities), Halifax West (13.1 percent), Charlottetown (8.9 percent), Dartmouth — Cole Harbour (7.9 percent) and Fredericton (5.2 percent).

New Brunswick, PEI and Newfoundland and Labrador have no visible minority members in their legislatures, reflecting their low numbers of visible minorities (2.3 percent, 3.1 percent and 1.4 percent respectively. Representation of women also is lower than elsewhere in Canada, at about 20 percent.

Nova Scotia is the only Atlantic province with a significant visible minority presence, reflected in the legislature and Cabinet.

ATLANTIC CANADA: PROVINCIAL POLITICAL REPRESENTATION 2014 (PRINCE EDWARD ISLAND 2015)

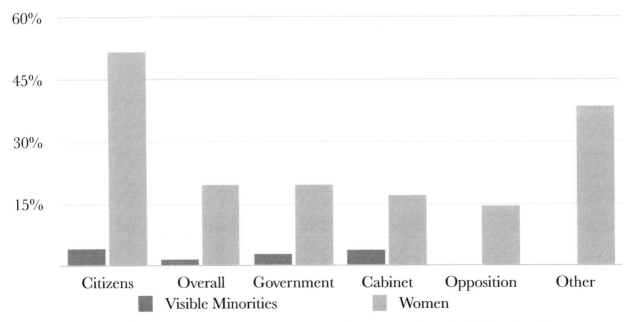

Visible Minorities   Women

With respect to public service employment equity, the low number of visible minorities means less comprehensive reporting for all provinces except Nova Scotia, which publishes an annual report on its 12,000 employees. Given the sizeable Black community, Nova Scotia characterizes visible minorities as "African Nova Scotians and Other Visible Minorities." Their report does not include data on senior management positions, except by gender.[220]

New Brunswick only provides employment equity information for gender (52.1 percent of its 9,000 core public administration employees are women), with no breakdown for Aboriginals and visible minorities.[221]

Neither Prince Edward Island, with its 8,000 employees, nor Newfoundland and Labrador, with its 12,000 employees, report on employment equity, with the exception (in Newfoundland and Labrador) of data on persons with disabilities.

National Household Survey public administration statistics for federal public

NOVA SCOTIA: 2012 CORE PUBLIC SERVICE EMPLOYMENT EQUITY

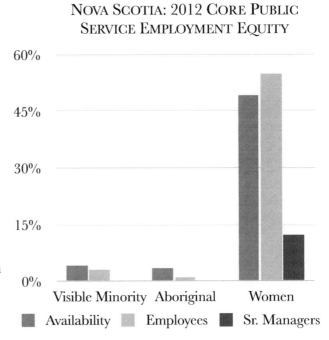

Availability   Employees   Sr. Managers

---

[220] Government of Nova Scotia, *Nova Scotia Employment Equity Report 2012-2013*.

[221] *Government of New Brunswick Workforce Profile 2013*.

---

servants in Atlantic Canada show that visible minorities comprise 2.8 percent of these employees, which is virtually identical to labour market availability (2.9 percent). The federal employment equity report, in contrast, which is based on core public administration, shows that 5.8 percent of employees are visible minorities (double the labour market availability). This overrepresentation of visible minorities in the core public administration is true of all provinces.

Looking at NHS public administration statistics, for federal public servants located in Atlantic Canada, visible minorities comprise 2.8 percent virtually identical to the 2.9 percent labour market availability. In contrast, the federal *Employment Equity in the Public Service of Canada* report, based on core public administration, shows 5.8 percent visible minorities, twice that of availability, as visible minorities are over-represented in all Atlantic provinces compared to labour market availability.

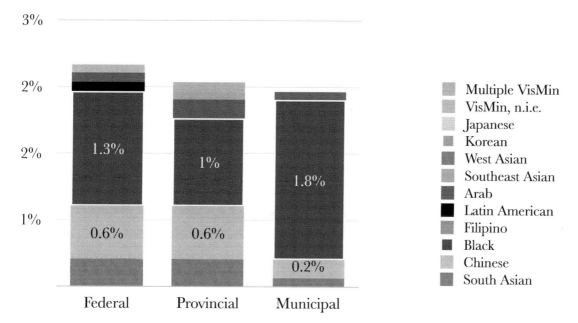

Representation of visible minorities in provincial and municipal public administration is at 2.7 percent and 3.0 percent, respectively.

As expected, the ethnic origin composition of visible minorities who do work in public administration reflects the population, with Black, South Asian and Chinese Canadians predominating.

Chapter 11 — The North: Aboriginal Nations and New Canadians

In contrast to the provinces, the Northwest Territories, Yukon and Nunavut only opened up for settlement following the advent of air travel to the North. Immigration really started up in the 1970s and 1980s, as the North developed and its labour needs increased.

The one wave of immigration prior took place in the Yukon during the Klondike Gold Rush of 1895. The Yukon's population increased to 27,219 in 1901, only to decline by two-thirds over the next decade.[222]

The North is characterized by a large Aboriginal population, and the challenges facing Aboriginal Peoples across a range of social and economic issues. While this analysis includes outcomes for Aboriginal Peoples, its focus will be on how well the small number of visible minorities in the North are doing.

Since most immigrants arrive in the North with employment secured, there are fewer economic integration issues for visible minorities and other groups that occur in the provinces.

---

[222] Robert Vineberg, "Immigration and Integration in Canada's Territories."

DEMOGRAPHICS

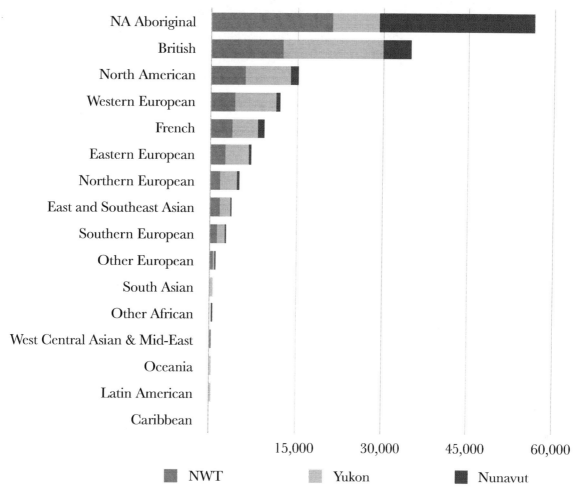

THE NORTH: ETHNIC ORIGINS 2011

This shows the overall ethnic origins reported by residents of the Northwest Territories, Yukon and Nunavut, including both single and multiple origins.

The majority Aboriginal population distinguishes the North, particularly in Nunavut (84 percent).

Recent immigrants, small in number, come mostly from Asia and Pacific, particularly the Philippines and China.

Appendix L lists the top 25 ethnic origins in the North.

Overall, 38.1 percent report multiple ethnic origins.

THE NORTH: RECENT ANNUAL AVERAGE IMMIGRANT INTAKE BY REGION 1988-2013

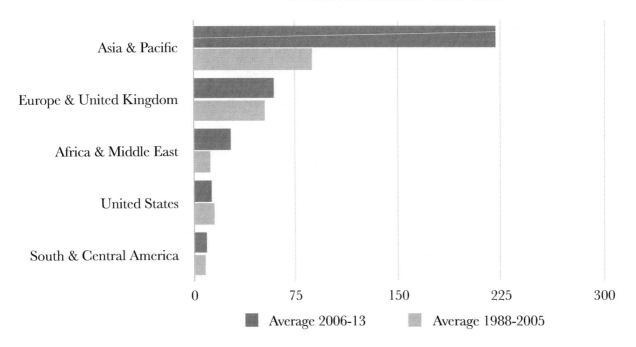

Religious Diversity

THE NORTH: RELIGIOUS DIVERSITY 2011

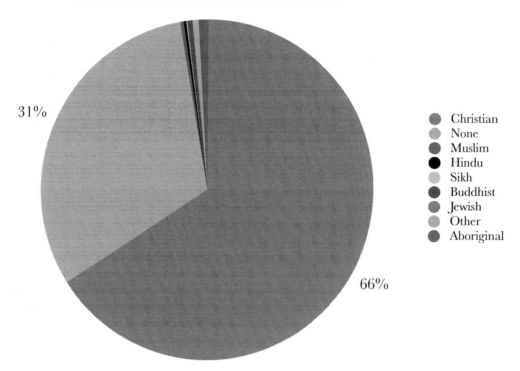

Most Northerners identify themselves as Christian, roughly in line with the national average of 67 percent.

About a third do not identify a religious affiliation.

Members of minority religions make up only about three percent of the population. Aboriginal spirituality is more prevalent than in other areas of Canada (but still has limited practitioners, at about one percent of the population). Other minority religions represented are Buddhism, Islam, Hinduism, Sikhism and Judaism.

ECONOMIC

For the North, I have only included South Asian, Black, Filipino and Chinese visible minorities, or those communities with over 250 working-age adults employed in the labour force. No individuals have incomes below the low-income cut-off.

With respect to unemployment, only Black Canadians have five percent unemployment, with the other groups (Filipino, Chinese, South Asian) fully employed. Unemployment of Aboriginal people (20.7 percent) is almost twice that of non-visible minorities (11.2 percent).

THE NORTH: 2011 VISIBLE MINORITY UNEMPLOYMENT RATE 25-64

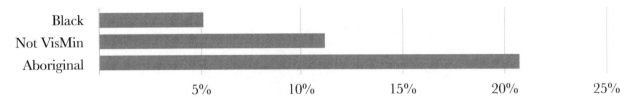

Median incomes tell a similar story. All visible minorities are doing better than non-visible minorities — this is true for both men and women. For all generations considered together, the median income in the North is $71,296 for non-visible minorities, compared to the Canadian median of $49,712 (see chart below, ranked by median incomes for women). For visible minorities, the median income in the North is $53,783, compared to $41,127 nationally. However, these higher median incomes are balanced by the higher living costs in the North.

The numbers for second-generation residents are too small for meaningful analysis. Only the data on Chinese Canadians allows for comparison, and it replicates the Canada-wide pattern: second-generation Chinese Canadian women do better (with a median income of $80,678) than non-visible minority women (at $70,242), while second-generation men in this cohort do less well (at $59,881, compared to $80,678 for non-visible minority men).

THE NORTH: 2011 MEDIAN INCOME FULL-TIME EMPLOYMENT VISIBLE MINORITY 25-64

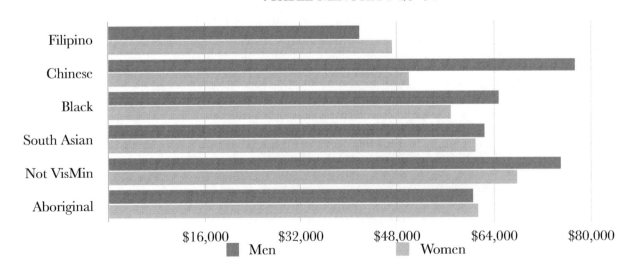

SOCIAL

THE NORTH: 2011 VISIBLE MINORITY LEVELS OF EDUCATION
25-64

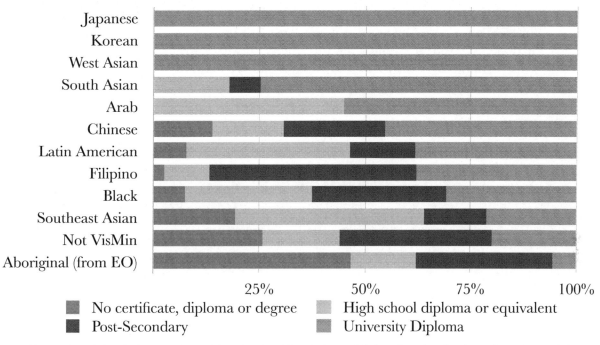

Visible minorities living and working in the North have higher levels of education than visible minorities living elsewhere. This is because the North does not attract general immigration — those moving there do so for skilled or professional positions..

THE NORTH: 2011 HEALTHCARE AND SOCIAL
SERVICES REPRESENTATION 15 AND OLDER

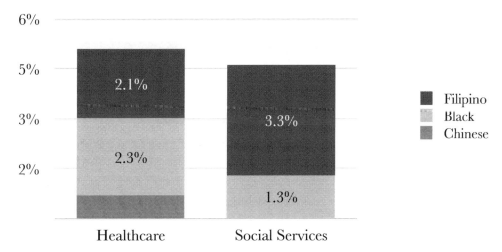

While we have generated the standard healthcare and social services chart, it should be re-emphasized that the numbers of visible minorities are small (i.e., 100 or fewer Chinese, Black and

Filipino). But it is not surprising that these groups are comprised only of professionals with university degrees, since it is likely that their qualifications were needed in the North.

Visible minorities are over-represented in relation to the overall population in healthcare (where they make up 7.8 percent of employees) and social services (8.8 percent), higher than the labour market availability of 5.9 percent.

For education, there are no community colleges or universities in the North and we only have information for elementary and secondary schools. The only visible minorities employed there are Black Canadians, and they make up a mere 0.3 percent of the workforce.

POLITICAL

THE NORTH: 2015 FEDERAL RIDINGS VISIBLE
MINORITY CONCENTRATION

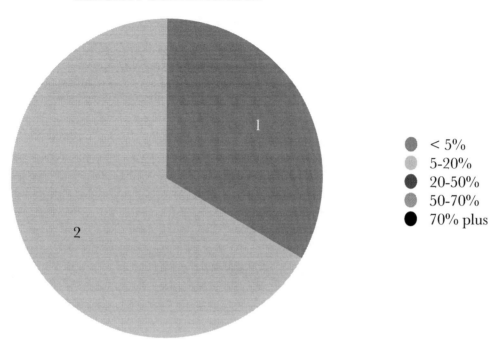

- ● < 5%
- ○ 5-20%
- ● 20-50%
- ● 50-70%
- ● 70% plus

Like in Atlantic Canada, the small visible minority population in the North means that these group do not factor into elections and political choices. These are dominated, instead, by the large Aboriginal population and the concerns of its members. Because of this — and the fact that there are no political parties in the Northwest Territories and Nunavut — I have not conducted an analysis of the territorial legislatures.

In terms of public administration, there is slight under-representation of visible minorities, likely reflecting an understandable priority given to Aboriginal Peoples, who have much higher labour market availability (40.6 percent).

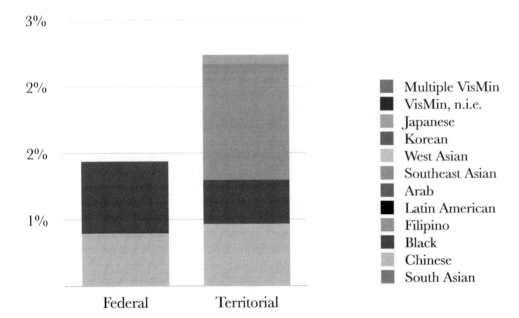

THE NORTH: 2011 PUBLIC
ADMINISTRATION REPRESENTATION
15 AND OLDER

Legend:
- Multiple VisMin
- VisMin, n.i.e.
- Japanese
- Korean
- West Asian
- Southeast Asian
- Arab
- Latin American
- Filipino
- Black
- Chinese
- South Asian

Federal | Territorial

Chapter 12 — Policy Reflections and Implications

If multiculturalism is Canada's "national project," as Michael Adams argues, it is essential to Canada's future that multiculturalism and related policies continue to encourage inclusion, participation and connection to Canadian society.

Looking at the range of data and information, at both the national and regional levels, provides an assessment of how well different groups are doing from economic, social and political perspectives, and how well Canada is doing in adjusting and adapting to ever-increasing diversity. The degree to which Canada can continue to find the appropriate balance between integration and accommodation is important to ongoing political consensus regarding Canada's citizenship, immigration and multiculturalism policies and programs.

My data-driven approach aims to complement both qualitative analysis and anecdotes regarding the overall success (or failure) of multiculturalism, and the degree to which Canada's dynamic of integration and accommodation will allow it to remain one of the more successful societies at welcoming and integrating new immigrants and citizens.

As stated earlier, my starting assumption, and basic thesis, was that Canada has been doing a fairly good job of integrating its diverse population. International comparisons are a compelling demonstration of this relative success. I still wanted to recognize, however, that more recent immigrant communities, composed mostly of visible minorities, face challenges — particularly with respect to economic outcomes and political representation.

Considering data organized by ethnic origin, visible minorities and religious minorities, separated by gender and generation provides a perspective on how outcomes vary by the different group characteristics — absolutely and in relative terms. Provincial breakdowns provide another perspective from which we can assess the success of communities from province to province.

The data demonstrates that certain groups are 'under-performing' relative to others, in some cases across the board but in other cases by generation, gender or location. A greater understanding of the range of factors influencing the success of visible minorities — external ones like discrimination, and internal ones like education and values — is needed to help drive policy work and research into ways to remedy underperformance. While government has a large part to play in improving equality of opportunity, participation and social inclusion, it must also ensure a certain 'policy modesty' (realism in setting objectives and indicators) when it comes to its role and impact in affecting social change.

Reflection by members of more well-established communities on their contribution to making society more inclusive with greater equality of opportunity needs to be matched by reflection within and among the newer communities on how individuals within these communities themselves can be better prepared to overcome barriers. All individuals, whether from newer or well-established communities, need to consider how their individual (or group) attitudes and actions either contribute or fail to contribute to the creation of a more respectful and inclusive social culture. They must also consider, in the legitimate pursuit of their particular interests, their impact on society as a whole.

This chapter reflects on the implications of what the data shows and suggests possible research and policy responses.

It is divided into two distinct sections. The first section is a recap of the findings overall, and also expands on the discussion in *Chapter 3: Canada — A National Perspective* by adding provincial information, and high-level implications, when appropriate.

The second section explores, more in the nature of personal reflections, the ongoing issues and challenges raised in the conclusion to *Chapter 2: Theory, Police and Practice*, informed by the data and analysis presented in subsequent chapters. The purpose of this section is not to provide definitive answers or recommendations so much as to generate discussion about these challenges and whether adjustments to existing policy and programs, or new approaches, are needed.

Many of these issues pertain to the social fabric of Canada, starting with the longer-term implications of changing settlement patterns, the evolving balance between integration and accommodation, the challenge in reducing discrimination and prejudice, and the need for a more balanced approach to radicalization and extremism (moving beyond security measures to a focus on improving social inclusion).

A number of issues have both social and political elements. Issues of dual loyalties and diaspora politics can, if taken to excess, focus unduly on the particular rather than general interest and run the risk of being divisive. A decline in naturalization weakens attachment to Canada and raises the potential of marginalized communities. Ongoing attention is needed to further strengthen political and public sector representation. A weak multiculturalism focus implies limited attention to longer-term, multi-generational challenges.

Lastly, and perhaps most important to the ongoing success of Canadian multiculturalism, all Canadians, whatever their position and whatever their individual and group identities, need to model more respectful and inclusive public discourse.

The intent is to sketch out the general landscape of each of these issues, highlight a number of key aspects, indicate the likely or possible implications, and suggest, where appropriate, policy recommendations and considerations. In so doing, I hope to provide a basis to make more informed the necessary conversations regarding Canada's ongoing and evolving approach to multiculturalism and integration.

OVERALL FINDINGS FROM THE DATA

On the whole, the data suggests that Canada has been largely successful at building an inclusive, multicultural society that encourages participation and integration. Analysis of the data confirms this success, but not without raising some issues and risks.

Greater and more varied diversity: Diversity within Canada continues to evolve and is becoming more complex and varied, with over 250 ethnicities, an ever-larger visible minority population and increased religious diversity. Statistical groups of visible minorities and ethnic origins, while useful for broad comparisons, understate the degree of diversity within these groups, whether in terms of religion, country of origin, time of immigration to Canada, or individual values and perspectives.

While there are commonalities across regions, each province has its own particular "flavour" of diversity. British Columbia is more heavily Asian, Ontario has the greatest diversity, Alberta has overtaken Quebec both in numbers and diversity and Quebec's composition reflects a preference for French-speaking immigrants. The implications of these differences are more varied requests for accommodation and, consequently, debate and discussion.

Quebec needs to move beyond its somewhat caricatural portrait of multiculturalism and be more open to looking at what works (and what does not) in English Canada in its public debates and private discussions.

Changing urban mix: MTV (Montreal, Toronto, Vancouver) has been replaced by TVC (Toronto, Vancouver, Calgary), and Alberta has displaced Quebec as Canada's third most diverse province, reflecting greater economic growth in the former. Moreover, diversity continues to expand outwards from the largest cities and their suburbs, particularly in British Columbia, Ontario and Alberta, to more medium-sized cities. Quebec is an exception to this trend, with new Canadians concentrated in Montreal proper, rather than its suburbs (though this is starting to change). While rural Canada remains relatively untouched by immigration, its diversity is growing, and more and more communities are having to come to terms with change and accommodation.

Economic differences persist: Economic differences — whether evaluated by LICO prevalence, unemployment rates or median income — between visible minorities and those of Canadian or European origin persist, even if participation rates for visible minorities are stronger. This is also the case for most second-generation immigrants who have been schooled in Canada. However, some second-generation visible minority women are doing better than non-visible minority women. Moreover, many university-educated second-generation visible minorities aged 25 to 34 are doing as well or better than non-visible minorities. Visible minority seniors, particularly women, have higher levels of poverty than their counterparts who are not visible minorities.

This pattern persists across the country, although visible minorities in Quebec fare more poorly: LICO prevalence is 50 percent greater than elsewhere (save Atlantic Canada), the gap between visible minorities unemployed and non-visible minorities unemployed is greatest (6.8 percent), and second-generation median incomes of visible minorities are lower than in other provinces. Quebec policy makers need to consider the longer-term implications of this difference and possible responses.

Unsurprisingly, at least until the recent collapse in oil prices Alberta and Saskatchewan have had the strongest economic outcomes for visible minorities and non-visible minorities alike.

Given the role that economic integration plays in overall integration, the persistence of economic differences for certain groups will likely continue to impact social inclusion and cohesion, requiring more work on policy options to attenuate these integration issues.

Strong educational performance: Education outcomes for most visible minority groups are significantly stronger than for non-visible minority groups in terms of university education. In most groups, there is no major difference between levels of education for men and women.

Canada continues to do a good job of integrating young new Canadians in primary and secondary schools. Attention should be paid, however, to lower rates of university education among Black and Latin American Canadians.

There remains a disconnect between education (where many new Canadians excel) and economic outcomes (which are poorer for visible minorities). Further work in research and policy is needed to understand and address this disconnect.

Discrimination remains an issue: Reported hate crimes and perceived discrimination remain an issue. The official statistics have remained largely flat over the past four years, showing that hate crimes are more common in provinces with greater numbers of visible minorities and religious minorities, with the notable exception of Nova Scotia (which has more racially-motivated hate crimes) and Quebec (which has relatively few hate crimes).

These statistics, however, probably underestimate the number of hate crimes occurring, and do not account for other examples of religious and racial intolerance and discrimination, such as that illustrated by the blind C.V. test. Ongoing prejudice and discrimination account in part for the persistence of difference in economic outcomes for visible minority groups.

While bias and prejudice are hard to eradicate, organizations need to pay more attention to ensuring that hiring and other workplace processes are as fair as possible. Individuals, both in the workplace and in society in general, also need to become more mindful of their implicit or subconscious biases and prejudices to assist integration and inclusion. All policy makers and those in positions of authority should take the Implicit Association Test as a first step in improving mindfulness.

Improved representation in public services: Representation of visible minorities in the public institutions that Canadians interact with the most — healthcare, social services and education (particularly higher education) — is fairly close to being representative of the population in the larger provinces. While many visible minorities in these sectors are in more junior positions, a number of communities have strong representation in more highly-paid occupations. In other words, visible minorities accessing healthcare are more often than not served by a mix of visible minorities and non-visible minorities.

This mostly-positive picture is tempered by the fact that some immigrant groups are overly represented in support positions. Activists in these groups need to address some cultural factors that may discourage individuals from pursuing highly-qualified occupations, in addition to their current focus on structural barriers. More also needs to be done to increase the numbers of visible minority public school teachers at the primary and secondary levels to improve representation and provide role models for visible minority youth.

Enclaves at the riding level: While there are areas of ethnic group concentration (33 federal ridings in 2015 had visible minority populations above 50 percent), most ridings feature a mix of communities, some larger than others. While there are some ridings in British Columbia and Ontario that approach the classic definition of an ethnic enclave (at over 70 percent visible minorities), in only two of these — Surrey-Newton in British Columbia and Brampton East — does a single group comprise 50 percent or more of the population. More detailed studies at the census district level provide, however, examples of greater ethnic group concentration.

The urge to win means that candidates in these ridings will likely be part of the largest or most dominant ethnic origin group, which can run the risk of making politics in these areas overly particularized, undermining basic Canadian identity and marginalizing members of smaller groups. Political parties need to take care in finding the balance between "shopping for votes" and pan-Canadian engagement.

Declining naturalization: The Canadian model of immigration leading to citizenship is at risk given declining naturalization rates (from 56 percent for landing year 2005 to 47 percent for landing year 2008, measured by six years after landing), a problem exacerbated by policy and program changes that have made citizenship "harder to get and easier to lose."[223] Politicians often cite an 85.6 percent overall naturalization rate, which, while formally correct (taking into account all foreign-born residents), hides the more recent trend towards decreasing naturalization along with a decline in those applying for citizenship.

The longer-term implications of a declining naturalization rate and an increased percentage on non-citizen permanent residents, include less social inclusion and weaker social cohesion. This is particularly true when visible minority immigrants are disproportionately affected.

Political under-representation: Visible minorities ((and women across the board) continue to be underrepresented among federal and provincial political representatives, with the number of visible minority candidates stable at ten percent since 2004 among all major parties. Even the most diverse provinces, British Columbia and Ontario, have significant under-representation at both the federal and provincial levels. Typically — but not universally — visible minority MPs elected in the 2011 election tended to represent ridings with large populations of their ethnic-origin groups. On the bright side, Canada has no anti-immigration party and all parties are competing for the ethnic vote. Visible minorities (and women) are seriously under-represented in judicial appointments.

Ongoing under-representation weakens Canada's social fabric and, along with more restrictive citizenship, can diminish the diversity of voices in legislatures and the judiciary branch, eroding inclusion and increasing marginalization.

Public sector representation reasonably strong: Core public service employment of visible minorities in the federal government is roughly in line with (a conservative) labour market availability, with the exception of some federal departments and agencies (e.g.,

---

[223] Both figures are six years after landing.

Canadian Forces, RCMP). Governments of the larger provinces, with the exception of Quebec, are also reasonably representative.

While this picture is fairly positive, changing the benchmark for representation from the proportion of visible minority Canadian citizens (15.0 percent) to the entire visible minority population (19.1 percent) would challenge public services to strengthen further their employment equity initiatives.

The following table summarizes some of the key economic, social and political indicators of successful integration, comparing the national and provincial portraits and the outcomes for visible minorities with those of residents and citizens who are not visible minorities.[224]

TABLE 19: 2011 KEY INDICATORS COMPARIING VISIBLE MINORITIES TO NON-VISIBLE MINORITIES BY PROVINCE								
	CA	BC	AB	SK	MB	ON	QC	ATL
Economic								
Below pre-tax LICO 25-64	10.6%	9.4%	6.8%	10.6%	9.3%	9.7%	19.0%	15.0%
Participation Rate 2nd Generation 25-34	-1.3%	0.8%	0.9%	-1.9%	-1.0%	-2.1%	-3.0%	-0.9%
Unemployment 25-64	2.5%	0.8%	1.0%	-0.2%	1.6%	2.9%	6.8%	0.1%
Unemployment 2nd Generation 25-34	0.9%	-0.2%	-0.7%	-4.5%	1.7%	1.5%	2.2%	-2.3%
Median Income 25-64	83.4%	78.5%	77.1%	79.1%	80.2%	81.7%	79.1%	93.4%
Median Income 2nd Generation 25-64	91.0%	93.9%	93.7%	101.5%	88.1%	89.8%	84.6%	101.3%
Median Income 2nd Generation 25-34 University Diploma	101.1%	104.2%	99.7%	87.4%	94.7%	100.0%	95.2%	99.6%
Social								
University Graduation 25-64	15.1%	14.0%	18.5%	25.3%	16.3%	12.7%	13.7%	24.8%
Healthcare Representation compared to Labour Market Availability (LMA)	0.5%	0.5%	4.5%	1.5%	4.1%	-0.2%	0.6%	0.4%
Education Representation compared to LMA	-7.6%	-7.1%	-4.4%	-0.1%	-4.2%	-7.3%	-1.6%	1.2%
Political								
Naturalization Rate	85.6%	84.3%	83.8%	78.8%	80.8%	87.0%	85.1%	78.5%
Political Representation compared to visible minority citizens	-5.6%	-8.4%	-1.8%	-4.9%	-3.2%	-4.4%	-4.6%	-2.4%
Public Service Representation compared to LMA	-3.7%	-10.6%	-1.7%	-0.8%	-4.6%	-4.0%	-3.8%	-0.2%

---

[224] This table uses the same methodologies used in the detailed analysis of each chapter.

While not the focus of the book, one last finding needs to be noted: the sharp contrast between the outcomes for visible minorities and Aboriginal Peoples. By any measure, new Canadians are doing much better than Aboriginal Peoples, and this finding is included in a number of charts to highlight this disturbing contrast.

ONGOING AND EVOLVING POLICY ISSUES

At the end of the *Theory, Policy and Practice* chapter, a number of ongoing and evolving policy issues were raised that emerge from the data. The common theme underlying discussion of these policy issues relates to the implications and probably consequences of these findings for Canadian society, and the risks that the combination of demographic changes, mixed economic outcomes, varied social challenges and mixed political and public representation pose for social inclusion and cohesion. These personal reflections aim to provoke reflection and discussion on these broader issues.

Settlement Patterns and Enclaves Reflect Increased Concentration Along With Dispersion

As noted previously, the sheer variety and diversity of the various communities in Canada means that it does not have ethnic enclaves to the same degree as other countries do. However, as the riding-level analysis in this book and more specialized studies have shown, ethnic neighbourhoods continue to respond to the "bonding capital" (connections within communities) and support-network needs of new Canadians, causing them to grow. This is not new; concerns over ethnic neighbourhoods have always been part of Canada's history. While many Canadians may prefer to live in neighbourhoods with other members of their own ethnic group, they often work in other areas or are exposed to other Canadians in schools in universities.

Subsequent generations may choose to stay in the neighbourhood of first settlement or not, depending on a mix of personal preference and economic considerations. In our larger cities, many ethnic neighbourhoods have become centres for the broader community, places where people go to sample different cultures and foods — think of all the Chinatowns, little India's, and little Italy's.

The impact of globalization, cheaper travel, free communications, social networks and a multiverse of global media options mean greater fragmentation and the possibility to live in a virtual enclave as much as a physical one. There are fewer common social spaces than before.

Greater understanding and more research is needed regarding the impact of social media and similar networks on communities, and whether these strengthen or weaken connection to Canada and Canadians at large. As media and social media tend to address more specialized and fragmented audiences — tailoring themselves to specific communities, ethnic or otherwise — they may strengthen bonding capital at the expense of bridging capital (connections between communities.

Identity, always a fluid concept, will probably become even more so. Identities are increasingly varied, complex and diverse. We can expect our urban geography to continue to develop and evolve, a process that will generate greater concentration of ethnicities in neighbourhoods *and* greater dispersion of communities across Canadian cities as people follow economic opportunities. Others may move back and forth more frequently between Canada and their country of origin for similar reasons.

Immigration will continue to be driven by economic opportunity. In many ways, it is no surprise that Alberta, given its stronger economic growth, has surpassed Quebec in the diversity of its population. Equally, it is no surprise that Ontario's relative share of immigration has decreased from 59 percent in 2001 to about 40 percent in 2011, considering its less attractive economic opportunities and deliberate policy changes to encourage economic immigrants to settle outside of Toronto (like the other traditional magnet cities of Vancouver and Montreal). Efforts by Western provinces to draw in more immigrants, through provincial nominee programs tailored to meet labour market needs, have been instrumental in this shift.

Atlantic Canada's efforts to increase immigrant attraction (and retention) have had limited success.

Further shifts in immigration trends depend on short- and medium-term economic trends. For example, a sustained period of low oil prices and its impact on the Alberta economy will reduce immigration from within and outside Canada to Alberta (and Saskatchewan). It is unclear, however, whether this will also reduce overall immigration to Canada (which did not cut immigration levels following the 2008 recession).

Another shift is likely to be generated by the Express Entry immigration program, launched in 2015. This program has employers selecting immigrants by the extension of job offers. From what blind C.V. experiments have taught us, there is reason to be concerned that subconscious bias may cause a preference for prospective immigrants with European backgrounds (as Debbie Douglas and Ratna Omidvar argue).[225] Time will tell whether such a change occurs, as it did in Australia.[226]

Population shifts and preferences for certain groups of immigrants are to a large extent beyond the control of governments. Governments can, however, use policy and program choices to facilitate these shifts (e.g., provincial nomination programs, Express Entry) or impede them (the late unlamented Quebec Values Charter).

---

[225] See Ratna Omidvar, "Changing the rules on immigration changes Canada's narrative," *The Globe and Mail*, 13 February 2015 and Debbie Douglas, on TVO's *The Agenda*, 15 January 2015, transcript here.

[226] The Australian experience with its shift towards employer-driven selection and greater emphasis on language competency has shifted source countries towards a greater percentage of immigrants from English speaking countries. See Lesleyanne Hawthorne, *The Impact of Economic Selection Policy on Labour Market Outcomes for Degree-Qualified Migrants in Canada and Australia*, and, *Competing for Skills: Migration Policies and Trends in New Zealand and Australia* 195.

Ongoing Challenge of Balance Between Integration and Accommodation

Canadian multiculturalism reflects a deliberate choice in favour of integration and not assimilation, allowing individuals and communities to preserve and maintain their culture within the Canadian legal and human rights framework. In practice, this has meant a sometimes uneasy and shifting balance between integration and accommodation.

The increased diversity analyzed in past chapters highlights both the historic cultural and ethnic diversity that was the basis for Canadian multiculturalism, and the more recent trend toward religious diversity and the arrival of religious minorities.

Recent controversies and debates over multiculturalism are less existential than those in Europe, and are over the finer details of the balance between integration and accommodation. Sources of debate have included the issue of turban-wearing Sikhs in the RCMP (1991), or, more recently (in 2010 and 2014), the wearing of the niqab during citizenship ceremonies and the public debates over accommodation in Quebec (2008 and 2014). These reflect the natural process of adjustment to living in an increasingly diverse society, not a fundamental questioning of immigration and diversity as is occurring in Europe.

Part of the success of Canadian multiculturalism, but also part of the frustration for some, is that often new groups bring new demands for accommodation as they become more established and participate more in Canadian life. Beyond the legal interpretation of the 'duty to accommodate,' the definition of what is 'reasonable' accommodation and what is not continues to evolve along with Canadian values. What was controversial 25 years ago is largely accepted today, whether a RCMP officer in a turban or gay marriage.

A key objective of multicultural societies, particularly liberal democratic ones, is to ensure that all citizens have an equal opportunity to succeed. Taking a one-size-fits-all approach impedes the achievement of this objective (for instance, banning religious headgear or symbols poses an obstacle to participation for members of some groups). At the same time, however, absolutist claims about accommodation may not help individuals in those groups meet their potential either. Some individuals and communities may nevertheless choose to maintain a more separate identity and eschew complete integration, subject to the law and the balance between the different rights of the *Charter of Rights and Freedoms*.

One of the key principles of reasonable accommodation is that both sides share responsibility. Just as the "mainstream" has an obligation to be flexible and willingly accommodate difference, minorities have an obligation to be flexible to the norms of society and be reasonable in terms of their requests for accommodation. A request for accommodation does not lead to automatic acceptance, but rather to discussion and negotiation, and possible responses include modification or rejection of the request.

Given the integration objective of multiculturalism — we do not accommodate for accommodation's sake, but to promote integration and participation — there are a number of elements that need to be considered:

Common space: Accommodation that encourages common spaces, where people with different backgrounds mix, is preferred to accommodation that reinforces separate identity. A system of public schools, rather than publicly-funded but separate schools, is a good example at the government level; participation in social and workplace activities beyond one's community is another.

Common Norms: Whether in clothing or social etiquette, some degree of conformity facilitates integration. Not uniformity — expression of particular identities is still allowed, but within limits that evolve over time and through different contexts. At the societal level, codifying common norms, beyond legal and professional codes, becomes inherently controversial (the 2013 proposed Quebec values charter being the best example). At the individual level, insistence on gender separation or "extreme" clothing (e.g., the niqab) sends signals of separation, not integration.

Participation: Common space and common norms aim at encouraging participation in wider society, beyond one's own community. Whether in the workplace, the school, the political process or elsewhere, integration is a matter of "rubbing shoulders" with a wide range of Canadians and building shared experiences across communities. Governments, public and private institutions and other organizations, along with individuals, should encourage broad and inclusive participation.

Table 20 provides an illustrative list of reasonable accommodation. It does not attempt to be comprehensive but rather to capture a number of examples to provoke reflection and discussion.[227]

---

[227] The examples used are taken from media articles and commentary. For Thorncliffe Park school, see "Friday prayers return at Valley Park," *The Star*, 24 November 2011. For York University, see "Religious accommodation or 'accessory to sexism'? York student's case stirs debate," *The Globe and Mail*, 8 January 2014.

TABLE 20: REASONABLE ACCOMMODATION ILLUSTRATIVE LIST

Type	More Reasonable	Less Reasonable
Clothing	Hijab, kirpan, kippa, turban etc. Note: Laïcisme ouverte or other model	Face covering (burqa, niqab)
Food	Availability of different foods, dietary restrictions	Segregated dining
Identification	Removal of face covering for ID purposes (e.g., airports, government offices) - same sex when possible but this accommodation is not a right Private: not encouraged but allowed	Refusal to reveal face when same gender not available
Faith	Acknowledgement of other faiths as part of common humanity Common faith rooms	Exclusiveness and non-acceptance Separate faith rooms
Education	Language or faith modules added on to public school day Comparative and inter-faith learning	Publicly financed faith-based schools Religious instruction against charter values (e.g., gay rights, women - e.g., Thorncliffe Park) Joint study in mixed gender groups (e.g., York University case)
Health	Request for male or female medical staff	Insistence on male or female medical staff
Workplace	Common spaces Acceptance of other habits, foods, cultures	Segregated spaces Not willing to be at same table or place with others who do not share beliefs (e.g., ok if colleague eats pork, has a beer, or in a same-sex relationship)
Recreation	Same-gender activities where needed to increase participation	No common space for both genders

To reiterate: accommodation requests must always be understood in the context of Canadian laws and the Charter to ensure a balance between the fundamental rights and freedoms of the person making the request and to ensure that any accommodation does not encroach on the rights and freedoms of others.

Canada is fortunate to have two contrasting approaches to reasonable accommodation: the Anglo-Saxon *ad hoc* case-by-case approach, or the more prescriptive, Cartesian approach in

Quebec, which provides greater clarity on what is legitimate accommodation and what is not.[228] In general, the former approach, frustrating as it sometimes is (with certain decisions seeming to swing too far towards accommodation or restrictiveness, depending on one's perspective), provides more flexibility to address the range of accommodation requests and situations that exist. Even this approach has some limits that get tested through the political process, as both the 2005 Ontario rejection of sharia family law tribunals and the 2007 decision on the part of Ontario voters not to provide funding to religious minority schools, illustrate.

But just as the majority population needs to provide accommodation where reasonable and where it does not impact upon the rights of others, those requesting accommodation need to take into account whether their request supports and facilitates integration and participation, and recognize that requests must not be absolute and need to respect the rights of others.

---

[228] Within each approach, there are variants ranging from more generous to restrictive. The 2013 proposed Quebec Values Charter was an example a more restrictive approach; the current Quebec government's, the proposed Charte de la laïcité, a more generous approach.

Discrimination Remains an Issue

Visible and religious minorities, particularly those who are first-generation immigrants, have significantly poorer economic outcomes that other ethnic communities and the "mainstream." The experience varies by community, but the overall pattern is clear. Second-generation outcomes show smaller gaps, particularly for women in general and for university-educated men and women. In most communities there are few third-generation members and consequently little data so there is less evidence to go on, but one would expect income and related gaps to shrink further.

One contributing factor to the persistence of gaps is ongoing prejudice and discrimination.

As noted earlier, there is an increased body of psychological and neuroscience research demonstrating how unconscious prejudice and bias are hard-wired in our brains. This explains, at least partly, why human resource professionals are more likely to interview non-visible minorities (those with familiar names). These same biases and prejudices apply in a wide range of situations (e.g., policing), and the fact that they are often unconscious and automatic makes them particularly difficult to correct.

Though I have not seen any studies on prejudices and biases against religious minorities in the workplace, it is likely, in light of general attitudes towards Muslims and Sikhs, that similar instances of discrimination would arise. Some of these attitudes may be captured in blind C.V. tests, if the names tested included those like Mohammed or Singh. When data on visible minority groups and religions are correlated, second-generation university-educated Muslim Canadians have the highest unemployment rates across the range of visible minorities.

In other words, it is a mix of good and bad news. On the one hand, there is improved intergenerational mobility, particularly for the university-educated. On the other, there remain persistent economic differences that reflect, at least partly, inbuilt biases and prejudice that disproportionately affect some visible and religious minorities.

More effort needs to be made by all to achieve more equality of opportunity. The Royal Bank of Canada Ernst-Young report, *Outsmarting our brains: Overcoming hidden biases to harness diversity's true potential*, mentioned earlier, provides a series of useful checklists to follow, calling for more mindful and deliberative selection practices in the workplace and elsewhere:

> **Think differently**: Make a conscious effort to seek out people with different backgrounds, experiences and capabilities to collaborate on teams and projects.

> **Learn differently**: Seek out opportunities to immerse yourself and your team members in different environments outside your (or their) comfort zone.

> **Act differently**: Take deliberate actions that disrupt your normal process and help prevent biases from shaping your decisions and behaviour.

For governments and educators, it remains important both to address specific forms of prejudice and discrimination as well as to generate broader messaging that fosters an inclusive and respectful society. Traditional racial discrimination and prejudice, which shows itself in worse economic outcomes, high hate crime statistics, poor policing practices and other areas, remains an issue for Black Canadians and some other visible minorities. Despite the progress that has been made, messaging and programming needs to continue to address the persistence of these racial biases and prejudice

But equally, we need to recognize the bias and prejudice against minority religions, particularly antisemitism and anti-Muslim attitudes or Islamophobia. Much recent federal programming in Canada, and initiatives in other countries, has focussed on antisemitism — appropriately so, as the frequency of antisemitic incidents has increased, causing fear within Jewish communities here and elsewhere. But the paradox of the focus on antisemitism is that by any other measure of integration — economic, social, political — Canadian Jews rank among the most successful minorities, if not Canadians period.

On the other hand, Canadian Muslims are much less successful than other minority religions, and are subject to greater suspicion and mistrust, as shown in most polling and in some public commentary. Yet this community has been met with, at best, silence from governments; and, at worst, approaches like the Conservative government's identity politics and fear mongering.[229] This does not facilitate the success and integration of the Muslim community. Since Canadian Muslims make up, at over one million people, the largest religious minority in the country, their economic and social challenges and the risks of radicalization and violent extremism demand more programming and greater care in messaging on the subject. Messaging should reinforce inclusion and the participation of all members of Canadian society, and the reduction of prejudicial barriers to this integration.

---

[229] "PM Harper's 'dangerous' comments on Muslims show lack of understanding on culture, says Taylor," *The Hill Times*, 28 February 2015. "Emmett Macfarlane: Harper's needless niqab fight," *The National Post*, 23 March 2015.

More Balanced Approach to Radicalization and Extremism

There have always been elements of society that accept violence as a means to achieve their political goals. Extremists can be left or right wing, secular or religious, educated or not, and Canadian or foreign-born.

Radicalization is the extreme case of dual loyalties, taking the form of violent extremism. There can be a shift in loyalty towards foreign extremist and violent entities (e.g., the current risks related to ISIS and Al-Shabab) or politically-motivated violence (e.g., previous events such as the Air India bombing of 1985, the FLQ October crisis and the killing of Pierre Laporte and kidnapping of British diplomat James Cross in 1970, or European left-wing extremism in the 1970s and 1980s of the Red Brigades in Italy and the Baader-Meinhof gang in Germany).

Moreover, a recent internal CSIS report on lone-wolf attacks revealed that these have a range of motivations — Islamic-inspired extremism is just one.[230]

However, for understandable reasons, the current focus is on the risks related to Islamic-inspired extremism given that most contemporary organized extremism is inspired by Islamist ideologies.

In addition to violent extremism, there is also peaceful extreme fundamentalism that is largely incompatible with Canadian rights and values (e.g., Salafism, extreme orthodox Judaism and their equivalents in other religions).

The more clear-cut case is support for and participation in violent extremism. While this threat has been real for a number of years, the

Table 21: Ideological Source Lone-Wolf	
Ideological Source	**Percent**
Right-wing and white supremacist	17%
Islamic extremism	15%
Left-wing and "black power"	13%
Anti-abortion	8%
Nationalism or separatism	7%
No clear motivation	40%

recent upsurge in arrests related to planned attacks on Canadian soil, and the increased number of Canadians travelling abroad to join extremist entities in Iraq and Syria, demonstrate that Canada is not immune to violent extremism. The most recent manifestations were the the lone-wolf attacks of October 2014 at Parliament Hill and St-Jean-sur-Richelieu and the fear and public and political reactions these engendered. Approximately 140 persons are suspected of having terrorism links links, according to media accounts of public remarks by CSIS and the RCMP. Most of these people are motivated primarily by perceived injustices against Muslims.

The difficult history of foreign interventions in the Mid-East, ranging from the Sikes-Picot post-World War I creation of artificial states, Western-sponsored coups in countries such as Iran, unbalanced support for Israel, and more recent interventions such as the 2003 Iraq war and ongoing drone strikes among others have helped create anti-Western narratives.

---

[230] Cited in "CSIS highlights white supremacist threat ahead of radical Islam," *The Star*, 15 March 2015.

Most studies on why some people are drawn to these narratives and extremism more than others suggest that there are a range of different factors at play in radicalization. While Islamist ideology plays a significant part, most of these individuals do not have a good religious understanding. Some have come from difficult backgrounds, and radicalization offers a sense of purpose and identity. Most are naturalized Canadians, many of whom came to Canada as children, but a significant number are Canadian-born converts to Islam. It should be noted, however, that having radical thoughts does not necessarily lead to violent action.[231] Similar patterns are found in other countries.

While some have argued that multiculturalism encourages radicalization, the presence of radicalization and violent extremism in a range of countries, some with multicultural policies, some without, indicates a more complex array of factors. Nor, however, do multiculturalism and inclusive social policies inoculate against radicalization, although there is some evidence that countries such as Canada, Australia and the US have lower per-capita rates of radicalization, something that can be attributed to the greater integration of their Muslim communities.[232] But it is not surprising, given the size of Canada's Muslim population (over 1 million), that a (fortunately small) number of these individuals are being radicalized and planning or engaging in extremist violence.

While the bulk of resources is appropriately dedicated to "hard" security and intelligence work to detect and prevent acts of violence, most countries also have extensive "soft" programming to reduce the risk of radicalization and de-radicalize returning extremists.[233] These complementary approaches, taken together, are likely to be more effective than solely focussing on the security dimension, as Dawson and Hiebert, among others, have argued.[234] Other voices arguing for greater emphasis on prevention and de-radicalization have included the mother of

---

[231] This summary draws upon analysis by Lorne Dawson and Dan Hiebert of the Canadian Network for Research on Terrorism, Security and Society among other sources.

[232] For example, Belgium is estimated to some 380 extremists out of a population of 10 million who have left for Iraq and Syria ("Belgian town has become a 'laboratory' for countering ISIS recruitment, mayor tells anti-extremism summit," *National Post*, 18 February 2015). The UK is monitoring some 3,000 extremists feared to possible commit domestic terror ("UK puts 3,000 extremists on 'Jihadi John' watchlist," *Financial Times*, 27 February 2015. French Justice Minister Christiane Taubira noted in her visit to Canada April 2015 the link between marginalization and radicalization ("Racism fuels terrorism recruiting, says visiting French justice minister," *iPolitics*, 23 April 2015).

[233] "Deradicalization programs aim to 'get ahead of the curve' on extremists," CBC News, 31 October 2014, citing Saudi Arabia, Denmark, Germany and UK as examples.

[234] "'Soft security' measures also needed to battle home-grown radicalism, experts say," *The Star*, 27 February 2015.

dead extremist Damian Clermont, Christianne Boudreau, as well as Imam Syed Soharwardy among others.[235]

One common theme underlying the various approaches — whether the "hard" or "soft" perspective — is the need to work closely with the affected local Muslim communities to help identify those drawn towards radicalization and hopefully prevent some from becoming radicalized and engaging in violent acts.

Language and tone are important. The contrast between President Obama's care to distinguish between violent extremism and Islam, and Prime Minister Harper, who appears to use fear and xenophobia for electoral purposes, is the most obvious example.[236] Combined with messaging perceived as anti-Muslim, this could not be designed to do a better job of alienating the very communities that the Government must work with to combat radicalization.

But what about non-violent extremism that advocates change peacefully, or those who choose to live separately and not integrate? After all, every religion has its fundamentalist or conservative variants. Media attention may focus on Islamic fundamentalism, and its incompatibility with gender equality, gay rights, tolerance and acceptance of others and advocacy of sharia. But similar issues exist with orthodox Jews, conservative Christians, and traditional Sikhs. Most conservative variants of religions do not allow female faith leaders, many are intolerant towards homosexuals, some are opposed to contraception, some turn a relative blind-eye to spousal and family abuse and some portray other religions with intolerance.

From an integration perspective, the freedom to live one's life as one chooses can be respected to the extent that it does not impact on the rights of others. Matters that are internal to a faith such as not allowing female faith leaders can be respected (of course, one can argue that this does affect the lives of women in the faith, some of whom do want to be faith leaders).

In secular liberal democracies, however, while religions can have teachings on any number of issues and advocate for their views to be reflected in laws and regulations, it is ultimately up to the government and the court to decide which path to take, as recent debates (such as those on abortion, same-sex marriage and assisted suicide) have illustrated.

Followers should be free to follow their beliefs in their personal lives, as long as this does not impact on the rights of other individuals. If followers prefer to live more separately, as a way to live more deeply their beliefs, that is their right, as it is their right to *seek* accommodation for their religious practices, though this accommodation may or may not be deemed appropriate. The section on reasonable accommodation aims to provide some guidance in this regard beyond the formal legal requirements.

---

[235] "Mother of fallen Canadian jihadi launches de-radicalization effort," CBC News, 9 September 2014. "Imams divided on how much scrutiny to give would-be Muslim converts in wake of recent terror charges," *National Post,* 18 February 2015.

[236] William Saletan. "How Obama thinks about Islam and terrorism: Why he chooses his words so carefully," *Slate,* 20 February 2015. Footnote 227 with respect to PM Harper reference.

While not ideal from an integration perspective, allowing people to live more separately is part of the balance of rights and freedoms that we enjoy as Canadians.

Dual Loyalties Are Part of Canada's Reality

Canada, as a country composed of immigrants (and their descendants) from over 200 countries, has many citizens with a variety of identities and attachments. This leads to what some might consider a conditional loyalty to Canada.

Much of the debate over multiculturalism and citizenship has focussed on issues related to how the recognition and encouragement of diverse identities can undermine loyalty to Canadian values and social cohesion, and weaken what is perceived as an already-weak Canadian identity.

Questions about the loyalty of immigrants and their descendants are not new. Earlier waves of immigrants from Ireland, Eastern Europe, Germany and Italy, among others, raised similar concerns.

Yan Martel's characterization of Canada as "the greatest hotel on earth" — welcoming, with minimal expectations — explicitly pinpoints the issue of loyalty.

Overall, despite the Government's tightening of messaging and increased emphasis on the meaningfulness of citizenship, Canada remains very accepting of dual nationality and all political parties are responsive to "homeland" politics and the issues facing ethnic communities.

This fairly relaxed attitude to how Canadians view themselves, their identities and their interests means that Canadians generally do not object when new Canadians concern themselves with events happening in their country of origin, except when this concern takes extreme forms (as in the case of individuals who have, in recent years, left Canada to fight in Iraq or Syria).

The situations described above are obvious. What about those that are less clear, cases where loyalty to Canada may be less important than other loyalties? We can assess loyalty from four perspectives: cultural, social, economic and governmental (civic engagement).

Cultural: There are few loyalty issues involved when Canadians express their culture of origin. The richness of the different cultures, entertainment, food and folklore is welcomed as part of the Canadian mosaic. Traditional dress in this context is accepted; traditional dress in the workplace is largely accommodated.

Should we consider mixed loyalties an issue when it comes to world sporting events like the Olympics and World Cup soccer? Does it matter which team or country people cheer for? On the whole, no. There is little conflict when it comes to soccer given Canada is not a strong player, and most who cheer for another country in this sport will happily cheer for the Canadian hockey teams at the Olympics.

Social: Newcomers have always had a tendency to settle close to fellow newcomers. The various Chinatowns, Little Italy's, and so on, reflect this. When these communities were formed, we did not worry about ethnic enclaves, viewing them as part of a normal, multigenerational integration process. The children of immigrants in ethnic enclaves go to neighbourhood schools that, while they reflect community demographics, are generally not monolithic. They may choose to remain in the same neighbourhood as their parents, or may move elsewhere to pursue other opportunities. While there is a risk of ghettoization in some low-income neighbourhoods, where the barriers to integration may be higher, the evidence does not suggest that this is a serious issue.

We cannot regulate where people live, nor should we. The first generation will naturally prefer to settle where the local shops, services and organizations cater to the community and where newcomers may find stronger support networks. At any rate, newcomers often work in mixed environments where they have exposure to other communities.

Is the risk of enclaves greater in today's globalized world? Do people maintain closer links back to the "home" country given cheap travel, free communications and the wide range of speciality ethnic media? Yes, most likely, but in most cases newcomers consume a mix of "mainstream" and community-specific media, which makes this less of an issue. Some may choose to "self-exclude" for religious or other reasons, but this is largely limited to a minority within most communities.

Economic: While most new Canadians work and invest in Canada, many maintain economic and business links with their countries of origin. This ranges from small businesses (e.g., ethnic grocery stores, travel agents and the like) to trading companies that export from or import to Canada as well as other businesses. Some maintain property in their countries of origin. None of these activities raise dual loyalty issues, unless of course such trade contravenes Canadian laws and regulations (e.g., export and import controls).

Similarly, continuing to receive Canadian government benefits (like a pension) when retired abroad is not an issue. Recipients paid into these plans and benefits when they lived and worked in Canada.

Civic Engagement: Canada allows dual citizenship, in response to the practical realities of Canadians who need to maintain the citizenship of their country of origin for travel or other purposes. While some (Griffiths, Cohen) have argued against dual citizenship, this position does not have broad support, although issues have arisen with respect to spouses of former Governors General (e.g., Jean-Daniel Lafond) or political leaders (e.g., Stéphane Dion).

But it is in the details of dual nationality that questions emerge. Should citizens exercise their voting rights in more than one country? What about the overseas constituencies of countries like Italy and France, and the Canadian dual nationals elected in foreign countries to represent them? Should Canadians celebrate "homeland" national days, or just cultural and religious festivals? Should Canadians be active in "homeland" issues? If so, to what extent? What about participation in foreign governments? What about military service in another country, or participation in foreign conflicts?

While many of these issues are not "either/or", loyalty concerns do emerge if a Canadian only votes in her or his home country's elections, only celebrates "homeland" national days, and is exclusively focussed on "homeland" issues. In other words, it is the balance between civic engagement in Canada and the country of origin that matters. Some interest in and advocacy for issues in the country of origin is one thing; an exclusive focus on these is another.

Foreign military service or participation in foreign conflicts, which raise the question, "which country are you prepared to die for?", suggest greater loyalty to the foreign country.

Participation in foreign governments, like that of dual citizens from Eastern Europe and the Baltic states, has been largely accepted, as it is viewed as projecting Canadian values (such as democracy) abroad. But it does raise the question of where loyalty would lie should the country of origin come into conflict with Canadian interests.

Since Canada's diversity continues to grow as a result of ongoing immigration and increased intermarriage, identities will become more and more varied and, in some cases, blended. At the same time, interest in global events (and the ability to follow them, thanks to modern media) and the ability to participate in the political and social life of other countries also continues to increase.

In most cases, questions of dual loyalties do not arise. Canada welcomes the richness of our cultural and ethnic diversity. Canadians understand the historic reasons why newcomers have tended to settle first in communities of similar ethnic origin. We trust that subsequent generations will navigate their way through the mix of their Canadian and "homeland" identity and values.

Canada welcomes and encourages trade and investment links with countries of origin. Successive Canadian governments have accepted dual nationality for pragmatic reasons and to make life easier for Canadians with ongoing ties to their country of origin.

The current government has, however, set limits on what kind of behaviour is acceptable. In addition to the obvious one of not engaging in violent extremism, it phrased its general expectations as follows in *Discover Canada*:

> Some Canadians immigrate from places where they have experienced
> warfare or conflict. Such experiences do not justify bringing to Canada
> violent, extreme or hateful prejudices. In becoming Canadian, newcomers
> are expected to embrace democratic principles such as the rule of law.[237]

More broadly, most Canadians expect interest in countries of origin not to be exclusive, occurring at the expense of engagement in Canadian issues and debates. Canadian citizens are expected to vote in Canada and to participate in Canadian political, social and economic debates, and not only vote or advocate on behalf of "homeland" issues.

As Canadians continue to navigate and develop their various identities, they are expected to find a balance between their ethnic or country of origin identity and their Canadian identity. Canada has few hard and fast rules, given the complexity of lives and identities, and provides considerable scope for Canadians to express their attachment to their country of origin and its culture. This attachment should, however, be tempered by an ongoing commitment to participate in Canadian society.

---

[237] *Discover Canada* 12.

No Escaping Diaspora Politics But Need for Limits

Linked to the question of dual loyalties is the ongoing reality of diaspora politics, where Canadians of diverse ethnic origin advocate on behalf of the interests of their country of origin on various issues. In many ways, this is similar to any kind of interest-group politics, in which a group with sufficient numbers, riding and regional concentrations and focus can influence political decision-making.

It is no surprise that diaspora politics, and the interests of ethnic communities, are very much part of Canadian politics, and that governments tend to respond to these interests, much to the frustration of present and past diplomats.[238] The greater the diversity, the greater the challenge in managing the diverse, and often opposing, claims of different communities.

But governments make political choices when responding to these and other legitimate political pressures. What are the factors driving some of these choices? How do ideology and values manifest themselves? When should the government apply a "principles-based policy" (or values not interest-based) and when is another approach appropriate?[239] Which principles should govern decision-making? When should a government work with allies on diaspora issues, and when should it go it alone? And how do governments deal with conflicting interests between different communities?

Some factors help explain how governments make these choices.

The size of the community matters. Larger communities have more influence and weight. Chinese, South Asian and Ukrainian Canadian communities are large, and Filipino Canadians are growing in number.

Moreover, many of the larger groups are also concentrated in a number of cities and suburbs, where they have greater influence in election results than communities that are more dispersed across the country. As the examination of political representation indicated, many ridings, whether from an ethnic or visible minority perspective, the results in many ridings reflect their proportions of ethnic or visible minority groups, with elected members frequently representing the largest group. It is no surprise Chinese and South Asian Canadians in British Columbia's lower mainland and Ontario's Greater Toronto Area, Ukrainian Canadians in Western Canada and Haitian Canadians in Montreal can and do influence election results in more ridings than dispersed and diverse communities such as Arab Canadians.

The longer the community has been in Canada, and the stronger the tradition of political activism, the greater the effectiveness of its advocacy. Newer, less-established communities have less time and understanding and fewer resources than older ones. It is not only first-generation immigrants who remain interested in "homeland" issues; for many communities, this interest

---

[238] A recent example being former Ambassador to China, David Mulroney, noting that former leaders are unimpressed being used as "props" for "photo opportunities" aimed at Canadian ethnic media, quoted in "Harper inadequate, inconsistent on China, former adviser says," *Vancouver Sun*, 3 March 2015.

[239] "The mystery of Canada's "values" foreign policy," *The Globe and Mail* (editorial), 7 February 2014.

remains across generations. Ukrainian Canadians have been particularly successful at effecting change at the government level, thanks to their longstanding presence in Canada (dating back to the settling of the West) and their strong sense of community and identity.

In addition, the more a community can speak with a single voice, the more impact it is likely to have. While there is a diversity of views within all communities, the main organizations representing Ukrainian Canadians and Canadian Jews, for example, provide a central focus and internal community interest brokering around common positions that makes it easier for governments and political parties to respond.

These factors apply to all political parties, who largely go where the votes are. Increasingly, too, "shopping for votes" means the targeting and even micro-targeting of potential voters. While there is generally all-party support in cases of humanitarian crisis (e.g., Haiti earthquake, Philippines typhoon), political positions can differ, either in nuance or more substantively, on international political situations.

In the case of Ukraine, the community in Canada is strong, concentrated, long-standing and unified. Canada has no politically significant Russian Canadian community and comparatively limited economic and other interests with Russia. There was and is little conflict between the Government's worldview, its deeply felt distrust of former communist totalitarianism, and the views of the Ukrainian Canadian community. Opposition parties shared this general approach although the Government's language was characteristically stronger. G7 partners are largely aligned with this position and the US forcefully so. The Government, then, benefitted politically from being in step with our allies, and any risks particular to Canada are limited.

Other larger communities are different. While Chinese Canadians are concentrated in suburban areas outside Vancouver and Toronto, organizations tend to focus more on domestic issues than on China. The much smaller Tibetan Canadian community understandably focuses on Chinese treatment of Tibetans. Indo-Canadians, while concentrated in the same areas as Chinese Canadians, are more diverse in terms of faith and tend to be less unified in their advocacy. The shadow of past Sikh extremism such as the Air India bombing remains as an example of the kind of imported conflict to be rejected.[240]

Situations of conflict, like those in the Middle East, present challenges for political parties. While the Canadian Jewish community is small, it is nonetheless influential: the population is concentrated in a certain number of ridings, and the main Jewish organization present a fairly unified position. Palestinian and Arab Canadians are less concentrated and relatively new to the country, with no strong national organizations. But apart from politics, beliefs play a role. The Government has shifted Canadian Mid-East policy to align more with Israel and the current Israeli government, increasingly out of step with the US and Europe. The recent trip to

---

[240] Former Ambassador to the UN Paul Heinbecker in his yearly memorial address to fallen diplomats is characteristically forceful about the limits to diaspora politics for both members of diasporas as well as Canadian politicians. "At the Memorial Ceremony for Fallen Diplomats And in Commemoration of the Late Colonel Atilla Altikat," *Heinbecker and Associates*, 27 August 2014.

Jerusalem by PM Harper with some 200 Canadian Jews is the most recent manifestation. While other Canadian political parties strongly support Israel, their support is balanced by more recognition of Arab and Palestinian concerns.

Iran is largely viewed through a similar framework. Iran may be an increasing source of immigrants but overall numbers are still small. There are some concentrations of Iranians in North Vancouver and North York, but the community is new and has not yet organized. A decision to shut down diplomatic relations with Iran was relatively easy. The Government's blindness to the significance of Iranian President Rouhani's election, right after hosting an innovative on-line conversation and outreach with Iranians and Iranian Canadians, revealed the weakness and divisions within the community. And the Government's harsh rhetoric against US and European efforts to negotiate a nuclear agreement with Iran, echoing Israeli-government rhetoric, are a further reflection of its alignment with the Israeli government.

Other examples of conflicting interests include the Tamils and Singhalese in Sri Lanka, Ukrainian and Jewish sensitivities over war crimes and the Holocaust, and and divisions among Muslims of different sects and countries of origin.

The Conservative government is well attuned to diaspora issues because of the extensive outreach by Minister for Multiculturalism (and Economic and Social Development) Jason Kenney. Like all governments, it has its preferred target groups, on both political and ideological grounds. What makes it different is its greater willingness to pick sides on issues like how to deal with the threat of a nuclear-armed Iran and the conflict between Israel and Palestine, even at the risk of alienating allies and some Canadians. The Conservative government is also unique in its more explicit use of diaspora politics to "shop for votes".

Ironically, as the Government made citizenship "harder to get and easier to lose", suggesting a more exclusive attachment to Canada, its active engagement in diaspora politics reinforces a more fluid concept of identity and citizenship, one more attune with the complex identities many Canadians have.

Diaspora politics are a legitimate part of the Canadian landscape. While some may perceive them as "pandering," diaspora politics reflect the normal response to concerns of citizens. The challenge for all political parties is to balance the interests of individual communities with those of other communities, and with Canada's broader interests and values. Too strong a focus on "shopping for votes" risks undermining this balance and the ongoing priority on integration and participation in Canadian society and politics.

Moreover, this fragmentation of interests makes it more challenging to find policies and priorities that address broader foreign and domestic issues, which will become more so as newer communities become more established and politically active.

When communities press their claims and interests, they need to recognize that these must be balanced against the claims of other communities and overall Canadian interests, however defined. An exclusive focus on concerns specific to one community (even if dressed up as in the interest of Canada) and no interest in broad Canadian affairs or recognition of other communities is not conducive to creating an integrated and inclusive society.

"Harder to get and easier to lose" Citizenship: Declining Naturalization

As I have analyzed in some depth, the Canadian model of immigration to citizenship is at risk. This reflects both historic trends showing a decline in naturalization and a number of the policy and program changes introduced by the Conservative government. Canada, like Australia, has always cited a high naturalization rate as a significant indicator of integration, frequently contrasting this with the European approach of putting up greater barriers to citizenship, and the resulting integration issues

It is important to recognize that many of these policy and program changes were driven by valid concerns regarding the integrity of the citizenship program, and the perceived need to redress the balance in favour of more meaningful citizenship and a stronger engagement to Canada.

The 2014 *Citizenship Act* further reinforced this overall approach through a number of provisions:

- Longer residency (four out of the past six years, from three out of four), physical presence, extension of knowledge and language assessment to 14 to 64 (from 18 to 55 years old), an "intent to reside" commitment, and removal of credit for time spent prior to becoming a permanent resident towards citizenship for international students, live-in caregivers and some temporary foreign workers;

- A quintupling of fees (from $100 to $520 for adults, with no provision for refugees or other applicants of low income;

- Barring citizenship in cases of foreign criminality for equivalent Canadian offences;

- Increased ministerial discretion to revoke citizenship in case of fraud, with recourse to courts only through seeking judicial leave; and,

- More fundamentally, revocation for dual nationals convicted of terrorism or treason, at home or abroad, a major change in a long-standing policy (dating back to Diefenbaker's assertion that "a citizen is a citizen," whether with single or dual nationality).

The Government has made major progress in addressing the citizenship backlog in 2014 (over 260,000 new citizens, more than any other year in Canadian history). However, this reflects incremental funding and resources to address the backlog of applicants under the old rules. It will take a number of years to assess the full impact of the changes in the 2014 *Citizenship Act* because they are complex, and interact with one another.

However, an early indication of whether these changes are likely to reduce citizenship take-up further will be seen in the number of applications received. The last two full years show a significant decline of over 30 percent from a historic average of approximately 200,000, with only about 130,000 new applications received in both 2013 and 2014. At the time of writing (July

2015), CIC had not provided an explanation for this sharp decline. But a decline is consistent with the policy of making "citizenship harder to get."[241]

After all, the context has changed. Earlier waves of immigration tended to be one-way. Two-way travel opportunities were limited and expensive. Today's globalized world features free communications, low-cost travel and community-specific media (produced in Canada or internationally) that all make identities more fluid and complex. Governments may try to reinforce a strong sense of Canadian (or other) identity, but their policies hit up against this modern reality. This is particularly true of the well-educated, trained and mobile immigrants that we aim to attract.

Despite these trends and related phenomenon like circular migration (when immigrants return to their country of origin, as have many Hong Kong Chinese Canadians), it is likely that most immigrants who stay long enough to become citizens will likely remain in Canada at least until retirement age.[242]

But the broader question is whether a high naturalization rate is important or not. Does it really matter that fewer immigrants take up citizenship since any children they have in Canada will automatically be Canadian citizens by birth? Is the historic model of immigrating to Canada and becoming a citizen increasingly obsolete given greater globalization and mobility? Is citizenship becoming more instrumental, something to further the economic prospects of immigrants rather than affirm their Canadian identity? And what should the balance be between making citizenship more meaningful while providing flexibility to accommodate the varied lives and interests of those who come to Canada? Are social and economic outcomes more important to integration than citizenship?

The European experience of the (permanent) guest worker model suggests that permanent residency without a reasonable pathway to citizenship impedes integration and full participation, but there are a range of other issues involved (as briefly captured in the international comparisons section).[243] The ongoing controversies in the US over immigration and pathways to citizenship may be another illustration that the fact of citizenship matters to integration, and of the risk of having a large group of permanently marginalized residents.

As Canada continues to strengthen its emphasis on economic immigration, most recently through the introduction of Express Entry and its aim to select the highest ranking immigrants, the corollary is that Canada is selecting the most mobile with the most opportunities, and hence those with the most instrumental view of citizenship. For those at the other end of the scale

---

[241] From 211,000 in 2009 to 133,000 in 2013. 2010 applications only totalled 97,000.

[242] See "Canadians Abroad," *Statistics Canada*, 23 August 2014 which indicates that while up to 35 percent of male immigrants emigrate within 20 years of arrival, 60 percent do so within one year of arrival, with a second wave of emigration in some communities post-retirement.

[243] E.g., the Netherlands, despite its integration challenges, has a naturalization rate of 70 percent.

(particularly refugees), citizenship is much more meaningful, and yet successive changes have made it less attainable.

But citizenship does mean the right (and as *Discover Canada* states) the responsibility to participate in Canadian society and the political process. Ideally, it reinforces the connection to Canada and Canadian society, even though much of that connection is formed through day-to-day interactions in communities and workplaces. A lower naturalization rate suggests a devaluing of Canadian citizenship and the political participation that citizenship enables.

Emphasizing citizenship may, however, be more idealistic than realistic. After all, the trend is towards lower political participation and voting rates among Canadians born here and abroad. But naturalization is nonetheless a necessary condition for integration and, moreover, all political parties continue to reach out to the "ethnic vote" despite this overall decline in participation.

Apart from this general trend, it is worrisome to see a decline in citizenship disproportionately affecting visible minorities. Some groups are facing greater barriers to integration, especially when their communities are low-income. For many members of these groups, the increase in citizenship fees will likely be prohibitive. More detailed research and analysis is required to fully understand the range of factors involved, and what policy changes may need to be considered. Should this trend continue, the Canadian model risks becoming closer to the European reality — disenfranchised residents with less stake in society.

It is unclear whether, in making its various changes to citizenship, the Government has reflected on what it thinks is an appropriate naturalization rate for Canada. The total number, from Statistics Canada, of foreign-born residents who have taken up citizenship (at 85.6 percent) reflects historical rates of naturalization, not the present one (so too with Citizenship and Immigration Canada's operational statistics showing a more accurate figure of around 80 percent).

Given the various changes to the citizenship program and legislation and the trend towards a lower rate, it is likely the Government prefers something lower. But how much lower? A 69 percent naturalization rate, as in Australia? 49 percent as in the USA? Or 43 percent like the UK?

The challenge in answering this question lies in defining what is the appropriate balance between meaningfulness and facilitation. An excessive focus on meaningfulness — or an overly rigid definition or criteria of what meaningfulness means — can make it harder for permanent residents to become Canadian while pursuing a career or other aspirations; on the other hand, making citizenship too easy to acquire undermines connections to Canada. Arguably, the Conservative government, while providing a needed correction to previous government citizenship policy and lack of attention to integrity issues, overshot the mark: it has made citizenship too hard to get, and longer-term implications for social inclusion are to be expected should the naturalization rate continue to decrease.

Need to Improve Political and Public Service Representation

Ideally, public institutions and and political representatives should reflect the populations they serve, whether in terms of ethnic origin, gender or another source of diversity.

With respect to public services, as noted in the review of employment equity reports and NHS data, the federal government and a number of provincial governments have made progress in this regard. This progress has, however, been uneven in the core public administration, with considerable variation between departments. As for the government services that citizens interact with the most (healthcare and education), representation of visible minorities is relatively strong, although these groups are over-represented in lower-income occupational groups within these sectors (with some exceptions in healthcare).

Police forces, from the limited data we have, and the military have significant recruitment and retention challenges with respect to visible minorities, although municipal police forces in the major cities of Toronto and Montreal are doing better than the RCMP (which provides services in many parts of rural Canada).

In the federal core public administration, it is striking that representation of women appears to have plateaued at the level of more senior positions. In contrast, representation of visible minorities will likely continue to improve (because of their younger demographic), although some visible minority groups appear to be doing better than others. The current lack of emphasis by the federal government on employment equity is unlikely to change the overall trend.

There is not reliable data on religious minorities although this could be derived, albeit imperfectly, from the NHS. It is likely that a similar pattern to that of the visible minorities would apply to both the core public administration and the broader public sector for religious minorities.

Federal and provincial reporting does not provide a breakdown by gender for visible minorities. Current reports do not allow us to compare visible minority women with non-visible minority women, and the same applies for men. This effectively understates some of the gaps. Separating out gender for visible minorities and Aboriginal Peoples should be part of future reports, so that we can see whether additional efforts are required, or whether demographic changes alone will cause representation to improve.

With respect to political representation, the good news compared to other countries is that Canada has no anti-immigration political party. Looking at the divisive immigration politics in the US, or the rise of anti-immigrant parties like UKIP in Britain or the Front national in France, is a sobering reminder of what can happen when the public is not comfortable with immigration.

And, at least until the 2015 politicization of security legislation, the wearing of the niqab at citizenship ceremonies, and the Government's stirring up xenophobia in its fundraising, the Government had managed to make significant reforms to immigration and citizenship while maintaining overall supportive messaging, including the announced increase in immigration levels.

All political parties continue to target immigrant and visible (and religious) minority voters, to the extent that party leaders are spending considerable time with the voters in ridings with high visible or religious minority concentration. Each party, naturally enough, focuses more on the communities that it feels are aligned to its values and beliefs. And each party considers ethnic group factors in candidate selection in those ridings where one group is more significant than others.

However, the 2004-11 comparison of party candidates showed a plateauing of visible minority candidates. Whether nominated candidates in 2015 will have a proportion of visible minorities commensurate with the increase in the visible minority population is as yet unknown.

Political parties have to balance their "ethnic shopping for votes" strategies with the broader electoral strategy and the risk of undermining support among other groups and the general voter. While ideally, a visible minority candidate should not necessarily have to come from one of the 33 ridings with more than 50 percent visible minorities, the practical electoral reality, and the wish to appear representative of the local population, will mean that this will continue (just as candidates in rural Canada reflect the non-visible minority local population).

Ongoing Need for an Active Multiculturalism Policy and Program

As noted earlier, the shift towards greater emphasis on integration between and among ethnic and faith communities (rather than between the "mainstream" and visible minorities"), from employment equity in the public service to improvements in the responsiveness of institutions to serving the needs of a diverse population, to actively engaging in internal discussions on diversity, has not made much of a difference. This is because of the small size of the Multiculturalism Grants and Contribution Program (less than $10 million annually, with frequent lapses).

However, the machinery change moving the multiculturalism program from Canadian Heritage to Citizenship and Immigration (as I argued in _Policy Arrogance or Innocent Bias: Resetting Citizenship and Multiculturalism_) has reduced the importance of multiculturalism in Canadian government policy-making.

Combined with successful rounds of resource reallocation and cuts, and the somewhat convoluted roles being played by an array of ministers (senior Minister Jason Kenney retains leadership on political and program issues, CIC Minister Alexander heads the department where Multiculturalism resides, and junior Ministers play a largely ceremonial role), it is no surprise that there is little to no policy leadership in the public service that brings a multiculturalism — or longer-term integration — perspective to policy debates. While Multiculturalism always had a strong political element (it is no accident that multiculturalism grants and contributions were never delegated to officials but had to be signed off by Ministers), there had always been a significant policy element that contributed to government-wide discussion and analysis.

Does the absence of a multiculturalism policy focus matter? Has multiculturalism become so part of the mainstream, so much part of the way of doing things, that a separate multiculturalism "lens" and voice is no longer needed?

While all departments play in diversity/multiculturalism space to a certain degree, given the diverse nature of the public being served, this tends to be driven by the concerns of individual departments. For example, Public Safety and other security agencies have understandably and appropriately focussed more on "hard" security responses than "soft" prevention and de-radicalization ones in their approach to radicalization and extremism. In the past, the Multiculturalism program provided a focus for these softer aspects of a strategy for countering violent extremism. It did so imperfectly and inadequately, but at least ensured that there was a voice at the table, and an expectation that the softer perspective would be brought up.

Beyond this specific example, the decline of the program has meant the absence of a focal point for overall assessment and consideration about the broader picture of how well Canadian multiculturalism is working in practice, what the ongoing and emerging policy issues or gaps are, and how these gaps might be addressed.

In one sense, this book is a refutation of the argument that a centre of expertise in multiculturalism is not needed. By drawing on the wide range of data and statistics available, I have highlighted where visible minorities are doing well and where they are doing relatively poorly, as well as the variations among the different groups of visible minorities.

The analysis of the impact of citizenship changes on different communities illustrates that taking a multiculturalism perspective can bring out issues that otherwise go unnoticed. Canadian Immigration and Citizenship, despite the best of intentions, will always focus on immigration-related issues (whether internally or in interdepartmental discussions), giving comparatively little attention to the longer-term integration and participation issues faced by second and subsequent generations. Having a centre of expertise to provide a framework for applying a multiculturalism or diversity lens to the success of visible minorities and non-visible minorities is essential, just as gender-based analysis is for evaluating gaps in opportunity for Canadian men and women.[244] This book has shown considerable variation in outcomes across any number of areas and indicators, something that needs to become a greater part of mainstream policy analysis.

---

[244] An example of a diversity lens can be seen in *Advancing Equity and Inclusion A Guide for Municipalities*, City for All Women Initiative (CAWI), 2005 which provides good checklists of issues to consider along with some examples of how an equity and inclusion lens (broader than a multiculturalism lens) has been applied.

Public Discourse to be Clear and Respectful

Invariably, specific issues provoke media commentary and public debate, whether it be reasonable accommodation issues such as requests related to gender, or radicalization and extremism. Finding the balance in these debates and discussions remains a challenge. On the one hand, excessive political correctness can camouflage underlying issues; on the other, fanning xenophobic fears alienates communities.

By and large, some Sun Media and Quebec commentators aside, most media commentary has been sensitive in its portrayal of issues related to multiculturalism and particular communities, without dissimulating some of the underlying issues involved. The winter 2015 controversy over the niqab at citizenship ceremonies is a case in point. Many media commentators and editorials, to my surprise, were opposed to the Government's ban on wearing the niqab during ceremonies, and many articles provided considerable space for the words of Zunera Ishaq, the woman insisting on her right to wear the niqab. Quebec media commentators, not surprisingly, were less flexible (but moderate in comparison to some of the hysteria and media controversies highlighted in the Bouchard-Taylor report of 2008).

The Federal Government, on the other hand, deliberately used the niqab issue as part of its electoral strategy in Quebec and elsewhere. This was disappointing in light of its strong opposition to the 2014 *Quebec Values Charter*. Combined with some of the Government rhetoric (and legislation) on the threat of violent extremism, the overall messaging has singled out Canadian Muslims, and poisoned public discourse. Other examples include the reference to "barbaric cultural practices" in *Discover Canada* and in the name of the anti-forced-marriage bill, *Zero Tolerance for Barbaric Cultural Practices Act*. Both were designed as "bumper stickers" to drive home the Government's approach to the broader public. Instead, these issues should have been engaged framed in a manner to engage with the particular communities involved and address more effectively.

As noted in the section on radicalization, this kind of messaging is unlikely to help the Government engage with those in Muslim communities that it needs to work with in addressing and building resilience to the threat of violent extremism. So while the Government language aims to consolidate political support, it undermines the efforts of the security agencies and others to strengthen cooperation with those communities that are most affected by radicalization.

This is particularly unfortunate considering that the Conservative Party has made successful efforts to engage ethnic communities while also making significant changes to immigration and citizenship policy, and to strengthen the emphasis on integration for all Canadians. Some may argue otherwise, but overall, despite its obvious targeting of some communities and an exaggeration of the degree of fraud and abuse in citizenship, the Conservative Party's messaging has on the whole been supportive of Canada as a country based on immigration, and has recognized Canada's multicultural heritage.

Language and tone matter given that there will always be — and should always be — debate over what multiculturalism means, which accommodations are reasonable, and which are not.

Similarly, there will always be debate over what measures are needed to reduce the risk of violent extremism, and what the appropriate checks and balances on security agencies are. But both sets of issues have an ongoing impact on the kind of society we have, and are thus too important to be subject to overly partisan approaches.

Attention to how issues are presented and discussed is always needed. Being sensitive to language and wording does not necessarily mean extreme "political correctness." It simply means understanding that words matter, and remembering that the goal is not to fire people up but rather to engage with them in discourse to further the policy goals and objectives of society.

Summary

The large number of new Canadians and their children mean that the success of Canada's immigration, citizenship and multiculturalism policies is central to its overall success as a country. The success of immigrants is Canada's success, and, conversely, their failure would be our failure. As high levels of immigration continue, diversity — both ethnic and religious — will continue to increase, bringing with it some of the challenges related to diversity and integration.

Multiculturalism is not just a philosophy and a series of related policies and practices. It is the Canadian demographic reality, and will remain so. Equally, however, our fundamental policy framework (dating from the *Bilingualism and Biculturalism Commission*) remains valid: recognition to foster integration into Canadian society, and equality of opportunity to allow all to participate to the full extent of their abilities economically, socially and politically. Moreover, these principles have been largely embedded throughout Canadian legislation and policies. In a very real way, multiculturalism has become Canada's national project, one that ranks sixth in a recent poll of Canadians on "what makes you proud to be a Canadian."[245]

My national and regional overviews aimed to provide a detailed portrait of how effectively Canada is living up to the recognition and equality goals of multiculturalism from economic, social and political perspectives. While there are few surprises (the declining naturalization rate being perhaps the exception), the overall portrait compares favourably to other immigrant-based countries such as Australia and the United States, which are the most appropriate countries for comparison (as the history and demographics of European countries are very different).

As I have highlighted in this concluding chapter, however, this mostly-positive portrait is not without some warning signs and areas of risk:

- The persistence of inter-generational economic inequality for some groups (e.g., second-generation university-educated Black and Latin American Canadian men) and high levels of low-income prevalence among first-generation immigrants;

- The changing nature of accommodation requests (increasingly challenging other rights, whether substantively or philosophically, and often on religious grounds), and ongoing discussion of whether a more explicit "values charter" of some kind would provide more guidance for dealing with these requests than English Canada's *ad hoc* approach;

- The unconscious bias and prejudice that most of us have, as illustrated by human resources practices, which contributes to higher unemployment rates for some visible minorities;

- The preponderance of visible minorities in junior or support positions, despite relatively strong public-sector representation, which bears monitoring, though it should improve naturally over time;

---

[245] "Harper government poll for Canada's 150th birthday cites Liberal, NDP icons." *The Globe and Mail.* 15 June 2014. The top 10 were (in order): Medicare, peacekeeping, the 1982 Charter of Rights and Freedoms, contribution to the Second World War; the Canadarm; multiculturalism; contribution to the First World War; bilingualism; space exploration; and the Constitution Act of 1982.

- The possible increase, judging by recent trends, in ethnic enclaves at the census tract level (and lack of reliable data on media consumption and social media networks, which may reinforce ethnic enclaves);

- The declining citizenship naturalization rate (expected to continue because of changes to the *Citizenship Act*), likely to have an impact on the medium-term integration of immigrants;

- The ongoing challenges in ensuring that political representation more closely approximates the population, whether in terms of visible minority status or gender; and,

- Lastly, the unfortunate increased use of identity and wedge politics by some governments (PQ under former Premier Marois, Conservatives under PM Harper) as part of their electoral strategies.

Canadians need to reflect on these findings at a personal level, being more mindful of the attitudes and concerns of the various communities that form Canada. While the majority groups may have a greater responsibility to listen to minority group concerns, minority groups also need to be sensitive to the concerns of the majority. Overall, Canadians have been remarkably successful in this awareness and sensitivity. This does not mean excessive political correctness — frank and open discussion is part of democracy — but it does mean a greater awareness of the other, and being respectful in one's discourse.

While this book has focussed on the federal and provincial levels of government, all Canadian governments should consider what these findings and observations mean for their investments in research, policies and programs. A greater focus on Canada's ever-evolving diversity and an effort to consider whether policy adjustments or new instruments are needed will better prepare Canada for the future.

Like any public policy issues, there are different legitimate perspectives that can and should be brought to the table. While my bias and preference is for more inclusive approaches, which I believe are supported by the evidence, I nonetheless recognize other approaches and think that discussion and debate about possible options is needed.

My hope is that the evidence highlighted in this book will contribute to creating a more informed discourse as Canada — by most measures a remarkably successful, diverse and multicultural society — prepares for its 150th anniversary.

Acknowledgements

I have benefitted from the advice and expertise of many in the writing of this book.

To start with, special thanks to Kamal Dib for his initial idea for the book and his ongoing encouragement. Kamal was helpful in his written input for the "Theory, Policy and Practice" chapter, particularly with respect to multiculturalism theory and researching the policies of comparator countries. We had many lively and constructive debates to inform how best to frame some of the issues. Kamal also largely prepared the glossary.

This book would not have been possible without the strong support from Citizenship and Immigration Canada, in particular the Research and Evaluation Branch. Thanks to Ümit Kiziltan, Xiaoyi Yan, Lorna Jantzen, Ima Okkony and Znining Qi among others, along with their counterparts at Statistics Canada who prepared the data tables, and who were always patient and helpful.

A number of people were particularly helpful in the initial stages. Gustave Goldman and Richard Shillington helped me understand how to interpret and use NHS data. Others were helpful in providing more general advice on how to integrate the data with the overall storyline and provide me with feedback on early drafts. Michael Adams, Howard Duncan, Phil Ryan, Ratna Omidvar and Dana Wagner were particularly helpful in this regard. I would also like to thank the discussants at my Metropolis 2015 workshop on the key findings of my work — Annick Germain, Alden Habecon, Joe Garcea and David Ley — who provided invaluable feedback to my treatment of the issues. Others who were helpful included Jack Jedwab in terms of general advice and Dan Hiebert for his expertise on ethnic enclave methodology.

Ravi Pendakur deserves special mention for his review of my charts and his helpful suggestions to improve both the underlying analysis and the presentation. Diane Fulford was a consistent trusted reader who gave me invaluable advice in suggesting avenues to explore as well as how to strengthen the narrative.

At Labour Canada, Gert Zagler and Lona Touckly helped me understand the employment equity reports of federally-regulated sectors (banking, communications and transport). Wally Boxhill at CIC, drawing from his employment equity experience, provided helpful feedback.

Stephen Lautens helped strengthen the political representation section through his articles and advice on judicial appointments. Erin Tolley provided some initial guidance on issues and articles related to political representation.

A number of friends provided particular encouragement through regular walks and conversation, as well as being trusted readers. To Dennis Fox, Guy Levac and Ian Matheson, many thanks for your friendship and your advice and support in my writing of this book.

My regular copy editor, Madeleine Levac, lent her usual diligent eye to copy editing, improving the readability and clarity of the text, and providing an additional critical eye to the overall flow and argumentation. My daughter, Roxanne, reviewed and corrected the various references for consistency and accuracy.

Of course, any responsibility for errors of fact or interpretation is mine alone.

My brother Lorne and son Alex designed the cover and were ever-patient with my fine-tuning suggestions. Lorne also reviewed the layout of the book and suggested improvements as well as providing feedback on related material.

An ongoing thank-you to my medical team at the Ottawa Hospital for their support during my cancer journey.

Last, but not least, to my family, Nazanine, Alex and Roxanne, for their ongoing love, support and encouragement, and their patience with what quickly became my obsession.

Bibliography

Adams, Michael. *Unlikely Utopia: The Surprising Triumph of Canadian Pluralism.* Toronto: Viking Canada, 2007.

"An Examination of the Duty to Accommodate in the Canadian Human Rights Context." Ottawa: Library of Parliament Background Paper, Publication No. 2012-01-E, 10 January 2012.

Anderson, Alan. "Ethnic Bloc Settlements." *The Encyclopedia of Saskatchewan.* n.d. Web. 1 February 2015.

Anti-Defamation League. "Global 100: An Index of Antisemitism." 2014. Web. 15 January 2015.

Arab American Institute (polling done by Zogby Analytics). "American Attitudes Toward Arabs and Muslims." 29 July 2014. Web. 20 January 2015.

Australian Bureau of Statistics. "Estimates of Aboriginal and Torres Strait Islander Australians, June 2011." 14 November 2013. Web. 17 January 2015.

Australian Bureau of Statistics. "State And Territory Composition Of Country Of Birth," 2011 Census. 28 January 2015. Web. 10 February 2015.

Bell, Derek J. "York University, Religious Accommodation, and the Absence of Bright Lines." *Bennet Jones Thought Network*, 16 January 2014. Web. 23 January 2014

Bendel, Petra. *Coordinating immigrant integration in Germany Mainstreaming at the federal and local levels.* Brussels: Migration Policy Institute Europe, August 2014.

Berry, John. *Integration and Multiculturalism: Ways towards Social Solidarity*, Papers on Social Representations Volume 20, 2.1-2.21, 2011.

Biles, John, Erin Tolley, Caroline Andrew, Victoria Esses and Meyer Burstein "Integration and Inclusion in Ontario: The Sleeping Giant Stirs," *Integration and Inclusion of Newcomers and Minorities in Canada.* Ed. John Biles et al. Kingston: McGill-Queen's University Press, 2011.

Bissoondath, Neil. *Selling Illusions: The Cult of Multiculturalism in Canada.* Toronto: Penguin, 2002.

Black, Jerome. "Racial Diversity in the 2011 Federal Election: Visible Minority Candidates and MPs." *Canadian Parliamentary Review,* Vol. 36 No. 3, 2013.

Blacklumb, Penny. "Immigration: The Canada-Quebec Accord." Ottawa: Library of Parliament, October 2008.

Block, Sheila and Grace-Edward Galabuzi. *Canada's Colour Coded Labour Market: The Gap For Racialized Workers.* Toronto: Wellesley Institute and the Canadian Centre for Policy Alternatives, March 2011.

Bouchard, Gérard. "Steering Paper, International Symposium on Interculturalism." May 2011. Web. 14 November 2014.

Bouchard, Gérard. *Interculturalism: A View from Quebec.* Toronto: University of Toronto Press, 2014.

Judicial Council of British Columbia Annual Report 2013. 31 December 2013.

Brochu, Pierre Marie-Anne Deussing, Koffe Houme and Maria Chuy. _Measuring Up: Canadian Results of the OECD PISA Study 2012_. Toronto: Council of Ministers of Education Canada (CMEC), 2013.

Cairns Way, Rosemary. "Deliberate Disregard: Judicial Appointments Under the Harper Government," Ottawa Faculty of Law Working Paper 2014-08, 19 June 2014.

Canadian Security and Intelligence Service (CSIS) Annual Report to the Treasury Board on the Employment Equity Program, 2012-13. September 2013.

Carter, Tom and Benjamin Amoyaw, "Manitoba: The Struggle to Attract and Retain Immigrants." _Integration and Inclusion of Newcomers and Minorities in Canada_, Ed. Biles, John et al. Kingston: McGill-Queen's University Press, 2011.

Centraal Bureau voor de Statistiek "Bevolking; generatie, geslacht, leeftijd en herkomstgroepering, 1 januari 2014." 16 May 2014. Web. 10 January 2015.

City for All Women Initiative (CAWI). _Advancing Equity and Inclusion A Guide for Municipalities_. Ottawa, 2005.

Champion, C.P. _The Strange Demise of British Canada: The Liberals and Canadian Nationalism, 1964-68_. Montreal: McGill-Queen's, 2010.

Choudhry, Sujit. "Rights Adjudication in a Plurinational State: The Supreme Court of Canada, Freedom of Religion, and the Politics of Reasonable Accommodation." Toronto: Osgoode Hall Law Journal. 50:3 (Spring 2013).

Citizenship and Immigration Canada. _Annual Report of the Operation of the Canadian Multiculturalism Act 2013-14_ and earlier reports.

Citizenship and Immigration Canada. "CIC Annual Tracking Survey — Winter 2010 Final Report." Ekos. April 2010.

Citizenship and Immigration Canada. "CIC Annual Tracking Survey 2013 - 2014 - Methodology Report." Harris-Decima. 31 March 2014.

Citizenship and Immigration Canada, "Forging Our Legacy: Canadian Citizenship and Immigration, 1900–1977." 1 July 2006. Web. 11 February 2015.

Clarkson, Adrienne. _Belonging: The Paradox of Citizenship_. Toronto: Anansi Press, 2014.

Corak, Miles. "Immigration in the Long Run: The Education and Earnings Mobility of Second-Generation Canadians." IRPP Choices. 14:13. October 2008.

Cottrell, Michael. "History of Saskatchewan." _Encyclopedia of Saskatchewan_. n.d. Web. 1 February 2015.

Council of Ministers of Education, Canada. _Measuring up: Canadian Results of the OECD PISA Students 2012, First Results for Canadians Aged 15_. Toronto: CMEC, 2012.

Delacourt, Susan. _Shopping for Votes: How Politicians Choose Us and How We Choose Them_. Toronto: Douglas & McIntyre, 2013.

Department of National Defence. _Canadian Armed Forces Employment Equity Report 2012-13_. Ottawa: October 2013.

Deveson, Morris. "The History of Agriculture in Manitoba (1812-2007)." _Manitoba AG Hall of Fame_. October 2007. Web. 5 February 2015.

Dib, Kamal, Ian Donaldson and Brittany Turcotte. "Integration and Identity in Canada: The Importance of Multicultural Common Spaces." *Multicultural Discourses in Canada*, special edition of *Canadian Ethnic Studies special edition*. 40:1. 2008.

Dib, Kamal and Ian Donaldson. "The Adams-Cohen Debate on Canada's Identity and Diversity," *Canadian Diversity*. 6:4. (2008).

European Commission: Directorate-General Home Affairs. *Awareness of Home Affairs Report*. June 2012.

Finlayson, James Gordon. *Habermas: A Very Short Introduction*. Oxford: Oxford University Press, 2005.

Flanagan, Tom. "The Emerging Conservative Coalition." *Policy Options*, June 2011.

Fleras, A. and Jean Kunz. *Media and Minorities: representing diversity in a Multicultural Canada*. Toronto: Thompson Education Publishing, 2001.

Frey, William H. "Glimpses of a Ghetto-Free Future." *New Republic*, 26 November 2014. Web. 15 February 2015.

Frideres, Jim. "Four Strong Winds: Immigration Without Direction in Alberta." *Integration and Inclusion of Newcomers and Minorities in Canada*, Ed. John Biles et al. Kingston: McGill-Queen's University Press, 2011.

Funke, Alice. "Who Really One the Ethnic Vote in the May Election." *Pundits Guide*, 9 September 2011. Web. 14 October 2015.

Gagnon, Erica. "Settling the West: Immigration to the Prairies from 1867 to 1914." Halifax: *Pier21 Canadian Museum of Immigration*. n.d. Web. 14 February 2015.

Garcea, Joseph. "Settlement and Integration in Saskatchewan." *Integration and Inclusion of Newcomers and Minorities in Canada*. Ed. John Biles et al. Kingston: McGill-Queen's University Press, 2011.

Germain, Annick and Tuyet Trinh. "Immigration in Quebec: Profile and Players." *Integration and Inclusion of Newcomers and Minorities in Canada*. Ed. John Biles et al. Kingston: McGill-Queen's University Press, 2011.

Government of Alberta. "About Us: Careers with the Government of Alberta." Web. 12 November 2014.

Government of British Columbia Public Service. *Workforce Profile Report*. March 2011. Web. 10 November 2014.

Government of Canada. *Discover Canada: The Rights and Responsibilities of Citizenship*. Ottawa: 2010 and 2012.

Government of Manitoba. *Manitoba Civil Service Commission, Annual Report 2012-13*. n.d. Web. 10 November 2014.

Government of New Brunswick Department of Human Resources. *Government of New Brunswick Workforce Profile 2013*. n.d.

Government of Nova Scotia Public Service Commission. *Nova Scotia Employment Equity Report 2012-2013*. n.d. Web. 20 October 2014.

Government of Ontario OPS Diversity Office. *Inclusion Now! Ontario Public Service Inclusion Strategic Plan 2013–2016*. 2013.

Government of Ontario. *Ontario Judicial Appointments Committee Annual Report 2012*. Toronto: January 2013.

Government of Quebec Ministry of Immigration, Diversity et Inclusion. "Historic Overview Quebec Immigration." 10 June 2006. Web. 20 January 2015.

Government of Quebec Secrétariat du Conseil du trésor. *L'effectif de la fonction publique du Québec 2011-2012*. 2013.

Griffith, Andrew. *Policy Arrogance or Innocent Bias: Resetting Citizenship and Multiculturalism*. Ottawa: Anar Press, 2013.

Grubel, Herbert and Patrick Grady. "Fiscal Transfers to Immigrants in Canada: Responding to Critics and a Revised Estimate." Vancouver: Fraser Institute, 15 March 2012.

Habermas, Jurgen. "Struggles for Recognition in Constitutional States." *International European Journal of Philosophy.* n° 128, 1993.

Habermas, Jurgen. "Apologetic tendencies," and "Historical Consciousness and Post-Traditional identity: Orientation Towards the West in West Germany." *The New Conservatism: Cultural Criticism and the Historians' Debate*. Boston: The MIT Press, 1991.

Hawthorne, Lesleyanne. "The Impact of Economic Selection Policy on Labour Market Outcomes for Degree-Qualified Migrants in Canada and Australia. " *IRPP Choices*. 14:5. 12 May 2008. Web. 7 April 2015.

Hawthorne, Lesleyanne. *Competing for Skills: Migration Policies and Trends in New Zealand and Australia,* Canberra: Australian Government Department of Immigration and Citizenship, 2011.

Heath, Anthony. "Has multiculturalism failed in the UK? Not really." *The Guardian*, 10 August 2012.

Hiebert, Dan. "Exploring Minority Enclave Areas in Montréal, Toronto, and Vancouver." *Citizenship and Immigration Canada*. March 2009. Web. 10 November 2014. Updates to study presented to Metropolis 2015 Conference, March 2015.

Hill, Lawrence. *Blood.* Toronto: Anansi Press, 2013.

Hill, Lawrence. *The Book of Negroes.* Toronto: Harper-Collins 2007.

Iceland, John. *Residential Segregation: A Transatlantic Analysis*. Washington, DC: Migration Policy Institute, September 2014.

INSEE. "Immigrés et descendants d'immigrés en France, édition 2012." Paris: 2012. Web. 20 January 2015.

INSEE. "Population immigré 2012." Paris: 2012. Web. 20 January 2015.

Institute for Canadian Citizenship (Environics). "Canadians on Citizenship." Toronto: February 2012.

Ipsos-MORI. "Britain is most concerned about immigration control." 30 December 2013. Web. 15 February 2015.

Javdani, Mohsen and Krishna Pendakur. "Fiscal Transfers to Immigrants in Canada." Metropolis British Columbia Working Paper Series 11:08. July 2011.

Javdani, Mohsen and Krishna Pendakur. "Fiscal Effects of Immigrants in Canada." May 2013. Web. 20 January 2015.

Jewish Virtual Library. "Manitoba." *Encyclopaedia Judaica*. Farmington Hills: Gale, 2008. Web. 7 February 2015.

Kahneman, Daniel. *Thinking, Fast and Slow*. New York: Farrar, Straus & Giroux Inc, 2011.

Kelley, Ninette and Michael Trbilcock. *The Making of the Mosaic: A History of Canadian Immigration Policy.* Toronto: University of Toronto Press, 1998.

Knowles, Valerie. *Strangers at our Gates: Canadian Immigration and Immigration Policy.* Toronto: Dundurn Press, 2007.

Kogawa, Joy. *Obasan*. Toronto: Penguin Canada, 1983.

Kymlicka, Will. "The Current State of Multiculturalism," Multicultural Directions, special edition of *Canadian Journal for Social Research*. 2:1. Available online at The Current State of Multiculturalism in Canada and Research Themes in Canadian Multiculturalism 2008-10. *Citizenship and Immigration Canada* 2010.

Kymlicka, Will. "The New Debate on Minority Rights," *Multiculturalism and Political Theory*, Ed. A. S. Laden and D. Owen. Cambridge: Cambridge University Press, 2007.

Labour Canada. *2011 Employment Equity Data Report*. 28 November 2014. Web. 10 December 2015.

Labour Canada. *Employment Equity Act: Annual Report 2013*. 11 December 2014. Web. 15 December 2014.

Lautens, Stephen. "How do we get more diversity on the bench when there's no transparency in the appointments process?" *Canadian Lawyer*, 1 September 2014.

Leman, Marc. "Canadian Multiculturalism." Ottawa: Parliament of Canada, 15 February 1999.

Li, Peter. *Destination Canada: Immigration Debate and Issues*. Toronto: Oxford University Press, 2003.

Lupul, Manoly R. *The Politics of Multiculturalism: A Ukrainian Canadian Memoir*. Edmonton: Canadian Institute of Ukrainian Studies Press, 2005.

Manitobia. "Immigration and Settlement: 1870-1919." *Manitobia: Digital Resources on Manitoba History*. n.d. Web. 10 February 2015.

Mansur, Salim. *Delectable Lie - a liberal repudiation of multiculturalism*. Brantford: Mantua Books, 2011.

Markus, Andrew. *Mapping Social Cohesion 2014: National Report*. Caulfield East: Scanlon Foundation, 2014.

Marwah, Inder, Phil Triadafilopoulos and Stephen White. "Immigration, Citizenship, and Canada's New Conservative Party." Rayside, David. *Conservatism in Canada*. Toronto: UofT Press, 2013.

Mooney, Chris. "The Science of Why Cops Shoot Young Black Men." *Mother Jones*, 1 December 2014.

OECD. *Naturalisation: A Passport for the Better Integration of Immigrants?* Paris: OECD 11 March 2011. Web. 10 February 2015.

OECD. *Settling In: OECD Indicators of Immigrant Integration 2012*. Paris: OECD, 3 December 2012. Web. 10 February 2015.

OECD. *PISA 2012 Results in Focus*. Paris: OECD, 2014.

Palmer, Howard and Tamara Jeppson. *Peoples of Alberta: Portraits of Cultural Diversity.* Saskatoon: Western Producer Prairie Books, 1985.

Paquet, Gilles. *Deep Cultural Diversity: A Governance Challenge.* Ottawa: Invenire Press, 2008.

Pendakur, Krishna and Ravi Pendakur. "Colour By Numbers: Minority Earnings in Canada 1996-2006." Metropolis British Columbia Working Paper Series, 11:5 May 2011.

Pew Research. "5 facts about the Muslim population in Europe." 15 January 2015. Web. 12 February 2015.

Pew Research. "A Fragile Rebound for EU Image on Eve of European Parliament Elections." 12 May 2014. Web. 13 February 2015.

Poupeau, Franck. "French sociology under fire: a preliminary diagnosis of the November 2005 'urban riots'." *Riots in France.* 11 June 2006. Web. 16 February 2015.

Public Policy Forum. *Edging Towards Diversity: A Statistical Breakdown of Canada's 41st Parliament, with Comparisons to the 40th Parliament.* Ottawa, June 2011.

Public Service Commission. "Appointments to the Public Service by Employment Equity Designated Group for 2012-2013 – Statistical Update." 10 March 2014. Web. 9 September 2014.

Public Service Commission. "Study on Members of Employment Equity Groups: Chances of Promotion." March 2014. Web. 9 September 2014.

Public Service Commission. "Study on Members of Employment Equity Groups: Perceptions of Merit and Fairness in Staffing Activities." March 2014. Web. 10 September 2014.

Ralston Saul, John. *A Fair Country: Telling Truths about Canada.* Toronto: Penguin Canada, 2008.

Ralston Saul, John. *The Comeback.* Toronto: Penguin Canada, 2014.

RCMP (Members) Employment Equity Report Fiscal Year 2012-2013. Ottawa: September 2013.

Resnick, P. *The European Roots of Canadian Identity.* Peterborough: Broadview Press, 2005.

Richez, Emanuelle. "The Impact of Constitutional Multiculturalism after Three Decades of Existence." Canadian Political Science Association (CPSA) papers 2012. Web. 10 January 2015.

Rienzo, Cinzia and Carlos Vargas-Silva. "Migrants in the UK: An Overview." Oxford: Migration Observatory. 19 December 2014. Web. 23 January 2015.

Roy, Maya, Navjeet Sidhu and Beth Wilson. "The Economy And Resilience of Newcomers (EARN): Exploring Newcomer Entrepreneurship." Toronto: Social Planning Toronto, 2014.

Royal Bank and Ernst & Young. "Outsmarting our brains: Overcoming hidden biases to harness diversity's true potential." 2013. Web. 20 February 2015.

Royal Commission on Bilingualism and Biculturalism, Chapter IV. *The Cultural Contribution of the Other Ethnic Groups.* Ottawa: Queen's Printer, October 23, 1969.

Ryan, Phil. *Multicultiphobia.* Toronto: University of Toronto Press, 2010.

Salanié, Bernard. "The Riots in France: An Economist's View." Riots in France. 11 June 2006. Web. 16 February 2014.

Saunders, Doug. *The Myth of the Muslim Tide.* Toronto: Alfred E. Knopf Canada, 2012.

Sedghi, Ami. "Neighbourhood ethnic segregation: has it decreased?" (Gemma Catney quote). *The Guardian*, 27 February 2013.

Soroka, Stuart, et al. "Capturing change (and stability) in the 2011 campaign." *Policy Options,* June 2011. Web. 18 November 2014.

Statistics Canada. "Factors Associated with Voting." February 2012, updated 13 April 2015. Web. 10 October 2014.

Statistics Canada. "Low income cut-offs (LICO)." 2 May 2013.

Statistics Canada. "Mixed unions in Canada." 2 June 2014. Web. 20 November 2014.

Statistics Canada. "Obtaining Canadian citizenship." 14 January 2014. Web. 12 December 2014.

Statistics Canada. "Police Resources in Canada, 2012." 20 March 2013. Web. 2 March 2015.

Statistics Canada. "Police-reported hate crime in Canada, 2012" and 2007-11 annual reports. 26 June 2014. Web. 9 September 2014.

Statistics Canada. "Population Projections for Canada (2013 to 2063), Provinces and Territories (2013 to 2038)." 17 September 2014.

Steyn, Mark. *Lights Out: Islam, Free Speech And The Twilight Of The West.* Montreal: Stockade Books, 2009.

Taylor, Charles, et al. *Multiculturalism: Examining The Politics of Recognition.* Princeton: Princeton University Press, 1994.

Taylor, Zack, Phil Triadafilopoulos and Christopher Cochrane. "On the Backs of Immigrants? Conservative Politics and New Canadian Voters." CPSA 2012. Web. 15 October 2014.

Tolley, Erin. "Partisan Players Or Political Pawns? Immigrants, Minorities And Conservatives In Canada." Revised Version Of A Paper Presented At The Annual Meeting Of The Atlantic Provinces Political Science Association. Charlottetown, Prince Edward Island. 2014.

Treasury Board Secretariat. *Annual Report to Parliament: Employment Equity in the Public Service of Canada 2012–13.* 1 April 2014. Web. 20 September 2014.

UK Office for National Statistics. "Population By Country of Birth and Nationality tables January 2013 to December 2013." 28 August 2014. Web. 5 February 2015.

United States Census Bureau. "Foreign-Born Population by Sex, Age, and World Region of Birth: 2012." "Population by Sex, Age, Nativity, and U.S. Citizenship Status: 2012." n.d. Web. 10 February 2015.

United States CIA World Fact Book. "United States," 2007 data. Web. 10 February 2015.

Vineberg, Robert. "Immigration and Integration in Canada's Territories." *Integration and Inclusion of Newcomers and Minorities in Canada.* Ed. John Biles et al. Kingston: McGill-Queen's University Press, 2011.

Vineberg, Robert. *Responding to Immigrant Settlement Needs: The Canadian Experience.* Springer, 2012.

Westlake, Daniel Jesse. *Building multiculturalism : the contribution of the Ukrainian Canadian Community to a rethinking of Canadian identity,* MA Thesis. UBC, 2010.

Appendices

APPENDIX A — GLOSSARY

Multidisciplinary research covers a wide spectrum of social, economic, civic and cultural issues that have implications for Canada, in the present and in the future. This annex provides a compilation of terms and their definitions. While these terms and their definitions are neither legal nor government definitions, except where indicated, they aim to increase understanding of current notions and concepts used in multidisciplinary research on Canada. They may also apply to other multicultural societies.

ANTISEMITISM: Antisemitism is a certain perception of Jews that may be expressed as hatred towards Jews. Rhetorical and physical manifestations of antisemitism are directed toward Jewish or non-Jewish individuals and/or their property, or toward Jewish community institutions and religious facilities. From the European Forum on Antisemitism.

BIGOTRY: Dislike or hatred of a person because of her/his membership in a particular group.

BULLYING: Bullying is characterized by repeated physical or verbal interactions that are meant to be hostile, and cause distress. They involve a power differential between bully and victim. Bullying can occur in many forms across the lifespan, from playground interactions to dating violence, workplace harassment and elder abuse.

CANADIAN CHARTER OF RIGHTS AND FREEDOMS: The Canadian Charter of Rights and Freedoms, which forms Part I of Canada's 1982 constitution, sets out most of the rights and freedoms that all governments of Canada must respect. It includes certain fundamental freedoms, such as freedom of religion, expression and association, as well as certain democratic, mobility, legal, equality, linguistic and Aboriginal rights. The Charter also makes reference to the fact that it should be "interpreted in a manner consistent with the preservation and enhancement of the multicultural heritage of Canadians." The courts, not human rights commissions, enforce the Charter.

CULTURAL RELATIVISM: Cultural relativism is a concept that refers to the fact that what is regarded as true, valued or expected in one social system may not be so in another. It is important for several reasons, the most important being that if we are more aware of cultural relativism, we tend to be less blind and arrogant in relation to other societies and less rigid in evaluating the idea of changing our own.[246]

DISCRIMINATION: Discrimination involves formally and informally classifying people into different groups with the intent or effect of according the members of each group unequal treatment, rights or obligations. The criteria delineating the groups determine the kind of discrimination. Types of discrimination include: race (racism), gender (sexism), religion (religious discrimination), height, ethnic background, national origin, disability, or sexual orientation, among others. However, there is also discrimination based on grounds that are not reflected in laws, and these include preference or behaviour, results of IQ testing, age or political views, among others.

Discrimination can either be individual or systemic. For example, past eligibility criteria for police officers and firefighters often included height and other physical conditions that discriminated against minorities and women.

---

[246] From About.Com Sociology.

DIVERSITY: The term diversity, when associated with human diversity, relates to specific social, economic, cultural and political contexts. It is a term that applies to a range of human perspectives, backgrounds and experiences as reflected in characteristics such as age, class, ethnic origin, race, gender, nationality, physical and learning ability, Aboriginal status, region, religion, sexual orientation, marital status, education and employment, as well as cultural values, beliefs and practices. The idea of diversity is passive, while multiculturalism includes active notions of respect, recognition, equality, social justice, integration and participation.

ETHNIC: Of or relating to people grouped according to a single or a combination of common racial, national, tribal, religious, linguistic and/or cultural origin.

ETHNIC ENCLAVE: Ethnic enclave is a neutral term referring to the a geographic concentration of an ethnic group. Unlike ghettos, enclaves tend to exist by conscious choice, not by coercion or poverty. The development of such enclaves is related to the history of immigration and settlement in Canada (i.e., where the Irish, French, Ukrainians, Poles, Germans, etc., chose to settle). Large Canadian cities have neighbourhoods with certain concentrations, such as so-called Chinatowns and Little Italy's, a trend that has expanded to their suburbs.

ETHNIC ORIGIN: In 2011, Canadians reported over 206 ethnic origins, with roots in all parts of the world. These origins were mostly in Europe (English, Irish, French, Polish, Italian, Hungarian, etc.), but also in Asia (Pakistani, Afghan, East Indian, Japanese, etc.), Africa (Ugandan, Nigerian, Ghanaian, Ethiopian, Somali, etc.), Latin America (Chilean, Brazilian, Argentinean, etc.), Caribbean (Haitian, Jamaican, etc.), and the Middle East (Iraqi, Turkish, Egyptian, Iranian, etc.). Ethnic origin is one of the 11 prohibited grounds of discrimination in the Canadian Human Rights Act, and is referred to in the legislation as "national or ethnic origin".

ETHNOCENTRISM: The attitude of prejudice or mistrust towards outsiders that may exist within a social group; a way of perceiving one's own cultural group in relation to others. An attitude that one's own culture, society, or group is inherently superior to all others. Ethnocentrism refers to the inability to appreciate others whose cultural attributes may include a different racial group, ethnic group, religion, morality, or language — hence the tendency of a host or mainstream culture to dismiss or diminish other perspectives.

EUROCENTRISM: The practice of consciously or unconsciously privileging the cultures of Europe over other cultures. Eurocentrism is a belief in the superiority of European-based moral thoughts and practices, and treats them as a norm that provides the standard by which others are judged and interpreted. For example, terms such as Orient, Far East and Middle East locate Asia in relation to Europe. Referring to the Americas as the "New World" and Europe as the "Old World" ignores the ancient civilizations of the Americas. The term "Third World", in turn, suggests a hierarchy. Europe is not alone in this regard; other societies also have their "centrisms."

FOREIGN NATIONAL/FOREIGNER: A person who is neither a Canadian citizen nor a permanent resident. Such a person could be a visitor or a student. The word "foreigner," like its US counterpart "alien national," should be avoided except when used in context (foreign visitors, foreign students, etc.). It has been largely replaced by "international," reflecting globalization.

GHETTOIZATION: The conscious or unconscious phenomenon of segregating members of a group from the larger community, which confines them to specific geographic location, deprives them of the elements of social, economic and political participation of the wider mainstream society, and abandons them to face poverty and need. Ghettoization as a social process is coercive and not solely a question of choice for those who live in the resulting ghettos.

EMPLOYMENT EQUITY: Employment equity encourages the establishment of working conditions that are free of barriers, corrects the conditions of disadvantage in employment and promotes the principle that employment equity requires special measures and the accommodation of differences for the four designated employment equity groups in Canada. The Employment Equity Act governs employment equity in Canada.

HATE SPEECH/HATE CRIMES: In Canada, four specific offences are listed as hate crimes in the Criminal Code: advocating genocide, public incitement of hatred, wilful promotion of hatred and mischief in relation to religious property. In addition, section 718.2(a)(i) of the Criminal Code allows for increased penalties when sentencing any criminal offence (such as assault or mischief) where there is evidence that the offence was motivated by bias, prejudice or hatred toward a particular group.[247]

HISTORICAL RECOGNITION: In general, refers to actions by communities and governments to recognize injustices in the past that involved discrimination against or mistreatment of particular communities. In Canada, the community and national historical recognition programs aimed at increasing awareness of wartime internment measures and immigration restrictions that affected Chinese Canadians, Indo-Canadians, Italian Canadians, Canadian Jews and those interned during World War 1 (primarily Ukrainian Canadians) are notable examples.

HUMAN RIGHTS: Human rights refer to fundamental rights regarded as belonging to all people. Human rights are defined in the Universal Declaration of Human Rights, adopted by the United Nations in 1948. In Canada human rights are entrenched at the federal level in the Charter of Rights and Freedoms and the Canadian Human Rights Act, and in provincial human rights codes.

IDENTITY (CULTURAL, RELIGIOUS): Identity or feeling of belonging to, as part of the self-conception and self-perception of nationality, an ethnicity, religion, social class, generation, locality and any kind of social group that has its own distinct culture. In this way, cultural identity refers both to a characteristic of the individual and to a culturally-identical group, members of which share a cultural identity. Cultural identity is similar to, and overlaps with, identity politics.[248]

IMMIGRANT: At the more technical level, refers to a person who is, or has been, a landed immigrant in Canada. A landed immigrant is a person who has been granted the right to live in Canada permanently by the immigration authorities. Recent immigrant refers to a person who immigrated to Canada in the 5 years preceding a given census, excluding the census year itself (e.g., recent immigrants in 2001 were those who immigrated from 1996 to 2000). In more general use, an immigrant in Canada is someone who was born somewhere else. In contrast, in most European countries the term immigrant may be used to describe those who do not belong to the national ethnic group, even if they were born in the country and hold its citizenship.

---

[247] Statistics Canada Police-Reported Hate Crimes 2011.

[248] Wikipedia.

INTERCULTURALISM: The Quebec variant of multiculturalism, making a stronger reference to the "reigning historical identity" than multiculturalism. Still, like multiculturalism, interculturalism provides a voice for all citizens, whatever their identity. In practice, official Canadian multiculturalism has recently stressed Canadian historical identity and values, thus making the difference even more nuanced. See comparative table in Chapter 9 — Quebec.

INTOLERANCE: An unwillingness to consider, endure and/or respect the beliefs and practices of an individual or group. Racial intolerance refers to an unwillingness to permit equal opportunity and full societal participation to members of other racial groups; religious intolerance is the unwillingness to accept, endure or respect those of other religious beliefs. Intolerance can work in all directions, against all groups.

ISLAMOPHOBIA: Distrust and suspicion of Muslims and Muslim communities in the West, referred to as Islamophobia, is a variant of attitudes of prejudice, hatred and intolerance. While there is no uniformly agreed-upon definition, one of the better ones comes from the Runnymede Trust. It defines Islamophobia as including a view of Islam as a static, separate, inferior, violent and political ideology, with hostility towards Muslims used to justify discrimination (complete definition can be downloaded here).

LABOUR MARKET AVAILABILITY (LMS): According to Statistics Canada, "the workforce availability estimates are derived based on the following principles: First, availability is derived from the part of the population that has recent, relevant experience in their occupation of choice. Second, availability estimates vary according to the skills that employers hire and where their operations are located. Some employers also may have justifiable restrictions on the pools from which they recruit." Furthermore, "The availability benchmarks are derived from estimates of workers with relevant recent experience. As a result, the workforces for women, Aboriginal Peoples, and members of visible minorities were derived from the non-student population aged 15 and over who worked some time within the 17 months previous to the Census."

LOW-INCOME CUT-OFF: Represents an income threshold where a family is likely to spend 20 percent more of its income on food, shelter and clothing than the average family, leaving less income available for other expenses such as health, education, transportation and recreation. LICOs are calculated for families and communities of different sizes.

MARGINALIZATION: This occurs when individuals or groups end up in positions of lesser importance, influence or power because they have been excluded from decision-making or have not had an equal opportunity to participate. Marginalization exists when the voices of a group are separated and contained apart from the problem-solving and central decision-making process of an institution or a society. Marginalization refers to the experience of certain groups that do not have full and equal access to and cannot participate in the social, economic, cultural and political institutions of society. Individuals can also be marginalized.

MEMBERS OF VULNERABLE GROUPS: Groups who are socially excluded from the benefits and privileges enjoyed by the mainstream society, and who therefore are at higher risk of being subjected to discriminatory practices, violence, natural or environmental disasters, or economic hardship. Alternately, during periods of conflict and crisis, this term can refer to members of any group or sector of society such as women, children or the elderly that is at higher risk. Measures to promote social inclusion can be difficult and lengthy.

MINORITIES: Beyond the mathematical definition (numerically smaller), generally used to refer to groups and communities that have less influence, whose members possess different ethnic, racial, religious or linguistic characteristics from the majority "mainstream" population, and who, if only implicitly, maintain a sense of solidarity directed towards preserving their group's culture, traditions, religion or language.

MINORITIES, VISIBLE: According to Statistics Canada, a member of a visible minority group in Canada is someone (other than an Aboriginal person) who is non-white in colour/race, regardless of place of birth. This includes persons from the following visible minority groups or origins: Black, Chinese, Filipino, Japanese, Korean, South Asian/East Indian, Southeast Asian, West Central Asian and Middle Eastern, Non-White Latin American, visible minority, n.i.e. ('n.i.e.' means 'not included elsewhere') and multiple visible minorities. Visible minority persons could be first-generation Canadians (i.e., born outside Canada) or second and more generations (Canadian born). The term 'visible minority' is not a synonym of 'immigrant' and vice versa. See Appendix B for detailed breakdown of broad ethnic origin and visible minority groups.

MULTICULTURALISM (AS POLICY): The federal Canadian Multiculturalism Act affirms the value and dignity of all Canadian citizens regardless of their racial or ethnic origins, their language or their religious affiliation, and promotes attempts to ensure that the public sector reflects Canada's diversity. The Act also confirms the rights of Aboriginal Peoples and the status of Canada's linguistic duality.

Multiculturalism exists in the context of the Canadian Constitution, Charter and laws, reflecting the fundamental belief that all citizens are equal. It recognizes that Canadians have different cultural identities, take pride in their ancestry and feel a sense of belonging to Canada.

Through acceptance and accommodation (within limits), multiculturalism gives Canadians a feeling of security and self-confidence, making them more open to, and accepting of, diverse cultures. Overall, the Canadian experience has shown that multiculturalism encourages racial and ethnic harmony and cross-cultural understanding, and discourages ghettoization, hatred, discrimination and violence.

MULTICULTURALISM (AS IDEOLOGY): Multiculturalism provides a framework for societies with a diversity of racial, ethnic, religious or cultural groups. At a minimum, it promotes tolerance and cross-cultural understanding, but usually also strives to welcome and leverage diversity as an asset to society. It has strong equality goals, which it works toward by fostering full participation in all aspects of Canadian society for all Canadians, regardless of their background and culture. Multiculturalism recognizes that diversity is a fundamental characteristic of Canadian society and of our national character.

But multiculturalism is not "anything goes": it is situated within the Canadian legal framework, among others.

MULTICULTURALISM (AS DEMOGRAPHIC REALITY): Multiculturalism is used to characterize a society with ethnic or cultural heterogeneity. It has been used in Canada as an attribute of Canadian society for at least the last four decades. Canada has become a multi-ethnic, multi-racial and multi-religious society, and is expected to become more diverse in the coming decade. Statistics Canada predicts that visible minorities will represent 20 to 25 percent of the population of Canada in 2017, and religious minorities will represent 10 to 12 percent by the same date.

NORMS/VALUES: Norms are rules for accepted and expected behaviour, prescribing "proper" behaviour. Values are culturally defined standards held by individuals, groups or organizations about what is desirable, proper, beautiful and good (or bad). They serve as broad guidelines for social life. Many norms and values are incorporated into laws. Norms should not be confused with national values, such as respect for law and order or the embrace of parliamentary democracy, which exist at the level of political culture. Part of the normal dynamic is the challenging of norms and values, often on religious grounds, which can either be accommodated or not, depending on the balance between competing interests and rights.

PERMANENT RESIDENTS: A permanent resident is someone who has been given permanent resident status by immigrating to Canada, but is not a Canadian citizen. Permanent residents are citizens of other countries. A person in Canada temporarily, like a student or foreign worker, is not a permanent resident.

PLURALISM: An approach in which some degree of cultural, ethnic, linguistic, religious or other group distinction is maintained and valued by groups and individuals. This is a concept used to express the notion of a society in which groups can remain voluntarily apart from each other when it comes to traditions, cultural practices and beliefs, while sharing a set of commonly held principles and a consensus on social and political values. Pluralism can either be relatively shallow (cultural recognition, but common institutions, like public education) or deeper (a larger number of separate institutions, like faith-based schools).

PREJUDICE: Prejudice is an unjustified and usually negative attitude directed toward others because of their social category or group memberships. Similar to intolerance.

RACIAL DISCRIMINATION: According to the International Convention on the Elimination of All Forms of Racial Discrimination (1965), to which Canada is a signatory, the term racial discrimination refers to any distinction, exclusion, restriction or preference based on race, colour, descent, or national or ethnic origin that has had the purpose or effect of nullifying or impairing the recognition, enjoyment or exercise, on an equal footing, of human rights and fundamental freedoms in the political, economic, social, cultural or any other field of public life.

RACIAL PROFILING: Judgments about an individual or group based solely on ethnicity or skin colour; racial profiling also refers to actions based on such judgments. Often used in a law enforcement context, the Ontario Human Rights Commission defines racial profiling as "any action taken for reasons of safety, security or public protection that relies on stereotypes about race rather than on reasonable suspicion, to single out an individual for greater security or different treatment".

RACIALIZED COMMUNITIES: Terms used as a replacement for visible minorities, taking into account that "race" is a social construct of differences among people (e.g., accent or manner of speech, name, clothing, diet, beliefs and practices, leisure preferences, places of origin). Racialization is "the process by which societies construct races as real, different and unequal in ways that matter to economic, political and social life."[249]

RADICALIZATION/EXTREMISM: The word "radicalization" has many definitions in intelligence and law enforcement communities. The FBI defines it as "the process by which individuals come

---

[249] Racial discrimination, race and racism, Ontario Human Rights Commission, Web 10 October 2014.

to believe their engagement in or facilitation of non-state violence to achieve social and political change is necessary and justified." German law enforcement and intelligence agencies describe it as the "turning of individuals or groups to an extremist mind-set and course of action and the growing readiness to facilitate or engage in nondemocratic methods up to the execution of violence to achieve their goals."[250]

REASONABLE ACCOMMODATION: Reasonable accommodation results in greater equality of opportunity and participation in employment, services and housing by persons with special needs.

Reasonable accommodation often involves a simple and inexpensive change to how something is typically done, which takes into account a need a person or group has that is based on a protected characteristic. An example is an employer allowing an employee to take a day's leave to observe a religious holiday. An accommodation is "reasonable" when there is an adequate process of accommodation, and the effort and measures taken are sufficient.[251]

SEGREGATION: The economic, physical, political, and social separation of diverse groups or individuals, particularly referring to ideological and structural barriers to civil liberties, equal opportunity and participation by minorities within a majority ethnic, linguistic, racial, religious or social group.

SOCIAL EXCLUSION: Social exclusion refers to multi-dimensional disadvantages of substantial duration that involve dissociation from the major social and occupational milieu of society. It is a shorthand term for what can happen to people or areas from a combination of linked problems such as unemployment, poor skills, low incomes, poor housing, high crime, bad health, family breakdown and/or racism.

SOCIAL INTEGRATION: Integration in the context of multiculturalism is not equivalent to assimilation. Social integration refers to the creation of a society that respects cultural diversity and at the same time promotes the goal of equal opportunity across private and public domains.

STEREOTYPE: Stereotypes are false or generalized conceptions of groups of people, which results in the unconscious or conscious categorization of each member of that group, without regard for individual differences. Stereotyping may relate to race or age; ethnic, linguistic, religious, geographical, or national groups; social, marital or family status; sexual orientation; physical, developmental or mental abilities; and/or gender. Stereotypes can be positive or negative.

TEMPORARY RESIDENTS: Includes those staying in Canada on a temporary basis, either as workers, live-in caregivers or international students.

TOLERANCE: The term tolerance suggests agreement to disagree and acceptance that others have different opinions or preferences that may differ from our own. While tolerance is an element of respect, it has been considered in the multiculturalism discourse as a passive, or even grudging, acceptance of diversity (e.g., quiet resentment of the presence of members of visible minority or Aboriginal groups in the workplace).

---

[250] FBI Law Enforcement Bulletin September 2011.

[251] Manitoba Human Rights Commission.

WHITE POWER: Originally coined in 1966 by American Nazi Party leader George Lincoln Rockwell, and used by White nationalists to "argue that every nationality feels a natural affection for its own kind." They advocate racial self-preservation and claim that culture is a product of race. Has also been used by some to denote the dominant social and economic positions held by "whites" ("white priviledge"). Multidisciplinary research covers a wide spectrum of social, economic, civic, and cultural issues that have implications for Canada, in the present and in the future. This annex provides a compilation of terms and their definitions. While these terms and their definitions are neither legal nor government definitions, except where indicated, they aim to increase understanding current notions and concepts used in multidisciplinary research on Canada. They may also apply to other multicultural societies.

APPENDIX B — ETHNIC ORIGIN AND VISIBLE MINORITY DEFINITIONS[252]

Visible minority refers to whether a person belongs to a visible minority group as defined by the Employment Equity Act and, if so, the visible minority group to which the person belongs. The Employment Equity Act defines visible minorities as "persons, other than Aboriginal Peoples, who are non-Caucasian in race or non-white in colour". The visible minority population consists mainly of the following groups: Chinese, South Asian, Black, Arab, West Asian, Filipino, Southeast Asian, Latin American, Japanese and Korean.

"**Not a visible minority**" is defined as: Includes respondents who reported 'Yes' to the Aboriginal identity question (Question 18) as well as respondents who were not considered to be members of a visible minority group. In this book I use "non-visible minorities" for readability reasons and the "Not VisMin" short-form for charts.

Ethnic origins are defined as follows, with linkage to Visible Minority where appropriate.

North American Aboriginal origins: First Nations (North American Indian), Inuit, and Métis.

First Nations and Métis form about 95 percent

Other North American origins: Acadian, American, Canadian, New Brunswicker, Newfoundlander, Nova Scotian, Ontarian, Québécois, Other North American origins, n.i.e.

Canadians form 95 percent.

EUROPEAN ORIGINS:
British Isles origins: Channel Islander, Cornish, English, Irish, Manx, Scottish, Welsh, British Isles origins, n.i.e.

English, Scottish and Irish form the vast majority.

French origins: Alsatian, Breton, French

Western European origins (except French origins): Austrian, Belgian, Dutch, Flemish, Frisian, German, Luxembourger, Swiss, Western European origins, n.i.e.

German and Dutch form the vast majority.

Northern European origins (except British Isles origins): Danish, Finnish, Icelandic, Norwegian, Swedish, Northern European origins, n.i.e.

Norwegian, Swedish and Danish are the three top origins.

Eastern European origins: Bulgarian, Byelorussian, Czech, Czechoslovakian, n.o.s., Estonian, Hungarian, Latvian, Lithuanian Moldovan, Polish, Romanian, Russian, Slovak, Ukrainian, Eastern European origins, n.i.e.

Ukrainian, Polish, and Russian are the three top origins.

---

[252] From Statistics Canada

Southern European origins: Albanian, Bosnian, Croatian, Cypriot, Greek, Italian, Kosovar, Macedonian, Maltese, Montenegrin, Portuguese, Serbian, Sicilian, Slovenian, Spanish, Yugoslavian, n.o.s., Southern European origins, n.i.e.

Italian, Portuguese and Spanish are the three top origins.

Other European origins: Basque, Jewish, Roma (Gypsy), Slavic, n.o.s., Other European origins, n.i.e.

Jewish is over 80 percent.

Caribbean origins: Antiguan, Bahamian, Barbadian, Bermudan, Carib, Cuban, Dominican, Grenadian, Haitian, Jamaican, Kittitian/Nevisian, Martinican, Montserratan, Puerto Rican, St. Lucian, Trinidadian/Tobagonian, Vincentian/Grenadinian, West Indian, n.o.s., Caribbean origins, n.i.e.

Jamaican, Haitian and Trinidadian/Tobagonian are the three top origins. Covered by Black for visible minority.

Latin, Central and South American origins: Aboriginal from Central/South America (except Maya), Argentinian, Belizean, Bolivian, Brazilian, Chilean, Colombian, Costa Rican, Ecuadorian, Guatemalan, Guyanese, Hispanic, Honduran, Maya, Mexican, Nicaraguan, Panamanian, Paraguayan, Peruvian, Salvadorean, Uruguayan, Venezuelan, Latin, Central and South American origins, n.i.e.

Mexican, Columbian and Guyanese are the three top origins.

AFRICAN ORIGINS

Central and West African origins: Akan, Angolan, Ashanti, Beninese, Burkinabe, Cameroonian, Chadian, Congolese, Gabonese, Gambian, Ghanaian, Guinean, Ibo, Ivorian, Liberian, Malian, Nigerian, Peulh, Senegalese, Sierra Leonean, Togolese, Yoruba, Central and West African origins, n.i.e.

Nigerian, Ghanian and Congolese are the three top origins.

Southern and East African origins: Afrikaner, Amhara, Bantu, n.o.s., Burundian, Eritrean, Ethiopian, Harari, Kenyan, Malagasy, Mauritian, Oromo, Rwandan, Seychellois, Somali, South African, Tanzanian, Tigrian, Ugandan, Zambian, Zimbabwean, Zulu, Southern and East African origins, n.i.e.

Somali, South African and Ethiopian are the three top origins.

Other African origins: Black, n.o.s., Other African origins, n.i.e.

For visible minority, most covered by Black category (e.g., apart from Africaners, white Zimbabweans etc)

North African origins: Algerian, Berber, Coptic, Dinka, Egyptian, Libyan, Maure, Moroccan, Sudanese, Tunisian, North African origins, n.i.e.

Egyptian, Moroccan and Algerian are the three top origins.

For visible minority, covered under Arab.

ASIAN ORIGINS

West Central Asian and Middle Eastern origins: Afghan, Arab, n.o.s., Armenian, Assyrian, Azerbaijani, Georgian, Iranian, Iraqi, Israeli, Jordanian, Kazakh, Kurd, Kuwaiti, Lebanese, Palestinian, Pashtun, Saudi Arabian, Syrian, Tajik, Tatar, Turk, Uighur, Uzbek, Yemeni, West Central Asian and Middle Eastern origins, n.i.e.

Lebanese, Iranian and Afghan are the three top origins.

For visible minority, West Asian and Arab are separated out into different categories.

South Asian origins: Bangladeshi, Bengali, East Indian, Goan, Gujarati, Kashmiri, Nepali, Pakistani, Punjabi, Sinhalese, Sri Lankan, Tamil, South Asian origins, n.i.e.

East Indian, Pakistani and Sri Lankan are the three top origins.

Same definition used for visible minority.

East and Southeast Asian origins: Burmese, Cambodian (Khmer), Chinese, Filipino, Hmong, Indonesian, Japanese, Korean, Laotian, Malaysian, Mongolian, Singaporean, Taiwanese, Thai, Tibetan, Vietnamese, East and Southeast Asian origins, n.i.e.

Chinese, Filipino and Vietnamese are the three top origins, followed by Korean and Japanese.

For visible minority, Chinese, Filipino, Korean and Japanese are separated out, with Southeast Asian referring to remaining groups.

Other Asian origins: Other Asian origins, n.i.e.

Oceania origins: Australian, New Zealander, Pacific Islands origins, Fijian, Hawaiian, Maori, Polynesian, n.o.s., Samoan, Pacific Islands origins, n.i.e.

Australian, Pacific Islands and New Zealander are the three top origins.

Other (for Visible Minority: Includes Visible Minority, n.i.e. (Not Identified Elsewhere), and Multiple Visible Minority

APPENDIX C — METHODOLOGY

General

This book relies principally on the Statistics Canada 2011 National Household Survey, government employment equity reports and operational statistics from Citizenship and Immigration Canada. The methodology followed in this book emulates standard analysis and procedures already established in the field by academics, researchers, and others. Visible minority, ethnic origin, and religious affiliation lenses are used.

In contrast to the previous mandatory Censuses, the NHS is voluntary. The 2006 Census had a response rate of 96.5 percent. The NHS overall response rate was 68 percent, prompting Statistics Canada to issue a note on the limitations of the NHS, particularly for small communities. Given that this book does not focus on smaller communities, this is not a major issue, as most of the provinces and communities analyzed have a non-response rate of between 25-30 percent. This is much higher than for a Census, but well below the threshold at which Statistics Canada does not publish data (50 percent). See NHS User Guide: Chapter 6 – Data dissemination for NHS standard products.

The NHS was conducted between May and August 2011.

Major events, both domestic and international, can influence how people report their ethnic origin. During the time of the NHS, major Canadian events included the aftermath of the May 2nd Federal Election (Harper majority government, resignation of Gilles Duceppe and Michael Ignatieff, and physical decline and eventual death of Jack Layton), the British Columbia sales tax referendum and the visit of the Duke and Duchess of Cambridge. World events included the killing of Osama Bin Laden, the volcano in Iceland shutting down air traffic, the ongoing US debt crisis, the "Arab Spring" and armed conflict particularly in Libya and Syria and the Breivik killings in Norway.

With the exception of the "Immigrants as a Percentage of the Canadian Population — Since Confederation" and "Evolution of Canadian Diversity" charts, this book does not compare Census data with NHS data. The "Evolution of Canadian Diversity" chart shows considerable variation between the 2006 Census and the 2011 NHS with respect to those of "Other European" origin. The projections for 2017 and 2031 are taken from the relevant Statistics Canada studies and, like all projections, are illustrative. Given that Statistics Canada projections use a number of different scenarios, I have used the reference scenario for the chart.

Ethnic origin has the advantage that it more accurately reflects the diversity of Canada, capturing both visible minorities and the diversity among Canadians of European origin. It also captures the reality that many Canadians have multiple ethnic origins (42 percent). But ethnic origin tends to be less precise given that many identify multiple ethnic origins, compared to visible minorities who largely identify only with one visible minority group.

Moreover, individuals may self-identify differently depending on current events. Such "ethnic mobility" could happen, for example, during the World Cup or the Olympics when Canadian audiences cheer for a particular team or country.

"Ethnic transfer" can occur between generations, as more recent generations may identify less with the ethnic origin of their ancestors.

Ethnic origin was used in lieu of "visible minority" where needed to reflect the full diversity of Canada. However, visible minorities were considered where appropriate — in economic indicators, employment equity reports and parliamentary representation, for example. Apart from the demographic overviews, the categories of "Visible Minority n.i.e." (not identified elsewhere) or "Multiple Visible Minority" were not used, as these two categories together only account for under five percent of the total visible minority population.

The one problematic ethnic origin category was "North American," 95 percent who identify themselves as "Canadian" or "Canadien." 44.8 percent of those with Canadian/Canadien ancestry have multiple ethnic origins. Only three percent of those identifying their ethnic origin as "Canadian" are first-generation.

43.1 percent of those identifying themselves as Canadian/Canadien live in Quebec, compared to 27.6 percent who live in Ontario, indicating the degree to which Canadian/Canadien is linked to a Quebec sense of identity.

Religion statistics are from the NHS. Aboriginal spirituality has only been included in the demographic data, as the absolute numbers are too small (less than five percent of the total Aboriginal population) to be meaningful for economic and social outcomes analysis. "Other religions" also have not been included as they only account for 0.4 percent of the total population. For the provincial and municipal charts, the focus is on minority religions, not including Christians or "no religious affiliation," given that these are the focus of most accommodation and other debates.

Immigration statistics are taken from Citizenship and Immigration Canada's CIC's Facts and Figures series or obtained directly from the Department. For the Canada overview, country of birth has been mapped against broad ethnic origin categories, which may overstate some ethnic origins (i.e., American and various European origins may include those of other ethnicities).

For provincial immigration (numbers of Permanent Residents), source countries (where the application was made) have been used, not country of birth. The number of "West Asian and Mid-East" may be overstated given the large number of expatriates working in the region; while some are from the region (e.g., Palestinians, Lebanese, Syrians), others are not (e.g., Pakistanis and other Asians).

Economic

For income, the book focusses on unemployment rates, median incomes and percentage Low-Income Cut-Off (LICO) before tax as the main indicators.

LICO is adjusted on the basis of seven family sizes and five different populations of the area of residence. The baseline dates from 1992, when average families spent 43 percent of their income on food, shelter and clothing. The LICO is 20 percentage points above this average.[253]

While LICO is not a perfect measure of inequality and low income (or "straightened circumstances," as Statistics Canada puts it) given that it has not been rebased since 1992 and

---

[253] "Low income cut-offs," *Statistics Canada*, 2 May 2013.

thus arguably understates poverty, other indices (e.g., Low Income Measures, Market Based Measures) are less well-known. Comparing LICO provides insight into relative low-income levels, making it adequate for my purposes.

I chose to use the LICO rate before tax, rather than after tax, as the latter understates poverty (by reducing the low-income threshold).[254]

In order to reduce the impact of differences in language, Canadian experience and education, the book concentrates on second-generation working-age adults, defined as between 25 and 64 years old. First-generation Canadians are used for comparative purposes. For visible minorities, only identified visible minority groups are analyzed — not "multiple visible minorities" or "not otherwise identified," since these last two categories comprised less than four percent of visible minorities in Canada. The analysis separates out first- and second-generation immigrants and also breaks down some outcomes by gender. Second-generation university educated Canadians aged 25-34 are also assessed in order to to provide a better sense of how younger and more educated second-generation immigrants are doing.

Regression analysis was considered to isolate more clearly some of the factors that impact on different economic outcomes, but the approximation used in this book was judged sufficient for the purpose of illustrating variations in outcomes and suggesting areas for further work.

Earlier studies based on Censuses from 2006 and earlier on income disparities between foreign and Canadian-born residents, and between visible minorities and non-visible minorities, include those by Miles Corak (Immigration in the Long Run: The Education and Earnings Mobility of Second-Generation Canadians),[255] Krishna and Ravi Pendakur (Colour By Numbers: Minority Earnings in Canada 1996-2006)[256] and Sheila Block and Grace-Edward Galabuzi (Canada's Colour Coded Labour Market: The Gap For Racialized Workers).[257]

Corak notes that second-generation immigrants in general (men and women) are better-educated than those with Canadian-born parents. In most communities, Canadian-born children of immigrants with relatively low levels of schooling attain more years of schooling than the Canadian-born average. Corak's analysis confirms that second-generation members of most communities do better than their parents and as well or better than those with Canadian-born parents (this is particularly true of women).

Pendakur and Pendakur use regression analysis to isolate the factor of ethnic origin and visible minority status, showing the persistence of earning gaps between visible minorities and non-visible minorities. They found more variation among men than women. Visible minority men, in particular, have a significant earnings gap compared to non-visible minority men.

---

[254] For a discussion of the impact of the various indices, before and after tax, see Richard Shillington, "Defining Poverty and Determining the Number Poor Long-Term Trends," Tristat Resources, 2011.

[255] IRPP Choices, Vol. 14 No. 13, October 1988.

[256] Metropolis British Columbia Working Paper, No. 11-05, May 2011.

[257] Canadian Centre for Policy Alternatives and The Wellesley Institute, March 2011

Block and Galabuzi paint a bleaker picture of an enduring gap between visible minorities and non-visible minorities, although this gap narrows for the second-generation and virtually disappears for the third generation and beyond.

All studies largely confirm the general patterns of this book's analysis in terms of an enduring — but lessening — gap over generations, with some communities doing better than others.

I have provided a similar analysis based on religion, and which also correlates visible minorities with religious affiliations, has been conducted.

For seniors, government transfer rates refer to individual rather than household transfers. Taxation is also for individuals.

For employment equity in the federally regulated sector (i.e., banking, communications, transport), the Treasury Board Secretariat's Employment Equity Act: Annual Report 2013, using 2011 labour market availability (LMA), has been the basis of my analysis. "Persons with disabilities" has not been used as a comparator given the particular challenges of that group compared to the others. Nor have I included the "other" category, due to its diverse nature. Given, however, that many of the companies in question are resource-based, Aboriginal employment is higher than labour market availability.

Women and Aboriginal Peoples have been used as the main comparator groups for visible minorities, as well as men in some cases. As none of the reports separate out male and female visible minorities from non-visible minority men and women (the same is true for Aboriginal people), the comparisons are valid but have some margin of error. For the federally regulated sectors, this likely means an underestimation of the various indicators, as 17 percent of men are Visible Minority, and 21 percent of women are Visible Minority.

2011 labour market availability comes from Labour Canada's 2011 Employment Equity Data Report.

Social

I have used NHS data on education levels separated out by visible minorities, non-European ethnic origins and religion, also allowing for analysis of gender differences.

Hate crimes statistics are from the separate StatsCan Police-Reported Hate Crimes 2012 analysis. Data used has been averaged over the five-year period of this survey. This has been supplemented with information from the CIC Annual Tracking Survey — Winter 2010 Final Report.

To gauge the representativeness of public services (healthcare, social services, and education), I used NHS data (covering individuals aged 15 and over) on the national and provincial levels, broken down by visible minority group (in turn broken down by gender). I have used regional Federally Regulated Sector LMAs for comparative purposes.

I used NHS data at the federal riding level (from both the 2008 and 2015 elections) as a proxy for evaluating ethnic community concentration. In so doing, I used the framework developed by Dan Hiebert ("Exploring Minority Enclave Areas in Montréal, Toronto, and Vancouver," CIC, March 2009), who in turn adapted methodology from Poulson, Johnston and Forrest (2001), which was adapted for Canada by Walks and Bourne (2006).

I created one new category: ridings with less than five percent diversity. I introduced this category to capture the many rural ridings that have limited diversity.

Three different views are presented: ethnic origin (to capture historic waves of immigration), visible minorities (to capture post 1970s immigration) and religious minorities (to provide context for current debates).

Political

The NHS Citizenship data table provides the basis for the 85.6 percent overall naturalization rate, also offering breakdowns for three different groups: those with Canadian citizenship only, those without Canadian citizenship and those who are dual nationals. The related analytical note, Obtaining Canadian citizenship, provides some useful insights and captures recent trends of declining naturalization.

This has been supplemented with CIC operational statistics. Looking at citizenship take-up rates, the percentage of "Permanent Residency Granted Date to Citizenship Case Signed Date," using 2008 as the last year when most Permanent Residents will have applied for citizenship, has been used. Historic data shows that between 75-80 percent of Permanent Residents have their case signed off within six years. This somewhat distorts the picture, as as those who became Permanent Residents in 2008 had six years to become citizens, those from 2007 had seven years, and those in 2006 had eight years. However, the difference between those permanent residents that become citizens after six and subsequent years is relatively small: 3.5 percent for the seventh year, and additional 4.3 percent for the eighth year, after which the yearly increase in citizenship take-up is two percent or less. The overall decline from 79 percent for 2000 Permanent Residents to 49 percent for 2008 Permanent Residents cannot be explained by this factor.

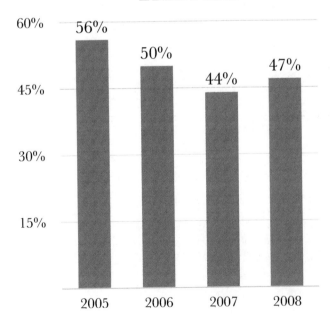

IMMIGRANTS WITH CITIZENSHIP SIX YEARS SINCE LANDING IN CANADA BY LANDING YEAR

CIC has also analyzed the percentage of immigrants who obtain citizenship within six years of landing in Canada by landing year (to remove any distortions caused by immigrants who have more time in Canada than others). This analysis shows a similar decline with an uptick in 2008, likely reflecting the 2014 push to address the citizenship application backlog.

CIC operational statistics were also used to assess the impact of the changes to the citizenship study guide and citizenship test. Citizenship test pass rates and acquisition by country of birth were examined, and countries of birth were made to line up with ethnic origin categories. The data has been separated for the period before 2009 and the period following, when the new study guide, *Discover Canada*, and related test were introduced, and then augmented with up-front language competency requirements and more anti-fraud measures.

For data on the federal parliament, my main source was the IRPP study, Edging Towards Diversity: A Statistical Breakdown of Canada's 41st Parliament, with Comparisons to the 40th Parliament (June 2011), which I compared with population figures from the 2011 NHS. For voting patterns, I used the Statistics Canada analytical note, Factors Associated with Voting.

As a benchmark for representation, I used the total number of visible minorities, adjusted for the number who are Canadian citizens (78.3 percent, data table 99-010-X2011038). I obtained this data from Immigration and Ethnocultural Diversity in Canada and Obtaining Canadian citizenship. As a result of my adjustment, the benchmark figure for visible minority political representation is 15.0 percent, lower than the total visible minority population (which includes non-citizens) of 19.1 percent.

I derived my data on provincial representation through a mix of provincial legislature websites and provincial party websites. I determined visible minority status based on a mix of name and head shot — an inexact method, but comparable to that used by the Institute for Research on Public Policy federally.

For 2015 electoral ridings, the appropriate NHS data table was Canada, provinces, territories and federal electoral districts (2013 Representation Order), with ridings sorted by percentage of visible minorities, correlated with ethnic origin and religion.

My public service employment equity data is taken from Appointments to the Public Service by Employment Equity Designated Group for 2012-2013 – Statistical Update and the TBS Annual Report to Parliament: Employment Equity in the Public Service of Canada 2012–13 for the public service.

Labour market availability from Labour Canada's 2011 Employment Equity Data Report, at 17.8 percent, was not used, and the the most recent report, Employment Equity in the Public Service of Canada 2013–14 did not update the 2006 LMA for the public service. Instead, I used the number of visible minorities who are citizens (15.0 percent), which is a more conservative figure yet realistic figure given that preference is given to citizens over permanent residents.

Public service reporting is less comprehensive than the federally regulated sectors. There is no published information on the gender breakdown for visible minorities (and Aboriginal people), and there are no published statistics on the number of male (or female) visible minorities. This means that use of women (or men) as comparator groups is more approximate than exact, but it does capture the general picture.

Provincial data is taken from the relevant provincial public sector reports.

I supplemented this data with NHS employment in the federal, provincial and municipal public services, for those aged 15 or over, broken down by visible minority groupings to provide more granularity than in the formal employment equity reports. Federal statistics include the broader public service, minus the defence sector.

I used the RCMP (Members) Employment Equity Report Fiscal Year 2012-2013 and the Canadian Armed Forces Employment Equity Report 2012-13 (neither are published on websites but are available from the Library of Parliament).

For police services, the Statistics Canada <u>Police resources in Canada, 2013</u> provided limited high level information on representation, which I compared to overall 2011 LMA. This has been supplemented by statistics obtained from the Toronto, Montreal and Vancouver police forces.

Data and Analysis Gaps

In reviewing the data, a number of gaps emerged. The most obvious, of course, was the poorer quality of data obtained with the voluntary National Household Survey compared to that of the previous mandatory census.

With respect to employment equity reports, the Treasury Board of Canada Secretariat (TBS) annual report would benefit from separating out gender from other equity groups, i.e., being able to compare visible minorities, Aboriginal people and persons with disabilities by gender compared to men and women who are not part of these employment equity groups (Labour Canada does this for the federally-regulated sectors). It would also be helpful, although not necessary, for TBS to have the key data — representation, hiring, promotions and separations — in a 25-year historical time series to make it easier for researchers to examine trends. TBS should also look at NHS public administration data to see how this can supplement the direct input from departments.

The usefulness of using a calculated labour market availability (LMA) rather than just the general demographic data to indicate how representative public services are of the publics they serve is questionable. The main advantage of using the LMA is that representation looks better than it is, if the overall goal is to have public services fully reflective of the population.

Police forces in Canada's major centres need to collect better data regarding employment equity, and automatically publish this information, ideally in a more consistent manner across police forces. This remains a major gap because of mixed reporting by police forces and the apparent cancellation of the Statistics Canada Police Resources in Canada survey.

There is no reliable consolidated data on visible minority representation in the judiciary. While there is no such data for political representation either (MPs and their provincial counterparts), it is relatively easy to compile this information from names and head shots, which is not the case for the judiciary.

With respect to police-reported hate crimes, should the current funding for Statistics Canada not continue, alternatives should be found to ensure that governments and others do not have to rely on anecdotes or reporting by individual groups.

While the data shows a decline in citizenship take-up rates and different outcomes for visible minorities compared to non-visible minorities for the citizenship test, there is little data explaining the reasons. CIC needs to monitor recent trends in citizenship take-up — by immigration class, gender, labour force participation, and ethnic origin or visible minority status — to understand better the factors at work and identify whether policy responses are necessary. The same kind of analysis has to be applied to citizenship test pass rates. In general, CIC needs to ensure that its various databases and statistics can be easily correlated with ethnic origin to make possible the application of a diversity lens, just as it currently applies gender-based analysis.

Another cross-cutting gap is the need for more attitudinal research. Angus-Reid's 2015 poll on religious beliefs and practices provides useful insights into the religiosity of believers, not just formal adherence. The forthcoming General Social Survey and World Values Survey will provide useful information in a variety of areas. Areas where attitudinal research is needed include, among others:

- Measuring interaction between and among different ethnic groups;

- Relative weight of country of origin and Canadian identity or feeling of belonging;

- Value and benefits of citizenship given declining take-up; and,

- More consistent tracking of general support for immigration, citizenship and multiculturalism, along with greater clarity on what that support includes and what it does not.

A more ambitious agenda of addressing data gaps would consider conducting an updated version of the 2003 Ethnic Diversity Survey, which provided a wealth of data to better understand how people's backgrounds affect their participation in the social, economic and cultural life of Canada and how Canadians of different ethnic backgrounds interpret and report their ethnicity.

APPENDIX D — CANADIAN ETHNIC ORIGINS

Ethnic Origin	Population	Multiple Origins
Canadian	10,563,805	44.8%
English	6,509,500	79.8%
French	5,065,690	77.0%
Scottish	4,714,970	88.5%
Irish	4,544,870	88.9%
German	3,203,330	81.0%
Italian	1,488,425	52.9%
Chinese	1,487,580	18.6%
First Nations	1,369,115	62.2%
Ukrainian	1,251,170	77.9%
East Indian	1,165,145	21.1%
Dutch	1,067,245	72.1%
Polish	1,010,705	74.8%
Filipino	662,600	23.6%
British Isles, n.i.e.	576,030	77.8%
Russian	550,520	80.5%
Welsh	458,705	93.7%
Norwegian	452,705	90.3%
Métis	447,655	84.8%
Portuguese	429,850	41.8%
American	372,575	91.2%
Spanish	368,305	81.9%
Swedish	341,845	92.4%
Hungarian	316,765	74.6%
Jewish	309,650	62.7%
Jamaican	256,915	44.4%
Greek	252,960	44.0%
Vietnamese	220,425	28.6%
Romanian	204,625	59.4%
Danish	203,080	84.6%
Austrian	197,990	88.4%

Ethnic Origin	Population	Multiple Origins
Québécois	193,885	34.5%
Lebanese	190,275	39.6%
Other African, n.i.e.	177,195	65.4%
Belgian	176,615	81.5%
Korean	168,890	8.6%
Iranian	163,290	19.7%
Pakistani	155,310	29.4%
Swiss	146,830	82.5%
Central and West African	142,780	25.9%
Sri Lankan	139,415	22.1%
Haitian	137,995	21.1%
Finnish	136,215	80.0%
Acadian	115,895	76.1%
Croatian	114,880	54.9%
Japanese	109,740	50.0%
Mexican	96,055	53.5%
Czech	94,805	76.6%
Arab, n.o.s.	94,640	39.0%
Icelandic	94,205	90.3%

APPENDIX E — BRITISH COLUMBIA TOP 50 ETHNIC ORIGINS

Ethnic Origin	Population	Multiple Origins
English	1,199,955	51.2%
Scottish	833,290	51.4%
Canadian	826,340	50.1%
Irish	643,470	52.6%
German	567,670	51.1%
Chinese	464,805	52.6%
French	369,100	52.3%
East Indian	274,060	50.0%
Dutch	204,700	50.4%
Ukrainian	203,585	52.2%
First Nations	202,530	51.7%
Italian	150,660	49.8%
Filipino	135,990	57.0%
Norwegian	134,430	51.5%
Polish	133,505	51.9%
Russian	120,835	52.0%
British Isles origins, n.i.e	107,925	51.8%
Welsh	107,780	52.8%
Swedish	106,085	53.1%
American	77,955	51.5%
Métis	70,200	52.2%
Spanish	60,175	54.9%
Danish	57,765	50.9%
Korean	55,450	52.8%
Hungarian	51,025	50.6%
Japanese	45,895	56.5%
Austrian	45,675	51.3%
Iranian	39,285	49.7%
Portuguese	36,550	50.3%
Vietnamese	35,855	52.7%
Jewish	31,865	49.5%

Ethnic Origin	Population	Multiple Origins
Finnish	31,610	51.0%
Swiss	29,705	51.4%
Romanian	28,330	51.0%
Punjabi	24,240	50.0%
Icelandic	22,600	51.8%
Greek	20,075	48.6%
Croatian	19,855	49.2%
Czech	19,570	49.5%
Belgian	19,055	50.5%
Pacific Islands origins	17,695	52.1%
Taiwanese	17,210	52.1%
Mexican	15,950	50.6%
Other African origins, n.i.e.	14,505	50.6%
Fijian	13,905	51.4%
Australian	12,760	50.3%
Northern European origins, n.i.e.	12,080	48.7%
Other European origins, n.i.e.	11,375	45.2%
South African	10,335	52.4%
Serbian	10,155	48.9%
Slovak	9,950	52.3%

The following table provides the top 20 ethnicities for the major cities of British Columbia.

Vancouver CMA	Vancouver	Surrey	Burnaby	Richmond	Abbotsford
2,280,695	590,205	463,340	220,260	189,305	130,950
English	Chinese	East Indian	Chinese	Chinese	English
Chinese	English	English	English	English	East Indian
Scottish	Scottish	Canadian	Canadian	Canadian	Canadian
Canadian	Canadian	Scottish	Scottish	Scottish	German
Irish	Irish	Irish	East Indian	Filipino	Scottish
East Indian[22]	German	German	Irish	East Indian	Irish
German	Filipino	Chinese	Filipino	Irish	Dutch
French	French	Filipino	German	German	French
Filipino	East Indian	French	Italian	French	Ukrainian
Ukrainian	Italian	Ukrainian	French	Japanese	Russian
Italian	Ukrainian	Dutch	Korean	Ukrainian	Norwegian
Dutch	Polish	Punjabi	Ukrainian	Russian	Polish
Polish	Vietnamese	Polish	Russian	Spanish	Swedish
Russian	British Isles, n.i.e	Italian	Spanish	Dutch	First Nations
Korean	Dutch	Norwegian	Polish	Polish	Punjabi
British Isles, n.i.e.	Russian	First Nations	Japanese	Jewish	Italian
Norwegian	Spanish	Vietnamese	Dutch	Taiwanese	Chinese
First Nations	Japanese	Korean	Taiwanese	Italian	British Isles, n.i.e
Welsh	First Nations	Pacific Islands	Iranian	British Isles	Welsh
Spanish	Jewish	Fijian	Vietnamese	Welsh	American

APPENDIX F — ALBERTA TOP 50 ETHNIC ORIGINS

Ethnic Origin	Population	Multiple Origins
English	886,760	83.6%
Canadian	776,695	55.8%
German	683,830	80.6%
Scottish	670,955	90.8%
Irish	565,120	91.9%
French	396,115	89.3%
Ukrainian	345,410	77.3%
Dutch	182,270	71.8%
First Nations	177,140	58.3%
Polish	174,380	83.4%
Chinese	155,960	23.4%
Norwegian	152,640	90.4%
East Indian	125,105	17.4%
Filipino	113,205	21.1%
Russian	99,780	87.1%
Swedish	96,890	93.0%
Métis	94,615	83.3%
Italian	88,705	74.1%
British Isles origins, n.i.e.	79,300	80.5%
Welsh	75,875	94.6%
American	71,435	91.1%
Danish	59,060	86.4%
Hungarian	52,025	79.3%
Spanish	39,325	81.8%
Austrian	36,670	91.1%
Vietnamese	32,505	32.8%
Romanian	29,425	77.1%

Ethnic Origin	Population	Multiple Origins
Lebanese	25,955	33.1%
Swiss	23,020	88.1%
Belgian	20,390	91.0%
Czech	18,910	83.3%
Portuguese	18,770	60.2%
Pakistani	17,825	27.2%
Icelandic	17,075	93.2%
Other African origins, n.i.e.	16,925	57.4%
Finnish	16,285	87.1%
Korean	15,865	11.2%
Jewish	15,815	77.6%
Japanese	15,650	55.0%
Mexican	14,460	53.0%
Northern European origins, n.i.e.	12,815	83.5%
Greek	12,395	64.7%
Jamaican	11,400	58.9%
Slovak	10,085	75.6%
Croatian	10,055	60.7%
Czechoslovakian, n.o.s.	9,470	87.2%
Iranian	9,215	27.2%
Punjabi	8,730	40.8%
Colombian	8,270	25.1%
Ethiopian	7,760	19.5%
Arab, n.o.s.	7,570	41.9%

The following table provides the top 20 ethnicities for the major cities of Alberta.

Calgary	Edmonton	Red Deer	Lethbridge
1,199,125	1,139,585	88,730	81,390
English	English	English	English
Canadian	Canadian	Canadian	German
Scottish	German	Scottish	Scottish
German	Scottish	German	Canadian
Irish	Irish	Irish	Irish
French	Ukrainian	French	French
Chinese	French	Ukrainian	Dutch
Ukrainian	Polish	Norwegian	Ukrainian
East Indian	Chinese	Dutch	Norwegian
Filipino	Dutch	First Nations	Polish
Polish	East Indian	Polish	Russian
Dutch	First Nations	Swedish	First Nations
Norwegian	Filipino	Métis	Italian
Italian	Norwegian	Filipino	Hungarian
Russian	Métis	Russian	Swedish
British Isles, n.i.e	Italian	British Isles, n.i.e	American
First Nations	Swedish	Danish	Welsh
Swedish	Russian	American	Danish
Welsh	British Isles, n.i.e	Welsh	British Isles, n.i.e
American	Welsh	Italian	Japanese

Appendix G — Saskatchewan Top 20 Ethnic Origins

Ethnic Origin	Population	Multiple Origins
German	288,790	76.8%
English	251,190	85.9%
Scottish	190,450	92.5%
Canadian	189,165	54.6%
Irish	156,655	93.7%
Ukrainian	136,415	76.0%
French	122,620	89.0%
First Nations	122,340	33.8%
Norwegian	69,490	88.7%
Polish	58,085	88.9%
Métis	45,955	78.8%
Russian	38,935	88.6%
Dutch	34,490	82.7%
Swedish	32,705	92.5%
Hungarian	27,770	82.0%
Austrian	18,600	87.6%
Welsh	17,420	95.9%
Filipino	16,705	15.7%
American	15,340	91.3%
Chinese	13,990	31.9%

The following table provides the top 20 ethnicities for the major cities of Saskatchewan.

Saskatoon	Regina
256,430	207,215
German	German
English	English
Scottish	Scottish
Canadian	Canadian
Irish	Irish
Ukrainian	Ukrainian
French	French
Norwegian	First Nations
First Nations	Polish
Polish	Norwegian
Russian	Hungarian
Métis	Russian
Dutch	Métis
Swedish	Austrian
Filipino	Swedish
Chinese	Dutch
Hungarian	Romanian
Welsh	Chinese
British Isles, n.i.e	Filipino
Austrian	Welsh

APPENDIX H — MANITOBA TOP 20 ETHNIC ORIGINS

Ethnic Origin	Population	Multiple Origins
English	255,535	85.7%
German	218,490	72.1%
Canadian	216,860	61.5%
Scottish	210,815	91.1%
Ukrainian	174,995	76.0%
Irish	155,455	93.8%
French	147,775	87.8%
First Nations	130,070	33.7%
Polish	85,410	85.9%
Métis	77,025	82.4%
Filipino	61,270	16.6%
Dutch	54,990	78.7%
Russian	50,640	84.0%
Icelandic	30,025	87.7%
Chinese	22,600	33.8%
Swedish	22,575	93.7%
Italian	21,960	69.3%
East Indian	21,705	20.3%
Norwegian	20,790	92.8%
Belgian	20,455	86.6%

The following table provides the top 20 ethnicities for the major cities of Manitoba.

Winnipeg	Brandon
714,640	51,980
English	English
Scottish	Scottish
Canadian	Canadian
German	Irish
Ukrainian	German
French	Ukrainian
Irish	French
Filipino	Polish
Polish	First Nations
Métis	Métis
First Nations	Dutch
Dutch	Chinese
Russian	Russian
Chinese	Welsh
East Indian	Belgian
Italian	Norwegian
Icelandic	Salvadorean
Swedish	Swedish
British Isles, n.i.e	Icelandic
Norwegian	British Isles, n.i.e

APPENDIX I — ONTARIO TOP 50 ETHNIC ORIGINS

Ethnic Origin	Population	Multiple Origins
Canadian	2,946,095	57.3%
English	2,925,660	79.3%
Scottish	2,080,545	88.4%
Irish	2,069,110	89.3%
French	1,362,320	87.3%
German	1,154,550	82.8%
Italian	883,990	48.3%
Chinese	713,245	18.5%
East Indian	678,465	23.2%
Dutch	508,595	68.4%
Polish	475,565	66.1%
First Nations	345,875	76.0%
Ukrainian	342,005	77.2%
Filipino	295,700	24.7%
Portuguese	295,030	37.6%
British Isles origins, n.i.e.	293,170	76.3%
Jamaican	218,060	41.4%
Welsh	192,645	93.5%
Russian	186,940	75.7%
Jewish	173,780	61.9%
Spanish	164,655	81.8%
Hungarian	148,960	70.8%
Greek	140,965	43.8%
American	136,505	91.6%
Sri Lankan	112,465	22.8%
Pakistani	109,295	29.0%
Vietnamese	100,520	28.3%
Métis	97,040	92.0%
Other African origins, n.i.e.	93,355	66.9%
Iranian	92,635	19.0%
Romanian	85,115	55.5%

Ethnic Origin	Population	Multiple Origins
Korean	82,640	8.7%
Finnish	74,505	77.6%
Croatian	74,020	51.1%
Lebanese	73,290	41.3%
Austrian	68,785	87.0%
Swedish	67,795	92.5%
Guyanese	67,045	52.9%
Swiss	57,270	81.6%
Serbian	56,760	39.1%
Norwegian	56,215	92.7%
Danish	53,145	83.1%
Belgian	52,635	81.2%
Trinidadian/Tobagonian	51,340	59.8%
West Indian, n.o.s.	46,390	48.5%
Tamil	43,450	45.6%
South Asian origins, n.i.e.	42,235	28.6%
Afghan	40,375	14.7%
Czech	39,800	72.8%
Arab, n.o.s.	39,315	43.2%
Egyptian	39,275	34.5%

The following table provides the top 20 ethnicities for the major cities of Ontario.

Toronto CMA						
Toronto	Mississauga	Brampton	Markham	Ottawa	Hamilton	London
2,576,025	708,725	521,315	300,135	867,090	708,170	467,260
British	British	East Indian	Chinese	British	British	British
English	East Indian	British	British	Canadian	English	English
Chinese	Canadian	Canadian	East Indian	English	Canadian	Canadian
Canadian	English	English	Canadian	Irish	Scottish	Scottish
Irish	Chinese	Jamaican	English	French	Irish	Irish
Scottish	Irish	Scottish	Scottish	Scottish	Italian	German
East Indian	Scottish	Irish	Irish	German	German	French
Italian	Italian	Italian	Sri Lankan	Italian	French	Dutch
Filipino	Polish	Portuguese	Italian	Chinese	Polish	Italian
German	Filipino	Filipino	Filipino	British Isles n.i.e.	Dutch	Polish
French	Portuguese	Punjabi	German	Polish	Ukrainian	British Isles n.i.e.
Polish	Pakistani	French	Greek	Dutch	Portuguese	Portuguese
Portuguese	German	German	Jamaican	First Nations	First Nations	First Nations
Jamaican	French	Chinese	Iranian	East Indian	British Isles n.i.e.	Ukrainian
Jewish	Jamaican	Pakistani	French	Lebanese	East Indian	Welsh
Ukrainian	Ukrainian	Other African	Tamil	Ukrainian	Chinese	Chinese
Russian	Spanish	Polish	Jewish	Welsh	Hungarian	East Indian
Sri Lankan	Vietnamese	Sri Lankan	Pakistani	Russian	Welsh	Hungarian
Spanish	Sri Lankan	Spanish	Polish	American	Croatian	American
Greek	Egyptian	Guyanese	Russian	Jewish	Filipino	Spanish

Appendix J — Quebec Top 50 Ethnic Origins

Ethnic Origin	Population	Multiple Origins
Canadian	4,571,990	31.0%
French	2,246,705	64.0%
Irish	428,570	81.7%
Italian	307,810	46.5%
First Nations	261,505	71.4%
English	240,945	84.7%
Scottish	196,670	86.5%
Québécois	183,350	32.2%
German	132,945	82.3%
Haitian	119,185	20.0%
Chinese	101,875	22.3%
Spanish	79,200	76.1%
Lebanese	70,205	32.8%
Greek	69,615	32.3%
Jewish	67,115	52.2%
Polish	65,445	68.8%
Moroccan	59,475	27.8%
Portuguese	59,400	41.8%
Belgian	49,255	71.1%
East Indian	48,535	32.7%
Russian	45,115	68.5%
Algerian	44,560	25.6%
American	44,555	87.8%
Vietnamese	42,480	24.8%
Romanian	41,605	35.4%
Arab, n.o.s.	38,465	34.1%
Métis	35,660	76.0%
Filipino	34,140	21.7%
Acadian	34,075	68.2%
Other African origins, n.i.e.	33,490	53.1%
Ukrainian	32,265	73.7%

Ethnic Origin	Population	Multiple Origins
British Isles origins, n.i.e.	28,305	84.7%
Colombian	26,570	22.9%
Armenian	25,155	39.1%
Mexican	25,045	37.8%
Dutch	24,835	79.2%
Berber	23,790	36.6%
Egyptian	23,225	49.0%
Hungarian	22,955	69.2%
Swiss	22,065	73.4%
Syrian	17,990	51.7%
Iranian	17,825	22.7%
Salvadorean	16,630	35.2%
Sri Lankan	16,455	14.6%
Peruvian	15,690	40.6%
Inuit	15,310	34.8%
Cambodian (Khmer)	14,695	40.6%
Turk	14,180	48.9%
Breton	13,455	65.4%
Congolese	13,330	21.0%
Jamaican	12,725	52.5%

The following table provides the top 20 ethnicities for the major cities of Quebec.

Montreal CMA	Montreal	Laval	Longueuil	Quebec	Gatineau	Sherbrooke
3,752,475	1,612,640	392,725	227,970	746,685	310,830	196,675
Canadian	Canadian	Canadian	Canadian	Canadian	Canadian	Canadian
French	French	French	French	French	French	French
Italian	Italian	Italian	Irish	Irish	Irish	Irish
Irish	Irish	Greek	Italian	Québécois	English	First Nations
English	Haitian	Haitian	First Nations	First Nations	First Nations	English
Scottish	Chinese	Lebanese	Québécois	Scottish	Scottish	Québécois
Haitian	English	Irish	English	English	German	Scottish
Chinese	Scottish	Armenian	Scottish	German	Italian	Italian
Québécois	Québécois	Québécois	Haitian	Italian	Métis	German
First Nations	Spanish	Portuguese	German	Spanish	Lebanese	Belgian
German	Moroccan	English	Chinese	Belgian	Québécois	Colombian
Greek	German	Moroccan	Spanish	Acadian	Portuguese	Spanish
Jewish	First Nations	First Nations	Moroccan	Chinese	Spanish	American
Spanish	Lebanese	Scottish	Portuguese	American	Polish	Polish
Lebanese	Algerian	German	Polish	Colombian	Haitian	Chinese
Moroccan	Greek	Spanish	Belgian	Métis	Chinese	Métis
Polish	Jewish	Romanian	East Indian	Portuguese	American	Acadian
Portuguese	Vietnamese	Chinese	Algerian	Breton	Belgian	Moroccan
East Indian	East Indian	Algerian	Colombian	Moroccan	Dutch	Congolese
Algerian	Polish	Syrian	Greek	Polish	British Isles, n.i.e	Dutch

APPENDIX K — ATLANTIC CANADA TOP 25 ETHNIC ORIGINS

Nova Scotia		New Brunswick		Newfoundland		PEI	
Origin	Pop.	Origin	Pop.	Origin	Pop.	Origin	Pop
English	279,420	English	190,610	Canadian	248,370	Scottish	53,960
Irish	201,655	Irish	159,195	English	219,925	Canadian	50,555
French	154,095	Scottish	146,230	Irish	110,370	English	42,700
German	97,605	German	34,870	Scottish	32,810	Irish	41,715
First Nations	41,395	First Nations	32,365	First Nations	29,295	French	28,950
Dutch	32,520	Acadian	32,005	French	28,840	German	7,160
Acadian	20,505	Dutch	16,370	Inuit	8,930	Dutch	4,240
British Isles, n.i.e.	17,960	Welsh	11,115	German	8,190	Acadian	3,760
Welsh	17,455	British Isles, n.i.e.	10,480	Métis	7,050	First Nations	3,750
Italian	14,305	Italian	7,195	Newfoundlander	4,375	Welsh	2,475
Métis	10,650	American	6,550	Welsh	4,070	Chinese	1,920
Polish	10,265	Métis	5,230	British Isles n.i.e.	4,035	British Isles origins, n.i.e.	1,855
Other African	9,405	Polish	4,035	American	2,010	Polish	960
Ukrainian	8,520	Danish	3,800	Chinese	1,970	Italian	955
Lebanese	7,245	Ukrainian	3,035	Dutch	1,860	Danish	880
American	7,120	Chinese	2,945	Italian	1,825	Ukrainian	855
Chinese	7,065	Norwegian	2,865	East Indian	1,400	American	785
Norwegian	5,190	Lebanese	2,645	Norwegian	1,230	Lebanese	700
East Indian	4,635	Swedish	2,640	Polish	1,160	Swedish	600
Spanish	4,265	East Indian	2,605	Swedish	955	Métis	505
Russian	4,035	Spanish	2,110	Ukrainian	885	Belgian	495
Swedish	3,815	Korean	1,865	Russian	855	Spanish	430
Jewish	3,665	Russian	1,765	Spanish	800	Portuguese	430
Danish	3,565	Other African	1,760	Portuguese	775	Hungarian	415
Russian	1,765	Jewish	3,665	Lebanese	630	Russian	370
Other African	1,760	Danish	3,565	Danish	465	Iranian	335

The following table provides the top 20 ethnicities for the major cities of Atlantic Canada.

Appendix K — Atlantic Canada Top 25 Ethnic Origins

Halifax	St. John's	Moncton	Saint John	Charlottetown
384,545	193,830	135,515	125,005	63,015
Canadian	English	Canadian	Canadian	Scottish
English	Canadian	French	English	Irish
Scottish	Irish	English	Irish	Canadian
Irish	Scottish	Irish	Scottish	English
French	French	Scottish	French	French
German	First Nations	Acadian	German	German
First Nations	German	German	First Nations	Dutch
Dutch	Newfoundlander	First Nations	Dutch	Chinese
British Isles, n.i.e	Welsh	Dutch	Welsh	Acadian
Welsh	British Isles, n.i.e	British Isles, n.i.e	British Isles, n.i.e	Welsh
Acadian	Inuit	Welsh	Acadian	First Nations
Italian	Chinese	Italian	Italian	British Isles, n.i.e
Other African, n.i.e.	Métis	Métis	Lebanese	Lebanese
Chinese	Italian	American	American	Ukrainian
Polish	Dutch	Polish	Swedish	Polish
Lebanese	American	Ukrainian	Chinese	Swedish
Ukrainian	East Indian	Danish	Polish	Italian
American	Norwegian	Korean	Métis	American
East Indian	Polish	East Indian	Norwegian	Iranian
Métis	Russian	Norwegian	Spanish	Danish

341

APPENDIX L — THE NORTH TOP 25 ETHNIC ORIGINS

Ethnic Origin	Population	Multiple Origins
Inuit	32,125	16.9%
First Nations	22,850	37.5%
English	16,790	83.6%
Scottish	16,445	89.6%
Canadian	13,585	55.1%
Irish	13,545	88.7%
French	9,240	86.6%
German	9,225	83.2%
Métis	3,720	68.7%
Ukrainian	3,220	84.0%
Dutch	2,400	79.4%
Norwegian	2,070	90.1%
British Isles origins, n.i.e.	1,945	72.2%
Polish	1,895	85.2%
Filipino	1,850	17.3%
Welsh	1,615	91.0%
Swedish	1,520	94.4%
Italian	1,485	88.2%
Russian	1,250	89.6%
Chinese	1,200	50.4%
American	1,195	92.5%
Danish	810	90.7%
Other European origins, n.i.e.	800	48.8%
Hungarian	775	86.5%
Austrian	595	88.2%
Finnish	560	87.5%

APPENDIX M — TOP 30 VISIBLE MINORITY RIDINGS (2011 ELECTION)

Riding	V.M.	Communities	MP	Party
		Highlight indicates dominant community twice as large as next Visible Minority		
Scarborough - Rouge River (ON)	91.0%	South Asian (33% Chinese (31%)	Sitsabaiesan, Rathika	NDP
Markham - Unionville (ON)	81.1%	Chinese (44%) South Asian (25%)	McCallum, John	Liberal
Scarborough - Agincourt (ON)	78.8%	Chinese (47%) South Asian (15%)	Jim Karygiannis Chan, Arnold (2014)	Liberal
Vancouver South (BC)	77.5%	Chinese (42%) South Asian (16%)	Young, Wai	Conservative
Richmond (BC)	73.9%	Chinese (55%) Filipino (6%)	Wong, Alice	Conservative
Etobicoke North (ON)	72.9%	South Asian (31%) Black (21%)	Duncan, Kirsty	Liberal
Bramalea - Gore - Malton (ON)	72.7%	South Asian (45%) Black (13%)	Gosal, Bal	Conservative
York West (ON)	72.2%	Black (22%) South Asian (16%)	Sgro, Judy	Liberal
Vancouver Kingsway (BC)	67.1%	Chinese (37%) Filipino (12%)	Davies, Don	NDP
Scarborough - Guildwood (ON)	65.8%	South Asian (31%) Black (15%)	McKay, John	Liberal
Mississauga - Brampton South (ON)	65.8%	South Asian (31%) Chinese (8%)	Adams, Eve	Conservative
Scarborough Centre (ON)	65.0%	South Asian (24%) Chinese (11%)	James, Roxanne	Conservative
Brampton - Springdale (ON)	64.4%	South Asian (38%) Black (12%)	Gill, Parm	Conservative
Willowdale (ON)	63.7%	Chinese (30%) West Asian (9%)	Leung, Chungsen	Conservative
Brampton West (ON)	63.2%	South Asian (33%) Black (16%)	Seeback, Kyle	Conservative
Newton - North Delta (BC)	62.6%	South Asian (49%) Chinese (5%)	Sims, Jinny J.	NDP
Surrey North (BC)	61.1%	South Asian (34%) Filipino (8%)	Sandhu, Jasbir	NDP
Calgary Northeast (AB)	60.0%	South Asian (29%) Filipino (8%)	Shory, Devinder	Conservative
Burnaby - New Westminster (BC)	59.8%	Chinese (26%) South Asian (11%)	Julian, Peter	NDP

Riding	V.M.	Communities	MP	Party
Don Valley East (ON)	59.4%	Chinese (18%) South Asian (12%)	Daniel, Joe	Conservative
Mississauga - Erindale (ON)	58.5%	South Asian (23%) Chinese (11%)	Dechert, Bob	Conservative
Fleetwood - Port Kells (BC)	57.0%	South Asian (29%) Chinese (8%)	Grewal, Nina	Conservative
Mississauga East - Cooksville (ON)	55.2%	South Asian (20%) Filipino (7%)	Lizon, Wladyslaw	Conservative
Burnaby - Douglas (BC)	54.7%	Chinese (30%) South Asian (6%)	Stewart, Kennedy	NDP
Richmond Hill (ON)	54.5%	Chinese (26%) West Asian (9%)	Menegakis, Costas	Conservative
York South - Weston (ON)	54.3%	Black (21%) Latin American (9%)	Sullivan, Mike	NDP
Oak Ridges - Markham (ON)	53.1%	Chinese (25%) South Asian (13%)	Calandra, Paul	Conservative
Mississauga - Streetsville (ON)	52.9%	South Asian (21%) Chinese (7%)	Butt, Brad	Conservative
Scarborough Southwest (ON)	51.4%	South Asian (18%) Black (9%)	Harris, Dan	NDP
Saint-Laurent - Cartierville (QC)	50.3%	Arab (15%) Black (10%)	Dion, Stéphane	Liberal

APPENDIX N — 2015 RIDINGS WITH MORE THAN 50% VISIBLE MINORITIES

	Riding	Top 2 Visible Minorities	Religious Minorities > 5%
Greater than 70% Visible Minority		Highlight indicates dominant community twice as large as next Visible Minority (no threshold) or Religious Minority (20 percent threshold)	
ON	Scarborough North	Chinese (44%) South Asian (25%)	Hindu (15%) Muslim (7%) Buddhist (7%)
ON	Brampton East	South Asian (60%) Black (13%)	Sikh (34%) Hindu (20%) Muslim (8%)
ON	Markham-Thornhill	Chinese (35%) South Asian (31%)	Hindu (17%) Muslim (10%) Buddhist (6%)
BC	Vancouver South	Chinese (40%) South Asian (18%)	Sikh (12%) Buddhist (7%)
ON	Scarborough-Agincourt	Chinese (46%) South Asian (15%)	Hindu (8%) Muslim (7%) Buddhist (6%)
ON	Markham-Unionville	Chinese (57%) South Asian (11%)	Buddhist (5%) Hindu (5%) Muslim (5%)
ON	Mississauga-Malton	South Asian (38%) Black (10%)	Muslim (13%) Hindu (13%) Sikh (12%)
ON	Etobicoke North	South Asian (30%) Black (21%)	Hindu (15%) Muslim (14%) Sikh (9%)
BC	Surrey-Newton	South Asian (59%) Filipino (3.9%)	Sikh (44%) Muslim (7%) Hindu (6%)
ON	York West	Black (22%) South Asian (16%)	Muslim (11%) Hindu (8%) Buddhist (6%)
ON	Brampton West	South Asian (34%) Black (21%)	Sikh (13%) Hindu (12%) Muslim (7%)
BC	Vancouver Kingsway	Chinese (38%) Filipino (13%)	Buddhist (10%)
BC	Steveston-Richmond East	Chinese (43%) South Asian (11%)	Buddhist (6%) Sikh (6%)
BC	Richmond Centre	Chinese (51%) Filipino (6%)	Buddhist (7%)

	Riding	Top 2 Visible Minorities	Religious Minorities > 5%
ON	Scarborough-Rouge Park	South Asian (31%) Black (14%)	Hindu (19%) Muslim (9%)
50-70% Visible Minority			
ON	Scarborough-Guildwood	South Asian (32%) Black (14%)	Hindu (16%) Muslim (15%)
ON	Don Valley North	Chinese (32%) South Asian (10%)	Muslim (11%)
ON	Mississauga Centre	South Asian (26%) Chinese (12%)	Muslim (17%) Hindu (9%)
ON	Scarborough Centre	South Asian (25%) Filipino (11%)	Hindu (13%) Muslim (12%)
BC	Burnaby South	Chinese (34%) South Asian (8%)	Buddhist (5%)
BC	Fleetwood-Port Kells	South Asian (27%) Chinese (11%)	Sikh (20%)
ON	Brampton North	South Asian (37%) Black (11%)	Sikh (20%) Hindu (11%) Muslim (6%)
ON	Willowdale	Chinese (23%) Korean (10%)	Muslim (12%) Jewish (7%)
BC	Surrey Centre	South Asian (33%) Filipino (8%)	Sikh (24%)
AB	Calgary Skyview	South Asian (31%) Filipino (8%)	Sikh (16%) Muslim (14%)
ON	Brampton South	South Asian (36%) Black (12%)	Sikh (19%) Hindu (10%) Muslim (6%)
ON	Mississauga-Erin Mills	South Asian (24%) Chinese (10 %)	Muslim (16%) Hindu (6%)
ON	Don Valley East	South Asian (16%) Black (9%)	Muslim (19%)
ON	Richmond Hill	Chinese (28%) South Asian (7%)	Muslim (11%) Jewish (5%)
ON	York South-Weston	Black (21%) Latin American (9%)	Muslim (8%)
ON	Brampton Centre	South Asian (26%) Black (12 %)	Hindu (10%) Muslim (9%) Sikh (8%)
ON	Scarborough Southwest	South Asian (18%) Black (10%)	Muslim (12%) Hindu (7%)

	Riding	Top 2 Visible Minorities	Religious Minorities > 5%
QC	Saint-Laurent	Arab (15%) Chinese (8%)	Muslim (17%) Jewish (7%)

APPENDIX O — 2015 RIDINGS WITH MORE THAN 20% MINORITY RELIGIONS

		Muslim	Hindu	Sikh	Buddhist	Jewish	Total
50-70% Minority Religions		Highlight indicates dominant religious minority twice as large as next religious minority					
ON	Brampton East	7.7%	19.5%	33.8%	1.3%	0.1%	62.7%
BC	Surrey-Newton	7.2%	6.2%	44.3%	1.1%	0.1%	59.3%
20-50% Minority Religions							
ON	Thornhill	4.3%	3.4%	0.5%	2.0%	37.1%	47.8%
QC	Mont-Royal	7.4%	2.8%	0.0%	2.1%	30.7%	43.2%
ON	Markham-Thornhill	10.4%	16.8%	2.7%	5.5%	4.9%	40.9%
ON	Mississauga-Malton	13.0%	12.8%	11.5%	3.1%	0.1%	40.9%
ON	Etobicoke North	14.3%	14.5%	8.9%	1.6%	0.1%	39.8%
ON	Brampton North	6.1%	10.9%	20.3%	1.3%	0.2%	38.9%
AB	Calgary Skyview	14.3%	4.5%	16.3%	2.2%	0.1%	37.8%
BC	Surrey Centre	4.5%	4.9%	23.7%	3.0%	0.2%	36.9%
ON	Brampton South	6.1%	9.5%	19.2%	1.1%	0.1%	36.3%
ON	Scarborough-Guildwood	14.8%	16.2%	0.9%	1.2%	0.2%	33.9%
ON	Brampton West	7.2%	11.8%	13.0%	1.5%	0.1%	33.9%
QC	Saint-Laurent	17.0%	3.2%	0.1%	4.3%	7.4%	32.3%
ON	Mississauga Centre	16.5%	8.9%	2.8%	2.9%	0.2%	31.8%
ON	Scarborough-Rouge Park	9.4%	18.6%	1.3%	1.0%	0.1%	30.7%
BC	Fleetwood-Port Kells	3.7%	3.3%	19.6%	3.6%	0.1%	30.7%
ON	Scarborough North	7.3%	14.5%	0.7%	6.5%	0.1%	29.4%
ON	York Centre	4.1%	2.2%	0.1%	2.9%	19.0%	28.5%
ON	York West	10.7%	8.4%	2.4%	6.0%	0.3%	28.1%
ON	Brampton Centre	8.5%	9.6%	7.8%	1.3%	0.3%	27.8%
ON	Scarborough Centre	11.9%	13.2%	0.3%	1.7%	0.2%	27.6%
ON	Eglinton-Lawrence	3.3%	0.9%	0.1%	1.1%	22.0%	27.6%
ON	Mississauga-Erin Mills	16.2%	5.7%	2.0%	2.1%	0.3%	27.0%
ON	Don Valley East	19.4%	4.0%	0.2%	1.9%	0.9%	27.0%
ON	Don Valley West	13.9%	1.8%	0.2%	1.2%	8.8%	26.4%
AB	Calgary Forest Lawn	11.6%	2.2%	4.7%	6.1%	0.1%	25.4%

		Muslim	Hindu	Sikh	Buddhist	Jewish	Total
BC	Vancouver South	2.3%	3.4%	12.0%	6.8%	0.5%	25.4%
AB	Edmonton Mill Woods	6.4%	4.8%	11.7%	1.1%	0.1%	24.6%
QC	Pierrefonds-Dollard	9.1%	4.0%	1.7%	1.0%	8.5%	24.6%
ON	Willowdale	11.6%	1.8%	0.1%	2.9%	6.6%	23.6%
QC	Papineau	13.5%	4.3%	1.7%	3.5%	0.2%	23.5%
QC	Outremont	9.5%	1.2%	0.0%	1.3%	11.0%	23.3%
ON	Don Valley North	10.5%	3.8%	0.2%	2.9%	4.5%	23.0%
QC	Saint-Léonard-Saint-Michel	17.3%	1.0%	0.1%	3.8%	0.1%	22.4%
ON	Richmond Hill	10.8%	1.9%	0.6%	3.0%	5.2%	22.4%
ON	Scarborough Southwest	12.2%	7.3%	0.2%	1.5%	0.3%	22.0%
ON	Mississauga-Cooksville	10.3%	6.5%	1.0%	2.7%	0.2%	21.0%
ON	Scarborough-Agincourt	6.5%	7.9%	0.3%	5.6%	0.1%	20.7%
BC	Mission-Matsqui-Fraser Canyon	0.4%	1.0%	17.1%	0.4%	0.1%	20.6%
ON	St. Paul's	2.5%	1.4%	0.1%	1.2%	14.7%	20.6%
ON	Aurora-Oak Ridges-Richmond Hill	9.9%	2.3%	0.2%	2.2%	4.8%	20.2%
ON	Ottawa South	15.3%	1.4%	0.2%	1.5%	1.2%	20.1%
ON	King-Vaughan	6.9%	4.8%	1.1%	2.5%	4.5%	20.0%

Note: We have not included Aboriginal spirituality given that this is only 1.1 percent in Mission-Matsqui-Fraser Canyon (British Columbia) 0.2 percent in Scarborough-Guildwood (ON) with a handful of ridings at 0.1 percent.

APPENDIX P — ECONOMIC OUTCOMES SENIORS

Visible Minority	Unemployment	LICO	Government transfers	Income taxes	Median income
Not VisMin	6.9%	13.1%	40.6%	12.2%	$24,385
South Asian	10.3%	10.0%	44.8%	10.8%	$17,546
Southeast Asian	10.0%	18.1%	56.1%	8.1%	$16,879
Chinese	7.5%	19.4%	48.8%	9.3%	$16,752
Filipino	6.6%	8.8%	47.5%	9.1%	$18,601
Korean	7.4%	26.4%	48.1%	9.0%	$17,835
West Asian	9.6%	28.6%	49.7%	9.9%	$16,359
Japanese	1.7%	8.0%	35.9%	11.9%	$28,834
Arab	8.7%	25.3%	45.2%	11.2%	$17,524
Black	9.1%	16.8%	47.1%	10.2%	$21,455
Latin American	10.0%	23.1%	53.7%	9.2%	$18,025
VisMin n.i.e.	11.1%	15.5%	50.7%	8.8%	$20,005
Multiple VisMin	6.5%	13.9%	50.1%	8.7%	$19,046

Made in the USA
San Bernardino, CA
03 September 2016